# The Life of the Mind

*Books by Hannah Arendt*

The Origins of Totalitarianism

The Human Condition

Between Past and Future

On Revolution

Eichmann in Jerusalem

Men in Dark Times

On Violence

Crises of the Republic

Rahel Varnhagen

The Life of the Mind:

    One / Thinking
    Two / Willing

# One / Thinking

# Two / Willing

*One-volume Edition*

*A Harvest/HBJ Book*

# Hannah Arendt

# The Life of the Mind

*Harcourt Brace Jovanovich*

*New York and London*

*Thinking* appeared originally in
*The New Yorker* in somewhat different form.

The quotations from W. H. Auden are from *Collected Poems,*
by W. H. Auden, edited by Edward Mendelson. Copyright
© 1976 by Edward Mendelson, William Meredith and Monroe K.
Spears, Executors of the Estate of W. H. Auden. The quotation from
Rainer Maria Rilke is from *Duino Elegies,* by Rainer Maria Rilke,
translated by J. B. Leishman and Stephen Spender, copyright 1939
by W. W. Norton & Company, Inc., copyright renewed 1967 by
Stephen Spender and J. B. Leishman, and is reprinted with the
permission of W. W. Norton & Company, Inc., and The Hogarth Press.

Requests for permission to make copies of any part of the work
should be mailed to: Permissions, Harcourt Brace Jovanovich, Inc.,
757 Third Avenue, New York, N.Y. 10017

Printed in the United States of America

Library of Congress Cataloging in Publication Data

Arendt, Hannah.
　　The life of the mind.

　　(A Harvest/HBJ book)
　　Originally published in two separate volumes with
subtitles: Thinking, and Willing.
　　Includes bibliographical references and indexes.
　　1.　Philosophy—Collected works.　I.　Title.
B29.A73　1981　　110　　80-25403
ISBN 0-15-651992-5

First Harvest/HBJ edition 1981

B C D E F G H I J

*Numquam se plus agere quam nihil cum ageret, numquam minus solum esse quam cum solus esset.*

CATO

Every one of us is like a man who sees things in a dream and thinks that he knows them perfectly and then wakes up to find that he knows nothing.

PLATO, *Statesman*

# Contents

## II Mental Activities in a World of Appearances

## III What Makes Us Think?

## IV Where Are We When We Think?

# Two / Willing

# III  Will and Intellect

# IV  Conclusions

# Editor's Note

As Hannah Arendt's friend and literary executor, I have prepared *The Life of the Mind* for publication. In 1973 *Thinking* was delivered in briefer form as Gifford Lectures at the University of Aberdeen, and in 1974 the opening part of *Willing* as well. Both *Thinking* and *Willing*, again in briefer form, were given as lecture courses at the New School for Social Research in New York in 1974–5 and 1975. The history of the work and of its editorial preparation will be related in the editor's postface to be found at the end of each volume. The second volume contains an appendix on Judging, drawn from a lecture course on Kant's political philosophy given in 1970 at the New School.

On Hannah Arendt's behalf, thanks are extended to Professor Archibald Wernham and Professor Robert Cross of the University of Aberdeen, and to Mrs. Wernham and Mrs. Cross, for their kindness and hospitality during the periods she spent there as Gifford Lecturer. Thanks are due, too, to the Senatus Academicus of the University, which was responsible for the invitation.

My own thanks, as editor, are extended, above all, to Jerome Kohn, Dr. Arendt's teaching assistant at the New School for his continuing helpfulness in resolving some difficult textual questions and for his industry and care in hunting down and checking references. And I am grateful to him and to Larry May for preparing the index. My particular thanks go also to Margo Viscusi for her saintly patience in retyping a heavily worked-over manuscript, with many insertions and interlineations in different handwritings, and for her searching editorial questions. I thank her husband, Anthony Viscusi, for the loan of his college textbooks, which much facilitated the checking of some elusive quotations. I thank my own husband, James West, for the windfall of *his* college textbooks in philosophy and for his readiness to discuss the manuscript and its occasional perplexities, and I thank him also for his decisiveness in cutting several Gordian knots in the general plan and lay-out of these volumes. I am grateful to Lotte Köhler, my co-executor, for making the relevant books from Hannah Arendt's library available to the publisher's editors, and for her overall helpfulness and devotion. Great appreciation is due Roberta Leighton and her staff at Harcourt Brace Jovanovich for the enormous pains and the intelligence they have brought to bear on the manuscript, far surpassing normal editorial practice. I warmly thank William Jovanovich for the personal interest he has always taken in *The Life of the Mind,* already evident in his presence in Aberdeen at three of the Gifford Lectures. Hannah Arendt was much more than an "author" to him, and she, on her side, valued not only his friendship but also his comments on and critical insights into her text. Since her death, he has encouraged and fortified me by his attentive reading of the edited text and by his suggestions for handling the Judgment material from the Kant lectures. Over and above that, there has been his willingness to share the burdens of decision on some minute points as well as on larger ones. I must thank too my friends Stanley Geist and Joseph Frank for being available for consultation on linguistic problems raised by the manuscript. And, for giving a hand with the German, my friend Werner Stemans of the Goethe Institute in Paris. Acknowledgments are due *The New Yorker,* which has published *Thinking* with a few slight changes; I feel gratitude to William Shawn for his enthusiastic response to the manuscript—a reaction that would have been very satisfying to the author. Finally, and most of all, I thank Hannah Arendt for the privilege of working on her book.

MARY McCARTHY

# One / Thinking

*Thinking does not bring knowledge as do the sciences.*

*Thinking does not produce usable practical wisdom.*

*Thinking does not solve the riddles of the universe.*

*Thinking does not endow us directly with the power to act.*

MARTIN HEIDEGGER

# Introduction

The title I have given this lecture series, *The Life of the Mind*, sounds pretentious, and to talk about Thinking seems to me so presumptuous that I feel I should start less with an apology than with a justification. No justification, of course, is needed for the topic itself, especially not in the framework of eminence inherent in the Gifford Lectures. What disturbs me is that *I* try my hand at it, for I have neither claim nor ambition to be a "philosopher" or be numbered among what Kant, not without irony, called *Denker von Gewerbe* (professional thinkers).[1] The question then is, should I not have left these problems in the hands of the experts, and the answer will have to show what prompted me to venture from the relatively safe fields of political science and theory into these rather awesome matters, instead of leaving well enough alone.

Factually, my preoccupation with mental activities has two rather different origins. The immediate impulse came from my attending the Eichmann trial in Jerusalem. In my report of it[2] I spoke of "the banality of evil." Behind that phrase, I held no thesis or doctrine, although I was dimly aware of the fact that it went counter to our tradition of thought—literary, theological, or philosophic—about the phenomenon of evil. Evil, we have learned, is something demonic; its incarnation is Satan, a "lightning fall from heaven" (Luke 10:18), or Lucifer, the fallen angel ("The devil is an angel too"—Unamuno) whose sin is pride ("proud as Lucifer"), namely, that *superbia* of which only the best are capable: they don't want to serve God but to be like Him. Evil men, we are told, act out of envy; this may be resentment at not having turned out well through no fault of their own (Richard III) or the envy of Cain, who slew Abel because "the Lord had regard for Abel and his

1. Notes are on pages 217–238.

offering, but for Cain and his offering he had no regard."
Or they may be prompted by weakness (Macbeth). Or, on the
contrary, by the powerful hatred wickedness feels for sheer
goodness (Iago's "I hate the Moor: my cause is hearted"; Clag-
gart's hatred for Billy Budd's "barbarian" innocence, a hatred
considered by Melville a "depravity according to nature"), or
by covetousness, "the root of all evil" (*Radix omnium malorum
cupiditas*). However, what I was confronted with was utterly
different and still undeniably factual. I was struck by a manifest shallowness in the doer that made it impossible to trace the
uncontestable evil of his deeds to any deeper level of roots or
motives. The deeds were monstrous, but the doer—at least the
very effective one now on trial—was quite ordinary, common-
place, and neither demonic nor monstrous. There was no sign
in him of firm ideological convictions or of specific evil motives,
and the only notable characteristic one could detect in his past
behavior as well as in his behavior during the trial and throughout the pre-trial police examination was something entirely
negative: it was not stupidity but *thoughtlessness*. In the setting of Israeli court and prison procedures he functioned as
well as he had functioned under the Nazi regime but, when
confronted with situations for which such routine procedures
did not exist, he was helpless, and his cliché-ridden language
produced on the stand, as it had evidently done in his official
life, a kind of macabre comedy. Clichés, stock phrases, adher-
ence to conventional, standardized codes of expression and
conduct have the socially recognized function of protecting us
against reality, that is, against the claim on our thinking attention that all events and facts make by virtue of their existence.
If we were responsive to this claim all the time, we would soon
be exhausted; Eichmann differed from the rest of us only in
that he clearly knew of no such claim at all.

It was this absence of thinking—which is so ordinary an experience in our everyday life, where we have hardly the time,
let alone the inclination, to *stop* and think—that awakened
my interest. Is evil-doing (the sins of omission, as well as the
sins of commission) possible in default of not just "base motives" (as the law calls them) but of any motives whatever, of
any particular prompting of interest or volition? Is wickedness,

however we may define it, this being "determined to prove a villain," *not* a necessary condition for evil-doing? Might the problem of good and evil, our faculty for telling right from wrong, be connected with our faculty of thought? To be sure, not in the sense that thinking would ever be able to produce the good deed as its result, as though "virtue could be taught" and learned—only habits and customs can be taught, and we know only too well the alarming speed with which they are unlearned and forgotten when new circumstances demand a change in manners and patterns of behavior. (The fact that we usually treat matters of good and evil in courses in "morals" or "ethics" may indicate how little we know about them, for morals comes from *mores* and ethics from *ēthos*, the Latin and the Greek words for customs and habit, the Latin word being associated with rules of behavior, whereas the Greek is derived from habitat, like our "habits.") The absence of thought I was confronted with sprang neither from forgetfulness of former, presumably good manners and habits nor from stupidity in the sense of inability to comprehend—not even in the sense of "moral insanity," for it was just as noticeable in instances that had nothing to do with so-called ethical decisions or matters of conscience.

The question that imposed itself was: Could the activity of thinking as such, the habit of examining whatever happens to come to pass or to attract attention, regardless of results and specific content, could this activity be among the conditions that make men abstain from evil-doing or even actually "condition" them against it? (The very word "con-science," at any rate, points in this direction insofar as it means "to know with and by myself," a kind of knowledge that is actualized in every thinking process.) And is not this hypothesis enforced by everything we know about conscience, namely, that a "good conscience" is enjoyed as a rule only by really bad people, criminals and such, while only "good people" are capable of having a bad conscience? To put it differently and use Kantian language: after having been struck by a fact that, willy-nilly, "put me in possession of a concept" (the banality of evil), I could not help raising the *quaestio juris* and asking myself "by what right I possessed and used it."[3]

The Eichmann trial, then, first prompted my interest in this subject. Second, those moral questions, arising from factual experience, and going counter to the wisdom of the ages—not only to the various traditional answers that "ethics," a branch of philosophy, has offered to the problem of evil, but also to the much larger answers that philosophy has ready for the much less urgent question What is thinking?—were apt to renew in me certain doubts that had been plaguing me ever since I had finished a study of what my publisher wisely called "The Human Condition," but which I had intended more modestly as an inquiry into "The Vita Activa." I had been concerned with the problem of Action, the oldest concern of political theory, and what had always troubled me about it was that the very term I adopted for my reflections on the matter, namely, *vita activa*, was coined by men who were devoted to the contemplative way of life and who looked upon all kinds of being alive from that perspective.

Seen from that perspective, the active way of life is "laborious," the contemplative way is sheer quietness; the active one goes on in public, the contemplative one in the "desert"; the active one is devoted to "the necessity of one's neighbor," the contemplative one to the "vision of God." (*Duae sunt vitae, activa et contemplativa. Activa est in labore, contemplativa in requie. Activa in publico, contemplativa in deserto. Activa in necessitate proximi, contemplativa in visione Dei.*) I have quoted from a medieval author[4] of the twelfth century, almost at random, because the notion that contemplation is the highest state of the mind is as old as Western philosophy. The thinking activity—according to Plato, the soundless dialogue we carry on with ourselves—serves only to open the eyes of the mind, and even the Aristotelian *nous* is an organ for seeing and beholding the truth. In other words, thinking aims at and ends in contemplation, and contemplation is not an activity but a passivity; it is the point where mental activity comes to rest. According to traditions of Christian time, when philosophy had become the handmaiden of theology, thinking became meditation, and meditation again ended in contemplation, a kind of blessed state of the soul where the mind was no longer stretching out to know the truth but, in anticipation of a future state, received it temporarily in intuition. (Descartes, characteristically, still influenced by this tradition, called the treatise in which he set out to demonstrate God's existence *Méditations*.) With the rise of the modern age, thinking became chiefly the hand-maiden of science, of organized knowledge; and even though thinking then grew extremely active, following modernity's crucial conviction that I can know only what I myself make, it was Mathematics, the non-empirical science par excellence, wherein the mind appears to play only with itself, that turned out to be the Science of sciences, delivering the key to those laws of nature and the universe that are concealed by appear-ances. If it was axiomatic for Plato that the invisible eye of the soul was the organ for beholding invisible truth with the certainty of knowledge, it became axiomatic for Descartes—during the famous night of his "revelation"—that there existed "a fundamental accord between the *laws* of nature [which are concealed by appearances and deceptive sense perceptions] and the laws of mathematics";[5] that is, between the laws of dis-cursive thinking on the highest, most abstract level and the laws of whatever lies behind mere semblance in nature. And he actually believed that with this kind of thinking, with what Hobbes called "reckoning with consequences," he could deliver certain knowledge about the existence of God, the nature of the soul, and similar matters.

What interested me in the Vita Activa was that the contrary notion of complete quietness in the Vita Contemplativa was so overwhelming that compared with this stillness all other dif-ferences between the various activities in the Vita Activa dis-appeared. Compared to this quiet, it was no longer important whether you labored and tilled the soil, or worked and pro-duced use-objects, or acted together with others in certain enterprises. Even Marx, in whose work and thought the ques-tion of action played such a crucial role, "uses the expression 'Praxis' simply in the sense of 'what man does' as opposed to 'what man thinks.' "[6] I was, however, aware that one could look at this matter from an altogether different viewpoint, and to indicate my doubts I ended this study of active life with a curious sentence that Cicero ascribed to Cato, who used to say that "never is a man more active than when he does nothing, never is he less alone than when he is by himself" (*Numquam se plus agere quam nihil cum ageret, numquam minus solum esse quam cum solus esset*).[7] Assuming Cato was right, the questions are obvious: What are we "doing" when we do nothing but think? Where are we when we, normally always surrounded by our fellow-men, are together with no one but ourselves?

Obviously, to raise such questions has its difficulties. At first glance, they seem to belong to what used to be called "philosophy" or "metaphysics," two terms and two fields of inquiry that, as we all know, have fallen into disrepute. If this were merely a matter of modern positivist and neo-positivist assaults, we perhaps need not be concerned. Carnap's statement that metaphysics should be regarded as poetry certainly goes counter to the claims usually made by metaphysicians; but these, like Carnap's own evaluation, may be based on an underestimation of poetry. Heidegger, whom Carnap singled out for attack, retorted by stating that philosophy and poetry were indeed closely related; they were not identical but sprang from the same source—which is thinking. And Aristotle, whom so far no one has accused of writing "mere" poetry, was of the same opinion: poetry and philosophy somehow belong together. Wittgenstein's famous aphorism "What we cannot speak of we must be silent about," which argues on the other side, would, if taken seriously, apply not only to what lies beyond sense experience but even more to objects of sensation. Nothing we see or hear or touch can be expressed in words that equal what is given to the senses. Hegel was right when he pointed out that "the This of sense . . . cannot be reached by language."[8] Was it not precisely the discovery of a discrepancy between words, the medium in which we think, and the world of appearances, the medium in which we live, that led to philosophy and metaphysics in the first place? Except that in the beginning, it was thinking, in the form either of *logos* or of *noēsis*, that was held to reach truth or true Being, while by the end the emphasis had shifted to what is given to perception and to the implements by which we can extend and sharpen our bodily senses. It seems only natural that the former will discriminate against appearances and the latter against thought.

Our difficulties with metaphysical questions are caused not so much by those to whom they are "meaningless" anyhow as by the party under attack. For just as the crisis in theology reached its climax when theologians, as distinguished from the old crowd of non-believers, began to talk about the "God is dead" proposition, so the crisis in philosophy and metaphysics came into the open when the philosophers themselves began to declare the end of philosophy and metaphysics. By now this is an old story. (The attraction of Husserl's phenomenology sprang from the anti-historical and anti-metaphysical implications of the slogan "*Zu den Sachen selbst*"; and Heidegger, who "seemingly remained on the metaphysical track," actually also aimed at "overcoming metaphysics," as he has repeatedly proclaimed since 1930.[9])

It was not Nietzsche but Hegel who first declared that the "sentiment underlying religion in the modern age [is] the sentiment: God is dead."[10] Sixty years ago, the Encyclopaedia Britannica felt quite safe in treating "metaphysics" as philosophy "under its most discredited name,"[11] and if we wish to trace this disrepute further back, we encounter Kant most prominently among the detractors, not the Kant of the *Critique of Pure Reason*, whom Moses Mendelssohn called the "all-destroyer," the *alles Zermalmer*, but Kant in his pre-critical writings, where he quite freely admits that "it was [his] fate to fall in love with metaphysics" but also speaks of its "bottomless abyss," its "slippery ground," its utopian "land of milk and honey" (*Schlaraffenland*) where the "Dreamers of reason" dwell as though in an "airship," so that "there exists no folly which could not be brought to agree with a groundless wisdom."[12] All that needs to be said today on this subject has been admirably said by Richard McKeon: In the long and complicated history of thought, this "awesome science" has never produced "general conviction concerning [its] function . . . nor indeed much consensus of opinion concerning its subject matter."[13] In view of this history of detraction, it is rather surprising that the very word "metaphysics" has been able to survive at all. One almost suspects that Kant was right when as a very old man, after having dealt a deathblow to the "awesome science," he prophesied that men will surely return to metaphysics "as one returns to one's mistress after a quarrel" (*wie zu einer entzweiten Geliebten*).[14]

I do not think this very likely or even desirable. Yet before we begin to speculate about the possible advantages of our present situation, it may be wise to reflect upon what we really mean when we observe that theology, philosophy, metaphysics have reached an end—certainly not that God has died, something about which we can *know* as little as about God's existence (so little, in fact, that even the word "existence" is misplaced), but that the way God had been thought of for thousands of years is no longer convincing; if anything is dead, it can only be the traditional *thought* of God. And something similar is true of the end of philosophy and metaphysics: not that the old questions which are coeval with the appearance of men on earth have become "meaningless," but that the way they were framed and answered has lost plausibility.

What has come to an end is the basic distinction between the sensory and the suprasensory, together with the notion, at least as old as Parmenides, that whatever is not given to the senses—God or Being or the First Principles and Causes (*archai*) or the Ideas—is more real, more truthful, more meaningful than what appears, that it is not just *beyond* sense perception but *above* the world of the senses. What is "dead" is not only the localization of such "eternal truths" but also the distinction itself. Meanwhile, in increasingly strident voices the few defenders of metaphysics have warned us of the danger of nihilism inherent in this development; and although they themselves seldom invoke it, they have an important argument in their favor: it is indeed true that once the suprasensory realm is discarded, its opposite, the world of appearances as understood for so many centuries, is also annihilated. The sensory, as still understood by the positivists, cannot survive the death of the suprasensory. No one knew this better than Nietzsche, who, with his poetic and metaphoric description of the assassination of God,[15] has caused so much confusion in these matters. In a significant passage in *The Twilight of Idols*, he clarifies what the word "God" meant in the earlier story. It was merely a symbol for the suprasensory realm as understood by metaphysics; he now uses, instead of "God," the expression "true world" and says: "We have abolished the true world. What has remained? The apparent one perhaps? Oh no! With the true world we have also abolished the apparent one."[16]

This insight of Nietzsche's, namely, that "the elimination of the suprasensory also eliminates the merely sensory and thereby the difference between them" (Heidegger),[17] is actually so obvious that it defies every attempt to date it historically; all thinking in terms of two worlds implies that these two are inseparably connected with each other. Thus, all the elaborate modern arguments against positivism are anticipated by the unsurpassed simplicity of Democritus' little dialogue between the mind, the organ for the suprasensory, and the senses. Sense perceptions are illusions, says the mind; they change according to the conditions of our body; sweet, bitter, color, and so on exist only *nomō*, by convention among men, and not *physei*, according to true nature behind the appearances. Whereupon the senses answer: "Wretched mind! Do you overthrow us while you take from us your evidence [*pisteis*, everything you can trust]? Our overthrow will be your downfall."[18] In other words, once the always precarious balance between the two worlds is lost, no matter whether the "true world" abolishes the "apparent one" or vice versa, the whole framework of reference in which our thinking was accustomed to orient itself breaks down. In these terms, nothing seems to make much sense any more.

These modern "deaths"—of God, metaphysics, philosophy, and, by implication, positivism—have become events of considerable historical consequence, since, with the beginning of our century, they have ceased to be the exclusive concern of an intellectual elite and instead are not so much the concern as the common unexamined assumption of nearly everybody. With this political aspect of the matter we are not concerned here. In our context, it may even be better to leave the issue, which actually is one of political authority, outside our considerations, and to insist, rather, on the simple fact that, however seriously our ways of thinking may be involved in this crisis, our *ability* to think is not at stake; we are what men always have been—thinking beings. By this I mean no more than that men have an inclination, perhaps a need, to think beyond the limitations of knowledge, to do more with this ability than use it as an instrument for knowing and doing. To talk about nihilism in this context is perhaps just unwillingness to part company with concepts and thought-trains that actually died quite some time ago, though their demise has been publicly acknowledged only recently. If only, one would like to imagine, we could do in this situation what the modern age did in its early stage, that is, treat each and every subject "as though no one had touched the matter before me" (as Descartes proposes in his introductory remarks to "*Les Passions de l'âme*")! This has become impossible, partly because of our enormously enlarged historical consciousness, but primarily because the only record we possess of what thinking as an activity meant to those who had chosen it as a way of life is what we would call today the "metaphysical fallacies." None of the systems, none of the doctrines transmitted to us by the great thinkers may be convincing or even plausible to modern readers; but none of them, I shall try to argue here, is arbitrary and none can be simply dismissed as sheer nonsense. On the contrary, the metaphysical fallacies contain the only clues we have to what thinking means to those who engage in it—something of great importance today and about which, oddly enough, there exist few direct utterances.

Hence, the possible advantage of our situation following the demise of metaphysics and philosophy would be twofold. It would permit us to look on the past with new eyes, unburdened and unguided by any traditions, and thus to dispose of a tremendous wealth of raw experiences without being bound by any prescriptions as to how to deal with these treasures. "*Notre héritage n'est précédé d'aucun testament*" ("Our inheritance comes to us by no will-and-testament").[19] The advantage would be even greater had it not been accompanied, almost inevitably, by a growing inability to move, on no matter what level, in the realm of the invisible; or, to put it another way, had it not been accompanied by the disrepute into which everything that is not visible, tangible, palpable has fallen, so that we are in danger of losing the past itself together with our traditions.

For even though there has never been much consensus about the subject matter of metaphysics, at least one point has been taken for granted: that these disciplines—whether you called them metaphysics or philosophy—dealt with matters that were not given to sense-perception and that their understanding transcended common-sense reasoning, which springs from sense experience and can be validated by empirical tests and means. From Parmenides till philosophy's end, all thinkers were agreed that, in order to deal with such matters, man had to detach his mind from the senses by detaching it both from the world as given by them and from the sensations—or passions—aroused by sense-objects. The philosopher, to the extent that he is a philosopher and not (what of course he also is) "a man like you and me," withdraws from the world of appearances, and the region he then moves in has always, since philosophy's beginning, been described as the world of the few. This age-old distinction between the many and the "professional thinkers" specializing in what was supposedly the highest activity human beings could attain to—Plato's philosopher "shall be called the friend of the god, and if it ever is given to man to put on immortality, it shall be given to him"[20]—has lost its plausibility, and this is the second advantage in our present situation. If, as I suggested before, the ability to tell right from wrong should turn out to have anything to do with the ability to think, then we must be able to "demand" its exercise from every sane person, no matter how erudite or ignorant, intelligent or stupid, he may happen to be. Kant—in this respect almost alone among the philosophers—was much bothered by the common opinion that philosophy is only for the few, precisely because of its moral implications, and he once observed that "stupidity is caused by a wicked heart."[21] This is not true: absence of thought is not stupidity; it can be found in highly intelligent people, and a wicked heart is not its cause; it is probably the other way round, that wickedness may be caused by absence of thought. In any event, the matter can no longer be left to "specialists" as though thinking, like higher mathematics, were the monopoly of a specialized discipline.

Crucial for our enterprise is Kant's distinction between *Vernunft* and *Verstand*, "reason" and "intellect" (not "understanding," which I think is a mistranslation; Kant used the

German *Verstand* to translate the Latin *intellectus,* and *Verstand,* though it is the noun of *verstehen,* hence "understanding" in current translations, has none of the connotations that are inherent in the German *das Verstehen*). Kant drew this distinction between the two mental faculties after he had discovered the "scandal of reason," that is, the fact that our mind is not capable of certain and verifiable knowledge regarding matters and questions that it nevertheless cannot help thinking about, and for him such matters, that is, those with which mere thought is concerned, were restricted to what we now often call the "ultimate questions" of God, freedom, and immortality. But quite apart from the existential interest men once took in these questions, and although Kant still believed that no "honest soul ever lived that could bear to think that everything is ended with death,"[22] he was also quite aware that "the urgent need" of reason is both different from and "more than mere quest and desire for knowledge."[23] Hence, the distinguishing of the two faculties, reason and intellect, coincides with a distinction between two altogether different mental activities, thinking and knowing, and two altogether different concerns, meaning, in the first category, and cognition, in the second. Kant, though he had insisted on this distinction, was still so strongly bound by the enormous weight of the tradition of metaphysics that he held fast to its traditional subject matter, that is, to those topics which could be *proved* to be unknowable, and while he justified reason's need to think beyond the limits of what can be known, he remained unaware of the fact that man's need to reflect encompasses nearly everything that happens to him, things he knows as well as things he can never know. He remained less than fully aware of the extent to which he had liberated reason, the ability to think, by justifying it in terms of the ultimate questions. He stated defensively that he had "found it necessary to deny *knowledge* . . . to make room for *faith,*"[24] but he had not made room for faith; he had made room for thought, and he had not "denied knowledge" but separated knowledge from thinking. In the notes to his lectures on metaphysics he wrote: "The aim of metaphysics . . . is to extend, albeit only negatively, our use of reason beyond the limitations of the sensorily given world, that is, *to eliminate the obstacles by which reason hinders itself"* (italics added).[25]

The great obstacle that reason (*Vernunft*) puts in its own way arises from the side of the intellect (*Verstand*) and the entirely justified criteria it has established for its own purposes, that is, for quenching our thirst, and meeting our need, for knowledge and cognition. The reason neither Kant nor his successors ever paid much attention to thinking as an activity and even less to the experiences of thinking ego is that, all distinctions notwithstanding, they were demanding the kind of results and applying the kind of criteria for certainty and evidence that are the results and the criteria of cognition. But if it is true that thinking and reason are justified in transcending the limitations of cognition and the intellect—justified by Kant on the ground that the matters they deal with, though unknowable, are of the greatest existential interest to man—then the assumption must be that thinking and reason are not concerned with what the intellect is concerned with. To anticipate, and put it in a nutshell: *The need of reason is not inspired by the quest for truth but by the quest for meaning. And truth and meaning are not the same.* The basic fallacy, taking precedence over all specific metaphysical fallacies, is to interpret meaning on the model of truth. The latest and in some respects most striking instance of this occurs in Heidegger's *Being and Time,* which starts out by raising "anew the question of the meaning of Being."[26] Heidegger himself, in a later interpretation of his own initial question, says explicitly: " 'Meaning of Being' and 'Truth of Being' say the same."[27]

The temptations to make the equation—which comes down to a refusal to accept and think through Kant's distinction between reason and intellect, between the "urgent need" to think and the "desire to know"—are very great, and by no means due only to the weight of tradition. Kant's insights had an extraordinary liberating effect on German philosophy, touching off the rise of German idealism. No doubt, they had made room for speculative thought; but this thought again became a field for a new brand of specialists committed to the notion that philosophy's "subject proper" is "the actual knowledge of what truly is."[28] Liberated by Kant from the old school dogmatism and its sterile exercises, they erected not only new systems but a new "science"—the original title of the greatest of their works, Hegel's *Phenomenology of Mind,* was "Science of the Experience of Consciousness"[29]— eagerly blurring Kant's distinction between reason's concern with the unknowable and the intellect's concern with cognition. Pursuing the Cartesian ideal of certainty as though Kant had never existed, they believed in all earnest that the results of their speculations possessed the same kind of validity as the results of cognitive processes.

*Does God ever judge us by*

*appearances? I suspect*

*that he does.*

W. H. AUDEN

# Appearance     I

# 1 The world's phenomenal nature

The world men are born into contains many things, natural and artificial, living and dead, transient and sempiternal, all of which have in common that they *appear* and hence are meant to be seen, heard, touched, tasted, and smelled, to be perceived by sentient creatures endowed with the appropriate sense organs. Nothing could appear, the word "appearance" would make no sense, if recipients of appearances did not exist—living creatures able to acknowledge, recognize, and react to—in flight or desire, approval or disapproval, blame or praise—what is not merely there but appears to them and is meant for their perception. In this world which we enter, appearing from a nowhere, and from which we disappear into a nowhere, *Being and Appearing coincide.* Dead matter, natural and artificial, changing and unchanging, depends in its being, that is, in its appearingness, on the presence of living creatures. Nothing and nobody exists in this world whose very being does not presuppose a *spectator.* In other words, nothing that is, insofar as it appears, exists in the singular; everything that is is meant to be perceived by somebody. Not Man but men inhabit this planet. Plurality is the law of the earth.

Since sentient beings—men and animals, to whom things appear and who as recipients guarantee their reality—are themselves also appearances, meant and able both to see and be seen, hear and be heard, touch and be touched, they are never mere subjects and can never be understood as such; they are no less "objective" than stone and bridge. The worldliness of living things means that there is no subject that is not also an object and appears as such to somebody else, who guarantees its "objective" reality. What we usually call "consciousness," the fact that I am aware of myself and therefore in a sense can appear to myself, would never suffice to guarantee reality. (Descartes' *Cogito me cogitare ergo sum* is a non sequitur for the simple reason that this *res cogitans* never appears at all unless its *cogitationes* are made manifest in sounding-out or written-down speech, which is already meant for and presupposes auditors and readers as its recipients.) Seen from the perspective of the world, every creature born into it arrives well equipped to deal with a world in which Being and Appearing coincide; they are fit for worldly existence. Living beings, men and animals, are not just in the world, they are *of the world,* and this precisely because they are subjects and objects—perceiving and being perceived—at the same time.

Nothing perhaps is more surprising in this world of ours than the almost infinite diversity of its appearances, the sheer entertainment value of its views, sounds, and smells, something that is hardly ever mentioned by the thinkers and philosophers. (Only Aristotle at least incidentally counted the life of passive enjoyment of the pleasures our bodily organs provide as among the three ways of life that can be elected by those who, not being subject to necessity, can devote themselves to the *kalon,* to what is beautiful in opposition to what is necessary and useful.[1]) This diversity is matched by an equally astounding diverseness of sense organs among the animal species, so that what actually appears to living creatures assumes the greatest variety of form and shape: every animal species lives in a world of its own. Still, all sense-endowed creatures have appearance as such in common, first, an appearing world and second, and perhaps even more important, the fact that they themselves are appearing and disappearing creatures, that there always was a world before their arrival and there always will be a world after their departure.

To be alive means to live in a world that preceded one's own arrival and will survive one's own departure. On this level of sheer being alive, appearance and disappearance, as they follow upon each other, are the primordial events, which as such mark out time, the time span between birth and death. The finite life span allotted to each living creature determines not merely its life expectancy but also its time experience; it provides the secret prototype for all time measurements no matter how far these then may transcend the allotted life span into past and future. Thus, the lived experience of the length of a year changes radically throughout our life. A year that to a five-year-old constitutes a full fifth of his existence must seem much longer than when it will constitute a mere twentieth or thirtieth of his time on earth. We all know how the years revolve quicker and quicker as we get older, until, with the approach of old age, they slow down again because we begin to measure them against the psychologically and somatically anticipated date of our departure. Against this clock, inherent in living beings who are born and die, stands "objective" time, according to which the length of a year never changes. This is the time of the world, and its underlying assumption—regardless of any religious or scientific beliefs—is that the world has neither beginning nor end, an assumption that seems only natural for beings who always come into a world that preceded them and will survive them.

In contrast to the inorganic thereness of lifeless matter, living beings are not mere appearances. To be alive means to be possessed by an urge toward self-display which answers the fact of one's own appearingness. Living things *make their appearance* like actors on a stage set for them. The stage is common to all who are alive, but it *seems* different to each species, different also to each individual specimen. Seeming— the it-seems-to-me, *dokei moi*—is the mode, perhaps the only possible one, in which an appearing world is acknowledged and perceived. To appear always means to seem to others, and this seeming varies according to the standpoint and the perspective of the spectators. In other words, every appearing thing acquires, by virtue of its appearingness, a kind of disguise that may indeed—but does not have to—hide or disfigure it. Seeming corresponds to the fact that every appearance, its identity notwithstanding, is perceived by a plurality of spectators.

The urge toward self-display—to respond by showing to the overwhelming effect of being shown—seems to be common to men and animals. And just as the actor depends upon stage, fellow-actors, and spectators, to make his entrance, every living thing depends upon a world that solidly appears as the location for its own appearance, on fellow-creatures to play with, and on spectators to acknowledge and recognize its existence. Seen from the viewpoint of the spectators to whom it appears and from whose view it finally disappears, each individual life, its growth and decline, is a developmental process in which an entity unfolds itself in an upward movement until all its properties are fully exposed; this phase is followed by a period of standstill—its bloom or epiphany, as it were—which in turn is succeeded by the downward movement of disintegration that is terminated by complete disappearance. There are many perspectives in which this process can be seen, examined, and understood, but our criterion for what a living thing essentially is remains the same: in everyday life as well as in scientific study, it is determined by the relatively short time span of its full appearance, its epiphany. The choice, guided by the sole criteria of completeness and perfection in appearance, would be entirely arbitrary if reality were not first of all of a phenomenal nature.

The primacy of appearance for all living creatures to whom the world appears in the mode of an it-seems-to-me is of great relevance to the topic we are going to deal with—those mental activities by which we distinguish ourselves from other animal species. For although there are great differences among these activities, they all have in common a *withdrawal* from the world as it appears and a bending back toward the self. This would cause no great problem if we were mere spectators, godlike creatures thrown into the world to look after it or enjoy it and be entertained by it, but still in possession of some other region as our natural habitat. However, *we are of the world and not merely in it;* we, too, are appearances by virtue of arriving and departing, of appearing and disappearing; and while we come from a nowhere, we arrive well equipped to deal with whatever appears to us and to take part in the play of the world. These properties do not vanish when we happen to be engaged in mental activities and close the eyes of our body, to use the Platonic metaphor, in order to be able to open the eyes of the mind. The two-world theory belongs among the metaphysical fallacies but it would never have been able to survive for so many centuries if it had not so plausibly corresponded to some basic experiences. As Merleau-Ponty once put it, "I can flee being only into being,"[2] and since Being and Appearing coincide for men, this means that I can flee appearance only into appearance. And that does not solve the problem, for the problem concerns the fitness of thought to appear at all, and the question is whether thinking and other invisible and soundless mental activities are meant to appear or whether in fact they can never find an adequate home in the world.

## 2   *(True) being and (mere) appearance: the two-world theory*

We may find a first consoling hint regarding this subject if we turn to the old metaphysical dichotomy of (true) Being and (mere) Appearance, because it, too, actually relies on the primacy, or at least on the priority, of appearance. In order to find out what truly *is,* the philosopher must *leave* the world of appearances among which he is naturally and originally at home— as Parmenides did when he was carried upward, beyond the gates of night and day, to the divine way that lay "far from the beaten path of men,"[3] and as Plato did, too, in the Cave parable.[4] The world of appearances is *prior* to whatever region the philosopher may *choose* as his "true" home but into which he was not born. It has always been the very appearingness of this world that suggested to the philosopher, that is, to the human mind, the notion that something must exist that is not appearance: *"Nehmen wir die Welt als Erscheinung so beweiset sie gerade zu das Dasein von Etwas das nicht Erscheinung ist"* ("If we look upon the world as appearance, it demonstrates the existence of something that is not appearance"), in the words of Kant.[5] In other words, when the philosopher takes leave of the world given to our senses and does a turnabout (Plato's *periagōgē*) to the life of the mind, he takes his clue from the former, looking for something to be revealed to him that would explain its underlying truth. This truth—*a-lētheia,* that which is disclosed (Heidegger)—can be conceived only as another "appearance," another phenomenon originally hidden but of a supposedly higher order, thus signifying the lasting predominance of appearance. Our mental apparatus, though it can withdraw from *present* appearances, remains geared to Appearance. The mind, no less than the senses, in its search—Hegel's *Anstrengung des Begriffs*—expects that something will appear to it.

Something quite similar seems to be true for science, and especially for modern science, which—according to an early remark of Marx's—relies on Being and Appearance having parted company, so that the philosopher's special and individual effort is no longer needed to arrive at some "truth" behind the appearances. The scientist, too, depends on appearances, whether, in order to find out what lies beneath the surface, he cuts open the visible body to look at its interior or catches hidden objects by means of all sorts of sophisticated equipment that deprives them of the exterior properties through which they show themselves to our natural senses. The guiding notion of these philosophical and scientific efforts is always the same: Appearances, as Kant said, "must themselves have grounds which are not appearances."[6] This, in fact, is an obvious generalization of the way natural things grow and "appear" into the light of day out of a ground of darkness, except that it was now assumed that this ground possessed a higher rank of reality than what merely appeared and after a while disappeared again. And just as the philosophers' "conceptual efforts" to find something beyond appearances have always ended with rather violent invectives against "mere appearances," the eminently practical achievements of the scientists in laying bare what appearances themselves never show without being interfered with have been made at their expense.

The primacy of appearance is a fact of everyday life which neither the scientist nor the philosopher can ever escape, to which they must always return from their laboratories and studies, and which shows its strength by never being in the least changed or deflected by whatever they may have discovered when they withdrew from it. "Thus the 'strange' notions of the new physics . . . [surprise] common sense . . . without changing anything of its categories."[7] Against this unshakable common-sense conviction stands the age-old theoretical supremacy of Being and Truth over mere appearance, that is, the supremacy of the *ground* that does not appear over the surface that does. This ground supposedly answers the oldest question of philosophy as well as of science: How does it happen that something or somebody, including myself, appears at all and what makes it appear in this form and shape rather than in any other? The question itself asks for a *cause* rather than a base or ground, but the point of the matter is that our tradition of philosophy has transformed the base from which something rises into the cause that produces it and has then assigned to this producing agent a higher rank of reality than is given to what merely meets the eye. The belief that a cause should be of higher rank than the effect (so that an effect can easily be disparaged by being retraced to its cause) may belong to the oldest and most stubborn metaphysical fallacies. Yet here again we are not dealing with a sheer arbitrary error; the truth is, not only do appearances never reveal what lies beneath them of their own accord but also, generally speaking, they never just reveal; they also conceal—"No thing, no side of a thing, shows itself except by actively hiding the others."[8] They expose, and they also protect from exposure, and, as far as what lies beneath is concerned, this protection may even be their most important function. At any rate, this is true for living things, whose surface hides and protects the inner organs that are their source of life.

The elementary logical fallacy of all theories that rely on the dichotomy of Being and Appearance is obvious and was early discovered and summed up by the sophist Gorgias in a fragment from his lost treatise *On Non-Being or On Nature*—supposedly a refutation of Eleatic philosophy: "Being is not manifest since it does not appear [to men: *dokein*]; appearing [to men] is weak since it does not succeed in being."[9]

Modern science's relentless search for the base underneath mere appearances has given new force to the old argument. It has indeed forced the ground of appearances into the open so that man, a creature fitted for and dependent on appearances, can catch hold of it. But the results have been rather perplexing. No man, it has turned out, can live among "causes" or give full account in normal human language of a Being whose truth can be scientifically demonstrated in the laboratory and tested practically in the real world through technology. It does look as though Being, once made manifest, overruled appearances—except that nobody so far has succeeded in *living* in a world that does not manifest itself of its own accord.

## 3   *The reversal of the metaphysical hierarchy: the value of the surface*

The everyday common-sense world, which neither the scientist nor the philosopher ever eludes, knows error as well as illusion. Yet no elimination of errors or dispelling of illusions can arrive at a region beyond appearance. "For when an illusion dissipates, when an appearance suddenly breaks up, it is always for the profit of a new appearance which takes up again for its own account the ontological function of the first. . . . The dis-illusion is the loss of one evidence only because it is the acquisition of *another evidence* . . . there is no *Schein* without an *Erscheinung*, every *Schein* is the counterpart of an *Erscheinung*."[10] That modern science, in its relentless search for *the* truth behind *mere* appearances, will ever be able to resolve this predicament is, to say the least, highly doubtful, if only because the scientist himself belongs to the world of appearances although his perspective on this world may differ from the common-sense perspective.

Historically speaking, it seems that an irremovable doubt has been inherent in the whole enterprise ever since its beginnings with the rise of science in the modern age. The first entirely new notion brought in by the new age—the seventeenth-century idea of an unlimited *progress,* which after a few centuries became the most cherished dogma of *all* men living in a scientifically oriented world—seems intended to take care of the predicament: though one expects to progress further and further, no one seems ever to have believed in reaching a final absolute goal of truth.

It is obvious that consciousness of the predicament should be most acute in the sciences that deal directly with men, and the answer—reduced to its lowest common denominator— of the various branches of biology, sociology, and psychology is to interpret all appearances as functions of the life process. The great advantage of functionalism is that it presents us again with a unitary world view, and the old metaphysical dichotomy of (true) Being and (mere) Appearance, together with the old prejudice of Being's supremacy over appearance, is still kept intact, albeit in a different manner. The argument has shifted; appearances are no longer depreciated as "secondary qualities" but understood as necessary conditions for essential processes that go on inside the living organism.

This hierarchy has recently been challenged in a way that seems to me highly significant. Could it not be that appearances are not there for the sake of the life process but, on the contrary, that the life process is there for the sake of appearances? Since we live in an *appearing* world, is it not much more plausible that the relevant and the meaningful in this world of ours should be located precisely on the surface?

In a number of publications on the various shapes and forms in animal life, the Swiss zoologist and biologist Adolf Portmann has shown that the facts themselves speak a very different language from the simplistic functional hypothesis that holds that appearances in living beings serve merely the twofold purpose of self-preservation and preservation of the species. From a different and, as it were, more innocent viewpoint, it rather looks as though, on the contrary, the inner, non-appearing organs exist only in order to bring forth and maintain the appearances. "Prior to all functions for the purpose of preservation of the individual and the species . . . we find the simple fact of appearing as self-display *that makes these functions meaningful*" (italics added).[11]

Moreover, Portmann demonstrates with a great wealth of fascinating example, what should be obvious to the naked eye—that the enormous variety of animal and plant life, the very richness of display in its sheer functional *superfluity*, cannot be accounted for by the common theories that understand life in terms of functionality. Thus, the plumage of birds, "which, at first, we consider to be of value as a warm, protective covering, is thus in addition so formed that its visible parts—and these only—build up a coloured garment, the intrinsic worth of which lies solely in its visible appearance."[12] Generally speaking, "the functional form pure and simple, so much extolled by some as befitting Nature [adequate to nature's purpose], is a rare and special case."[13] Hence, it is wrong to take into account only the functional process that goes on inside the living organism and to regard everything that is outside and "offers itself to the senses as the more or less subordinate consequence of the much more essential, 'central,' and 'real' processes."[14] According to that prevailing misinterpretation, "the external shape of the animal serves to conserve the essential, the inside apparatus, through movement and intake of food, avoidance of enemies, and finding sexual partners."[15] Against this approach Portmann proposes his "morphology," a new science that would reverse the priorities: *"Not what something is, but how it 'appears' is the research problem"* (italics added).[16]

This means that the very shape of an animal "must be appraised as a special organ of reference in relationship to a beholding eye. . . . The eye and what is to be looked at form a functional unit which is fitted together according to rules as strict as those obtaining between food and digestive organs."[17] And in accordance with this reversal, Portmann distinguishes between "authentic appearances," which come to light of their own accord, and "inauthentic" ones, such as the roots of a plant or the inner organs of an animal, which become visible only through interference with and violation of the "authentic" appearance.

Two facts of equal importance give this reversal its main plausibility. First, the impressive phenomenal difference between "authentic" and "inauthentic" appearances, between outside shapes and the inside apparatus. The outside shapes are infinitely varied and highly differentiated; among the higher animals we can usually tell one individual from another. Outside features of living things, moreover, are arranged according to the law of symmetry so that they appear in a definite and pleasing order. Inside organs, on the contrary, are never pleasing to the eye; once forced into view, they look as though they had been thrown together piecemeal and, unless deformed by disease or some peculiar abnormality, they appear alike; not even the various animal species, let alone the individuals, are easy to tell from each other by the mere inspection of their intestines. When Portmann defines life as "the appearance of an inside in an outside,"[18] he seems to fall victim to the very views he criticizes; for the point of his own findings is that what appears outside is so hopelessly *different* from the inside that one can hardly say that the inside ever appears at all. The inside, the functional apparatus of the life process, is covered up by an outside which, as far as the life process is concerned, has only one function, namely, to hide and protect it, to prevent its exposure to the light of an appearing world. If this inside were to appear, we would all look alike.

There is, second, the equally impressive evidence for the existence of an innate impulse—no less compelling than the merely functional instinct of preservation—which Portmann calls "the urge to self-display" (*Selbstdarstellung*). This instinct is entirely gratuitous in terms of life-preservation; it far transcends what may be deemed necessary for sexual attraction. These findings suggest that the predominance of outside appearance implies, in addition to the sheer receptivity of our senses, a spontaneous activity: *whatever can see wants to be seen, whatever can hear calls out to be heard, whatever can touch presents itself to be touched.* It is indeed as though everything that is alive—in addition to the fact that its surface is made for appearance, fit to be seen and meant to appear to others—has an *urge to appear,* to fit itself into the world of appearances by displaying and showing, not its "inner self" but itself as an individual. (The word "self-display," like the German *Selbstdarstellung,* is equivocal: it can mean that I actively make my presence felt, seen, and heard, or that I display my *self,* something inside me that otherwise would not appear at all—that is, in Portmann's terminology, an "inauthentic" appearance. In the following we shall use the word in

the first meaning.) It is precisely this self-display, quite prominent already in the higher forms of animal life, that reaches
its climax in the human species.

Portmann's morphological reversal of the usual priorities
has far-reaching consequences, which he himself, however—
perhaps for very good reasons—does not elaborate. They point
to what he calls "the value of the surface," that is, to the fact
that "the appearance shows a maximum power of expression
compared with the internal, whose functions are of a more
primitive order."[19] The use of the word "expression" shows
clearly the terminological difficulties an elaboration of these
consequences is bound to encounter. For an "expression" cannot but express something, and to the inevitable question, What
does the expression express? (that is, press out), the answer
will always be: something inside—an idea, a thought, an emotion. The expressiveness of an appearance, however, is of a
different order; it "expresses" nothing but itself, that is, it
exhibits or displays. It follows from Portmann's findings that
our habitual standards of judgment, so firmly rooted in metaphysical assumptions and prejudices—according to which the
essential lies beneath the surface, and the surface is "superficial"
—are wrong, that our common conviction that what is inside
ourselves, our "inner life," is more relevant to what we "are"
than what appears on the outside is an illusion; but when it
comes to correcting these fallacies, it turns out that our
language, or at least our terminological discourse, fails us.

## 4 *Body and soul; soul and mind*

Besides, the difficulties are far from being merely terminological. They are intimately related to the problematic beliefs
we hold with regard to our psychic life and the relationship of
soul and body. To be sure, we are inclined to agree that no
bodily inside ever appears authentically, of its own accord, but
if we speak of an inner life that is expressed in outward appearance, we mean the life of the soul; the inside-outside relation,

true for our bodies, is not true for our souls, even though we speak of our psychic *life* and its location "inside" ourselves in metaphors obviously drawn from bodily data and experiences. The same use of metaphors, moreover, is characteristic of our conceptual language, designed to make manifest the life of the mind; the words we use in strictly philosophical discourse are also invariably derived from expressions originally related to the world as given to our five bodily senses, from whose experience they then, as Locke pointed out, are "transferred"—*metapherein*, carried over—"to more abstruse significations, and made to stand for ideas that come not under the cognizance of our senses." Only by means of such transference could men "conceive those operations they experimented in themselves, which made no outward sensible appearances."[20] Locke relies here on the old tacit assumption of an identity of soul and mind, both being opposed to the body by virtue of their invisibility.

Upon closer examination, however, it turns out that what is true for the mind, namely, that metaphorical language is the only way it has to make an "outward sensible appearance"— even silent, non-appearing activity already consists in speech, the soundless dialogue of me with myself—is not at all true for the life of the soul. Conceptual metaphorical speech is indeed adequate to the activity of thinking, the operations of our mind, but the life of our soul in its very intensity is much more adequately expressed in a glance, a sound, a gesture, than in speech. What becomes manifest when we speak about psychic experiences is never the experience itself but whatever we *think* about it when we reflect upon it. Unlike thoughts and ideas, feelings, passions, and emotions can no more become part and parcel of the world of appearances than can our inner organs. What appears in the outside world in addition to physical signs is only what we make of them through the operation of thought. Every *show* of anger, as distinct from the anger I feel, already contains a reflection on it, and it is this reflection that gives the emotion the highly individualized form which is meaningful for all surface phenomena. To show one's anger is one form of self-presentation: I decide what is fit for appearance. In other words, the emotions

I feel are no more *meant* to be shown in their unadulterated state than the inner organs by which we live. To be sure, I could never transform them into appearances if they did not prompt it and if I did not feel them as I do other sensations that make me aware of the life process within me. But the way they become manifest without the intervention of reflection and transference into speech—by glance, gesture, inarticulate sound—is no different from the way the higher animal species communicate very similar emotions to each other as well as to men.

Our mental activities, by contrast, are conceived in speech even before being communicated, but speech is meant to be heard and words are meant to be understood by others who also have the ability to speak, just as a creature endowed with the sense of vision is meant to see and to be seen. Thought without speech is inconceivable; "thought and speech anticipate one another. They continually take one another's place";[21] they actually take each other for granted. And although the power of speech can be physically located with greater assurance than many emotions—love or hatred, shame or envy—the locus is not an "organ" and lacks all the strictly functional properties that are so characteristic of the whole organic life process. It is true that all mental activities withdraw from the world of appearances, but this withdrawal is not toward an interior of either the self or the soul. Thought with its accompanying conceptual language, since it occurs in and is spoken by a being at home in a world of appearances, stands in need of metaphors in order to bridge the gap between a world given to sense experience and a realm where no such immediate apprehension of evidence can ever exist. But our soul-experiences are body-bound to such an extent that to speak of an "inner life" of the soul is as unmetaphorical as to speak of an inner sense thanks to which we have clear sensations of the functioning or non-functioning of our inner organs. It is obvious that a mindless creature cannot possess anything like an experience of personal identity; it is at the complete mercy of its inner life process, its moods and emotions, whose continual change is in no way different from the continual change of our bodily organs. Every emotion is a somatic experience; my heart aches when I am grieved, gets warm with sympathy, opens itself up in rare moments when love or joy overwhelms me, and similar physical sensations take possession of me with anger, wrath, envy, and other affects. The language of the soul in its mere expressive stage, prior to its transformation and transfiguration through thought, is not metaphorical; it does not depart from the senses and uses no analogies when it talks in terms of physical sensations. Merleau-Ponty, to my knowledge the only philosopher who not only tried to give an account of the organic structure of human existence but also tried in all earnest to embark upon a "philosophy of the flesh," was still misled by the old identification of mind and soul when he defined "the mind as the *other side* of the body" since "there is a body of the mind, and a mind of the body and a chiasm between them."[22] Precisely the lack of such chiasmata or crossings over is the crux of mental phenomena, and Merleau-Ponty himself, in a different context, recognized the lack with great clarity. Thought, he writes, is " 'fundamental' because it is not borne by anything, but not fundamental as if with it one reached a foundation upon which one ought to base oneself and stay. As a matter of principle, fundamental thought is bottomless. It is, if you wish, an abyss."[23] But what is true of the mind is not true of the soul and vice versa. The soul, though perhaps much darker than the mind will ever manage to be, is not bottomless; it does indeed "overflow" into the body; it "encroaches upon it, is hidden in it—and at the same time needs it, terminates in it, is *anchored* in it."[24]

Such insights, incidentally, into the forever troublesome body-soul problem are very old. Aristotle's *De Anima* is full of tantalizing hints at psychic phenomena and their close interconnection with the body in contrast with the relation or, rather, non-relation between body and mind. Discussing these matters in a rather tentative and uncharacteristic way, Aristotle declares: ". . . there seems to be no case in which the soul can act or be acted upon without the body, e.g., anger, courage, appetite, and sensation generally. [To be active without involving the body] seems rather a property of the mind [*noein*]. But if the mind [*noein*] too proves to be some imagination [*phantasia*] or impossible without imagination, it [*noein*] too could not be without the body."[25] And somewhat later, summing up: "Nothing is evident about the mind [*nous*] and the theoretical faculty, but it seems to be a different kind of soul, and only this kind can be separated [from the body], as what is eternal from what is perishable."[26] And in one of the biological treatises he suggests that the soul—its vegetative as well as its nutritive and sensitive part—"came into being in the embryo without existing previously outside it, but the *nous* entered the soul from outside, thus granting to man a kind of activity which had no connection with the activities of the body."[27] In other words, there are no sensations corresponding to mental activities; and the sensations of the psyche, of the soul, are actually feelings we sense with our bodily organs.

In addition to the urge toward self-display by which living things fit themselves into a world of appearances, men also *present* themselves in deed and word and thus indicate how they *wish* to appear, what in their opinion is fit to be seen and what is not. This element of deliberate choice in what to show and what to hide seems specifically human. *Up to a point* we can choose how to appear to others, and this appearance is by no means the outward manifestation of an inner disposition; if it were, we probably would all act and speak alike. Here, too, we owe to Aristotle the crucial distinctions. "What is spoken out," he says, "are symbols of affects in the soul, and what is written down are symbols of spoken words. As writing, so also is speech not the same for all. *That however of what these primarily are symbols, the affections [pathēmata] of the soul, are the same for all.*" These affections are "naturally" expressed by "inarticulate noises [which] also reveal something, for instance, those made by animals." Distinction and individuation occur through speech, the use of verbs and nouns, and these are not products or "symbols" of the soul but of the mind: "Nouns themselves and verbs resemble [*eoiken*] . . . thoughts [*noēmasin*]" (italics added).[28]

If the inner psychic ground of our individual appearance were not always the same, there could be no science of psychology which qua science relies on a psychic "inside we are all alike,"[29] just as the science of physiology and medicine relies on the sameness of our inner organs. Psychology, depth psychology or psychoanalysis, discovers no more than the ever-changing moods, the ups and downs of our psychic life, and its results and discoveries are neither particularly appealing nor very meaningful in themselves. "Individual psychology," on the other hand, the prerogative of fiction, the novel and the drama, can never be a science; as a science it is a contradiction in terms. When modern science finally began to illuminate the Biblical "darkness of the human heart"—of which Augustine said: *"Latet cor bonum, latet cor malum, abyssus est in corde bono et in corde malo"* ("Hidden is the good heart, hidden is the evil heart, an abyss is in the good heart and in the evil heart")[30] —it turned out to be "a motley-colored and painful storehouse and treasure of evils," as Democritus already suspected.[31] Or to put it in a somewhat more positive way: *"Das Gefühl ist herr-lich, wenn es im Grunde bleibt; nicht aber wenn es an den Tag tritt, sich zum Wesen machen und herrschen will"* ("The emotions are glorious when they stay in the depths, but not when they come forth into the day and wish to become of the essence and to rule").[32]

The monotonous sameness and pervasive ugliness so highly characteristic of the findings of modern psychology, and contrasting so obviously with the enormous variety and richness of overt human conduct, witness to the radical difference between the inside and outside of the human body. The passions and emotions of our soul are not only body-bound, they seem to have the same life-sustaining and preserving functions as our inner organs, with which they also share the fact that only disorder or abnormality can individualize them. Without the sexual urge, arising out of our reproductive organs, love would not be possible; but while the urge is always the same, how great is the variety in the actual appearances of love! To be sure, one may understand love as the sublimation of sex if only one keeps in mind that there would be nothing that we understand as sex without it, and that without some intervention of the mind, that is, without a deliberate choice between what pleases and what displeases, not even the selection of a sexual partner would be possible. Similarly fear is an emotion indispensable for survival; it indicates danger, and without that warning sense no living thing could last long. The courageous man is not one whose soul lacks this emotion or who can overcome it once and for all, but one who has decided that fear is not what he wants to show. Courage can then become second nature or a habit but not in the sense that fearlessness replaces fear, as though it, too, could become an emotion. Such choices are determined by various factors; many of them are predetermined by the culture into which we are born—they are made because we wish to please others. But there are also choices not inspired by our environment; we may make them because we wish to please ourselves or because we wish to set an example, that is, to persuade others to be pleased with what pleases us. Whatever the motives may be, success and failure in the enterprise of self-presentation depend on the consistency and duration of the image thereby presented to the world.

Since appearances always present themselves in the guise of seeming, pretense and willful deception on the part of the performer, error and illusion on the part of the spectator are, inevitably, among the inherent potentialities. Self-presentation is distinguished from self-display by the active and conscious choice of the image shown; self-display has no choice but to show whatever properties a living being possesses. Self-presentation would not be possible without a degree of self-awareness—a capability inherent in the reflexive character of mental activities and clearly transcending mere consciousness, which we probably share with the higher animals. Only self-presentation is open to hypocrisy and pretense, properly speaking, and the only way to tell pretense and make-believe from reality and truth is the former's failure to endure and remain consistent. It has been said that hypocrisy is the compliment vice pays to virtue, but this is not quite true. All virtue begins with a compliment paid to it, by which I express my being pleased with it. The compliment implies a promise to the world, to those to whom I appear, to act in accordance with my pleasure, and it is the breaking of the implied promise that characterizes the hypocrite. In other words, the hypocrite is not a villain who is pleased with vice and hides his pleasure from his surroundings. The test applying to the hypocrite is indeed the old Socratic *"Be* as you wish to appear," which means appear *always* as you wish to appear to others even if it happens that you are alone and appear to no one but yourself. When I make such a decision, I am not merely reacting to whatever qualities may be given me; I am making an act of deliberate choice among the various potentialities of conduct with which the world has presented me. Out of such acts arises finally what we call character or personality, the conglomeration of a number of identifiable qualities gathered together into a comprehensible and reliably identifiable whole, and imprinted, as it were, on an unchangeable substratum of gifts and defects peculiar to our soul and body structure. Because of the undeniable relevance of these self-chosen properties to our appearance and role in the world, modern philosophy, starting with Hegel, has succumbed to the strange illusion that man, in distinction from other things, has created himself. Obviously, self-presentation and the sheer thereness of existence are not the same.

## 5  *Appearance and semblance*

Since choice as the decisive factor in self-presentation has to do with appearances, and since appearance has the double function of concealing some interior and revealing some "surface"—for instance of concealing fear and revealing courage, that is, hiding the fear by showing courage—there is always the possibility that what appears may by disappearing turn out finally to be a mere *semblance*. Because of the gap between inside and outside, between the ground of appearance and appearance—or to put it differently, no matter how different and individualized we appear and how deliberately we have chosen this individuality—it always remains true that "inside we are all alike," unchangeable except at the cost of the very functioning of our inner psychic and bodily organs or, conversely, of an intervention undertaken to remove some dysfunction. Hence, there is always an element of semblance in all appearance: the ground itself does not appear. From this it does not follow that all appearances are mere semblances. Semblances are possible only in the midst of appearances; they presuppose appearance as error presupposes truth. Error is the price we pay for truth, and semblance is the price we pay for the wonders of appearance. Error and semblance are closely connected phenomena; they correspond with each other.

Semblance is inherent in a world ruled by the twofold law of appearing to a plurality of sensitive creatures each equipped with the faculties of perception. Nothing that appears manifests itself to a single viewer capable of perceiving it under all its inherent aspects. The world appears in the mode of it-seems-to-me, depending on particular perspectives determined by location in the world as well as by particular organs of perception. This mode not only produces error, which I can correct by changing my location, drawing closer to what appears, or by improving my organs of perception with the help of tools and implements, or by using my imagination to take other perspectives into account; it also gives birth to true semblances, that is, to deceptive appearance, which I cannot correct like an error since they are caused by my permanent location on the earth and remain bound up with my own existence as one of the earth's appearances. "Semblance" (*dokos,* from *dokei moi*), said Xenophanes, "is wrought over all things," so that "there is no man, nor will there ever be one who knows clearly about the gods and about everything I speak of; for even if someone should chance to say what appears in its total reality, he himself would not know it."[33]

Following Portmann's distinction between authentic and inauthentic appearances, one would like to speak of authentic and inauthentic semblances: the latter, mirages like some Fata Morgana, will dissolve of their own accord or can be dispelled upon closer inspection; the former, on the contrary, like the movement of the sun, its rise in the morning and setting in the evening, will not yield to any amount of scientific information, because that is the way the *appearance* of sun and earth inevitably *seems* to an earth-bound creature that cannot change its abode. Here we are dealing with those "natural and unavoidable illusions" of our sense apparatus to which Kant referred in his introduction to the transcendental dialectic of reason. The illusion in transcendent judgment he called "natural and unavoidable," because it was "inseparable from human reason, and . . . even after its deceptiveness has been exposed, will not cease to play tricks with reason and continually entrap it into momentary aberrations ever and again calling for correction."[34]

That natural and inevitable semblances are inherent in a world of appearances from which we can never escape is perhaps the strongest, certainly the most plausible, argument against the simple-minded positivism that believes it has found a firm ground of certainty if it only excludes all mental phenomena from consideration and holds fast to observable facts, the everyday reality given to our senses. All living creatures, capable both of receiving appearance through sense organs and displaying themselves as appearances, are subject to authentic illusions, which are by no means the same for each species but connected with the form and mode of their specific life process. Animals are also able to produce semblances—quite a number of them can even counterfeit a physical appearance—and men and animals both possess an innate ability to manipulate appearance for the sake of deception. To uncover the "true" identity of an animal behind its adaptive temporary color is not unlike the unmasking of the hypocrite. But what then appears under a deceptive surface is not an inside self, an authentic appearance, changeless and reliable in its thereness. The uncovering destroys a deception; it does not discover anything authentically appearing. An "inside self," if it exists at all, never appears to either the inner or the outward sense, since none of the inner data possess stable, relatively permanent features which, being recognizable and identifiable, characterize individual appearance. "No fixed and abiding self can present itself in this flux of inner appearances," as Kant observed repeatedly.[35] Actually it is misleading to speak even of inner "appearances"; all we know are inner sensations whose relentless succession prevents any of them from assuming a lasting, identifiable shape. ("For where, when, and how has there ever been a vision of the inside? . . . The 'psychism' is opaque to itself."[36]) Emotions and "inner sensations" are "un-worldly" in that they lack the chief worldly property of "stand-ing still and remaining" at least long enough to be clearly per-ceived—and not merely sensed—to be intuited, identified, and acknowledged; again according to Kant, "time, the only form of inner intuition, has nothing permanent."[37] In other words, when Kant speaks of time as the "form of inner intuition," he speaks, though without being aware of it, metaphorically, and he draws his metaphor from our spatial experiences, which have to do with outside appearances. It is precisely the ab-sence of form and hence of any possibility of intuition that characterizes our experience of inner sensations. In inner ex-perience, the only thing to hold onto, to distinguish something at least resembling reality from the incessantly passing moods of our psyche, is persistent repetition. In extreme cases repeti-tion can become so persistent that it results in the unbroken permanence of one mood, one sensation; but this invariably indicates a grave disorder of the psyche, the euphoria of the maniac or the depression of the melancholic.

## 6   *The thinking ego and the self: Kant*

In the work of no other philosopher has the concept of ap-pearance, and hence of semblance (of *Erscheinung* and *Schein*), played so decisive and central a role as in Kant. His notion of a "thing in itself," something which *is* but does not appear although it causes appearances, can be, and has been, explained on the grounds of the theological tradition: God is "something"; He is "not nothing." God can be thought, but only as that which does not appear, is not given to our experi-ence, hence is "in itself," and, as He does not appear, He is not *for us.* This interpretation has its difficulties. For Kant, God is an "Idea of reason" and as such *for us:* to think God and speculate about a hereafter is, according to Kant, inherent in human thought insofar as reason, man's speculative capacity, necessarily transcends the cognitive faculties of his intellect:

only what appears and, in the mode of it-seems-to-me, is given to experience can be known; but thoughts also "are," and certain thought-things, which Kant calls "ideas," though never given to experience and therefore unknowable, such as God, freedom, and immortality, are *for us* in the emphatic sense that reason cannot help thinking them and that they are of the greatest interest to men and the life of the mind. It may therefore be advisable to examine to what extent the notion of a non-appearing "thing in itself" is given in the very understanding of the world as a world of appearances, regardless of the needs and assumptions of a thinking being and of the life of the mind.

There is first the everyday fact—rather than Kant's conclusion mentioned above (page 24)—that every living thing because it appears possesses a "ground which is not appearance" but which can be forced to the light of day and then becomes what Portmann called an "inauthentic appearance." To be sure, in Kant's understanding, things that do not appear of their own accord but whose existence can be demonstrated—inner organs, roots of trees and plants, and the like—are also appearances. Still, his conclusion that appearances "must themselves have grounds which are not appearances" and therefore must "rest upon a transcendent object[38] which determines them as mere representations,"[39] that is, upon something which in principle is of an altogether different ontological order, seems clearly drawn in analogy to phenomena of this world, which contains both authentic and inauthentic appearances, and in which the inauthentic appearances, insofar as they contain the very apparatus of the life process, seem to *cause* the authentic ones. The theological bias (in Kant's case the need to make the arguments favor the existence of an intelligible world) enters here in the word "*mere* representations"—as though he had forgotten his own central thesis: "We assert that the conditions of the *possibility of experience* in general are likewise conditions of the *possibility of the objects of experience,* and that for this reason they have objective validity in a synthetic *a priori* judgment."[40] The plausibility of Kant's argument, that what causes something to appear must be of a different order from the appearance itself, rests on our experience with these life phenomena, but the hierarchical order between the "transcendent object" (the thing in itself) and "mere representations" does not, and it is this order of priorities that Portmann's thesis reverses. Kant was carried away by his great desire to shore up each and every argument which, without being able to arrive at a definite proof, may at least make it overwhelmingly plausible that "there *undoubtedly* is something distinct from the world which contains the ground of the order of the world,"[41] and therefore is itself of a higher order. If we trust only our experiences with appearing and non-appearing things and start speculating on the same lines, we can just as well, actually with much stronger plausibility, conclude that there may indeed exist a fundamental ground behind an appearing world, but that this ground's chief and even sole significance lies in its effects, that is, in what it causes to appear, rather than in its sheer creativity. If the divine is what causes appearances and does not appear itself, then man's inner organs could turn out to be his true divinities.

In other words, the common philosophical understanding of Being as the ground of Appearance is true to the phenomenon of Life, but the same cannot be said of the evaluation of Being *versus* Appearance which is at the bottom of all two-world theories. That traditional hierarchy arises not from our ordinary experiences with the world of appearances, but, rather, from the not-at-all ordinary experience of the thinking ego. As we shall see later, the experience transcends not only Appearance but Being as well. Kant himself explicitly identifies the phenomenon that gave him the actual basis for his belief in a "thing in itself" behind "mere" appearances. It was the fact that "in the consciousness of myself in the sheer thinking activity [*beim blossen Denken*], I am the thing itself [*das Wesen selbst*, i.e. *das Ding an sich*] although nothing of myself is thereby given for thought."[42] If I reflect on the relation of me to myself obtaining in the thinking activity, it may well seem as though my thoughts were "mere representations" or manifestations of an ego that itself remains forever concealed, for thoughts of course are never anything like properties that can be predicated of a self or a person. The thinking ego is indeed Kant's "thing in itself": it does not appear to others and, unlike the self of self-awareness, it does not appear to it-self, and yet it is "not nothing."

The thinking ego is sheer activity and therefore ageless, sexless, without qualities, and without a life story. Etienne Gilson, asked to write his autobiography, responded: "A man of seventy-five should have many things to say about his past, but . . . if he has lived only as a philosopher, he immediately realizes that he has no past."[43] For the thinking ego is not the self. There is an incidental remark—one of those on which we are so dependent in our inquiry—in Thomas Aquinas that sounds rather mysterious unless we are aware of this distinc-tion between the thinking ego and the self: "My soul [in Thomas the organ for thought] is not I; and if only souls are saved, I am not saved, nor is any man."[44]

The inner sense that might let us get hold of the thinking activity in some sort of inner intuition has nothing to hold on to, according to Kant, because its manifestations are utterly unlike "the appearance confronting external sense [which finds] something still and remaining . . . while time, the only form of inner intuition, has nothing permanent."[45] Hence, "I am conscious of myself, not as I appear to myself, nor as I am in myself, but only that I am. This *representation* is a *thought*, not an *intuition*." And he adds in a footnote: "The 'I think' expresses the act of determining my existence. Exis-tence is already given thereby, but the mode in which I am . . . is not thereby given."[46] Kant stresses the point repeatedly in the *Critique of Pure Reason*—nothing permanent "is given in inner intuition insofar as I think myself"[47]—but we will do better to turn to his pre-critical writings to find an actual de-scription of the sheer experiences of the thinking ego.

In the *Träume eines Geistersehers, erläutert durch Träume der Metaphysik* (1766), Kant stresses the "immateriality" of the *mundus intelligibilis*, the world in which the thinking ego moves, in contrast to the "inertia and constancy" of dead mat-ter that surrounds living beings in the world of appearances. In this context, he distinguishes between the "notion the soul of man has of itself as mind [*Geist*] through an immaterial intuition, and the consciousness through which it presents itself as a man by means of an image having its source in the sensation of physical organs and conceived in relation to material things. It is, therefore, indeed always the same subject that is both a member of the visible and the invisible world, but not the same person, since . . . what I as mind think is not remembered by me as man, and, conversely, my actual state as man does not enter my notion of myself as mind." And he speaks in a strange footnote of a "certain double personality which belongs to the soul even in this life"; he compares the state of the thinking ego to the state of sound sleep "when the external senses are completely at rest." The ideas in sleep, he suspects, "may be clearer and broader than the very clearest in the waking state," precisely because "man, at such times, is not sensible of his body." And of these ideas, on waking up, we remember nothing. Dreams are something still different; they "do not belong here. For then man does not wholly sleep . . . and weaves the actions of his mind into the impressions of the external senses."[48]

These notions of Kant's, if understood as constituting a dream theory, are patently absurd. But they are interesting as a rather awkward attempt to account for the mind's experiences of withdrawal from the real world. Because an account does have to be given of an activity that, unlike any other activity or action, never meets the resistance of matter. It is not even hindered or slowed down by sounding out in words, which are formed by sense organs. The experience of the activity of thought is probably the aboriginal source of our notion of spirituality in itself, regardless of the forms it has assumed. Psychologically speaking, one of the outstanding characteristics of thought is its incomparable *swiftness*—"swift as a thought," said Homer, and Kant in his early writings speaks repeatedly of the *Hurtigkeit des Gedankens*.[49] Thought is swift, clearly, because it is immaterial, and this in turn goes a long way toward explaining the hostility of so many of the great metaphysicians to their own bodies. From the viewpoint of the thinking ego, the body is nothing but an obstacle.

To conclude from this experience that there exist "things in themselves" which, in their own intelligible sphere, *are* as we "are" in a world of appearances belongs among the metaphysical fallacies, or, rather, semblances of reason, whose very existence Kant was the first to discover, to clarify, and dispel. It seems only proper that this fallacy, like most of the others that have afflicted the tradition of philosophy, should have its source in the experiences of the thinking ego. This one, at any rate, bears an obvious resemblance to a simpler and more common one, mentioned by P. F. Strawson in an essay on Kant: "It is, indeed, an old belief that reason is something essentially out of time and yet in us. Doubtless it has its ground in the fact that . . . we grasp [mathematical and logical] truths. But . . . [one] who grasps timeless truths [need not] himself be timeless."[50] It is characteristic of the Oxford school of criticism to understand these fallacies as logical non sequiturs—as though philosophers throughout the centuries had been, for reasons unknown, just a bit too stupid to discover the elementary flaws in their arguments. The truth of the matter is that elementary logical mistakes are quite rare in the history of philosophy; what appear to be errors in logic to minds disencumbered of questions that have been uncritically dismissed as "meaningless" are usually caused by semblances, unavoidable for beings whose whole existence is determined by appearance. Hence, in our context the only relevant question is whether the semblances are inauthentic or authentic ones, whether they are caused by dogmatic beliefs and arbitrary assumptions, mere mirages that disappear upon closer inspection, or whether they are inherent in the paradoxical condition of a living being that, though itself part of the world of appearances, is in possession of a faculty, the ability to think, that permits the mind to withdraw from the world without ever being able to leave it or transcend it.


7    *Reality and the thinking ego: the Cartesian doubt and the* sensus communis

Reality in a world of appearances is first of all characterized by "standing still and remaining" the same long enough to become an *object* for acknowledgment and recognition by a *subject.* Husserl's basic and greatest discovery takes up in exhaustive detail the intentionality of all acts of consciousness, that is, the fact that no subjective act is ever without an object: though the seen tree may be an illusion, for the act of seeing it is an object nevertheless; though the dreamt-of landscape is visible only to the dreamer, it is the object of his dream. Objectivity is built into the very subjectivity of consciousness by virtue of intentionality. Conversely and with the same justness, one may speak of the intentionality of appearances and their built-in subjectivity. All objects because they appear indicate a subject, and, just as every subjective act has its intentional object, so every appearing object has its intentional subject. In Portmann's words, every appearance is a "conveyance for receivers" (a *Sendung für Empfangsapparate*). Whatever appears is meant for a perceiver, a potential subject no less inherent in all objectivity than a potential object is inherent in the subjectivity of every intentional act.

That appearance always demands spectators and thus implies an at least potential recognition and acknowledgment has far-reaching consequences for what we, appearing beings in a world of appearances, understand by reality, our own as well as that of the world. In both cases, our "perceptual faith,"[51] as Merleau-Ponty has called it, our certainty that what we perceive has an existence independent of the act of perceiving, depends entirely on the object's also appearing as such to others and being acknowledged by them. Without this tacit acknowledgment by others we would not even be able to put faith in the way we appear to ourselves.

This is why all solipsistic theories—whether they radically claim that nothing but the self "exists" or, more moderately, hold that the self and its consciousness of itself are the primary objects of verifiable knowledge—are out of tune with the most elementary data of our existence and experience. Solipsism, open or veiled, with or without qualifications, has been the most persistent and, perhaps, the most pernicious fallacy of philosophy even before it attained in Descartes the high rank of theoretical and existential consistency. When the philosopher speaks of "man," he has in mind neither the species-being (the *Gattungswesen*, like horse or lion, which, according to

Marx, constitutes man's fundamental existence) nor a mere paradigm of what, in the philosopher's view, all men should strive to emulate. To the philosopher, speaking out of the experience of the thinking ego, man is quite naturally not just word but *thought made flesh,* the always mysterious, never fully elucidated incarnation of the thinking capability. And the trouble with this fictitious being is that it is neither the product of a diseased brain nor one of the easily dispelled "errors of the past," but the entirely authentic semblance of the thinking activity itself. For while, for whatever reason, a man indulges in sheer thinking, and no matter on what subject, he lives completely in the singular, that is, in complete solitude, as though not men but Man inhabited the earth. Descartes himself explained and justified his radical subjectivism by the decisive loss of certainties entailed by the great scientific discoveries of the modern age, and I have, in a different context, followed up Descartes' reasoning.[52] However, when—beset by the doubts inspired by the beginnings of modern science—he decided "*à rejeter la terre mouvante et le sable pour trouver le roc ou l'argile*" ("to reject the quicksand and mud in order to find the rock or clay"), he certainly rediscovered rather familiar territory in withdrawing to a place where he could live "*aussi solitaire et retiré que dans les déserts les plus écartés*" ("as solitary and retired as in the most remote deserts").[53] Withdrawal from the "beastliness of the multitude" into the company of the "very few"[54] but also into the absolute solitude of the One has been the most outstanding feature of the philosopher's life ever since Parmenides and Plato discovered that for those "very few," the *sophoi,* the "life of thinking" that knows neither joy nor grief is the most divine of all, and *nous,* thought itself, is "the king of heaven and earth."[55]

Descartes, true to the radical subjectivism that was the philosophers' first reaction to the new glories of science, no longer ascribed the gratifications of this way of life to the objects of thinking—the everlastingness of the *kosmos* that neither comes into being nor ever vanishes from it and thus gives those few who have decided to spend their lives as its spectators their share of immortality. His very modern suspicion of man's cognitive and sensory apparatus made him define with greater clarity than anyone before him as properties of the *res cogitans* certain characteristics that were by no means unknown to the ancients but that now, perhaps for the first time, assumed a paramount importance. Outstanding among these was self-suf- ficiency, namely, that this ego has "no need of any place, nor does it depend on any material thing," and, next, worldlessness, namely, that in self-inspection, "*examinant avec attention ce que j'étais,*" he could easily "*feindre que je n'avais aucun corps et qu'il n'y avait aucun monde ni aucun lieu où je fusse*" ("feign that I had no body, and that there was no world nor place where I would be").[56]

To be sure, none of these discoveries, or, rather, re-dis- coveries, was of great importance in itself to Descartes. His main concern was to find something—the thinking ego or, in his words, "*la chose pensante,*" which he equated with the soul —whose reality was beyond suspicion, beyond the illusions of sense perception: even the power of an all-powerful *Dieu trom- peur* would not be able to shatter the certainty of a conscious- ness that had withdrawn from all sense experience. Although everything given may be illusion and dream, the dreamer, if he will only consent not to demand reality of the dream, must be real. Hence, "*Je pense, donc je suis,*" "I think, therefore I am." So strong was the experience of the thinking activity itself, on the one hand, so passionate on the other the desire to find certainty and some sort of abiding permanence after the new science had discovered "*la terre mouvante*" (the shifting quicksand of the very ground on which we stand), that it never occurred to him that no *cogitatio* and no *cogito me cogitare,* no consciousness of an acting self that had suspended all faith in the reality of its intentional objects, would ever have been able to convince him of his own reality had he actually been born in a desert, without a body and its senses to perceive "material" things and without fellow-creatures to assure him that what he perceived was perceived by them too. The Cartesian *res cogitans,* this fictitious creature, bodiless, senseless, and for- saken, would not even know that there is such a thing as reality and a possible distinction between the real and the unreal, be- tween the common world of waking life and the private non- world of our dreams. What Merleau-Ponty had to say against

Descartes is brilliantly right: "To reduce perception to the thought of perceiving . . . is to take out an insurance against doubt whose premiums are more onerous than the loss for which it is to indemnify us: for it is to . . . move to a type of certitude that will never restore to us the 'there is' of the world."[57]

Moreover, it is precisely the thinking activity—the experiences of the thinking ego—that gives rise to doubt of the world's reality and of my own. Thinking can seize upon and get hold of everything real—event, object, its own thoughts; their realness is the only property that remains stubbornly beyond its reach. The *cogito ergo sum* is a fallacy not only in the sense that, as Nietzsche remarked, from the *cogito* only the existence of *cogitationes* could be inferred; the *cogito* is subject to the same doubt as the *sum*. The I-am is presupposed in the I-think; thought can seize on this presupposition but it can neither prove nor disprove it. (Kant's argument against Descartes was entirely right, too: The thought "*I am not* . . . cannot exist; for if I am not, it follows that I cannot become aware that I am not."[58]) Reality cannot be derived; thought or reflection can accept or reject it, and the Cartesian doubt, starting from the notion of a *Dieu trompeur*, is but a sophisticated and veiled form of rejection.[59] It remained for Wittgenstein, who had set out to investigate "how much truth there is in solipsism" and thus became its most relevant contemporary representative, to formulate the existential delusion underlying all its theories: "At death the world does not alter, but comes to an end." "Death is not an event in life; we do not live our death."[60] This is the basic premise of all solipsistic thinking.

Although everything that appears is perceived in the mode of it-seems-to-me, hence open to error and illusion, appearance as such carries with it a prior indication of *realness*. All sense experiences are normally accompanied by the additional, if usually mute, sensation of reality, and this despite the fact that none of our senses, taken in isolation, and no sense-object, taken out of context, can produce it. (Art therefore, which transforms sense-objects into thought-things, tears them first of all out of their context in order to de-realize and thus prepare them for their new and different function.)

The reality of what I perceive is guaranteed by its worldly context, which includes others who perceive as I do, on the one hand, and by the working together of my five senses on the other. What since Thomas Aquinas we call common sense, the *sensus communis*, is a kind of sixth sense needed to keep my five senses together and guarantee that it is the same object that I see, touch, taste, smell, and hear; it is the "one faculty [that] extends to all objects of the five senses."[61] This same sense, a mysterious "sixth sense"[62] because it cannot be localized as a bodily organ, fits the sensations of my strictly private five senses—so private that sensations in their mere sensational quality and intensity are incommunicable—into a common world shared by others. The subjectivity of the it-seems-to-me is remedied by the fact that the same object also appears to others though its mode of appearance may be different. (It is the inter-subjectivity of the world, rather than similarity of physical appearance, that convinces men that they belong to the same species. Though each single object appears in a different perspective to each individual, the context in which it appears is the same for the whole species. In this sense, every animal species lives in a world of its own, and the individual animal does not need to compare its own physical characteristics with those of its fellow-members in order to recognize them as such.) In a world of appearances, filled with error and semblance, reality is guaranteed by this three-fold commonness: the five senses, utterly different from each other, have the same object in common; members of the same species have the context in common that endows every single object with its particular meaning; and all other sense-endowed beings, though perceiving this object from utterly different perspectives, agree on its identity. Out of this threefold commonness arises the *sensation* of reality.

To each of our five senses corresponds a specific, sensorily perceptible property of the world. Our world is visible because we have vision, audible because we have hearing, touchable and full of odors and tastes because we have touch, smell, and taste. The sixth sense's corresponding worldly property is *realness*, and the difficulty with this property is that it cannot be perceived like other sensory properties. The sense of realness is not a sensation strictly speaking; reality "is *there* even if we can never be certain that we know it" (Peirce),[63] for the "sensation" of reality, of sheer thereness, relates to the *context* in which single objects appear as well as to the context in which we ourselves as appearances exist among other appearing creatures. The context qua context never appears entirely; it is elusive, almost like Being, which qua Being never appears in a world filled with beings, with single entities. But Being, since Parmenides the highest concept of Western philosophy, is a thought-thing that we do not expect to be perceived by the senses or to cause a sensation, whereas realness is akin to sensation; a feeling of realness (or irreality) actually accompanies all the sensations of my senses, which without it would not make "sense." This is why Thomas Aquinas defined common sense, his *"sensus communis,"* as an "inner sense"—*sensus interior*—that functioned as "the common root and principle of the exterior senses" (*"Sensus interior non dicitur communis . . . sicut genus; sed sicut communis radix et principium exteriorum sensuum"*).[64]

To equate this "inner sense," which cannot be physically localized, with the faculty of thought is tempting indeed, because among the chief characteristics of thinking, occurring in a world of appearances and performed by an appearing being, is that it is itself invisible. From this property of invisibility, shared by common sense with the faculty of thought, Peirce concludes that "reality has a relationship to human thought," ignoring the fact that thinking is not only itself invisible but also deals with invisibles, with things not *present* to the senses though they may be, and mostly are, also sense-objects, remembered and collected in the storehouse of memory and thus prepared for later reflection. Thomas Landon Thorson elaborates Peirce's suggestion and comes to the conclusion that "reality bears a relationship to the thought process like the environment does to biological evolution."[65]

These remarks and suggestions are based on the tacit assumption that thought processes are in no way different from common-sense reasoning; the result is the old Cartesian illusion in modern disguise. Whatever thinking can reach and whatever it may achieve, it is precisely reality as given to common sense, in its sheer thereness, that remains forever beyond its grasp, indissoluble into thought-trains—the stumbling block that alerts them and on which they founder in affirmation or negation. Thought processes, unlike common sense, can be physically located in the brain, but nevertheless transcend all biological data, be they functional or morphological in Portmann's sense. Common sense, on the contrary, and the feeling of realness belong to our biological apparatus, and common-sense reasoning (which the Oxford school of philosophy mistakes for thinking) could certainly bear the same relation to reality that biological evolution does to environment. With respect to common-sense reasoning, Thorson is right: "We may indeed be talking about more than an analogy; we may be describing two aspects of the same process."[66] And if language, in addition to its treasure of words for things given to the senses, did not offer us such thought-words, technically called "concepts," as justice, truth, courage, divinity, and so on, which are indispensable even in ordinary speech, we would certainly lack all tangible evidence for the thinking activity and hence might be justified in concluding with the early Wittgenstein: *"Die Sprache ist ein Teil unseres Organismus"* ("language is a part of our organism").[67]

Thinking, however, which subjects everything it gets hold of to doubt, has no such natural, matter-of-fact relation to reality. It was thought—Descartes' reflection on the *meaning* of certain scientific discoveries—that destroyed his common-sense trust in reality, and his error was to hope he could overcome his doubt by insisting on withdrawing from the world altogether, eliminating every worldly reality from his thoughts and concentrating only on the thinking activity itself. (*Cogito cogitationes*, or *cogito me cogitare, ergo sum*, is the correct form of the famous formula.) But thinking can neither prove nor destroy the *feeling* of realness arising out of the sixth sense, which the French, perhaps for this reason, also call *le bon sens*, the good sense; when thinking withdraws from the world of appearances, it withdraws from the sensorily given and hence also from the feeling of realness, given by common sense. Husserl claimed that the *suspension* [*epochē*] of this feeling was the methodological foundation of his phenomenological science. For the thinking ego, this suspension is a matter of course and by no means a special method to be taught and learned; we know it as the quite ordinary phenomenon of absent-mindedness, to be observed in anyone who happens to be absorbed in no matter what sort of thought. In other words, the loss of common sense is neither the vice nor the virtue of Kant's "professional thinkers"; it happens to everybody who ever reflects on something; it only happens more often to professional thinkers. These we call philosophers, and their way of life will always be "the life of a stranger" (*bios xenikos*), as Aristotle called it in his *Politics*.[68] And the reason that strangeness and absent-mindedness are not more dangerous, that all "thinkers," professionals and laymen alike, survive so easily the loss of the feeling of realness, is just that the thinking ego asserts itself only temporarily: every thinker no matter how eminent remains "a man like you and me" (Plato), an appearance among appearances equipped with common sense and knowing enough common-sense reasoning to survive.

## 8 *Science and common sense; Kant's distinction between intellect and reason; truth and meaning*

Something very similar seems, at first glance, to be true of the modern scientist who constantly destroys authentic semblances without, however, destroying his own sensation of reality, telling him, as it tells us, that the sun rises in the morning and sets in the evening. It was thinking that enabled men to penetrate the appearances and unmask them as semblances, albeit authentic ones; common-sense reasoning would never have dared to upset so radically all the plausibilities of our sensory apparatus. The famous "quarrel between the ancients and the moderns" actually turns on the question of what the aim of knowledge is; is it "to save the phenomena," as the ancients believed, or to discover the hidden functional apparatus which makes them appear? Thought's doubt of the reliability of sense experience, its suspicion that things might be quite different from the way they appear to human senses, was by no means uncommon in antiquity. Democritus' atoms were not only indivisible but invisible, moving in a void, infinite in number, and, through various configurations and combinations, producing impressions on our senses; Aristarchus in the third century B.C. first proposed the heliocentric hypothesis. It is interesting that the consequences of such daring were rather unpleasant: Democritus was suspected of being insane, and Aristarchus was threatened with an indictment for impiety. But the relevant point is of course that no attempt was made to prove these hypotheses and no science came out of it.

Thinking, no doubt, plays an enormous role in every scientific enterprise, but it is the role of a means to an end; the end is determined by a decision about what is worthwhile knowing, and this decision cannot be scientific. Moreover, the end is cognition or knowledge, which, having been obtained, clearly belongs to the world of appearances; once established as truth, it becomes part and parcel of the world. Cognition and the thirst for knowledge never leave the world of appearances altogether; if the scientists withdraw from it in order to "think," it is only in order to find better, more promising approaches, called methods, toward it. Science in this respect is but an enormously refined prolongation of common-sense reasoning in which sense illusions are constantly dissipated just as errors in science are corrected. The criterion in both cases is evidence, which as such is inherent in a world of appearances. And since it is in the very nature of appearances to reveal *and to conceal,* every correction and every *dis*-illusion "is the loss of one evidence only because it is the acquisition of *another evidence,"* in the words of Merleau-Ponty.[69] Nothing, even in science's own understanding of the scientific enterprise, guarantees that the new evidence will prove to be more reliable than the discarded evidence.

The very concept of an *unlimited progress,* which accompanied the rise of modern science, and has remained its dominant inspiring principle, is the best documentation of the fact that all science still moves within the realm of common sense experience, subject to corrigible error and deception. When the experience of constant correction in scientific research is generalized, it leads into the curious "better and better," "truer and truer," that is, into the boundlessness of progress with its inherent admission that *the* good and *the* true are unattainable. If they were ever attained, the thirst for knowledge would be quenched and the search for cognition would come to an end. This, of course, is unlikely to happen, in view of the enormous amount of the unknown, but it is quite likely that particular sciences may reach definite limits of what is knowable to man. Yet the point is that the modern idea of progress implicitly denies such limitations. Unquestionably the notion of progress was born as the result of the tremendous advances of scientific knowledge, a veritable avalanche of discoveries, in the sixteenth and seventeenth centuries, and I think it quite possible that it was the relentlessness inherent in sheer thinking, whose need can never be assuaged, that, once it had invaded the sciences, drove the scientists to ever-new discoveries, each one giving rise to a new theory, so that those caught in the movement were subject to the illusion of a never-ending process—the *process* of progress. Here we should not forget that the later notion of an unending perfectibility of the human species, so prominent in the eighteenth-century Enlightenment, was absent from the sixteenth and seventeenth centuries' rather pessimistic evaluation of human nature.

One consequence, however, of this development seems to me obvious and of considerable importance. The very notion of *truth*, which somehow had survived so many turning-points of our intellectual history, underwent a decisive change: it was transformed or, rather, broken down into a string of verities, each one in its time claiming general validity even though the very continuity of the research implied something merely provisional. This is a strange state of affairs. It may even suggest that if a given science accidentally reached its goal, this would by no means stop the workers in that field, who would be driven past their goal by the sheer momentum of the illusion of unlimited progress, a kind of semblance rising out of their activity.

The transformation of truth into mere verity results primarily from the fact that the scientist remains bound to the common sense by which we find our bearings in a world of appearances. Thinking withdraws radically and for its own sake from this world and its evidential nature, whereas science profits from a possible withdrawal for the sake of specific results. In other words, it is common-sense reasoning ultimately that ventures out into the realm of sheer speculation in the theories of the scientists, and the chief weakness of common sense in this sphere has always been that it lacks the safeguards inherent in sheer thinking, namely, thinking's critical capacity, which, as we shall see, harbors within itself a highly self-destructive tendency. But to go back to the assumption of unlimited progress, the basic fallacy was early discovered. It is well known that not progress per se, but the notion of its limitlessness would have made modern science unacceptable to the ancients. It is less well known that the Greeks had some reason for their "prejudice" against the infinite. (Plato discovered that everything permitting of a comparative is by nature unlimited, and limitlessness was to him as to all Greeks the cause of all evils.[70] Hence, his great confidence in number and measurement: it sets limits on what of itself [pleasure, for instance] "does not and never will contain and derive from itself either beginning [*archē*] or middle or end [*telos*]."[71])

That modern science, always hunting for manifestations of the invisible—atoms, molecules, particles, cells, genes—should have added to the world a spectacular, unprecedented quantity of new perceptible things is only seemingly paradoxical. In order to prove or disprove its hypotheses, its "paradigms" (Thomas Kuhn), and to discover what makes things work, it began to imitate the working processes of nature. For that purpose it produced the countless and enormously complex implements with which to *force* the non-appearing to appear (if only as an instrument-reading in the laboratory), as that was the sole means the scientist had to persuade himself of its reality. Modern technology was born in the laboratory, but this was not because scientists wanted to produce appliances or change the world. No matter how far their theories leave common-sense experience and common-sense reasoning behind, they must finally come back to some form of it or lose all sense of realness in the object of their investigation. And this return is possible only via the man-made, artificial world of the laboratory, where that which does not appear of its own accord is forced to appear and to disclose itself. Technology, the "plumber's" work held in some contempt by the scientist, who sees practical applicability as a mere by-product of his own efforts, introduces scientific findings, made in "unparalleled insulation . . . from the demands of the laity and of everyday life,"[72] into the everyday world of appearances and renders them accessible to common-sense experience; but this is possible only because the scientists themselves are ultimately dependent on that experience. Seen from the perspective of the "real" world, the laboratory is the anticipation of a changed environment; and the cognitive processes using the human abilities of thinking and fabricating as means to their end are indeed the most refined modes of common-sense reasoning. The activity of knowing is no less related to our sense of reality and no less a world-building activity than the building of houses.

The faculty of thinking, however, which Kant, as we have seen, called *Vernunft* (reason) to distinguish it from *Verstand* (intellect), the faculty of cognition, is of an altogether different nature. The distinction, on its most elementary level and in Kant's own words, lies in the fact that "concepts of reason serve us to conceive [*begreifen*, comprehend], as concepts of the intellect serve us to apprehend perceptions" (*"Vernunftbegriffe dienen zum Begreifen, wie Verstandesbegriffe zum Verstehen der Wahrnehmungen"*).[73] In other words, the intellect (*Verstand*) desires to grasp what is given to the senses, but reason (*Vernunft*) wishes to understand its *meaning*. Cognition, whose highest criterion is truth, derives that criterion from the world of appearances in which we take our bearings through sense perceptions, whose testimony is self-evident, that is, unshakeable by argument and replaceable only by other evidence. As the German translation of the Latin *perceptio*, the word *Wahrnehmung* used by Kant (what is given me in perceptions and ought to be *true* [*Wahr*]) clearly indicates, truth is located in the evidence of the senses. But that is by no means the case with meaning and with the faculty of thought, which searches for it; the latter does not ask what something is or whether it exists at all—its existence is always taken for granted—*but what it means for it to be.* This distinction between truth and meaning seems to me to be not only decisive for any inquiry into the nature of human thinking but also to be the necessary consequence of Kant's crucial distinction between reason and intellect. Admittedly, Kant himself never pursued that particular implication of his own thought; in fact, a clear-cut line of demarcation between these two altogether different modes cannot be found in the history of philosophy. The exceptions—occasional remarks by Aristotle in *On Interpretation*—remained without significance for Aristotle's later philosophy. In that early treatise on language he writes: Every "*logos* [sentence, in the context] is a significant sound (*phōnē sēmantikē*)"; it gives a sign, points out something. But "not every *logos* is revealing (*apophantikos*), only those in which true speech or false speech (*alētheuein* or *pseudesthai*) holds sway. This is not always the case; for example, a prayer is a *logos* [it is significant] but neither true nor false."[74]

The questions raised by our thirst for knowledge arise from our curiosity about the world, our desire to investigate whatever is given to our sensory apparatus. The famous first sentence of Aristotle's *Metaphysics*, "*Pantes anthrōpoi tou eidenai oregontai physei*"[75]—"All men by nature desire to know"—literally translated reads: "All men desire to see and to have seen [that is, to know]," and Aristotle immediately adds: "An indication of this is our love of the senses; for they are loved for their own sake, quite apart from their use." The questions raised by the desire to know are in principle all answerable by common-sense experience and common-sense reasoning; they are exposed to corrigible error and illusion in the same way as sense perceptions and experiences. Even the relentlessness of modern science's Progress, which constantly corrects itself by discarding the answers and reformulating the questions, does not contradict science's basic goal—to see and to know the world as it is given to the senses—and its concept of truth is derived from the common-sense experience of irrefutable evidence, which dispels error and illusion. But the questions raised by thinking and which it is in reason's very nature to raise—questions of meaning—are all unanswerable by common sense and the refinement of it we call science. The quest for meaning is "meaningless" to common sense and common-sense reasoning because it is the sixth sense's function to fit us into the world of appearances and make us at home in the world given by our five senses; there we are and no questions asked.

What science and the quest for knowledge are after is *irrefutable* truth, that is, propositions human beings are not free to reject—they are compelling. They are of two kinds, as we have known since Leibniz: truths of reasoning and truths of fact. The main distinction between them lies in the degree of their force of compulsion: the truths of "Reasoning are necessary and their opposite is impossible" while "those of Fact are contingent and their opposite is possible."[76] The distinction is very important although perhaps not in the sense Leibniz himself meant. Truths of fact, their contingency notwithstanding, are as compelling for anybody witnessing them with his own eyes as the proposition that two and two make four is for anybody in his right mind. The point is only that a fact, an event, can never be witnessed by everyone who may want to know about it, whereas rational or mathematical truth presents itself as self-evident to everyone endowed with the same brain power; its compelling nature is universal, while the compelling force of factual truth is limited; it does not reach those who, not having been witnesses, have to rely on the testimony of others, whom one may or may not believe. The true opposite of factual, as distinguished from rational, truth is not error or illusion but the deliberate lie.

Leibniz' distinction between the truths of fact and the truths of reasoning, whose highest form is mathematical reasoning—which deals only with thought-things and needs neither witnesses nor the sensorily given—is based on the age-old distinction between necessity and contingency, according to which all that is necessary, and whose opposite is impossible, possesses a higher ontological dignity than whatever is but could also not be. This conviction that mathematical reasoning should serve as a paradigm for all thought is probably as old as Pythagoras; at any rate we find it in Plato's refusal to admit anyone to philosophy who has not been trained in mathematics. It is still at the root of the medieval *dictamen rationis,* the

dictate of reason. That truth compels with the force of necessity
(*anagkē*), which is far stronger than the force of violence
(*bia*), is an old *topos* in Greek philosophy, and it is always
meant as a compliment to truth that it can compel men with the
irresistible force of Necessity (*hyp' autēs alētheias anagkasthentes,* in the words of Aristotle[77]). "*Euclide,*" as Mercier de la
Rivière once noted, "*est un véritable despote; et les vérités
qu'il nous a transmises, sont des lois véritablement despo-
tiques.*"[78] The same notion led Grotius to the conviction that
"even God cannot cause two times two not to make four"—a
very questionable proposition not only because it would put
God under the dictate of necessity but because, if true, it
would be equally valid for the evidence of sense perception,
and it was on these grounds that Duns Scotus had questioned it.

The source of mathematical truth is the human brain, and
*brain power* is no less natural, no less equipped to guide us
through an appearing world, than our senses plus common
sense and the extension of it that Kant called intellect.
The best proof of this may lie in the otherwise quite mysterious fact that mathematical reasoning, the purest activity of our brain, and at first glance, because of its abstraction from all qualities given to our senses, the farthest removed
from sheer common-sense reasoning, could play such an
enormously liberating role in science's exploration of the
universe. The intellect, the organ of knowledge and cognition,
is still of this world; in the words of Duns Scotus, it falls under
the sway of nature, *cadit sub natura,* and carries with it all the
necessities to which a living being, endowed with sense organs
and brain power, is subject. The opposite of necessity is not
contingency or accident but freedom. Everything that appears
to human eyes, everything that occurs to the human mind,
everything that happens to mortals for better or worse is
"contingent," including their own existence. We all know:

> Unpredictably, decades ago, You arrived
> among that unending cascade of creatures spewed
> from Nature's maw. A random event, says Science.

But that does not prevent us from answering with the poet:

Random my bottom! A true miracle, say I,
for who is not certain that he was meant to be?[79]

But this being "meant to be" is not a truth; it is a highly meaningful proposition.

In other words, there are no truths beyond and above factual truths: all scientific truths are factual truths, those engendered by sheer brain power and expressed in a specially designed sign language not excluded, and only factual statements are scientifically verifiable. Thus the statement "A triangle laughs" is not untrue but meaningless, whereas the old ontological demonstration of the existence of God, as we find it in Anselm of Canterbury, is not valid and in this sense not true, but it is full of meaning. Knowing certainly aims at truth, even if this truth, as in the sciences, is never an abiding truth but a provisional verity that we expect to exchange against other, more accurate verities as knowledge progresses. To expect truth to come from thinking signifies that we mistake the need to think with the urge to know. Thinking can and must be employed in the attempt to know, but in the exercise of this function it is never itself; it is but the handmaiden of an altogether different enterprise. (Hegel seems to have been the first to protest against the modern development that tends to put philosophy in a position similar to the one it had in the Middle Ages. "Then, philosophy was supposed to be the handmaiden of theology, humbly accepting its achievements, and asked to bring them into a clean logical order and present them in a plausible, conceptually demonstrable context. Now, philosophy is supposed to be the handmaiden of the other sciences. . . . Its task is to demonstrate the methods of the sciences"—something Hegel denounces as "catching the shadow of shadows."[80])

Truth is what we are compelled to admit by the nature either of our senses or of our brain. The proposition that everybody who is "was meant to be" can easily be refuted; but the certainty of the I "was meant to be" will survive refutation intact because it is inherent in every thinking reflection on the I-am.

By drawing a distinguishing line between truth and meaning, between knowing and thinking, and by insisting on its importance, I do not wish to deny that thinking's quest for meaning and knowledge's quest for truth are connected. By posing the unanswerable questions of meaning, men establish themselves as question-asking beings. Behind all the cognitive questions for which men find answers, there lurk the unanswerable ones that seem entirely idle and have always been denounced as such. It is more than likely that men, if they were ever to lose the appetite for meaning we call thinking and cease to ask unanswerable questions, would lose not only the ability to produce those thought-things that we call works of art but also the capacity to ask all the answerable questions upon which every civilization is founded. In this sense, reason is the a priori condition of the intellect and of cognition; it is because reason and intellect are so connected, despite utter difference in mood and purpose, that the philosophers have always been tempted to accept the criterion of truth—so valid for science and everyday life—as applicable to their own rather extraordinary business as well. For our desire to know, whether arising out of practical or purely theoretical perplexities, can be fulfilled when it reaches its prescribed goal, and while our thirst for knowledge may be unquenchable because of the immensity of the unknown, the activity itself leaves behind a growing treasure of knowledge that is retained and kept in store by every civilization as part and parcel of its world. The loss of this accumulation and of the technical expertise required to conserve and increase it inevitably spells the end of this particular world. The thinking activity on the contrary leaves nothing so tangible behind, and the need to think can therefore never be stilled by the insights of "wise men." As far as positive results are concerned, the most we can expect from it is what Kant finally achieved in carrying out his purpose "to extend, albeit only negatively, our use of reason beyond the limitations of the sensorily given world, that is, to eliminate the obstacles by which reason hinders itself."[81]

Kant's famous distinction between *Vernunft* and *Verstand,* between a faculty of speculative thought and the ability to know arising out of sense experience—where "all thought is but a means to reach intuition" ("In whatever manner and by whatever means a cognition may relate to objects, *intuition* is that through which it is in immediate relation to them, and to which all thought is directed as a means")[82]—has consequences more far-reaching, and even perhaps quite other, than those he himself recognized.[83] (While discussing Plato, he once remarked "that it is by no means unusual, upon comparing the thoughts which an author has expressed in regard to his subject . . . to find that we understand him better than he has understood himself. As he has not sufficiently determined his concept, he has sometimes spoken, or even thought, in opposition to his own intention."[84] And this is of course applicable to his own work.) Although he insisted on the inability of reason to arrive at knowledge, especially with respect to God, Freedom, and Immortality—to him the highest objects of thought—he could not part altogether with the conviction that the final aim of thinking, as of knowledge, is truth and cognition; he thus uses, throughout the Critiques, the term *Vernunfterkenntnis,* "knowledge arising out of pure reason,"[85] a notion that ought to have been a contradiction in terms for him. He never became fully aware of having liberated reason and thinking, of having justified this faculty and its activity even though they could not boast of any "positive" results. As we have seen, he stated that he had "found it necessary to deny *knowledge* . . . to make room for *faith,*"[86] but all he had "denied" was knowledge of things that are unknowable, and he had not made room for faith but for thought. He believed that he had built the foundations of a future "systematic metaphysic" as "a bequest to posterity,"[87] and it is true that without Kant's unshackling of speculative thought the rise of German idealism and its metaphysical systems would hardly have been possible. But the new brand of philosophers—Fichte, Schelling, Hegel—would scarcely have pleased Kant. Liberated by Kant from the old school dogmatism and its sterile exercises, encouraged by him to indulge in speculative thinking, they actually took their cue from Descartes, went hunting for certainty, blurred once again the distinguishing line between thought and knowledge, and believed in all earnest that the results of their speculations possessed the same kind of validity as the results of cognitive processes.

What undermined Kant's greatest discovery, the distinction between knowledge, which uses thinking as a means to an end, and thinking itself as it arises out of "the very nature of our reason" and is done for its own sake, was that he constantly compared the two with each other. Only if truth (in Kant, intuition), and not meaning, is the ultimate criterion of man's mental activities does it make sense in this context to speak of deception and illusion at all. "It is impossible," he says, that reason, "this highest tribunal of all the rights and claims of speculation should itself be the source of deceptions and illusions."[88] He is right, but only because reason as the faculty of speculative thought does not move in the world of appearances and hence can produce non-sense and meaninglessness but neither illusion nor deception, which properly belong to the realm of sense perception and common-sense reasoning. He recognizes this himself when he calls the ideas of pure reason only "heuristic," not "ostensive" concepts;[89] they are tentative—they do not demonstrate or show anything. "They ought not to be assumed as existing in themselves, but only as having the reality of a schema . . . [and] should be regarded only as analoga of real things, not as in themselves real things."[90] In other words, they neither reach nor are able to present and represent reality. It is not merely the other-worldly transcendent things that they can never reach; the realness given by the senses playing together, kept in tune by common sense, and that is guaranteed by the fact of plurality—is beyond their grasp. But Kant does not insist on this side of the matter, because he is afraid that his ideas might then turn out to be "empty thought-things" (*leere Gedankendinge*)[91]—as indeed they invariably do when they dare to show themselves nakedly, that is, untransformed and in a way unfalsified by language, in our everyday world and in everyday communication.

It is perhaps for the same reason that he equates what we have here called meaning with Purpose and even Intention (*Zweck* and *Absicht*): The "highest formal unity, which rests solely on concepts of reason, is the *purposive* unity of things. The *speculative* interest of reason makes it necessary to regard all order in the world as if it had originated in the [intention] of a supreme reason."[92] Now, it turns out, reason pursues specific purposes, has specific intentions in resorting to its ideas; it is the need of human reason and its interest in God, Freedom, and Immortality that make men think, even though only a few pages later he will admit that "the mere speculative interest of reason" with respect to the three main objects of thought—"the freedom of the will, the immortality of the soul, and the existence of God"—"is very small; and for its sake alone we should hardly have undertaken the labor of transcendental investigations . . . since whatever discoveries might be made in regard to these matters, we should not be able to make use of them in any helpful manner *in concreto*."[93] But we do not have to go hunting for small contradictions in the work of this very great thinker. Right in the midst of the passages quoted above occurs the sentence that stands in the greatest possible contrast to his own equation of reason with Purpose: "Pure reason is in fact occupied with nothing but itself. It can have no other vocation."[94]

Mental
Activities in
a World of
Appearances

II

## 9   *Invisibility and withdrawal*

Thinking, willing, and judging are the three basic mental activities; they cannot be derived from each other and though they have certain common characteristics they cannot be reduced to a common denominator. To the question What makes us think? there is ultimately no answer other than what Kant called "reason's need," the inner impulse of that faculty to actualize itself in speculation. And something very similar is true for the will, which neither reason nor desire can move. "Nothing other than the Will is the total cause of volition" (*"nihil aliud a voluntate est causa totalis volitionis in voluntate"*), in the striking formula of Duns Scotus, or *"voluntas vult se velle"* ("the will wills itself to will"), as even Thomas, the least voluntaristic of those who thought about this faculty, had to admit.[1] Judgment, finally, the mysterious endowment of the mind by which the general, always a mental construction, and the particular, always given to sense experience, are brought together, is a "peculiar faculty" and in no way inherent in the intellect, not even in the case of "determinant judgments"—where particulars are subsumed under general rules in the form of a syllogism—because no rule is available for the *applications* of the rule. To know how to apply the general to the particular is an additional "natural gift," the want of which, according to Kant, is "ordinarily called stupidity, and for such a failing there is no remedy."[2] The autonomous nature of judgment is even more obvious in the case of "reflective judgment," which does not descend from the general to the particular but ascends "from the particular . . . to the universal" by deciding, without any over-all rules, This is beautiful, this is ugly, this is right, this is wrong; and here for a guiding principle, judging "can only give [it] as a law from and to itself."[3]

I called these mental activities basic because they are autonomous; each of them obeys the laws inherent in the activity itself, although all of them depend on a certain stillness of the soul's passions, on that "dispassionate quiet" (*"leidenschaftslose Stille"*) which Hegel ascribed to "merely thinking cognition."[4] Since it is always the same person whose mind thinks, wills, and judges, the autonomous nature of these activities has created great difficulties. Reason's inability to move the will, plus the fact that thinking can only "understand" what is past but neither remove it nor "rejuvenate" it— "the owl of Minerva begins its flight when dusk is falling"[5] —have led to the various doctrines asserting the mind's impotence and the force of the irrational, in brief to Hume's famous dictum that "Reason is and *ought* only to be the slave of the passions," that is, to a rather simple-minded reversal of the Platonic notion of reason's uncontested rulership in the household of the soul. What is so remarkable in all these theories and doctrines is their implicit monism, the claim that behind the obvious multiplicity of the world's appearances and, even more pertinently for our context, behind the obvious plurality of man's faculties and abilities, there must exist a oneness—the old *hen pan,* "the all is one"—either a single source or a single ruler.

The autonomy of mental activities, moreover, implies their being unconditioned; none of the conditions of either life or the world corresponds to them directly. For the "dispassionate quiet" of the soul is not a condition properly speaking; not only does the mere quiet never cause the mental activity, the urge to think; "reason's need" more often than not quiets the passions. To be sure, the objects of my thinking or willing or judging, the mind's subject matter, are given in the world, or arise from my life in this world, but they themselves as activities are not necessitated or conditioned by either. Men, though they are totally conditioned existentially— limited by the time span between birth and death, subject to labor in order to live, motivated to work in order to make themselves at home in the world, and roused to action in order to find their place in the society of their fellow-men— can mentally transcend all these conditions, but only mentally, never in reality or in cognition and knowledge, by virtue of which they are able to explore the world's realness and their own. They can judge affirmatively or negatively the realities they are born into and by which they are also conditioned; they can will the impossible, for instance, eternal life; and they can think, that is, speculate meaningfully, about the unknown and the unknowable. And although this can never directly change reality—indeed in our world there is no clearer or more radical opposition than that between thinking and doing—the principles by which we act and the criteria by which we judge and conduct our lives depend ultimately on the life of the mind. In short, they depend on the performance of these apparently profitless mental enterprises that yield no results and do "not endow us directly with the power to act" (Heidegger). Absence of thought is indeed a powerful factor in human affairs, statistically speaking the most powerful, not just in the conduct of the many but in the conduct of all. The very urgency, the *a-scholia,* of human affairs demands provisional judgments, the reliance on custom and habit, that is, on prejudices. As to the world of appearances, which affects our senses as well as our soul and our common sense, Heraclitus spoke truly, in words still unburdened by terminology: "The mind is separate from all things" (*sophon esti pantōn kechōrismenon*).[6] It is because of that complete separateness that Kant could believe so firmly in the existence of other intelligible beings in a different corner of the universe, namely, of creatures capable of the same kind of reasonable thought although without our sensory apparatus and without our intellectual brain power, that is, without our criteria for truth and error and our conditions for experience and scientific cognition.

Seen from the perspective of the world of appearances and the activities conditioned by it, the main characteristic of mental activities is their *invisibility*. Properly speaking, they never appear, though they manifest themselves to the thinking, willing, or judging ego, which is aware of being active, yet lacks the ability or the urge to appear as such. The Epicurean *lathē biōsas,* "live in hiding," may have been a counsel of prudence; it is also an at least negatively exact description of the *topos*, the locality, of the man who thinks; in fact, it is the very opposite of John Adams' *"spectemur agendo"* (let us be seen in action). In other words, to the invisible that manifests itself to thinking there corresponds a human faculty that is not only, like other faculties, invisible so long as it is latent, a mere potentiality, but remains non-manifest in full actuality. If we consider the whole scale of human activities from the viewpoint of appearance, we find many degrees of manifestation. Neither laboring nor fabrication requires display of the activity itself; only action and speaking need a space of appearance—as well as people who see and hear—in order to be actualized at all. But none of these activities is invisible. Were we to follow Greek linguistic custom, by which the "heroes," acting men in the highest sense, were called *andres epiphaneis,* men who are fully manifest, highly conspicuous, then we would call thinkers the inconspicuous men by definition and profession.[7]

In this, as in other respects, the mind is decisively different from the soul, its chief competitor for the rank of ruler over our inner, non-visible life. The soul, where our passions, our feelings and emotions arise, is a more or less chaotic welter of happenings which we do not enact but suffer (*pathein*) and which in cases of great intensity may overwhelm us as pain or pleasure does; its invisibility resembles that of our inner bodily organs of whose functioning or non-functioning we are also aware without being able to control them. The life of the mind, on the contrary, is sheer activity, and this activity, like other activities, can be started and stopped at will. The passions, moreover, though their seat is invisible, have an expressiveness of their own: we blush with shame or embarrassment, we grow pale with fear or anger, we can shine with happiness or look dejected, and we need a considerable training in self-control in order to prevent the passions from showing. The only outward manifestation of the mind is absent-mindedness, an obvious disregard of the surrounding world, something entirely negative which in no way hints at what is actually happening within us.

The mere fact of invisibility, that something can be without being manifest to the eye, must always have been striking. How much so may be gauged by the strange disinclination of our whole tradition to draw clear lines between soul, mind, and consciousness, so often equated as objects of our inner sense for no other reason than that they are non-appearing to the outer senses. Thus Plato concluded that the soul is invisible because it is made for the cognition of the invisible within a world of visible things. And even Kant, among the philosophers by far the most critical of traditional metaphysical prejudices, will occasionally enumerate two kinds of objects: " 'I', as thinking, am an object of inner sense, and am called 'soul'. That which is an object of the outer senses is called 'body'."[8] This, of course, is but a variation of the old metaphysical two-world theory. An analogy is made to the outwardness of sense experience, on the assumption that an internal space houses what is within us in the same way that external space provides for our bodies, so that an "inner sense," namely, the intuition of introspection, is pictured as fitted to ascertain whatever goes on "within" with the same reliability our outer senses have in dealing with the outer world. And for the soul, the analogy is not too misleading. Since feelings and emotions are not self-made but "passions" caused by outside events that affect the soul and bring about certain reactions, namely, the soul's *pathēmata*—its passive states and moods—these inner experiences may indeed be open to the inner sense of introspection precisely because they are possible, as Kant once remarked, "only on the assumption of outer experience."[9] Moreover, their very passivity, the fact that they are not liable to be changed by deliberate intervention, results in an impressive semblance of stability. This semblance then produces certain illusions of introspection, which in turn lead to the theory that the mind is not merely the master of its own activities but can rule the soul's passions—as though the mind were nothing but the soul's highest organ. This theory is very old and reached its climax in the Stoic doctrines of the mind's control of pleasure and pain; its fallacy—that you can *feel* happy when roasted in the Phalarian Bull—rests ultimately on the equation of soul and mind, that is, on ascribing to the soul and its essential passivity the powerful sovereignty of the mind.

No mental act, and least of all the act of thinking, is content with its object as it is given to it. It always transcends

the sheer givenness of whatever may have aroused its attention and transforms it into what Petrus Johannis Olivi, the
thirteenth-century Franciscan philosopher of the Will,[10] called
an *experimentum suitatis,* an experiment of the self with
itself. Since plurality is one of the basic existential conditions of human life on earth—so that *inter homines esse,* to
be among men, was to the Romans the sign of being alive,
aware of the realness of world and self, and *inter homines esse
desinere,* to cease to be among men, a synonym for dying—to
be by myself and to have intercourse with myself is the
outstanding characteristic of the life of the mind. The mind
can be said to have a life of its own only to the extent that it
actualizes this intercourse in which, existentially speaking,
plurality is reduced to the duality already implied in the
fact and the word "consciousness," or *syneidenai*—to know
with myself. I call this existential state in which I keep myself
company "solitude" to distinguish it from "loneliness," where
I am also alone but now deserted not only by human company
but also by the possible company of myself. It is only in loneliness that I feel *deprived* of human company, and it is only
in the acute awareness of such deprivation that men ever exist
really in the singular, as it is perhaps only in dreams or in
madness that they fully realize the unbearable and "unutter-
able horror" of this state.[11] Mental activities themselves all
testify by their *reflexive* nature to a *duality* inherent in consciousness; the mental agent cannot be active except by acting,
implicitly or explicitly, back upon himself. Consciousness, to
be sure—Kant's "I think"—not only accompanies "all other
representations" but all my activities, in which nevertheless
I can be entirely oblivious of my self. Consciousness as such,
before it is actualized in solitude, achieves nothing more than
an awareness of the sameness of the I-am—"I am conscious of
myself, not as I appear to myself, nor as I am in myself, but
only that I am"[12]—which guarantees the identical continuity
of a self throughout the manifold representations, experiences,
and memories of a lifetime. As such, it "expresses the act of
determining my existence."[13] Mental activities, and, as we
shall see later, especially thinking—the soundless dialogue of

the I with itself—can be understood as the actualization of the
original duality or the split between me and myself which
is inherent in all consciousness. But this sheer self-awareness,
of which I am, as it were, unconsciously conscious, is not an
activity; by accompanying all other activities it is the guaran-
tor of an altogether silent I-am-I.

The life of the mind in which I keep myself company may
be soundless; it is never silent and it can never be altogether
oblivious of itself, because of the reflexive nature of all its
activities. Every *cogitare,* no matter what its object, is also a
*cogito me cogitare,* every volition a *volo me velle,* and even
judgment is possible, as Montesquieu once remarked, only
through a *"retour secret sur moi-même."* This reflexivity seems
to point to a place of inwardness for mental acts, construed on
the principle of the outward space in which my non-mental
acts take place. But that this inwardness, unlike the passive
inwardness of the soul, could only be understood as a site
of activities is a fallacy, whose historical orgin is the discovery, in the early centuries of the Christian era, of the Will
and of the experiences of the willing ego. For I am aware of
the faculties of the mind and their reflexivity only as long as
the activity lasts. It is as though the very organs of thought
or will or judgment came into being only when I think, or will,
or judge; in their latent state, assuming that such latency
exists prior to actualization, they are not open to introspection. The thinking ego, of which I am perfectly conscious
so long as the thinking activity lasts, will disappear as though
it were a mere mirage when the real world asserts itself again.

Since mental activities, non-appearing by definition, occur
in a world of appearances and in a being that partakes of these
appearances through its receptive sense organs as well as
through its own ability and urge to appear to others, they
cannot come into being except through a deliberate *with-*
*drawal* from appearances. It is withdrawal not so much from
the world—only thought, because of its tendency to generalize, i.e., its special concern for the general as opposed to the
particular, tends to withdraw from the world altogether—as
from the world's being *present* to the senses. *Every mental*

*act rests on the mind's faculty of having present to itself what is absent from the senses.* Re-presentation, making present what is actually absent, is the mind's unique gift, and since our whole mental terminology is based on metaphors drawn from vision's experience, this gift is called *imagination,* defined by Kant as "the faculty of intuition even without the presence of the object."[14] The mind's faculty of making present what is absent is of course by no means restricted to mental images of absent objects; memory quite generally stores, and holds at the disposition of recollection, whatever is *no more,* and the will anticipates what the future may bring but is *not yet.* Only because of the mind's capacity for making present what is absent can we say "no more" and constitute a past for ourselves, or say "not yet" and get ready for a future. But this is possible for the mind only after it has withdrawn from the present and the urgencies of everyday life. Thus, in order to will, the mind must withdraw from the immediacy of desire, which, without reflecting and without reflexivity, stretches out its hand to get hold of the desired object; for the will is not concerned with objects but with projects, for instance, with the future availability of an object that it may or may not desire in the present. The will transforms the desire into an intention. And judgment, finally, be it aesthetic or legal or moral, presupposes a definitely "unnatural" and deliberate withdrawal from involvement and the partiality of immediate interests as they are given by my position in the world and the part I play in it.

It would be wrong, I believe, to try to establish a hierarchical order among the mind's activities, but I also believe that it is hardly deniable that an order of priorities exists. It is inconceivable how we would ever be able to will or to judge, that is, to handle things which are not yet and things which are no more, if the power of representation and the effort necessary to direct mental attention to what in every way escapes the attention of sense perception had not gone ahead and prepared the mind for further reflection as well as for willing and judging. In other words, what we generally call "thinking," though unable to move the will or provide judgment with general rules, must prepare the particulars given to the senses in such a way that the mind is able to handle them in their absence; it must, in brief, *de-sense* them.

The best description of this process of preparation I know of is given by Augustine. Sense perception, he says, "the vision, which was without when the sense was formed by a sensible body, is succeeded by a similar vision within," the image that re-presents it.[15] This image is then stored in memory, ready to become a "vision in thought" the moment the mind gets hold of it; it is decisive that "what remains in the memory"—the mere image of what once was real—is different from the "vision in thought"—the deliberately remembered object. "What remains in the memory . . . is one thing, and . . . something else arises when we remember,"[16] for "what is hidden and retained in the memory is one thing, and what is impressed by it in the thought of the one remembering is another thing."[17] Hence, the thought-object is different from the image, as the image is different from the visible sense-object whose mere representation it is. It is because of this twofold transformation that thinking "in fact goes even further," beyond the realm of all possible imagination, "when our reason proclaims the infinity of number which no vision in the thought of corporeal things has yet grasped" or "teaches us that even the tiniest bodies can be divided infinitely."[18] Imagination, therefore, which transforms a visible object into an invisible image, fit to be stored in the mind, is the condition *sine qua non* for providing the mind with suitable thought-objects; but these thought-objects come into being only when the mind actively and deliberately remembers, recollects and selects from the storehouse of memory whatever arouses its interest sufficiently to induce concentration; in these operations the mind learns how to deal with things that are absent and prepares itself to "go further," toward the understanding of things that are always absent, that cannot be remembered because they were never present to sense experience.

Although this last class of thought-objects—concepts, ideas, categories, and the like—became the special subject matter of "professional" philosophy, there is nothing in the ordinary life of man that cannot become food for thought, that is, be subjected to the twofold transformation that readies a sense-object to become a suitable thought-object. All the metaphysical questions that philosophy took as its special topics arise out of ordinary common-sense experiences; "reason's need"—the quest for meaning that prompts men to ask them—is in no way different from men's need to tell the story of some happening they witnessed, or to write poems about it. In all such reflecting activities men move outside the world of appearances and use a language filled with abstract words which, of course, had long been part and parcel of everyday speech before they became the special currency of philosophy. For thinking, then, though not for philosophy, technically speaking, withdrawal from the world of appearances is the only essential precondition. In order for us to think about somebody, he must be removed from our presence; so long as we are with him we do not think either of him or about him; thinking always implies remembrance; every thought is strictly speaking an after-thought. It may, of course, happen that we start thinking about a still-present somebody or something, in which case we have removed ourselves surreptitiously from our surroundings and are conducting ourselves as though we were already absent.

These remarks may indicate why thinking, the quest for meaning—as opposed to the thirst for knowledge, even for knowledge for its own sake—has so often been felt to be unnatural, as though men, whenever they reflect without purpose, going beyond the natural curiosity awakened by the manifold wonders of the world's sheer thereness and their own existence, engaged in an activity *contrary to the human condition.* Thinking as such, not only the raising of the unanswerable "ultimate questions," but every reflection that does not serve knowledge and is not guided by practical needs and aims, is, as Heidegger once observed, *"out of order"* (italics added).[19] It interrupts any doing, any ordinary activities, no matter what they happen to be. All thinking demands a *stop-and-think.* Whatever the fallacies and the absurdities of the two-world theories may have been, they arose out of these genuine experiences of the thinking ego. And since whatever prevents thinking belongs to the world of appearances and to those common-sense experiences I have in company with my fellow-men and that automatically guarantee my sense of the realness of my own being, it is indeed as though thinking paralyzed me in much the same way as an excess of consciousness may paralyze the automatism of my bodily functions, *"l'accomplissement d'un acte qui doit être réflexe ou ne peut être,"* as Valéry phrases it. Identifying the state of consciousness with the state of thinking, he added: *"on en pourrait tirer toute une philosophie que je résumerais ainsi: Tantôt je pense et tantôt je suis"* ("At times I think, and at times I am").[20] This striking observation, entirely based on equally striking experiences—namely, that the mere consciousness of our bodily organs is enough to prevent them from functioning properly—insists on an antagonism between being and thinking which we can trace back to Plato's famous saying that only the philosopher's body—that is, what makes him appear among appearances—still inhabits the city of men, as though, by thinking, men removed themselves from the world of the living.

Throughout the history of philosophy a very curious notion has persisted of an affinity between death and philosophy. Philosophy for many centuries was supposed to teach men how to die; it was in this vein that the Romans decided that the study of philosophy was a fit occupation only for the old, whereas the Greeks had held that it should be studied by the young. Still, it was Plato who first remarked that the philosopher appears to those who do not do philosophy as though he were pursuing death,[21] and it was Zeno, the founder of Stoicism, who, still in the same century, reported that the Delphic oracle, on his asking it what he should do to attain the best life, had answered: "Take on the color of the dead."[22] In modern times it is not uncommon to find people holding, with Schopenhauer, that our mortality is the eternal source of philosophy, that "death actually is the inspiring genius of philosophy . . . [and that] without death there would scarcely be any philosophizing."[23] Even the younger Heidegger of *Sein und Zeit* still treated the anticipation of death as the decisive experience through which man can attain an authentic self and be liberated from the inauthenticity of the They, quite unaware of the extent to which this doctrine actually sprang, as Plato had pointed out, from the opinion of the many.

## 10  *The intramural warfare between thought and common sense*

"Take on the color of the dead"—so indeed the philosopher's absent-mindedness and the style of life of the *professional* who devotes his entire life to thinking, thus monopolizing and raising to an absolute what is but one of the many human faculties, must appear to the common sense of common men, since we normally move in a world where the most radical experience of disappearing is death and withdrawal from appearance is dying. The very fact that there have always—at least since Parmenides—been men who chose this way of life deliberately without being candidates for suicide shows that this sense of an affinity with death does not come from the thinking activity and the experiences of the thinking ego itself. It is, rather, the philosopher's own common sense—his being "a man like you and me"—that makes him aware of being "out of order" while engaged in thinking. He is not immune from common opinion, because he shares, after all, in the "common-ness" of all men, and it is his own sense of realness that makes him suspect the thinking activity. And since thinking itself is helpless against the arguments of common-sense reasoning and the insistence on the "meaninglessness" of its quest for meaning, the philosopher is prone to answer in common-sense terms, which he simply turns upside down for the purpose. If common sense and common opinion hold that "death is the greatest of all evils," the philosopher (of Plato's time, when death was understood as the separation of soul from body) is tempted to say: on the contrary, "death is a deity, a benefactor to the philosopher, precisely because it dissolves the union of soul and body"[24] and thus seems to liberate the mind from bodily pain and pleasure, both of which prevent our mental organs from pursuing their activity, just as consciousness prevents our bodily organs from functioning properly.[25] The whole history of philosophy, which tells us so much about the objects of thought and so little about the process of thinking and the experiences of the thinking ego, is shot through with an *intramural warfare* between man's common sense, this sixth sense that fits our five senses into a common world, and man's faculty of thought and need of reason, which determine him to remove himself for considerable periods from it.

The philosophers have interpreted that intramural warfare as the natural hostility of the many and their opinions toward the few and their truth; but the historical facts to support this interpretation are rather scanty. There is, to be sure, the trial of Socrates, which probably inspired Plato to declare at the end of the Cave parable (when the philosopher returns from his solitary flight into the sky of the ideas to the darkness of the cave and the company of his fellow-men) that the many, if they only could, would lay hands on the few and kill them. This interpretation of Socrates' trial echoes through the history of philosophy up to and including Hegel. Yet, leaving aside some very justified doubts about Plato's version of the event,[26] the fact is, there are hardly any instances on record of the many on their own initiative declaring war on philosophers. As far as the few and the many are concerned, it has been rather the other way round. It was the philosopher who of his own accord quitted the City of men and then told those he had left behind that, at best, they were deceived by the trust they put in their senses, by their willingness to believe the poets and be taught by the populace, when they should have been using their minds, and that, at worst, they were content to live only for sensual pleasure and to be glutted like cattle.[27] It seems rather obvious that the multitude can never resemble a philosopher, but this does not mean, as Plato stated, that those who do philosophy are "necessarily blamed" and persecuted by the many "like a man fallen among wild beasts."[28]

The philosopher's way of life is solitary, but this solitude is freely chosen, and Plato himself, when he enumerates the natural conditions favorable to the development in "the noblest natures" of the philosophical gift, does not mention the hostility of the many. He speaks, rather, of exiles, of a "great mind born in a petty state whose affairs are beneath . . . notice," and of other circumstances such as ill health that cut such natures off from the public affairs of the many.[29] But this turning-of-the-tables, to make the warfare between thought and common sense the result of the few turning against the many, though perhaps a shade more plausible and better documented—to wit, on the philosopher's claim to rule—than the traditional persecution mania of the philosopher, is probably no nearer the truth. The most plausible explanation of the quarrel between common sense and "professional" thinking still is the point already mentioned (that we are dealing here with an intramural warfare) since surely the first to be aware of all the objections common sense could raise against philosophy must have been the philosophers themselves. And Plato—in a different context, where he is not concerned with a polity "worthy of the philosophical nature"—dismisses with laughter a question raised as to whether a man who is concerned with divine things is also good at things human.[30]

Laughter rather than hostility is the natural reaction of the many to the philosopher's preoccupation and the apparent uselessness of his concerns. This laughter is innocent and quite different from the ridicule frequently turned on an opponent in serious disputes, where it can indeed become a fearful weapon. But Plato, who argued in the *Laws* for the strict prohibition of any writing that would ridicule any of the citizens,[31] feared the ridicule in all laughter. What is decisive here are not the passages in the political dialogues, the *Laws* or the *Republic*, against poetry and especially comedians, but the entirely serious way in which he tells the story of the Thracian peasant girl who bursts out laughing when she saw Thales fall into a well while he was watching the motions of the heavenly bodies above him, "declaring that he was eager to know the things in the sky, but what was . . . just at his feet escaped him." And Plato adds: "Anyone who gives his life to philosophy is open to such mockery. . . . The whole rabble will join the peasant girl in laughing at

him . . . [as] in his helplessness he looks like a fool."[32]
It is strange that in the long history of philosophy it occurred only to Kant—who was so singularly free of all the
specifically philosophical vices—that the gift for speculative
thought could be like the gift "with which Juno honored
Tiresias, whom she blinded so that she might give him the
gift of prophecy." He suspected that intimate acquaintance
with another world could be "attained here only by forfeiting
some of the sense one needs for the present world." Kant, at
any rate, seems to have been unique among the philosophers
in being sovereign enough to join in the laughter of the
common man. Probably quite unaware of Plato's story of the
Thracian girl, he tells in perfectly good humor a virtually
identical tale about Tycho de Brahe and his coachman: the
astronomer had proposed that they take their bearings from
the stars to find the shortest way during a night journey, and
the coachman had replied: "My dear sir, you may know a
lot about the heavenly bodies; but here on earth you are a
fool."[33]

On the assumption that the philosopher does not need the
"rabble" to inform him of his "foolishness"—the common sense
he shares with all men must be alert enough for him to anticipate their laughter—on the assumption, in short, that what
we are dealing with is an intramural warfare between common-
sense reasoning and speculative thinking going on in the
mind of the philosopher himself, let us examine more closely
the affinity between death and philosophy. If we take our
perspective from the world of appearances, the common
world in which we appeared by birth and from which we shall
disappear by death, then the wish to know our common
habitat and amass all kinds of knowledge about it is natural.
Because of thinking's need to transcend it, we have turned
away; in a metaphorical sense, we have *dis*appeared from this
world, and this can be understood—from the perspective of the
natural and of our common-sense reasoning—as the anticipation of our final departure, that is, our death.

That is how Plato described it in the *Phaedo:* Seen from
the perspective of the multitude, the philosophers do nothing
but pursue death, from which the many, if they cared at

all, might conclude that philosophers had better die.[34] And
Plato is not so sure that the many are not right, except that
they do not know in what sense that is to be construed. The
"true philosopher," one who spends his whole life in thought,
has two desires: first, that he may be free from all kinds of
business and especially be rid of his body, which always demands to be taken care of, "falls in our way at every step . . .
and causes confusion and trouble and panic,"[35] and second,
that he may come to live in a hereafter where those things
with which thinking is concerned, such as truth, justice, and
beauty, will be no less accessible and real than what now
can be perceived with the bodily senses.[36] Even Aristotle, in
one of his popular writings, reminds his readers of those
"islands of the blessed" that are blessed because there "men
would not need anything and none of the other things could
be of any use to them so that only thinking and contemplating (*theōrein*) would be left, that is, what even now we call
a free life."[37] In short, the turning-about inherent in thinking is
by no means a harmless enterprise. In the *Phaedo* it reverses
all relationships: men, who naturally shun death as the greatest
of evils, are now turning to it as the greatest good.

All of this is of course spoken with tongue in cheek—or,
more academically, it is put into metaphorical language;
philosophers are not famous for their suicides, not even when
they hold with Aristotle (in a surprisingly personal remark in
the *Protreptikos*)[38] that those who want to enjoy themselves
should either philosophize or depart from life, all else seems
to be foolish talk and nonsense. But the metaphor of death,
or, rather, the metaphorical reversal of life and death—what
we usually call life is death, what we usually call death is life—
is not arbitrary, although one can see it a bit less dramatically:
If thinking establishes its own conditions, blinding itself
against the sensorily given by removing all that is close at
hand, it is in order to make room for the distant to become manifest. To put it quite simply, in the proverbial absent-
mindedness of the philosopher, everything present is absent
because something actually absent is present to his mind, and
among the things absent is the philosopher's own body. Both
the philosopher's hostility toward politics, "the petty affairs

of men,"[39] and his hostility toward the body have little to do with individual convictions and beliefs; they are inherent in the experience itself. While you are thinking, you are unaware of your own corporality—and it is this experience that made Plato ascribe immortality to the soul once it has departed from the body and made Descartes conclude "that the soul can think without the body except that so long as the soul is attached to the body it may be bothered in its operations by the bad disposition of the body's organs."[40]

*Mnemosyne*, Memory, is the mother of the Muses, and remembrance, the most frequent and also the most basic thinking experience, has to do with things that are absent, that have disappeared from my senses. Yet the absent that is summoned up and made present to my mind—a person, an event, a monument—cannot appear in the way it appeared to my senses, as though remembrance were a kind of witchcraft. In order to appear to my mind only, it must first be de-sensed, and the capacity to transform sense-objects into images is called "imagination." Without this faculty, which makes present what is absent in a de-sensed form, no thought processes and no trains of thought would be possible at all. Hence, thinking is "out of order" not merely because it stops all the other activities so necessary for the business of living and staying alive, but because it inverts all ordinary relationships: what is near and appears directly to our senses is now far away and what is distant is actually present. While thinking I am not where I actually am; I am surrounded not by sense-objects but by images that are invisible to everybody else. It is as though I had withdrawn into some never-never land, the land of invisibles, of which I would know nothing had I not this faculty of remembering and imagining. Thinking annihilates temporal as well as spatial distances. I can anticipate the future, think of it as though it were already present, and I can remember the past as though it had not disappeared.

Since time and space in ordinary experience cannot even be thought of without a continuum that stretches from the nearby into the distant, from the *now* into past or future, from *here* to any point in the compass, left and right, forward and backward, above and below, I could with some justification say that not only distances but also time and space themselves are abolished in the thinking process. As far as space is concerned, I know of no philosophical or metaphysical concept that could plausibly be related to this experience; but I am rather certain that the *nunc stans,* the "standing now," became the symbol of eternity—the "*nunc aeternitatis*" (Duns Scotus)— for medieval philosophy because it was a plausible description of experiences that took place in meditation as well as in contemplation, the two modes of thought known to Christianity.

Just now, I chose to speak first of de-sensed sense-objects, that is, of invisibles belonging to the world of appearances that have temporarily disappeared from or have not yet reached our field of perception and are drawn into our presence by remembering or anticipation. What actually occurs in these instances is told for all time in the story of Orpheus and Eurydice. Orpheus went down to Hades to recover his dead wife and was told he could have her back on condition that he would not turn to look at her as she followed him. But when they approached the world of the living, Orpheus did look back and Eurydice immediately vanished. More precisely than could any terminological language, the old myth tells what happens the moment the thinking process comes to an end in the world of ordinary living: all the invisibles vanish again. It is fitting, too, that the myth should relate to remembrance and not to anticipation. The faculty of anticipating the future in thought derives from the faculty of remembering the past, which in turn derives from the even more elementary ability to de-sense and have present *before* (and not just *in*) your mind what is physically absent. The ability to create fictive entities *in* your mind, such as the unicorn and the centaur, or the fictitious characters of a story, an ability usually called *productive* imagination, is actually entirely dependent upon the so-called reproductive imagination; in "productive" imagination, elements from the visible world are rearranged, and this is possible because the elements, now so freely handled, have already gone through the de-sensing process of thinking.

Not sense perception, in which we experience things directly and close at hand, but imagination, coming after it, prepares the objects of our thought. Before we raise such questions as What is happiness, what is justice, what is knowledge, and so on, we must have seen happy and unhappy people, witnessed just and unjust deeds, experienced the desire to know and its fulfillment or frustration. Furthermore, we must repeat the direct experience in our minds *after* leaving the scene where it took place. To say it again, every thought is an after-thought. By repeating in imagination, we *de-sense* whatever had been given to our senses. And only in this immaterial form can our thinking faculty now begin to concern itself with these data. This operation precedes all thought processes, cognitive thought as well as thought about meaning, and only sheer logical reasoning—where the mind in strict consistency with its own laws produces a deductive chain from a given premise—has definitely cut all strings to living experience; and it can do so only because the premise, either fact or hypothesis, is supposed to be self-evident, and therefore not subject to examination by thought. Even the simple *telling* of what has happened, whether the story then tells it as it was or fails to do so, is *preceded* by the de-sensing operation. The Greek language has this time element in its very vocabulary: the word "to know," as I pointed out earlier, is a derivative of the word "to see." To see is *idein*, to know is *eidenai*, that is, to *have* seen. First you see, then you know.

To vary this for our purposes: All thought arises out of experience, but no experience yields any meaning or even coherence without undergoing the operations of imagining and thinking. Seen from the perspective of thinking, life in its sheer thereness is meaningless; seen from the perspective of the immediacy of life and the world given to the senses, thinking is, as Plato indicated, a living death. The philosopher who lives in the "land of thought" (Kant)[41] will naturally be inclined to look upon these things from the viewpoint of the thinking ego, for which a life without meaning *is* a kind of living death. The thinking ego, because it is not identical with the real self, is unaware of its own withdrawal from the common world of appearances; from its perspective, it is rather as though the invisible had come forward, as though the innumerable entities making up the world of appearances, which through their very presence distract the mind and prevent its activity, had been positively concealing an always invisible Being that reveals itself only to the mind. In other words, what for common sense is the obvious withdrawal of the mind from the world appears in the mind's own perspective as a "withdrawal of Being" or "oblivion of Being"—*Seinsentzug* and *Seinsvergessenheit* (Heidegger). And it is true, everyday life, the life of the "They," is spent in a world from which all that is "visible" to the mind is totally absent.

And not only is the quest for meaning absent from and good for nothing in the ordinary course of human affairs, while at the same time its results remain uncertain and unverifiable; thinking is also somehow self-destructive. In the privacy of his posthumously published notes, Kant wrote: "I do not approve of the rule that if the use of pure reason has proved something, the result should no longer be subject to doubt, as though it were a solid axiom"; and "I do not share the opinion . . . that one should not doubt once one has convinced one-self of something. In pure philosophy this is impossible. *Our mind has a natural aversion to it*" (italics added).[42] From which it follows that the business of thinking is like Penelope's web; it undoes every morning what it has finished the night before.[43] For the need to think can never be stilled by allegedly definite insights of "wise men"; it can be satisfied only through thinking, and the thoughts I had yesterday will satisfy this need today only to the extent that I want and am able to think them anew.

We have been looking at the outstanding characteristics of the thinking activity: its withdrawal from the common-sense world of appearances, its self-destructive tendency with regard to its own results, its reflexivity, and the awareness of sheer activity that accompanies it, plus the weird fact that I know of my mind's faculties only so long as the activity lasts, which means that thinking itself can never be solidly established as one and even the highest property of the human species—man can be defined as the "speaking animal" in the Aristotelian sense of *logon echōn,* in possession of speech, but not as the thinking animal, the *animal rationale.* None of these charac-teristics has escaped the attention of the philosophers. The curious thing is, however, that the more "professional" the thinkers were and the greater they loom in our tradition of philosophy, the more they were inclined to find ways and means of reinterpreting these inherent traits so as to be armed against common-sense reasoning's objections to the uselessness and unreality of the whole enterprise. The lengths to which philosophers went in these reinterpretations as well as the quality of their arguments would be inexplicable if they had been directed at the famous multitude—which has never cared anyway and remained happily ignorant of philosophical argumentation—rather than prompted primarily by their own common sense and by the self-doubt which inevitably accompanies its suspension. The same Kant who confided his true thinking experiences to the privacy of his notebooks announced publicly that he had laid the foundations of all future metaphysical systems, and Hegel, the last and most ingenious among the system-builders, transformed thinking's undoing of its own results into the mighty power of the negative without which no movement and no development would ever come to pass. For him, the same inexorable chain of developmental consequences which rules organic nature from germ to fruit, in which one phase always "negates" and cancels out the earlier one, rules the undoing of the mind's thinking process, except that the latter, since it is "mediated through consciousness and will," through mental activities, can be seen as "making itself": "Mind is only that which it makes itself, and it makes itself actually into that which it is itself (potentially)." Which, incidentally, leaves unanswered the question of who made the potentiality of the mind to begin with.

I have mentioned Hegel because large portions of his work can be read as a running polemic against common sense, especially the Preface to the *Phenomenology of the Mind*. Very early (1801), he had asserted in a truculent mood, obviously still bothered by Plato's Thracian girl and her innocent laughter, that indeed "the world of philosophy [is for common sense] a world turned upside down."[44] Just as Kant had started out to remedy the "scandal of Reason," namely, that reason when it wished to know got trapped in its own antinomies, so Hegel set out to remedy the impotence of Kantian reason, that "it could achieve no more than an Ideal and an Ought," and declared that reason, on the contrary, by virtue of the Idea is *das schlechthin Mächtige,* the mighty as such.[45]

Hegel's significance in our context lies in the fact that he, perhaps more than any other philosopher, testifies to the intramural warfare between philosophy and common sense, and this by virtue of his being by nature equally gifted as a historian and as a thinker. He knew that the intensity of the thinking ego's experiences is due to their being sheer activity: the mind's "very essence . . . is *action.* It makes itself what it essentially is; it is its own product, its own work." And he knew about its reflexivity: "In this lust of activity it only deals with itself."[46] He even admitted in his own way the mind's tendency to destroy its results: "Thus the mind is at war with itself. It must overcome itself as its own enemy and formidable obstacle."[47] But these insights of speculative reason into what it is actually doing when to all appearances it is doing nothing he transformed into pieces of dogmatic knowledge, treating them as results of cognition, so as to be able to fit them into an all-comprehensive system where they would then have the same reality as the results of other sciences, results which, on the other hand, he denounced as essentially meaningless products of common-sense reasoning, or as "defective knowledge." And indeed the *system* with its strict architectonic organization can give the fleeting insights of speculative reason at least a semblance of reality. If truth is taken to be the highest object of thought, then it follows that "the true is real only as a system"; only as such a mental artifact does it have any chance to appear and acquire that minimum of durability that we demand of anything real—as a mere proposition it will hardly survive the battle of opinions. To make sure of having eliminated the common-sense notion that thinking deals with abstractions and irrelevancies, which indeed it does not, he asserted, always in the same polemical spirit, that "Being is Thinking" (*dass das Sein Denken ist*), that "the spiritual alone is the real," and that only those generalities with which we deal in thinking actually *are.*[48]

No one has fought with more determination against the particular, the eternal stumbling block of thinking, the undisputable thereness of objects that no thought can reach or explain. The highest function of philosophy, according to Hegel, is to eliminate the contingent, and all particulars, everything that exists, are contingent by definition. Philosophy deals with the particulars as parts of a whole, and the whole is the system, a product of speculative thought. This whole, scientifically speaking, can never be more than a plausible hypothesis, which by integrating every particular into an all-comprehensive thought transforms them all into thought-things and thus eliminates their most scandalous property, their realness, together with their contingency. It was Hegel who declared that "the time has come for the elevation of philosophy to a science," and who wished to transform philo-sophy, the mere love of wisdom, into wisdom, *sophia*. In this way he succeeded in persuading himself that "to think is to act"—which this most solitary occupation can never do, since we can act only "in concert," in company and agreement with our peers, hence in an existential situation that effectively prevents thinking.

In sharp contrast to all these theories, framed as a kind of apology for speculative thought, stands the famous, strangely unconnected and always mistranslated remark that occurs in the same Preface to the *Phenomenology* and that expresses directly, unsystematically, Hegel's original experiences in speculative thought: "The true is thus the bacchanalian revel, where no member [i.e., no particular thought] is not drunken, and since every member [every thought] no sooner separates itself [from the train of thought of which it is a mere part] than it dissolves straightaway, the revel is just as much a state of transparent, unbroken quiet." To Hegel, this was how the very "life of truth"—truth that has come alive in the process of thinking—manifests itself to the thinking ego. This ego may not know whether man and the world are real or—see especially Indian philosophy—a mere mirage; it knows only of being "alive" in an elation that always borders on "intoxication"—as Nietzsche once said. How deeply this feeling underlies the whole "system" may be gauged when we encounter it again at the end of the *Phenomenology*: there it is contrasted with the "lifeless"—the emphasis is always on *life*—and expresses itself in Schiller's verses, badly misquoted: "Out of the chalice of this spiritual kingdom / foams forth the mind's infinity." (*"Aus dem Kelche dieses Geisterreiches / schäumt ihm seine Unendlichkeit."*)

## 11 Thinking and doing: the spectator

I have been speaking of the special predicaments of thinking that may be ascribed to the radicalism of its withdrawal from the world. By contrast, neither willing nor judging, though dependent on thought's preliminary reflection upon their objects, is ever caught up in these reflections; their objects are particulars with an established home in the appearing world, from which the willing or judging mind removes itself only temporarily and with the intention of a later return. This is especially true of the will, whose withdrawal phase is characterized by the strongest form of reflexivity, an acting back upon itself: the *volo me velle* is much more characteristic of the will than the *cogito me cogitare* is of thinking. What all these activities have in common, however, is the peculiar *quiet*, absence of any doing or disturbances, the withdrawal from involvement and from the partiality of immediate interests that in one way or another make me part of the real world, a withdrawal referred to earlier (page 76) as the condition prerequisite for all judgment.

Historically, this kind of withdrawal from doing is the oldest condition posited for the life of the mind. In its early, original form it rests on the discovery that only the *spectator*, never the actor, can know and understand whatever offers itself as a spectacle. That discovery greatly contributed to the Greek philosophers' conviction of the superiority of the contemplative, merely onlooking, way of life, whose most elementary condition—according to Aristotle, who was the first to elaborate it[49]—was *scholē*. *Scholē* is not leisure time as we understand it, the leftover spare time of inactivity after a day's work "used for meeting the exigencies of existence,"[50] but the deliberate act of abstaining, of holding oneself back (*schein*) from the ordinary activities determined by our daily wants (*hē tōn anagkaiōn scholē*), in order to act out leisure (*scholēn agein*), which in turn was the true goal of all other activities, just as peace, for Aristotle, was the true goal of war. Recreation and play, in our understanding the natural activities of leisure, belonged, on the contrary, still to *a-scholia*, the state of being deprived of leisure, since play and recreation are necessary for the restoration of the human labor force charged with taking care of life's necessities.

We find this act of deliberate, active non-participation in life's daily business, probably in its earliest, certainly its simplest, form, in a parable ascribed to Pythagoras and reported by Diogenes Laertius:

Life . . . is like a festival; just as some come to the festival to compete, some to ply their trade, but the best people come as spectators [*theatai*], so in life the slavish men go hunting for fame [*doxa*] or gain, the philosophers for truth.[51]

What is stressed here as more noble than the competition for fame and gain is by no means a truth invisible and inaccessible to ordinary men; nor does the place the spectators withdraw to belong to any "higher" region such as Parmenides and Plato later envisioned; their place is in the world and their "nobility" is only that they do not participate in what is going on but look on it as a mere spectacle. From the Greek word for spectators, *theatai*, the later philosophical term "theory" was derived, and the word "theoretical" until a few hundred years ago meant "contemplating," looking upon something from the outside, from a position implying a view that is hidden from those who take part in the spectacle and actualize it. The inference to be drawn from this early distinction between doing and understanding is obvious: as a spectator you may understand the "truth" of what the spectacle is about; but the price you have to pay is withdrawal from participating in it.

The first datum underlying this estimate is that only the spectator occupies a position that enables him to see the whole play—as the philosopher is able to see the *kosmos* as a harmonious ordered whole. The actor, being part of the whole, must *enact* his part; not only is he a "part" by definition, he is bound to the particular that finds its ultimate meaning and the justification of its existence solely as a constituent of a whole. Hence, withdrawal from direct involvement to a standpoint outside the game (the festival of life) is not only a condition for judging, for being the final arbiter in the ongoing competition, but also the condition for understanding the meaning of the play. Second: what the actor is concerned with is *doxa*, a word that signifies both fame and opinion, for it is through the opinion of the audience and the judge that fame comes about. It is decisive for the actor, but not for the spectator, how he appears to others; he depends on the spectator's it-seems-to-me (his *dokei moi*, which gives the actor his *doxa*); he is not his own master, not what Kant would later call autonomous; he must conduct himself in accordance with what spectators expect of him, and the final verdict of success or failure is in their hands.

The withdrawal of judgment is obviously very different from the withdrawal of the philosopher. It does not leave the world of appearances but retires from active involvement in it to a privileged position in order to contemplate the whole. Moreover, and perhaps more significantly, Pythagoras' spectators are members of an audience and therefore quite unlike the philosopher who begins his *bios theōrētikos* by leaving the company of his fellow-men and their uncertain opinions, their *doxai* that can only express an it-seems-to-me. Hence the spectator's verdict, while impartial and freed from the interests of gain or fame, is not independent of the views of others— on the contrary, according to Kant, an "enlarged mentality" has to take them into account. The spectators, although disengaged from the particularity characteristic of the actor, are not solitary. Nor are they self-sufficient, like the "highest god" the philosopher tries to emulate in thought and who, according to Plato, "is forever . . . solitary by reason of his excellence, able to be together, he himself with himself, needing nobody else, neither acquaintance nor friend, he sufficient with himself."[52]

This distinction between thinking and judging only came to the fore with Kant's political philosophy—not surprisingly, since Kant was the first, and has remained the last, of the great philosophers to deal with judgment as one of the basic mental activities. For the point of the matter is that in the various treatises and essays, all written late in Kant's life, the spectator's viewpoint is not determined by the categorical imperatives of practical reason, that is, reason's answer to the question What ought I to do? That answer is moral and concerns the individual qua individual, in the full autonomous independence of reason. As such, in a moral-practical way, he can never claim the right to rebel. And yet, the same individual, when he happens not to act but to be a mere spectator, will have the right to judge and to render the final verdict on the French Revolution on no other grounds than his "wishful participation bordering on enthusiasm," his sharing in the "exaltation of the uninvolved public," his basing himself, in other words, on the judgment of his fellow-spectators, who also had not "the least intention of assisting" in the events. And it was their verdict, in the last analysis, and not the deeds of the actors, that persuaded Kant to call the French Revolution "a phenomenon in human history [which] is not to be forgotten."[53] In this clash between joint, participating action, without which, after all, the events to be judged would never have come into being, and reflecting, observing judgment, there is no doubt for Kant as to which should have the last word. Assuming that history is nothing but the miserable story of mankind's eternal ups and downs, the spectacle of sound and fury "may perhaps be moving for a while; but the curtain must eventually descend. For in the long run, it becomes a farce. And even if the actors do not tire of it—*for they are fools* —the spectator does, for any single act will be enough for him if he can reasonably conclude from it that the never-ending play will be of eternal sameness" (italics added).[54]

This is a telling passage indeed. And if we add to it Kant's conviction that human affairs are guided by the "ruse of nature," which leads the human species, behind the backs of acting men, into a perpetual progress, just as Hegel's "ruse of reason" leads them to the revelation of the Absolute Spirit, we may well be justified in asking if all actors are not fools, or if the spectacle, revealing itself only to the spectator, would not just as well be served by the acts of fools. With more or less sophisticated qualifications, this has always been the secret assumption of the philosophers of history, that is, of those thinkers of the modern age who, for the first time, decided to take the realm of human affairs—Plato's *ta tōn anthrōpōn pragmata*—seriously enough to reflect upon it. And are they right? Is it not true that "something else results from the actions of men than what they intend and achieve, something else than they know or want"? "To give an analogy, a man may set fire to the house of another out of revenge. . . . The immediate action is to hold a small flame to a small part of a beam. . . . [What follows is] a vast conflagration. . . . This result was neither part of the primary deed nor the intention of him who commenced it. . . . This example merely shows that in the immediate action something else may be involved than is consciously willed by the actor."[55] (These are Hegel's words, but they could have been written by Kant.) In either case it is not through acting but through contemplating that the "something else," namely, the meaning of the whole, is revealed. The spectator, not the actor, holds the clue to the meaning of human affairs—only, and this is decisive, Kant's spectators exist in the plural, and this is why he could arrive at a political philosophy. Hegel's spectator exists strictly in the singular: the philosopher becomes the organ of the Absolute Spirit, and the philosopher is Hegel himself. But even Kant, more aware than any other philosopher of human plurality, could conveniently forget that even if the spectacle were always the same and therefore tiresome, the audiences would change from generation to generation; nor would a fresh audience be likely to arrive at the conclusions handed down by tradition as to what an unchanging play has to tell it.

If we speak of the mind's withdrawal as the necessary condition of all mental activities, we can hardly avoid raising the question of the place or region toward which the movement of absenting oneself is directed. I have treated the withdrawal of judgment to the spectator's standpoint prematurely and yet at some length because I wanted to raise the question first in its simplest, most obvious form by pointing to cases where the region of withdrawal is clearly located within our ordinary world, the reflexivity of the faculty notwithstanding. There they are, in Olympia, on the ascending rows of theater or stadium, carefully separated from the ongoing games; and Kant's "uninvolved public" that followed events in Paris with "disinterested pleasure" and a sympathy "bordering on enthusiasm" was present in every intellectual circle in Europe during the early nineties of the eighteenth century—although Kant himself was probably thinking of the crowds in the streets of Paris.

But the trouble is that no such incontestable locality can be found when we ask ourselves where we are when we think or will, surrounded, as it were, by things which are no more or are not yet or, finally, by such everyday thought-things as justice, liberty, courage, that are nevertheless totally outside sense experience. The willing ego, it is true, early found an abode, a region of its own; as soon as this faculty was discovered, in the early centuries of the Christian era, it was localized *within* us, and if somebody were to write the history of inwardness in terms of an inner *life*, he would soon perceive that this history coincides with the history of the Will. But inwardness, as we have already indicated, has problems of its own even if one agrees that soul and mind are not the same. Moreover, the peculiar reflexive nature of the will, sometimes identified with the heart and almost always regarded as the organ of our innermost self, has made this region even harder to isolate. As for thinking, the question of where we are when we think seems to have been raised only by Plato, in the *Sophist*;[56] there, after having determined the sophist's locality, he promised to determine the philosopher's proper locality as well—the *topos noētos* he had mentioned in the earlier dialogues[57]—but he never kept this promise. It may have been that he simply failed to complete the trilogy of *Sophist-Statesman-Philosopher* or that he had come to believe that the answer was implicitly given in the *Sophist*, where he pictures the sophist as "at home in the darkness of Not-being," which "makes him so hard to perceive," "whereas the philosopher . . . is difficult to see because his region is so bright; for the eye of the many cannot endure to keep its gaze fixed on the divine."[58] That answer could indeed be expected from the author of the *Republic* and the Cave parable.


## 12 *Language and metaphor*

Mental activities, invisible themselves and occupied with the invisible, become manifest only through speech. Just as appearing beings living in a world of appearances have an urge to show themselves, so thinking beings, which still belong to the world of appearances even after they have mentally withdrawn from it, have an *urge to speak* and thus to make manifest what otherwise would not be a part of the appearing world at all. But while appearingness as such demands and presupposes the presence of spectators, thinking in its need of speech does not demand or necessarily presuppose auditors: communication with our fellow-men would not necessitate human language with its intricate complexity of grammar and syntax. The language of animals—sounds, signs, gestures—would be amply sufficient to serve all immediate needs, not only for self-preservation and the preservation of the species, but also for making evident the moods and emotions of the soul.

It is not our soul but our mind that demands speech. I referred to Aristotle when I drew a distinction between mind and soul, the thoughts of our reason and the passions of our emotional apparatus, and I called attention to the extent to which the key distinction in *De Anima* is reinforced by a passage in the introduction to his short treatise on language, *De Interpretatione*.[59] I shall come back to the same treatise, for its most interesting point is that the criterion of *logos*, coherent speech, is not truth or falsehood but meaning. Words as such are neither true nor false. The word "centaur," for instance (Aristotle uses the example of "goat-stag," an animal that is half-goat, half-stag), "means something, though nothing true or false, unless one adds 'non-being' or 'being' to it." *Logos* is speech in which words are put together to form a sentence that is totally meaningful by virtue of synthesis (*synthēkē*). Words, meaningful in themselves, and thoughts (*noēmata*) resemble each other (*eoiken*). Hence speech, though always "significant sound" (*phōnē semantikē*), is not necessarily *apophantikos*, a statement or a proposition in which *alētheuein* and *pseudesthai*, truth and falsehood, being and non-being, are at stake. This is not always the case: a prayer, as we saw, is a *logos*, but neither true nor false.[60] Thus implicit in the urge to speak is the quest for meaning, not necessarily the quest for truth. It is also note-worthy that nowhere in this discussion of the relation of lan-guage to thought does Aristotle raise the question of priorities; he does not decide whether thinking is the origin of speaking, as though speech were merely an instrument of communicating our thoughts, or whether thought is the consequence of the fact that man is a speaking animal. In any case, since words—carriers of meaning—and thoughts resemble each other, *think-ing beings have an urge to speak, speaking beings have an urge to think.*

Of all human needs, only "the need of reason" could never be adequately met without discursive thought, and discursive thought is inconceivable without words already meaningful, before a mind travels, as it were, through them—*poreuesthai dia logōn* (Plato). Language, no doubt, also serves communi-cation between men, but there it is needed only because men are thinking beings and as such in need of communicating their thoughts; thoughts do not have to be communicated in order to occur, but they cannot occur without being spoken—silently or sounding out in dialogue, as the case may be. It is because thinking, though it always takes place in words, does not need auditors that Hegel, in agreement with the testi-mony of almost all philosophers, could say that "philosophy is something solitary." And it is not because man is a thinking being but because he exists only in the plural that his reason, too, wants communication and is likely to go astray if deprived of it; for reason, as Kant observed, is indeed "not fit to isolate itself, but to communicate."[61] The function of that soundless speech—*tacite secum rationare*, to "reason silently with oneself," in the words of Anselm of Canterbury[62]—is to come to terms with whatever may be given to our senses in everyday appearances; the need of reason is to *give account, logon didonai,* as the Greeks called it with greater precision, of whatever there may be or may have occurred. This is prompted not by the thirst for knowledge—the need may arise in connection with well-known and entirely familiar phenomena—but by the quest for meaning. The sheer naming of things, the creation of words, is the human way of *appropriating* and, as it were, disalienating the world into which, after all, each of us is born as a newcomer and a stranger.

These observations on the interconnection of language and thought, which make us suspect that no speechless thought can exist, obviously do not apply to civilizations where the written sign rather than the spoken word is decisive and where, consequently, thinking itself is not soundless speech but mental dealing with images. This is notably true of China, whose philosophy may well rank with the philosophy of the Occident. There "the power of words is supported by the power of the written sign, the image," and not the other way round, as in the alphabetic languages, where script is thought of as secondary, no more than an agreed-upon set of symbols.[63] For the Chinese, every sign makes visible what we would call a concept or an essence—Confucius is reported to have said that the Chinese sign for "dog" is the perfect image of dog as such, whereas in our understanding "no image could ever be adequate to the concept" of dog in general. "It would never attain that universality of the concept which renders it valid of all" dogs.[64] "The concept 'dog,'" according to Kant, who in the chapter on Schematism in the *Critique of Pure Reason* clarifies one of the basic assumptions of all Western thinking, "signifies a rule according to which my imagination can delineate the figure of a four-footed animal in a general manner, without limitation to any single determinate figure such as experience, or any possible image that I can represent *in concreto,* actually presents." And he adds, "This schematism of our intellect . . . is an art concealed in the depths of the human soul, whose real modes of activity nature is hardly likely ever to allow us to discover, and to have open to our gaze."[65]

In our context, the relevance of the passage is that our mind's faculty of dealing with invisibles is needed even for ordinary sense experience, for us to recognize a dog as a dog no matter in what form the four-footed animal may present itself. It follows that we should be able to "intuit," in Kant's sense, the general character of an object that is never present to our senses. For these schemata—sheer abstractions—Kant used the word "monogram," and Chinese script can perhaps be best understood as monogrammatical, so to speak. In other words, what for us is "abstract" and invisible, is for the Chinese emblematically concrete and visibly given in their script, as when, for instance, the image of two united hands serves for the concept of friendship. They think in images and not in words. And this thinking in images always remains "concrete" and cannot be discursive, traveling through an ordered train of thought, nor can it give account of itself (*logon didonai*); the answer to the typically Socratic question What is friendship? is visibly present and evident in the emblem of two united hands, and "the emblem liberates a whole stream of pictorial representations" through plausible associations by which images are joined together. This can best be seen in the great variety of composite signs, when, for instance, the sign for "cold" combines "all those notions which are associated with thinking of cold weather" and the activities serving to protect men against it. Poetry, therefore, even if read aloud, will affect the hearer optically; he will not stick to the word he hears but to the sign he remembers and with it to the sights to which the sign clearly points.

These differences between concrete thinking in images and our abstract dealing with verbal concepts are fascinating and disquieting—I have no competence to deal with them adequately. They are perhaps all the more disquieting because amid them we can clearly perceive one assumption we share with the Chinese: the unquestioned priority of vision for mental activities. This priority, as we shall see shortly, remains absolutely decisive throughout the history of Western metaphysics and its notion of truth. What distinguishes us from them is not *nous* but *logos,* our necessity to give account of and *justify* in words. All strictly logical processes, such as the deducing of inferences from the general to the particular or inductive reasoning from particulars to some general rule, represent such justifications, and this can be done only in words. Only Wittgenstein, as far as I know, ever became aware of the fact that hieroglyphic writing corresponded to a notion of truth understood in the metaphor of vision. He writes: "In order to understand the essence of a proposition, we should consider hieroglyphic script, which depicts the facts that it describes. And alphabetic script developed out of it without losing what was essential to depiction."[66] This last remark is of course highly doubtful. What is less doubtful is that philosophy, as we know it, would hardly have come into existence without the Greeks' early reception and adaptation of the alphabet from Phoenician sources.

Yet language, the only medium through which mental activities can be manifest not only to the outside world but also to the mental ego itself, is by no means as evidently adequate for the thinking activity as vision is for its business of seeing. No language has a ready-made vocabulary for the needs of mental activity; they all borrow their vocabulary from words originally meant to correspond either to sense experience or to other experiences of ordinary life. This borrowing, however, is never haphazard or arbitrarily symbolic (like mathematical signs) or emblematic; all philosophic and most poetic language is metaphorical but not in the simple sense of the Oxford dictionary, which defines "Metaphor" as "the figure of speech in which a name or descriptive term is transferred to some object different from, but analogous to, that to which it is properly applicable." There is no analogy between, say, a sunset and old age, and when the poet in a hackneyed metaphor speaks of old age as the "sunset of life" he has in mind that the setting of the sun relates to the day that preceded it as old age relates to life. If therefore, as Shelley says, the poet's language is "vitally metaphorical," it is so to the extent that "it marks the before unapprehended *relations* of things and perpetuates their apprehension"

(italics added).[67] Every metaphor discovers "an intuitive perception of similarity in dissimilars" and, according to Aristotle,
is for this very reason a "sign of genius," "the greatest thing
by far."[68] But this similarity, for Aristotle, too, is not a similarity
present in otherwise dissimilar objects but a similarity of relations as in an *analogy* which always needs four terms and can
be presented in the formula B:A = D:C. "Thus a cup is in
relation to Dionysus what a shield is to Ares. The cup accordingly will be metaphorically described as the 'shield of
*Dionysus.'* "[69] And this speaking in analogies, in metaphorical language, according to Kant, is the only way through
which speculative reason, which we here call thinking, can
manifest itself. The metaphor provides the "abstract," image-
less thought with an intuition drawn from the world of appearances whose function it is "to establish the reality of our
concepts"[70] and thus undo, as it were, the withdrawal from
the world of appearances that is the precondition of mental
activities. This is comparatively easy as long as our thought
merely responds to the claims of our need to know and
understand what is given in the appearing world, that is, so
long as we remain within the limitations of common-sense
reasoning; what we need for common-sense thinking are
*examples* to illustrate our concepts, and these examples are
adequate because our concepts are drawn from appearances—
they are mere abstractions. It is altogether different if reason's
need transcends the boundaries of the given world and leads
us on to the uncertain sea of speculation where "no intuition
can be given which shall be adequate to [reason's ideas]."[71]
At this point metaphor comes in. The metaphor achieves the
"carrying over"—*metapherein*—of a genuine and seemingly
impossible *metabasis eis allo genos*, the transition from one
existential state, that of thinking, to another, that of being an
appearance among appearances, and this can be done only by
*analogies*. (Kant gives as an example of a successful metaphor
the description of the despotic state as a "mere machine (like a
hand mill)" because it is "governed by an individual absolute
will. . . . For between a despotic state and a hand mill there
is, to be sure, no similarity; but there is a similarity in the rules
according to which we reflect upon these two things and their

causality." And he adds: "Our language is full of indirect presentations of this sort," a matter that "has not been sufficiently analyzed hitherto, for it deserves a deeper investigation."[72]) The insights of metaphysics are "gained by *analogy*, not in the usual meaning of imperfect resemblance of two things, but of a *perfect resemblance of two relations between totally dissimilar things*."[73] In the often less precise language of the *Critique of Judgment* Kant also calls these "representations in accordance with a mere analogy" symbolical.[74]

All philosophical terms are metaphors, frozen analogies, as it were, whose true meaning discloses itself when we dissolve the term into the original context, which must have been vividly in the mind of the first philosopher to use it. When Plato introduced the everyday words "soul" and "idea" into philosophical language—connecting an invisible organ in man, the soul, with something invisible present in the world of invisibles, the ideas—he still must have heard the words as they were used in ordinary pre-philosophic language. *Psyche* is the "breath of life" exhaled by the dying, and idea or *eidos* is the shape or blueprint the craftsman must have in front of his mind's eye before he begins his work—an image that survives both the fabrication process and the fabricated object and can serve as model again and again, thus taking on an everlastingness that fits it for eternity in the sky of ideas. The underlying analogy of Plato's doctrine of the soul runs as follows: As the breath of life relates to the body it leaves, that is, to the corpse, so the soul from now on will be supposed to relate to the living body. The analogy underlying his doctrine of ideas can be reconstructed in a similar manner; as the craftsman's mental image directs his hand in fabrication and is the measurement of the object's success or failure, so all materially and sensorily given data in the world of appearances relate to and are evaluated according to an invisible pattern, localized in the sky of ideas.

We know that *noeomai* was first used in the sense of perceiving by the eyes, then transferred to perceptions of the mind in the sense of "apprehend"; finally it became a word for the highest form of thinking. Nobody, we can assume, thought that the eye, the organ of vision, and the *nous*, the

organ of thinking, were the same; but the word itself indicated that the relation between the eye and the seen object
was similar to the relation between the mind and its thought-
object—namely, yielded the same kind of evidence. We know
that no one before Plato had used the word for the artisan's
shape or blue print in philosophical language, just as no one
before Aristotle had used the word *energos,* an adjective indicating someone active, at work, busy, to frame the term
*energeia* denoting actuality in opposition to *dynamis,* mere
potentiality. And the same is true for such standard terms as
"substance" and "accident," derived from the Latin for *hypokeimenon* and *kata symbebēkos*—what underlies as distinct
from what accidentally accompanies. No one before Aristotle
had used in any other sense but accusation the word *katēgoria*
(category), signifying what was asserted in court procedures
about the defendant.[75] In Aristotelian usage this word became
something like "predicate," resting on the following analogy:
just as an indictment (*katagoreuein ti tinos*) hands something
down (*kata*) to a defendant that he is charged with, hence
that belongs to him, the predicate hands down the appropriate
quality to the subject. These examples are all familiar and
could be multiplied. I shall add one more that seems to me
especially telling because of its great importance for philosophical terminology; our word for the Greek *nous* is either
mind—from the Latin *mens,* indicating something like the
German *Gemüt*—or reason. I am concerned here with the latter
only. Reason comes from the Latin *ratio,* derived from the
verb *reor, ratus sum,* which means to calculate and also ratio-
cinate. The Latin translation has a totally different metaphorical content, which comes much closer to the Greek *logos*
than to *nous.* To those who have an understandable prejudice
against etymological arguments, I would like to recall the
common Ciceronian phrase *ratio et oratio,* which would make
no sense in Greek.

The metaphor, bridging the abyss between inward and
invisible mental activities and the world of appearances, was
certainly the greatest gift language could bestow on thinking
and hence on philosophy, but the metaphor itself is poetic
rather than philosophical in origin. It is therefore hardly sur-

prising that poets and writers attuned to poetry rather than to philosophy should have been aware of its essential function. Thus we read in a little-known essay by Ernest Fenollosa, published by Ezra Pound and so far as I know never mentioned in the literature on the metaphor: "Metaphor is . . . the very substance of poetry"; without it, "there would have been no bridge whereby to cross from the minor truth of the seen to the major truth of the unseen."[76]

The discoverer of this originally poetic tool was Homer, whose two poems are full of all kinds of metaphorical expressions. I shall choose from an *embarras de richesses* the passage in the *Iliad* where the poet likens the tearing onslaught of fear and grief on the hearts of men to the combined onslaught of winds from several directions on the waters of the sea.[77] Think of these storms that you know so well, the poet seems to tell us, and you will know about grief and fear. Significantly, the reverse will not work. No matter how long somebody thinks about grief and fear, he will never find out anything about the winds and the sea; the comparison is clearly meant to tell what grief and fear can do to the human heart, that is, meant to illuminate an experience that does not appear. The irreversibility of the analogy distinguishes it sharply from the mathematical symbol used by Aristotle in trying to describe the mechanics of metaphor. For no matter how successfully the metaphor may have hit upon a "perfect resemblance" of relation between two "totally dissimilar things" and how perfectly, therefore, since A obviously is not the same as C and B not the same as D, the formula $B{:}A = D{:}C$ may seem to express it, Aristotle's equation implies reversibility—if $B{:}A = D{:}C$, it follows that $C{:}D = A{:}B$. What is lost in the mathematical reckoning is the actual function of the metaphor, its turning the mind back to the sensory world in order to illuminate the mind's non-sensory experiences for which there are no words in any language. (The Aristotelian formula worked because it dealt only with visible things and actually was applied not to metaphors and their carrying over from one realm to another but to *emblems,* and emblems are already visible illustrations of something invisible—the cup of

Dionysus, a pictograph of the festive mood associated with wine; the shield of Ares, a pictograph of the fury of war; the scales of justice in the hands of the blind goddess, a pictograph of Justice, which weighs deeds without consideration of the persons who did them. The same is true of outworn analogies that have turned into idioms, as in the case in Aristotle's second example: "As old age (D) is to life (C), so is evening (B) to day (A).")

In common parlance of course there are a great many figurative expressions that resemble metaphors without exercising the true function of the metaphor.[78] They are mere figures of speech even if used by poets—"white like ivory," to remain with Homer—and they, too, are often characterized by a transference when some term belonging to one class of objects is referred to another class; thus we speak of the "foot" of a table, as if it were attached to a man or animal. Here the transference moves within the same realm, within the "genus" of visibles, and here the analogy is indeed reversible. But this is by no means always the case even with metaphors that do not directly point to something invisible. In Homer there is another, more complex kind of extended metaphor or simile which, though moving among visibles, points to a hidden story. For instance, the great dialogue between Odysseus and Penelope shortly before the recognition scene in which Odysseus, disguised as a beggar and saying "many false things," tells Penelope that he entertained her husband in Crete, whereupon we are told how "her tears ran" as she listened "and her body was melted, as the snow melts along the high places of the mountains when the West Wind has piled it there, but the South Wind melts it, and as it melts the rivers run full flood. It was even so that her beautiful cheeks were streaming tears, as Penelope wept for her man, who was sitting there by her side."[79] Here the metaphor seems to combine only visibles; the tears on her cheek are no less visible than the melting snow. The invisible made visible in the metaphor is the long winter of Odysseus' absence, the lifeless frigidity and unyielding hardness of those years, which now, at the first signs of hope for a renewal of life, begin to melt away. The tears themselves had only expressed sorrow; their meaning—the thoughts that caused them—became manifest in the metaphor of the snow melting and softening the ground before spring.

Kurt Riezler, who was the first to associate the "Homeric simile and the beginning of philosophy," insists on the *tertium comparationis*, necessary for every comparison, which permits "the poet to perceive and to make known soul as world and world as soul."[80] Behind the opposition of world and soul, there must be a unity that makes the correspondence possible, an "unknown law," as Riezler calls it, quoting Goethe, equally present in the world of the senses and the realm of the soul. It is the same unity that binds together all opposites—day and night, light and darkness, coldness and warmth—each of which is inconceivable in separation, unthinkable unless mysteriously related to its antithesis. This hidden unity becomes then, according to Riezler, the topic of the philosophers, the *koinos logos* of Heraclitus, the *hen pan* of Parmenides; perception of this unity distinguishes the philosopher's truth from the opinions of ordinary men. And in support he quotes Heraclitus: "The god is day night, winter summer, war peace, satiety hunger [all opposites, he is the *nous*]; he changes in the way that fire, when it is mixed with spices, is named according to the scent of each of them."[81]

Philosophy, one is inclined to agree, did go to Homer's school in order to emulate his example. And one's tendency to agree is considerably strengthened by the two earliest, most famous influential of all thought parables: Parmenides' voyage to the gates of day and night and Plato's Cave parable, the former being a poem and the latter essentially poetic, using Homeric language throughout. This suggests at least how right Heidegger was when he called poetry and thinking close neighbors.[82]

If we now try to examine more closely the various ways in which language succeeds in bridging the gulf between the realm of the invisible and the world of appearances, we may tentatively offer the following outline: From Aristotle's suggestive definition of language as a "meaningful sounding out" of words that in themselves are already "significant sounds" that "resemble" thoughts, it follows that thinking is the mental activity that actualizes those products of the mind that are inherent in speech and for which language, prior to any special effort, has already found an appropriate though provisional home in the audible world. If speaking and thinking spring from the same source, then the very gift of language could be taken as a kind of proof, or perhaps, rather, as a token, of men's being naturally endowed with an instrument capable of transforming the invisible into an "appearance." Kant's "land of thought"—*Land des Denkens*—may never appear or manifest itself to our bodily eyes; it is manifest, with whatever distortions, not just to our minds but to our bodily ears. And it is in this context that the mind's language by means of metaphor returns to the world of visibilities to illuminate and elaborate further what cannot be seen but can be said.

Analogies, metaphors, and emblems are the threads by which the mind holds on to the world even when, absent-mindedly, it has lost direct contact with it, and they guarantee the unity of human experience. Moreover, in the thinking process itself they serve as models to give us our bearings lest we stagger blindly among experiences that our bodily senses with their relative certainty of knowledge cannot guide us through. The simple fact that our mind is able to find such analogies, that the world of appearances reminds us of things non-apparent, may be seen as a kind of "proof" that mind and body, thinking and sense experience, the invisible and the visible, belong together, are "made" for each other, as it were. In other words, if the rock in the sea "which endures the swift courses of whistling winds and the swelling breakers that burst against it" can become a metaphor for endurance in battle, then "it is not . . . correct to say that the rock is viewed anthropomorphically, unless we add that our understanding of the rock is anthropomorphic for the same reason that we are able to look at ourselves petromorphically."[83] There is, finally, the fact of the irreversibility of the relationship expressed in metaphor; it indicates in its own manner the absolute primacy of the world of appearances and thus provides additional evidence of the extraordinary quality of thinking, of its being always out of order.

This last point is of special importance. If the language of thinking is essentially metaphorical, it follows that the world of appearances inserts itself into thought quite apart from the needs of our body and the claims of our fellow-men, which will draw us back into it in any case. No matter how close we are while thinking to what is far away and how absent we are from what is close at hand, the thinking ego obviously never leaves the world of appearances altogether. The two-world theory, as I have said, is a metaphysical delusion although by no means an arbitrary or accidental one; it is the most plausible delusion with which the experience of thought is plagued. Language, by lending itself to meta-phorical usage, enables us to think, that is, to have traffic with non-sensory matters, because it permits a carrying-over, *metapherein,* of our sense experiences. There are not two worlds because metaphor unites them.

## 13   *Metaphor and the ineffable*

Mental activities, driven to language as the only medium for their manifestation, each draw their metaphors from a different bodily sense, and their plausibility depends upon an innate affinity between certain mental and certain sensory data. Thus, from the outset in formal philosophy, thinking has been thought of in terms of *seeing,* and since thinking is the most fundamental and the most radical of mental activi-ties, it is quite true that vision "has tended to serve as the model of perception in general and thus as the measure of the other senses."[84] The predominance of sight is so deeply em-bedded in Greek speech and therefore in our conceptual language that we seldom find any consideration bestowed on it, as though it belonged among things too obvious to be noticed. A passing remark by Heraclitus, "The eyes are more exact witnesses than the ears,"[85] is an exception, and not a very helpful one. On the contrary, if one considers how easy it is for sight unlike the other senses to shut out the outside world and if one examines the early notion of the blind bard, whose stories are being listened to, one may wonder why hearing did not develop into the guiding metaphor for thinking.[86] Still, it is not altogether true that, in the words of Hans Jonas, "the mind has gone where vision pointed."[87] The metaphors used by the theoreticians of the Will are hardly ever taken from the visual sphere; their model is either desire as the quintessential property of all our senses— in that they serve the general appetitiveness of a needy and wanting being—or they are drawn from hearing, in line with the Jewish tradition of a God who is heard but not seen. (Metaphors drawn from hearing are very rare in the history of philosophy, the most notable modern exception being the late writings of Heidegger, where the thinking ego "hears" the call of Being. Medieval efforts to reconcile Biblical teaching with Greek philosophy testify to a complete victory of intuition or contemplation over every form of audition, and this victory was, as it were, foreshadowed by the early attempt of Philo of Alexandria to attune his Jewish creed to his Platonizing philosophy. He was still aware of the distinction between a Hebrew truth, which was heard, and the Greek *vision* of the true, and transformed the former into a mere preparation for the latter, to be achieved by divine intervention that had made man's ears into eyes to permit greater perfection of human cognition.[88])

Judgment, finally, in terms of discovery the late-comer of our mental abilities, draws, as Kant knew so well, its metaphorical language from the sense of *taste* (the *Critique of Judgment* was originally conceived as a "Critique of Taste"), the most intimate, private, and idiosyncratic of the senses, somehow the opposite of sight, with its "noble" distance. The chief problem of the *Critique of Judgment* therefore became the question of how propositions of judgment could possibly claim, as they indeed do, general agreement.

Jonas enumerates all the advantages of sight as the guiding metaphor and model for the thinking mind. There is first of all the indisputable fact that no other sense establishes such a safe distance between subject and object; distance is the most basic condition for the functioning of vision. "The gain is the concept of objectivity, of the thing as it is in itself as distinct from the thing as it affects me, and from this distinction arises the whole idea of *theōria* and theoretical truth." Moreover, sight provides us with a "co-temporaneous manifold," whereas all the other senses, and especially hearing, "construct their perceptual 'unities of a manifold' out of a temporal sequence of sensations." Sight permits "freedom of choice . . . dependent . . . on . . . the fact that in seeing I am not yet engaged by the seen object. . . . [The seen object] lets me be as I let it be," whereas the other senses affect me directly. This is especially important for hearing, the only possible competitor sight might have for pre-eminence but which finds itself disqualified because it "intrudes upon a passive subject." In hearing, the percipient is at the mercy of something or somebody else. (This, incidentally, may be why the German language derived a whole cluster of words indicating a position of non-freedom from *hören,* to hear: *gehorchen, hörig, gehören,* to obey, be in bondage, belong.) Most important in our context is the fact brought out by Jonas that seeing necessarily "introduces the beholder," and for the beholder, in contrast to the auditor, the *"present* [is not] the point-experience of the passing *now,"* but is transformed into a *"dimension* within which things can be beheld . . . as a lasting of the same." "Only sight therefore provides the sensual basis on which the mind may conceive the idea of the eternal, that which never changes and is always present."[89]

I mentioned before that language, the only medium in which the invisible can become manifest in a world of appearances, is by no means as adequate for that function as our senses are for their business of coping with the perceptible world, and I suggested that the metaphor in its own way can cure the defect. The cure has its dangers and is never wholly adequate either. The danger lies in the overwhelming evidence the metaphor provides by appealing to the unquestioned evidence of sense experience. Metaphors therefore can be used by speculative reason, which indeed cannot avoid them, but when they intrude, as is their tendency, on scientific reasoning, they are used and misused to create and provide plausible evidence for theories that are actually mere hypotheses that have to be proved or disproved by facts. Hans Blumenberg, in his *Paradigmen zu einer Metaphorologie,* has traced certain very common figures of speech, such as the iceberg metaphor or the various sea metaphors, through the centuries of Western thought, and thereby, almost incidentally, discovered to what an extent typically modern pseudo-sciences owe their plausibility to the seeming evidence of metaphor, which they substitute for the lacking evidence of data. His prime example is the consciousness theory of psychoanalysis, where consciousness is seen as the peak of an iceberg, a mere indication of the floating mass of unconsciousness beneath it.[90] Not only has that theory never been demonstrated but it is undemonstrable in its own terms: the moment a fragment of unconsciousness reaches the peak of the iceberg it has become conscious and lost all the properties of its alleged origin. Yet the evidence of the iceberg metaphor is so overwhelming that the theory needs neither argument nor demonstration; we would find the metaphor's use unobjectionable if we were told that we were dealing with speculations about something unknown—in the same way that former centuries used analogies for speculations about God. The only trouble is that every such speculation carries with it a mental construct in whose systematic order every datum can find its hermeneutic place with an even more stringent consistency than that provided by a successful scientific theory, since, being an exclusively mental construct without need of any real experience, it does not have to deal with exceptions to the rule.

It would be tempting to believe that metaphorical thought is only a danger when resorted to by the pseudo-sciences and that philosophic thought, if it does not claim demonstrable truth, is safe in using appropriate metaphors. Unfortunately this is not the case. The thought-systems of the great philosophers and metaphysicians of the past have an uncomfortable resemblance to the mental constructs of the pseudo-sciences, except that the great philosophers, in contrast to the cocksureness of their inferior brethren, have almost unanimously insisted on something "ineffable" behind the written words, something of which they, when they thought and did not write, were very clearly aware and which nevertheless refused to be pinned down and handed over to others; in short, they insisted that there was something that refused to lend itself to a transformation that would allow it to appear and take its place among the appearances of the world. In retrospect, we are tempted to see these ever-recurring utterances as attempts to warn the reader that he was in danger of a fatal mistake in understanding: what were offered him were thoughts, not cognitions, not solid pieces of knowledge which, once acquired, would dispel ignorance; what, as philosophers, they were primarily concerned with were matters that escape human knowledge, although they had not escaped but even haunted human reason. And since in pursuing these questions the philosophers inevitably discovered a great number of things that are indeed knowable, namely, all the laws and axioms of correct thinking and the various theories of knowledge, they themselves very early blurred the distinction between thinking and knowing.

While Plato still held that the true *archē,* beginning and principle of philosophy, is wonder,[91] Aristotle, in the opening paragraphs of the *Metaphysics,*[92] interpreted—and was the first to do so—this same wonder as mere astonishment or puzzlement (*aporein*); through astonishment men become aware of their ignorance of things that may be known, starting with "things close at hand" and then progressing "from there to greater matters such as the sun and the moon and the stars and the genesis of all things." Men, he said, "philosophized to escape ignorance," and the Platonic wonder was no longer understood as a principle but as a mere beginning: "all men begin by wondering . . . but one must end with the opposite and with what is better [than wondering], as is the case when men learn."[93] Hence, Aristotle, though he, too, in a different context, spoke of a truth *aneu logou,* a truth that refused to be expressed in discourse,[94] would not have said with Plato: Of the subjects that concern me nothing is known, since there exists nothing in writing about them, nor will there ever exist anything in the future. People who write about such things know nothing; they do not even know themselves. For there is no way of putting these things in words like other things that one can learn. Hence, no one who possesses the true faculty of

thinking (*nous*), and therefore knows the weakness of words,
will ever risk framing thoughts in discourse, let alone fix them
in so inflexible a form as that of written letters.[95]

We hear the same, almost in the same words, at the end
of this whole development. Thus Nietzsche, certainly no
Platonist, writes to his friend Overbeck: "My philosophy
. . . can no longer be communicated at least not in print,"[96]
and, in *Beyond Good and Evil:* "One no longer loves one's
insight enough when one communicates it."[97] And Heidegger writes, not about Nietzsche but about himself,
when he says: "The internal limit of all thinking . . . is
that the thinker never can say what is most his own . . .
because the spoken word receives its determination from the
ineffable."[98] To which we may add a few remarks by Wittgenstein, whose philosophical investigations center on the ineffable in a relentless effort to *say* what "the case may *be*":
"The results of philosophy are the uncovering . . . of *bumps* that
the intellect has got by running its head up against the limits
of language." These bumps are what we have called here
"metaphysical fallacies"; they are what "make us see the value
of the discovery." Or: "Philosophical problems arise when language goes on a holiday" (*wenn die Sprache feiert*). The German is equivocal: it can mean "to take a holiday," that is,
language ceases to work, and it can mean "to celebrate," and
would then signify almost the opposite. Or: "Philosophy is a
battle against the bewitchment of our intelligence by language."
The trouble is of course that this battle can be refought only
by language.[99]

Let us return to Plato, since he is, as far as I know, the
only philosopher of rank who has left us more than occasional
remarks on this subject. The main thrust of the argument in
the *Seventh Letter* is not against speaking but against writing.
This repeats in abbreviated form the objections already raised
against writing in the *Phaedrus*. There is first the fact that writing "will implant forgetfulness"; relying on the written word,
men "cease to exercise memory." There is second the written
word's "majestic silence"; it can neither give account of itself
nor answer questions. Third, it cannot choose whom to address,
falls into wrong hands, and "drifts all over the place"; ill-

treated and abused, it is unable to defend itself; the best one can say for it is to call it a harmless "pastime," collecting "a store of refreshment . . . against the day 'when oblivious age comes' " or a "recreation [indulged in] as others regale themselves with drinking parties and the like."[100] But in the *Seventh Letter,* Plato goes further; he does not mention his *agrapha dogmata,* which we know about through a remark by Aristotle,[101] but implicitly denies them, too, when he explicitly asserts that "these things cannot be put into words like other things we learn."

This indeed is very different from what we read in the Platonic dialogues (though that is no reason to believe that the *Seventh Letter* is spurious). Thus we read in the *Statesman* about "likenesses" between the visible and the invisible:

Likenesses which the senses can grasp are available in nature to those real existents . . . so that when someone asks for an account of these existents one has no trouble at all—one can simply indicate the sensible likeness and dispense with any account in words. But to the highest and most important class of existents there are no corresponding visible resemblances. . . . In these cases nothing visible can be pointed out to satisfy the inquiring mind. . . . Therefore we must train ourselves to give . . . an account in words of every existing thing. For the existents which have no visible embodiment, the existents which are of the highest value and the chief importance, are demonstrable only in speech [*logos*] and are not to be apprehended by any other means.[102]

In the *Phaedrus*[103] Plato contrasts the written word with the spoken word as used in "the art of talking things through" (*technē dialektikē*), the "living speech, the original, of which the written discourse may fairly be called a kind of image." The art of living speech is praised because it knows how to select its listeners; it is not barren (*akarpoi*) but contains a semen whence different *logoi,* words and arguments, grow up in different listeners so that the seed may become immortal. But if in thinking we carry out this dialogue with ourselves, it is as though we were "writing words in our souls"; at such times, "our soul is like a book," but a book that no longer contains words.[104] Following the writer, a second craftsman intervenes as we are thinking and he is a "painter," who paints in our soul those images that correspond to the written words. "This happens when we have drawn these opinions and spoken assertions away from sight or any other perception, so that we now somehow *see* the images of what we first opined and spoke about."[105]

In the *Seventh Letter* Plato tells us briefly how this two-fold transformation may possibly come about, how it is that our sense perception can be *talked about* and how this talking about (*dialegesthai*) is next transformed into an image visible only to the soul. We have names for what we see, for instance, the name "circle" for something round; this name can be explained in speech (*logos*) in sentences "composed of nouns and verbs," and we say the circle is a "thing which has every-where equal distances between its extremities and its center." These sentences can lead to the making of circles, of images (*eidōlon*) that can be "drawn and erased, turned out and destroyed," processes of course that do not affect *the* circle as such, which is different from all these circles. Knowledge and mind (*nous*) grasp the essential circle, that is, what all circles have in common, something that "lies neither in the sounds [of speech] nor in the shapes of bodies but in the soul," and this circle is clearly "different from the real circle," perceived first in nature by the eyes of the body, and different, too, from circles drawn according to verbal explanation. This circle in the soul is perceived by the mind (*nous*), which "is closest to it in affinity and likeness." And this inner intuition alone can be called truth.[106]

Truth of the evidential kind, construed on the principle of things perceived by our bodily vision, can be arrived at through the guidance (*diagōgē*) of words in the *dialegesthai*, the discursive train of thought that can be silent or spoken between teacher and disciple, "moving up and down," inquir-ing into "what is true and what is false." But the result, since it is supposed to be an intuition and not a conclusion, will follow suddenly after a long period of questions and answers: "when a flash of insight (*phronēsis*) about everything blazes up, and the mind . . . is flooded with light."[107] This truth itself is beyond words; names from which the thinking process starts are unreliable—"nothing prevents the things that are now called round from being called straight and the straight round"[108]—and words, the reasoned discourse of speech that seeks to explain, are "weak"; they offer no more than "a little guidance" to "kindle the light in the soul as from a leaping spark which, once generated, becomes self-sustaining."[109]

I have cited these few pages from the *Seventh Letter* at some length because they offer an otherwise unavailable insight into a possible incompatibility between intuition—the guiding metaphor for philosophical truth—and speech—the medium in which thinking manifests itself: the former always presents us with a co-temporaneous manifold, whereas the latter necessarily discloses itself in a sequence of words and sentences. That the latter was a mere instrument for the former was axiomatic even for Plato and remained axiomatic throughout the history of philosophy. Thus Kant still says: *"worauf alles Denken als Mittel abzweckt,* [*ist*] *die Anschauung,"* "all thinking is a means of reaching intuition."[110] And here is Heidegger: "The *dialegesthai* has in itself a tendency towards a *noein,* a seeing. . . . It lacks the proper means of *theōrein* itself. . . . This is the basic meaning of Plato's dialectic, that it tends towards a vision, a disclosure, that it prepares the original intuition through the discourses. . . . The *logos* remains tied to vision; if speech separates itself from the evidence given in intuition, it degenerates into idle talk which prevents seeing. *Legein* is rooted in seeing, *horan.*"[111]

Heidegger's interpretation is borne out by a passage in Plato's *Philebus*[112] where the inward dialogue of me with myself is once more mentioned but now on its most elementary level: A man sees an object in the distance and, *since he happens to be alone,* he asks *himself:* What is it that appears there? He answers his own question: It is a man. If "he had someone with him he would put what he said to himself into actual speech, addressed to his companion, audibly uttering the same thoughts. . . . Whereas if he is alone he continues thinking the same thing by himself." The truth here is the seen evidence, and speaking, as well as thinking, is authentic to the extent that it follows the seen evidence, appropriates it by translating it into words; the moment this speech becomes separated from the seen evidence, for instance, when other people's opinions or thoughts are repeated, it acquires the same inauthenticity that for Plato characterizes the image as compared to the original.

Among the outstanding peculiarities of our senses is the fact that they cannot be translated into each other—no sound can be seen, no image can be heard, and so on—though they are bound together by common sense, which for this reason alone is the greatest of them all. I have quoted Aquinas on the theme: "the one faculty [that] extends to all objects of the five senses."[113] Language, corresponding to or following common sense, gives an object its common name; this commonness is not only the decisive factor for intersubjective communication—the same object being perceived by different persons and common to them—but it also serves to identify a datum that appears altogether differently to each of the five senses: hard or soft when I touch it, sweet or bitter when I taste it, bright or dark when I see it, sounding in different tones when I hear it. None of these sensations can be adequately described in words. Our cognitive senses, seeing and hearing, have little more affinity with words than the lower senses of smell, taste, and touch. Something smells *like* a rose, tastes *like* pea soup, feels *like* velvet, that is as far as we can go. "A rose is a rose is a rose."

All this, of course, is only another way of saying that truth, in the metaphysical tradition understood in terms of the sight metaphor, is ineffable by definition. We know from the Hebrew tradition what happens to truth if the guiding metaphor is not vision but hearing (in many respects more akin than sight to thinking because of its ability to follow sequences). The Hebrew God can be heard but not seen, and truth therefore becomes invisible: "Thou shalt not make unto thee any graven image or any likeness of any thing that is in heaven above or that is on the earth beneath." *The invisibility of truth in the Hebrew religion is as axiomatic as its ineffability in Greek philosophy,* from which all later philosophy derived its axiomatic assumptions. And while truth, if understood in terms of hearing, demands obedience, truth understood in terms of vision relies on the same powerful self-evidence that forces us to admit the identity of an object the moment it is before our eyes. Metaphysics, the "awesome science" that "beholds what is insofar as it is" (*epistēmē hē theōrei to on hē on*),[114] could discover a truth which "forced men by the force of necessity" (*hyp' autēs tēs alētheias anagkazomenoi*)[115] because it relied on the same imperviousness to contradiction we know so well from sight experiences. For no discourse, whether dialectical in the Socratic-Platonic sense, or logical, using established rules to draw conclusions from accepted premises, or rhetorical-persuasive, can ever match the simple, unquestioned and unquestionable certainty of visible evidence. "What is it that appears there? It is a man." This is the perfect *adequatio rei et intellectus*,[116] "the agreement of knowledge with its object," which even for Kant was still the definite definition of truth. Kant, however, was aware that for this truth "no general criterion can be demanded. [It] would . . . be self-contradictory":[117] Truth as self-evidence does not need any criterion; it *is* the criterion, the final arbiter, of everything that then may follow. Thus Heidegger, discussing the traditional truth concept in *Sein und Zeit*, illustrates it as follows: "Let us suppose that someone with his back turned to the wall makes the true assumption that 'the picture on the wall is hanging askew.' The assertion is confirmed when the man who makes it turns around and perceives the picture hanging askew on the wall."[118]

The difficulties to which the "awesome science" of metaphysics has given rise since its inception could possibly all be summed up in the natural tension between *theōria* and *logos*, between seeing and reasoning with words—whether in the form of "dialectics" (*dia-legesthai*) or, on the contrary, of the "syllogism" (*syl-logizesthai*), i.e., whether it takes things, especially opinions, apart by means of words or brings them together in a discourse depending for its truth content on a primary premise perceived by intuition, by the *nous*, which is not subject to error because it is not *meta logou*, sequential to words.[119] If philosophy is the mother of the sciences, it is itself the science of the beginnings and principles of science, of the *archai;* and these *archai*, which then become the topic of Aristotelian metaphysics, can no longer be derived; they are given to the mind in self-evident intuition.

What recommended sight to be the guiding metaphor in philosophy—and, along with sight, intuition as the ideal of truth—was not just the "nobility" of this most cognitive of our senses, but the very early notion that the philosopher's quest for meaning was identical with the scientist's quest for knowledge. Here it is worth recalling the strange turn that Aristotle, in the first chapter of the *Metaphysics*, gave to Plato's proposition that *thaumazein*, wonder, is the beginning of all philosophy. But the identification of truth with meaning was made, of course, even earlier. For knowledge comes through searching for what we are accustomed to call truth, and the highest, ultimate form of cognitive truth is indeed intuition. All knowledge starts from investigating the appearances as they are given to our senses, and if the scientist then wants to go on and find out the causes of the visible effects, his ultimate aim is to make appear whatever may be hidden behind mere surfaces. This is true even of the most complicated mechanical instruments, which are designed to catch what is hidden from the naked eye. In the last analysis, confirmation of any scientist's theory comes about through sense evidence—just as in the simplistic model I took out of Heidegger. The tension I alluded to between vision and speech does not enter here; on this level, as in the example quoted, speech quite adequately translates vision (it would be different if the content of the painting and not just its position on the wall had to be expressed in words). The very fact that mathematical symbols can be substituted for actual words and be even more expressive of the underlying phenomena that are forced by instruments to appear, as it were, against their own bent demonstrates the superior efficacy of sight metaphors to make manifest whatever does not need speech as a conveyor.

Thinking, however, in contrast to cognitive activities that may use thinking as one of their instruments, needs speech not only to sound out and become manifest; it needs it to be activated at all. And since speech is enacted in sequences of sentences, the end of thinking can never be an intuition; nor can it be confirmed by some piece of self-evidence beheld in speechless contemplation. If thinking, guided by the old sight metaphor and misunderstanding itself and its function, expects "truth" from its activity, this truth is not only ineffable by definition. "Like children trying to catch smoke by closing their hands, philosophers so often see the object they would grasp fly before them"—Bergson, the last philosopher to believe firmly in "intuition," described very accurately what really happened to thinkers of that school.[120] And the reason for the "failure" is simply that nothing expressed in words can ever attain to the immobility of an object of mere contemplation. Compared to an object of contemplation, meaning, which can be said and spoken about, is slippery; if the philosopher wants to *see* and *grasp* it, it "slips away."[121]

Since Bergson, the use of the sight metaphor in philosophy has kept dwindling, not unsurprisingly, as emphasis and interest have shifted entirely from contemplation to speech, from *nous* to *logos*. With this shift, the criterion for truth has shifted from the agreement of knowledge with its object—the *adequatio rei et intellectus,* understood as analogous to the agreement of vision with the seen object—to the mere *form* of thinking, whose basic rule is the axiom of non-contradiction, of consistency with itself, that is, to what Kant still understood as the merely "negative touchstone of truth." "Beyond the sphere of analytic knowledge it has, as a *sufficient* criterion of truth, no authority and no field of application."[122] In the few modern philosophers who still cling, however tenuously and doubtfully, to the traditional assumptions of metaphysics, in Heidegger and Walter Benjamin, the old sight metaphor has not altogether disappeared but has shrunk, as it were: in Benjamin truth "slips by" (*huscht vorüber*); in Heidegger the moment of illumination is understood as "lightning" (*Blitz*), and finally replaced by an altogether different metaphor, *das Geläut der Stille,* "the ringing sound of silence." In terms of the tradition, the latter metaphor is the closest approximation to the illumination arrived at in speechless contemplation. For though the metaphor for the end and culmination of the thinking process is now drawn from the sense of hearing, it does not in the least correspond to listening to an articulated sequence of sounds, as when we hear a melody, but again to an immobile mental state of sheer receptivity. And since thinking, the silent dialogue of me with myself, is sheer activity of the mind combined with complete immobility of the body—"never am I more active than when I do nothing" (Cato)—the difficulties created by metaphors drawn from the sense of hearing would be as great as the difficulties created by the metaphor of vision. (Bergson, still so firmly attached to the metaphor of intuition for the ideal of truth, speaks of the "essentially active, I might almost say violent, character of metaphysical intuition" without being aware of the contradiction between the quiet of contemplation and any activity, let alone a violent one.[123]) And Aristotle speaks of "philosophical *energeia,* activity" as the "perfect and unhindered activity which [for this very reason] harbors within itself the sweetest of all delights (*"Alla mēn hē ge teleia energeia kai akōlytos en heautē echei to chairein, hōste an eiē hē theōrētikē energeia pasōn hēdistē"*).[124]

In other words, the chief difficulty here seems to be that for thinking itself—whose language is entirely metaphorical and whose conceptual framework depends entirely on the gift of the metaphor, which bridges the gulf between the visible and the invisible, the world of appearances and the thinking ego—there exists no metaphor that could plausibly illuminate this special activity of the mind, in which something invisible within us deals with the invisibles of the world. All metaphors drawn from the senses will lead us into difficulties for the simple reason that all our senses are essentially cognitive, hence, if understood as activities, have an end outside themselves; they are not *energeia,* an end in itself, but instruments enabling us to know and deal with the world.

Thinking is out of order because the quest for meaning produces no end result that will survive the activity, that will make sense after the activity has come to its end. In other words, the delight of which Aristotle speaks, though manifest to the thinking ego, is ineffable by definition. The only possible metaphor one may conceive of for the life of the mind is the sensation of being alive. *Without the breath of life the human body is a corpse; without thinking the human mind is dead.* This in fact is the metaphor Aristotle tried out in the famous seventh chapter of Book Lambda of the *Metaphysics:* "The activity of thinking [*energeia* that has its end in itself] is life."[125] Its inherent law, which only a god can tolerate forever, man merely now and then, during which time he is godlike, is "unceasing motion, which is motion in a circle"[126]— the only movement, that is, that never reaches an end or results in an end product. This very strange notion that the authentic process of thinking, namely, the *noēsis noēseōs*, turns in circles—the most glorious justification in philosophy of the circular argument—has oddly enough never worried either the philosophers or Aristotle's interpreters—partly, perhaps, because of the frequent mistranslations of *nous* and *theōria* as "knowledge," which always reaches an end and produces an end result.[127] If thinking were a cognitive enterprise it would have to follow a rectilinear motion, starting from the quest for its object and ending with cognition of it. Aristotle's circular motion, taken together with the life metaphor, suggests a quest for meaning that for man as a thinking being accompanies life and ends only in death. The circular motion is a metaphor drawn from the life process which, though it goes from birth to death, also turns in circles as long as man is alive. This simple experience of the thinking ego has proved striking enough for the notion of the circular movement to be repeated by other thinkers, even though it stands in flagrant contradiction to their traditional assumptions that truth is the result of thinking, that there is such a thing as Hegel's "speculative cognition."[128] We find Hegel saying, without any reference to Aristotle: "Philosophy forms a circle. . . . [It] is a sequence which does not hang in the air; it is not something which begins from nothing at all; on the contrary, *it circles back into itself*" (italics added).[129] And we find the same notion at the end of Heidegger's "What is Metaphysics?" where he defines the "basic question of metaphysics" as "Why is there anything and not rather nothing?"—in a way thinking's first question but at the same time the thought to which it "always has to swing back."[130]

Yet these metaphors, although they correspond to the speculative, non-cognitive way of thinking and remain loyal to the fundamental experiences of the thinking ego, since they relate to no cognitive capacity, remain singularly empty, and Aristotle himself used them nowhere else—except when he asserts that being alive is *energein,* that is, being active for its own sake.[131] Moreover, the metaphor obviously refuses to answer the inevitable question, Why do we think?, since there is no answer to the question, Why do we live?

In Wittgenstein's *Philosophical Investigations* (written after he had convinced himself of the untenability of his earlier attempt in the *Tractatus* to understand language, and hence thought, as a "picture of reality"—"A proposition is a picture of reality. A proposition is a model of reality as we conceive it"[132]), there is an interesting thought game that may help illustrate this difficulty. He asks: "What does man think for? . . . Does man think because he has found that thinking works? — Because he thinks it advantageous to think?" That would be like asking "Does he bring his children up because he has found it works?" Still, it must be admitted that "we do *sometimes* think because it has been found to work," implying by his italics that this is only "sometimes" the case. Hence: "How can we find out *why* man thinks?" Whereupon he answers: "It often happens that we only become aware of the important *facts,* if we suppress the question 'why?'; and then in the course of our investigations these facts lead us to an answer."[133] It is in a deliberate effort to suppress the question, *Why* do we think? that I shall deal with the question, *What* makes us think?

# What Makes III
# Us Think?

## 14  The pre-philosophic assumptions of
## Greek philosophy

Our question, What makes us think?, does not ask for either causes or purposes. Taking for granted man's need to think, it proceeds from the assumption that the thinking activity belongs among those *energeiai* which, like flute-playing, have their ends within themselves and leave no tangible outside end product in the world we inhabit. We cannot date the moment when this need began to be felt, but the very fact of language and all we know of pre-historical times and of mythologies whose authors we cannot name give us a certain right to assume that the need is coeval with the appearance of man on earth. What we can date, however, is the beginning of metaphysics and of philosophy, and what we can name are the answers given to our question at different periods of our history. Part of the Greek answer lies in the conviction of all Greek thinkers that philosophy enables mortal men to dwell in the neighborhood of immortal things and thus acquire or nourish in themselves "immortality in the fullest measure that human nature admits."[1] For the short time they can bear to engage in it, philosophizing transforms mortals into godlike creatures, "mortal gods," as Cicero says. (It is in this vein that ancient etymology repeatedly derived the key word *"theōrein"* and even *"theatron"* from *"theos."*[2]) The trouble with the Greek answer is that it is inconsistent with the very word "philosophy," love of or desire for wisdom, which cannot very well be ascribed to the gods; in the words of Plato, "No god philosophizes or desires to be wise; for he *is*."[3]

Let me first deal with that strange notion of *athanatizein*—immortalizing—whose influence on the legitimate subject matter of our traditional metaphysics can hardly be overrated. In an earlier chapter, you will remember, I interpreted the Pythagorean parable in terms of judgment, which as a separate

129

faculty was discovered late in the modern age, when Kant, following up the eighteenth-century interest in the phenomenon of taste and its role in aesthetics as well as social intercourse, wrote his *Critique of Judgment*. Historically speaking, this was quite inadequate. The Pythagorean notion of spectatorship had another and more far-reaching significance for the rise of philosophy in the West. Closely connected with the parable's main point of the supremacy of *theōrein,* of contemplating over doing, is the Greek notion of the divine. According to the Homeric religion, the gods were not transcendent, their home was not an infinite beyond but the "brazen sky . . . their sure citadel forever."[4] Men and gods were like each other, both of one kind (*hen andrōn, hen theōn genos*), drawing breath from one mother; the Greek gods, as Herodotus tells us,[5] had the same *physis* as men; but, though *anthrōpophysis,* of the same kind, they still, of course, had certain privileged peculiarities: unlike mortals they were deathless and enjoyed an "easy life." Free of mortal life's necessities, they could devote themselves to spectatorship, looking down from Olympus upon the affairs of men, which for them were no more than a spectacle for their entertainment. The Olympian gods' feeling for the world's spectacular quality—so different from other peoples' notions of divine occupations such as creating and law-giving, founding and governing communities —was a partiality they shared with their less fortunate brothers on earth.

That the passion for seeing, preceding (as we have noted) the thirst for knowledge even grammatically in the Greek language, was the basic Greek attitude to the world seems to me too obvious to require documentation. Whatever appeared —nature and the harmonious order of the *kosmos,* things that had come into being of their own accord and those that human hands had "led into being" ("*agein eis tēn ousian*")[6] (Plato's definition of fabrication [*to poiein*]) as well as whatever human excellence (*aretē*) brought forward in the realm of human affairs—was there primarily to be looked at and admired. What tempted men into a position of mere contemplation was the *kalon,* the sheer beauty of appearances, so that the "highest idea of the good" resided in what shone forth most (*tou ontos phanotaton*),[7] and human virtue, the *kalon k'agathon*, was assessed neither as an innate quality or intention of the actor, nor by the consequences of his deeds—only by the performance, by how he *appeared while* he was doing; virtue was what we would call virtuosity. As with the arts, human deeds had to "shine by their intrinsic merits," to use an expression of Machiavelli's.[8] Whatever existed was supposed, first of all, to be a spectacle fit for the gods, in which, naturally, men, those poor relations of the Olympians, wished to have their share.

Thus Aristotle ascribed the faculty of *logos*, reasoned speech, to the Greeks as distinguished from the barbarians, but the desire to see he ascribed to all men. Thus Plato's cave-dwellers are content to look at the *eidōla* on the screen before them without uttering a single word, unable even to turn to each other and communicate, being chained to their seats by the legs and neck. The many share in the divine passion to see. What was involved in the Pythagorean spectatorship, in the position outside all human affairs, was something divine. And the less time a man needed to take care of his body, and the more time he could devote to such a divine occupation, the closer he came to the way of life of the gods. Moreover, since men and gods were of the same kind, even the divine deathlessness seemed not altogether out of mortal reach; apart from being a constant source of envy, the great name, the precious reward for "great deeds and great words" (Homer), conferred potential immortality—to be sure, a poor substitute. This reward, again, was in the power of the spectator to bestow on the actor. For before the philosophers dealt with what is forever invisible and with what is not merely deathless but truly everlasting, *agenēton*, not only without end but also without beginning, that is, birthless—the Greek gods, as we know from Hesiod's *Theogony*, were deathless but not birthless—the poets and the historians had been dealing with what appears and, in the course of time, disappears from the visibility of the world. Hence, what was involved, prior to the rise of philosophy, in the notion of a position outside the realm of human affairs, can best be clarified if we briefly examine the Greek notion of the function of poetry and the position of the bard.

There exists a report of a lost poem by Pindar. It described a marriage feast of Zeus, where Zeus asked the assembled gods whether their happy blessedness still lacked something. Whereupon the gods begged him to create some new divine beings who would know how to beautify all his great works "with words and music." The new godlike beings Pindar had in mind were the poets[9] and bards who helped men to immortality, for "the story of things done outlives the act" and "a thing said walks in immortality if it has been said well."[10] The bards also, Homer-like, "straightened the story . . . in . . . magic words to charm all men thereafter."[11] They did not merely report, they also set it right (*orthōsas*)—Aias had slain himself from shame, but Homer had known better and "honored him above all men." A distinction is made between a thing done and a thing thought, and this thought-thing is accessible only to the "spectator," to the non-doer.

This concept of the bard comes right out of Homer. The crucial verses occur when Odysseus has come to the court of the Phaeacians and, at the king's order, is entertained by the bard, who sings some story of Odysseus' own life, his quarrel with Achilles: Odysseus, listening, covers his face and weeps, though he has never wept before, and certainly not when what he is now hearing actually happened. Only when he hears the story does he become fully aware of its meaning. And Homer himself says: The bard sings for men *and* gods what the Muse, Mnemosyne, who watches over Remembrance, has put into his mind. The Muse gave him good and bad: she deprived him of eyesight and gave him sweet song.

Pindar, in the lost Zeus poem, must have made clear the subjective as well as the objective side of these early thinking experiences: Both the world and men stand in need of praise lest their beauty go unrecognized. Since men appear in the world of appearances, they need spectators, and those who come as spectators to the festival of life are filled with admiring thoughts which are then uttered in words. Without spectators the world would be imperfect; the participant, absorbed as he is in particular things and pressed by urgent business, cannot see how all the particular things in the world and every particular deed in the realm of human affairs fit together and produce a harmony, which itself is not given to sense perception, and this invisible in the visible would remain forever unknown if there were no spectator to look out for it, admire it, straighten out the stories and put them into words.

To state this in conceptual language: The meaning of what actually happens and appears while it is happening is revealed when it has disappeared; remembrance, by which you make present to your mind what actually is absent and past, reveals the meaning in the form of a story. The man who does the revealing is not involved in the appearances; he is blind, shielded against the visible, in order to be able to "see" the invisible. And what he sees with blind eyes and puts into words is the story, *not* the deed itself and *not* the doer, although the doer's fame will reach the high heavens. Out of this then arises the typically Greek question: Who becomes immortal, the doer or the teller? Or: Who depends on whom? The doer on the poet, who gives him fame, or the poet on the doer, who must first accomplish things that deserve to be remembered? We need only read Pericles' funeral speech in Thucydides to learn that the question remained controversial, the answer depending on who replied—the man of action or the spectator. Pericles, at any rate, statesman and friend of philosophers, held that the greatness of Athens, the city that had become the "school of Hellas" (as Homer had been the teacher of all Greeks), was for that reason "far from needing a Homer . . . or other of his craft" to make it immortal; the Athenians by the sheer power of their daring had left "imperishable monuments" behind them on land and sea.[12]

It is the distinctive mark of Greek philosophy that it broke entirely with this Periclean estimate of the highest and most divine way of life for mortals. To quote but one of his contemporaries, Anaxagoras, who was also his friend: when asked why one should choose rather to be born than not—a question, incidentally, that seems to have preoccupied the Greek people and not merely philosophers and poets—he replied: " 'For the sake of viewing the heavens and the things there, stars and moon and sun,' as though nothing else were worth his while." And Aristotle agrees: "One should either philosophize or take one's leave of life and go away from here."[13]

What Pericles and the philosophers had in common was the general Greek estimate that all mortals should strive for immortality, and this was possible because of the affinity between gods and men. Compared to other living beings, man is a god;[14] he is a kind of "mortal god" (*quasi mortalem deum*, to quote Cicero's phrase again),[15] whose chief task therefore consists in an activity that could remedy his mortality and thus make him more like the gods, his closest relations. The alternative to that is to sink down to the level of animal life. "The best choose one thing in place of all else—everlasting fame among mortals; but the many are glutted like cattle."[16] The point here is that it was axiomatic in pre-philosophical Greece that the only incentive worthy of man qua man is the striving for immortality: the great deed is beautiful and praiseworthy not because it serves one's country or one's people but exclusively because it will "win eternal mention in the deathless roll of fame."[17] As Diotima points out to Socrates, "Do you suppose that Alcestis would have died to save Admetus, or Achilles to avenge Patroclus . . . if they had not believed that their excellence [*aretē*], would live for ever in men's memory, as in fact it does in ours?"[18] And all the various kinds of love, according to Plato's *Symposium*, are ultimately united by the striving for immortality of all things mortal.

I do not know who was really the first Greek to become aware of the decisive flaw in the praised and envied immortality of the gods: they were deathless (*a-thanatoi*, those who were forever *aien eontes*), but they were not eternal. "As the Theogony informs us in some detail, they have all been born: their vital duration had a temporal beginning. It is the philosophers who introduce an absolute *archē* or Beginning which is itself unbegun, a permanent and ungenerated source of generation. The initiator here is probably Anaximander,[19] but we can see the result more clearly in the poem of Parmenides.[20] His being *is forever* in the strong sense; it is ungenerated (*agenēton*) as well as unperishing (*anōlethron*).

Limited neither by birth nor by death, the duration of *What is* replaces and transcends the unending survival which characterized the Olympian gods."[21] In other words, *Being*, birthless as well as deathless, replaced for the philosophers the mere deathlessness of the Olympian gods; Being became the true divinity of philosophy because, in the famous words of Heraclitus, it was "made by none of the gods or men, but always was and is and shall be: an ever-living fire, fixed measures kindling and fixed measures going out."[22] The gods' immortality could not be trusted; what had come into being could also cease to be—were not the pre-Olympian gods dead and gone?—and it was this flaw in the gods' everlastingness (much more, I think, than their frequent immoral conduct) that made them so vulnerable to Plato's ferocious attacks. The Homeric religion was never a creed that could be replaced by another creed; "the Olympian gods were laid low by philosophy."[23] That the new and everlasting divinity, which Heraclitus in the fragment just quoted still calls *kosmos* (not the world or the universe but their order and harmony), is finally, starting with Parmenides, given the name "Being" seems due, as Charles Kahn suggests, to the *durative* connotations this word had from the beginning. It is indeed true, and by no means a matter of course, that "the durative aspect, being inseparable from the stem, colors every use of the verb, including every philosophical use."[24]

If Being replaced the Olympian gods, then philosophy replaced religion. Philosophizing became the only possible "way" of piety, and this new god's newest characteristic was that he was One. That this One was indeed a god and thus decisively different from what we understand by "being" becomes obvious when we see that Aristotle called his "First Philosophy" a "Theology," by which he did not mean a theory about the gods but what much later—in the eighteenth century—was called *ontologia* or "Ontology."

The great advantage of the new discipline was that man, to win his share of immortality, no longer needed to count on the uncertain ways of posterity. He could actualize it while he was alive without requiring any help from his fellow-men or from the poets, who in earlier days, by bestowing fame, could make his name last forever. The way to the new immortality was to take up one's abode with things that are forever, and the new faculty making this possible was called *nous* or mind. The term was borrowed from Homer, where *noos* encompasses all mental activities besides designating the specific mentality of one person. It is *nous* that corresponds to Being, and when Parmenides says *"to gar auto noein estin te kai einai"*[25] ("to be and to think [*noein*, the activity of *nous*] are the same"), he is already saying implicitly what Plato and Aristotle then said explicitly: that there is something in man that corresponds exactly to the divine because it enables him to live, as it were, in its neighborhood. It is this divinity that causes Thinking and Being to be the same. By using his *nous* and by withdrawing mentally from all perishable things, man assimilates himself to the divine. And the assimilation is meant pretty literally. For just as Being is the god, *nous,* according to Aristotle (quoting from either Ermotimos or Anaxagoras), is "the god in us," and "every mortal life possesses the part of some god."[26] *Nous,* "as all wise men agree," said Plato, "is the king of heaven and earth";[27] hence it is above the whole universe, just as Being is higher in rank than anything else. The philosopher, therefore, who has decided to risk the voyage beyond "the gates of Day and Night" (Parmenides), beyond the world of mortals, "shall be called the friend of god, and if ever it is given to man to put on immortality, it shall be given to him."[28] In short, to engage in what Aristotle called the *theōrētikē energeia* that is identical with the activity of the god (*hē tou theou energeia*) means to "immortalize" (*athanatizein*), engage in an activity that in itself makes us immortal "as far as that is possible, and [to] do our utmost to live in accordance with what is highest in us."[29]

For us, it is of some importance to note that the immortal and divine part within man does not exist unless it is actualized and focused on the divine outside; in other words, the *object* of our thoughts bestows immortality on thinking itself. The object is invariably the everlasting, what was and is and will be, and therefore cannot be otherwise than it is, and cannot *not* be. This everlasting object is primarily the "revolutions of the universe," which we can follow mentally, thus proving that we are "not an earthly but a heavenly growth," creatures who have their "kindred" not on earth but in heaven.[30] Behind this conviction, we can easily detect the aboriginal wonder, in itself philosophical. It is wonder that sends the scientist on his course of "dispelling ignorance" and that made Einstein say: "The eternal mystery of the world [i.e., the universe] is its comprehensibility." Hence all subsequent "development" of theories to match the universe's comprehensibility "is in a certain sense a continuous flight from 'wonder.'"[31] The God of the scientists, one is tempted to suggest, created man in his own image and put him into the world with only one Commandment: Now try to figure out by yourself how all this was done and how it works.

At any rate, to the Greeks, philosophy was "the achievement of immortality,"[32] and as such it proceeded in two stages. There was first the activity of *nous*, which consisted in contemplation of the everlasting and was in itself *aneu logou*, speechless; then followed the attempt to translate the vision into words. This was called *alētheuein* by Aristotle and does not just mean to tell things as they really are without concealing anything, but also applies only to propositions about things that always and necessarily are and cannot be otherwise. Man qua man, as distinct from other animal species, is a composite of *nous* and *logos*: "his essence is set in order according to *nous* and *logos*—*ho anthrōpos kai kata logon kai kata noun tetaktai autou hē ousia*.[33] Of these two, it is only *nous* that enables him to partake of the everlasting and the divine, while *logos*, designed "to say what is," *legein ta eonta* (Herodotus), is the specifically, uniquely human ability that is also applied to mere "mortal thought," opinions or *dogmata*, to what happens in the realm of human affairs and to what merely "seems" but *is* not.

*Logos* as distinguished from *nous* is not divine, and the translation of the philosopher's vision into speech—*alētheuein*, in the philosophers' strict sense—created considerable difficulties; the criterion of philosophical speech is *homoiōsis* (in opposition to *doxa* or opinion), "to make a likeness" or assimilate in words as faithfully as possible the vision provided by *nous*, which itself is without discourse, seeing "directly, without any process of discursive reasoning."[34] The criterion for the faculty of vision is not "truth" as suggested by the verb *alētheuein*, derived from the Homeric *alēthes* (truthful), where it is used only for the *verba dicendi*, in the sense of: tell me without hiding (*lanthanai*) within yourself, that is, do not deceive me—as though the common function of speech, here implied in the *alpha privativum*, were precisely deception. Truth remains the criterion of speech, though now, when it has to assimilate itself to and take its cue, as it were, from the vision of *nous*, it changes character. The criterion for vision is only the quality of everlastingness in the seen object; the mind can partake in that directly, but "if a man is engrossed in appetites and ambitions and spends all his pains on these . . . he cannot fall short of becoming mortal altogether, since he has nourished the growth of his mortality." But "if he has set his heart" on contemplating the everlasting objects, he cannot "fail to possess immortality in the fullest measure that human nature admits."[35]

It is generally admitted that philosophy, which since Aristotle has been the field of inquiry into things that came after the physical and transcended them (*tōn meta ta physika*, "about what comes after the physical"), is Greek in origin. And being Greek in origin it set itself the original Greek goal, immortality, which seemed even linguistically the most natural aim for men who understood themselves as *mortals, thnētoi* or *brotoi*, for whom, according to Aristotle, death was "the greatest of all evils," and who had as their kindred, their blood relations, as we would say, "drawing breath from one mother," the immortal gods. Philosophy did nothing to change this natural goal; it only proposed another way to attain it. Summarily speaking, the goal disappeared with the decline and fall of the Greek people and disappeared from philosophy altogether with the arrival of Christianity, bearing its "good news," telling men they were not mortals, that, contrary to their former pagan beliefs, the world was doomed to end, but they would be bodily resurrected after death. The last trace of the Greek quest for the everlasting may be seen in the *nunc stans*, the "standing now" of the medieval mystics' contemplation. The formula is striking, and we shall see later that it indeed corresponds to an experience highly characteristic of the thinking ego.

However, while the mighty incentive to philosophize disappeared, the topics of metaphysics remained the same and continued to prejudge throughout the centuries which things are worthy of being thought about and which are not. What for Plato was a matter of course—that "pure knowledge is concerned with the things that are always the same without change or mixture, or with what is most akin to them"[36]—remained in manifold variations the chief assumption of philosophy up to the last stages of the modern age. Excluded by definition were all matters concerning human affairs, because they were contingent; they could always be different from what they actually were. So even when Hegel, under the influence of the French Revolution—in which, according to him, eternal principles such as freedom and justice had been actualized—took history itself as his field of inquiry, he could do it only on the assumption that not only the revolutions of the skies and sheer thought-things such as numbers and the like followed the iron laws of necessity, but that the course of human affairs on earth also followed such laws, the laws of the incarnation of the Absolute Mind. From then on, the goal of philosophizing was not immortality but necessity: "Philosophical contemplation has no other intention than to eliminate the accidental."[37]

The originally divine metaphysical topics, the everlasting and the necessary, survived the need to "immortalize" through the mind's effort to "stay" and remain in the presence of the divine, an effort rendered otiose when, with the rise of Christianity, faith replaced thought as the bringer of immortality. And in a different way the evaluation of spectatorship as the essentially philosophical and best way of life also persisted.

In pre-Christian times that notion was still alive in the philosophical schools of late antiquity, when life in the world was no longer considered a blessing and involvement in human affairs no longer seen as a distraction from a more divine activity but, rather, as dangerous and joyless in itself. To keep yourself out of political involvement meant to occupy a position outside the turmoil and misery of human affairs and their inevitable shifts. The Roman spectators were no longer situated on the ascending rows of a theater where they could look down godlike on the game of the world; their place was now the secure shore or haven where they could watch, without being endangered, the wild and unpredictable upheavals of the storm-swept sea. These are the words of Lucretius praising the advantages of mere spectatorship: "What joy it is, when out at sea the stormwinds are lashing the waters, to gaze from the shore at the heavy stress some other man is enduring! Not that anyone's afflictions are in themselves a source of delight; but to realize from what troubles you yourself are free is joy indeed."[38] Here, of course, the philosophic relevance of spectatorship is entirely lost—a loss that befell so many Greek notions when they fell into Roman hands. What is lost is not only the spectator's privilege of judging, as we found it in Kant, and the fundamental contrast between thinking and doing, but also the even more fundamental insight that whatever appears is there to be seen, that the very concept of appearance demands a spectator, and that therefore to see and to behold are activities of the highest rank.

It was left to Voltaire to draw conclusions from Lucretius' proposition. According to him, the desire to see is nothing but cheap curiosity: it attracts people to the spectacle of a ship about to be shipwrecked; it drives people to climb trees or look at the massacres of battle or attend public executions. And this passion, according to Voltaire, man shares with monkeys and young dogs. In other words, if Lucretius is right and man's passion for seeing spectacles is due solely to his sense of safety, then the sheer lust for seeing can be ascribed only to an immature irrational drive that endangers our very existence. The philosopher, for whom Lucretius speaks, will not need to see the shipwreck to be warned against entrusting his safety to the wildness of the sea.

Unfortunately, it is in this rather shallow form that the beneficial and "noble" distance between the spectator and his object has been handed down in our tradition—if we leave out of consideration the high rank of contemplation in medieval philosophy with its altogether different connotations. And it is curious how frequently Lucretius is the implicit or explicit

passage itself is somewhat out of order, as happens frequently in Plato, where the most telling sentences can easily be isolated and sound out of context, especially when, after getting involved in the logical and other perplexities typical of his century and of which one could rightly say they are dated, he suddenly breaks off discussing them. Here Theaetetus has said that he was "wondering"—in the ordinary sense of being "puzzled"—whereupon Socrates compliments him: "This is the true mark of the philosopher," and never comes back to the issue under consideration. The short passage reads: "For this is chiefly the passion (*pathos*) of the philosopher, to wonder (*thaumazein*). There is no other beginning and principle (*archē*) of philosophy than this one. And I think he [namely Hesiod] was not a bad genealogist who made Iris [the Rainbow, a messenger of the gods] the daughter of Thaumas [the Wonderer]."[41] At first glance, this seems merely to say that philosophy as understood by the Ionian school is a child of astronomy; it springs from marveling at the miracles of the sky. As the rainbow connecting the sky with the earth brings its message to men, so thinking or philosophy, responding in wonder to the daughter of the Wonderer, connects the earth with the sky.

Upon closer inspection, these few words hint at much more. The word "Iris," rainbow, also occurs in the *Cratylus*,[42] where Plato derives it "from the verb *to tell* (*eirein*), because she was a messenger," whereas the word for "wonder" (*thaumazein*), which he here divests of the ordinary sense in which Theaetetus had used it by giving its genealogy, occurs regularly in Homer and is itself derived from one of the many Greek verbs for seeing in the sense of "beholding": *theasthai*—the same root we met earlier in Pythagoras' *theatai*, spectators. In Homer, this wonder-struck beholding is usually reserved for men to whom a god appears; it is also used as an adjective for men in the sense of O admirable one!—namely worthy of the admiring wonder we usually reserve for the gods, a godlike man. Moreover, the gods who appeared to men had this peculiarity: they appeared in familiar human disguise and were recognized as divinities only by those whom they approached. The responding wonder, therefore, is not something men can summon up by themselves; the wonder is a *pathos*, something to be suffered, not acted; in Homer, it is the god who acts, whose appearance men have to endure, from whom they must not run away.

In other words, what sets men wondering is something familiar and yet normally invisible, and something men are forced to *admire*. The wonder that is the starting-point of thinking is neither puzzlement nor surprise nor perplexity; it is an *admiring* wonder. What we marvel at is confirmed and affirmed by admiration which breaks out into speech, the gift of Iris, the rainbow, the messenger from above. Speech then takes the form of praise, a glorification not of a particularly amazing appearance or of the sum total of things in the world, but of the harmonious order behind them which itself is not visible and of which nevertheless the world of appearances gives us a glimpse. "For the appearances are a glimpse of the non-revealed" (*"opsis gar tōn adēlōn ta phainomena"*), in the words of Anaxagoras.[43] Philosophy begins with an awareness of this invisible harmonious order of the *kosmos*, which is manifest in the midst of the familiar visibilities as though these had become transparent. The philosopher marvels at the "non-visible harmony," which, according to Heraclitus, is "better than the visible" (*"harmoniē aphanēs phanerēs kreittōn"*).[44] Another early word for the invisible in the midst of the appearances is *physis*, nature, which according to the Greeks was the totality of all things that were not man-made and not created by a divine maker but that had come into being by themselves; and of this *physis* Heraclitus said that "it likes to hide itself,"[45] namely behind the appearances.

I have introduced Heraclitus by way of explication, because Plato himself does not specify what his admiring wonder is directed at. Nor does he say how this original marveling transforms itself into the dialogue of thinking. In Heraclitus, the significance of *logos* is at least suggested in the following context: Apollo, he says, "the lord of the Delphian oracle" and, we may add, the god of the poets, "does not speak out nor does he conceal but indicates" (*"oute legei oute kryptei alla sēmainei"*),[46] that is, hints at something ambiguously, to be understood only by those who have an understanding of mere hints (the god *winkt,* as Heidegger translates). Even more tantalizingly suggestive is another fragment: "Bad witnesses are eyes and ears for men if they have barbarian souls,"[47] that is, if they do not possess *logos*—for the Greeks not just speech but the gift of reasoned argument that distinguished them from the barbarians. In short, wonder has led to thinking in words; the experience of wonder at the invisible manifest in the appearances has been appropriated by speech, which at the same time is strong enough to dispel the errors and illusions that our organs for the visible, eyes and ears, are subject to unless thinking comes to their help.

From this, it should be obvious that the wonder that befalls the philosopher can never concern anything particular but is always aroused by the whole, which, in contrast to the sum total of entities, is never manifest. Heraclitus' harmony comes about through the sounding together of opposites—an effect that can never be the property of any particular sound. This harmony in a way is separate (*kechōrismenon*) from the sounds that produce it, just as the *sophon,* which one "may not and may call by the name of Zeus,"[48] is "set apart from all other things."[49] In terms of the Pythagorean parable, it is the beauty of the game of the world, the meaning and meaningfulness of all the particulars acting together. As such this is manifest only to a beholder in whose mind the particular instances and sequences are invisibly united.

Since Parmenides, the key word for this invisible imperceptible whole implicitly manifest in all that appears has been *Being*—seemingly the most empty and general, the least meaningful word in our vocabulary. What happens to a man who suddenly turns about to become aware of Being's all-pervasive presence in the world of appearances was described with great precision thousands of years after its first discovery in Greek philosophy. The passage is relatively modern and therefore more insistent on personal, subjective emotions than any Greek text would be, and for that very reason perhaps more persuasive to psychologically trained ears. Coleridge writes:

Hast thou ever raised thy mind to the consideration of existence, in and by itself, as the mere act of existing? Hast thou ever said to thyself thoughtfully, It is! Heedless in that moment, whether it were a man before thee, or a flower, or a grain of sand, — without reference, in short, to this or that particular mode or form of existence? If thou hast indeed attained to this, thou wilt have felt the presence of a mystery, which must have fixed thy spirit in awe and wonder. The very words, — There is nothing! or, — There was a time, when there was nothing! are self-contradictory. There is that within us which repels the proposition with as full and instantaneous a light, as if it bore evidence against the fact in the right of its own eternity.

Not to be, then, is impossible: to be, incomprehensible. If thou hast mastered this intuition of absolute existence, thou wilt have learnt likewise, that it was this, and no other, which in the earlier ages seized the nobler minds, the elect among men, with a sort of sacred horror. This it was that first caused them to feel within themselves a something ineffably greater than their own individual nature.[50]

The Platonic wonder, the initial shock that sends the philosopher on his way, was revived in our own time when Heidegger, in 1929, concluded a lecture entitled "What is Metaphysics?" with the words, already cited, "Why is there anything at all and not, rather, nothing?" and called this "the basic question of metaphysics."[51]

The question, expressing the philosopher's shock in modern terms, had been asked before him. It occurs in Leibniz' *"Principes de la nature et de la grâce"*: *"Pourquoi il y a plutôt quelque chose que rien?"* For since *"le rien est plus simple et plus facile que quelque chose,"*[52] this something must have a sufficient cause for its existence, and this cause in turn must have been caused by something else. Following this train of thought, one finally arrives at the *causa sui*, at something which is its own cause, so that Leibniz' answer arrives at the ultimate cause, called "God," an answer we already find in Aristotle's "unmoved mover"—the god of the philosophers. It was Kant, of course, who dealt the death blow to that god, and in his words on the subject we can clearly recognize what Plato only hinted at: the uncaused and "unconditioned necessity" our cause-and-effect thinking "so indispensably require[s] as the last bearer of all things, is for human reason the veritable abyss. . . . We cannot put aside, and yet also cannot endure the thought, that a being, which we represent to ourselves as supreme amongst all possible beings, should, as it were, say to itself: 'I am from eternity to eternity, and outside me there is nothing save what is there through my will, *but whence then am I?*' All support here fails us; and the *greatest* perfection, no less than the *least* perfection, is unsubstantial and baseless for the merely speculative reason, which makes not the least effort to retain either the one or the other, and feels indeed no loss in allowing them to vanish entirely."[53] What strikes us here as specifically modern is that in the restatement of Parmenides' early insight that nothingness is inconceivable, unthinkable, the emphasis has shifted, as it were, from nothingness to Being: Kant nowhere says that the abyss of nothing because of being inconceivable *is not,* and though he might have said that the antinomies of reason, rousing him from dogmatic slumber, had made him think, he nowhere says that the experience of this abyss—the other side of Plato's wonder—had done so.

Schelling quoted Kant's words emphatically and it was probably from this passage, rather than from the more casual remark in Leibniz, that he derived his own repeated insistence on this "ultimate question" of all thinking—Why is something at all, why is there not nothing?[54] He calls it the "most despairing question."[55] This reference to sheer despair, as arising out of thinking itself, occurs in Schelling's late writings, and it is so very significant because the same thought had haunted him earlier, in his youth when he still believed that no more was needed to banish nothingness than "absolute affirmation," which he called "the essence of our soul." By virtue of it "we recognize that non-being is forever impossible," neither knowable nor understandable. And for the young Schelling, this ultimate question—Why is there not nothing, why is there anything at all?—posed by the intellect seized with vertigo at the rim of the abyss—is forever suppressed by the insight that "*Being* is necessary, [made so] that is, by the absolute affirmation of Being in cognition."[56]

All this would suggest a simple return to the position of Parmenides if Schelling had not felt that only the "absolute *positing* of the idea of God" could guarantee this affirmation, which according to him is "the absolute negation of nothingness": it is "as certain that reason forever negates nothingness, and that nothingness is nothing, as it is certain that reason affirms the All and that God is eternal." Hence, the only "completely valid answer to the question, *Why is there not nothing, why is there anything at all?* is not the something but the All *or God.*"[57] Reason, unaided by the idea of God, according to "its mere nature," may "posit a Being that is forever," but then, confronting this thought which it is in reason's nature to posit, reason remains as it were "thunderstruck (*quasi attonita*), paralyzed, unable to move."[58] No Iris-like messenger, bringing the gift of speech, and with it the gift of reasoned argument and reasonable response, accompanies the philosophical shock; and the affirmation of Being, clearly corresponding to the element of admiration in Plato's wonder, needs faith in a Creator-God to save human reason from its speechless dizzy glance into the abyss of nothingness.

What happens to thought's "ultimate question," once this faith is resolutely rejected and human reason is left completely alone with its own capacities, we can trace in Sartre's *Nausea,* by far the most important of his philosophical works. There the hero of the novel, looking at the root of a chestnut tree, has been suddenly overcome by "what 'to exist' meant . . .; existence usually hides itself. It is there, around us, in us, it is *us,* you can't say two words without mentioning it, but you can never touch it." But now "existence had suddenly unveiled itself. It had lost the harmless look of an abstract category: it was the very paste of things. . . . Or rather the root, the park gates, the bench, the sparse grass, all that had vanished: the diversity of things, their individuality, were only an appearance, a veneer." The reaction of Sartre's hero is not admiration, and not even wonder, but nausea at the opaqueness of sheer existence, at the naked thereness of the factually given, which indeed no thought has ever succeeded in reaching, let alone illuminating and making transparent: "You couldn't even wonder where all that sprang from, or how it was that a world came into existence, rather than nothingness." Now that all marveling had been eliminated, it was the scandal of Being that nothingness was "unthinkable." There had been nothing *before* it. Nothing . . . That was what worried me: of course there was no *reason* for this flowing larval stuff to exist. *But it was impossible* for it not to exist. It was unthinkable: to imagine nothingness you had to be there already, in the middle of the world, alive, with your eyes wide open. . . . I felt with boredom that I had no way of understanding. No way. Yet it was there, waiting, looking at one." It is this completely meaningless thereness that makes the hero shout: " 'Filth! what rotten filth!' . . . but it held fast and there was so much, tons and tons of existence, endless."[59]

In this progressive shift from Being to nothingness, caused not by the loss of wonder or perplexity but by the loss of admiration and willingness to affirm in thought, it would be very tempting to see the end of philosophy, at least of that philosophy whose beginning Plato had fixed. No doubt, the turning from admiration to negation is easy enough to understand, not because it is occasioned by any tangible events or thoughts but because, as Kant had already observed, speculative reason in itself "feels no loss" and no gain in turning to either side of the matter. Hence, the notion that to think means to say "yes" and confirm the factuality of sheer existence is also found in many variations throughout the history of philosophy in the modern age. We find it notably in Spinoza's "acquiescence" in the process in which everything that is swings and in which the "big fish" forever eat the small fish. It appears in Kant's pre-critical writings when he tells the metaphysician that he should first ask: "Is it possible that nothing at all exists?" which then should lead him to the conclusion that "if no existence is given at all, there would also be nothing to think about," a thought that in turn leads to a "concept of absolutely necessary being "[60]—a conclusion Kant would hardly have recognized in the critical period. More interesting is a remark he makes a little earlier about living in "the best possible world": he repeats the old consoling thought, "that the whole is the best, and that everything is good for the sake of the whole," but seems himself not quite convinced of this ancient *topos* of metaphysics, for he suddenly injects: *"Ich rufe allem Geschöpfe zu* . . . : *Heil uns, wir sind!"*—"I call out to every creature . . . : Hail to us that we are!"[61]

This affirmation, or, rather, the need to reconcile thought

with reality, is one of the leitmotifs of the work of Hegel. It informs Nietzsche's *amor fati* and his notion of "eternal recurrence"—the "highest form of affirmation that can be reached"[62] precisely because it is at the same time the "heaviest weight."

> How, if a . . . demon were to . . . say to you "This life as you now live it . . . you will have to live . . . innumerable times more; and there will be nothing new in it, but every pain and every joy and every thought and sigh . . . must return to you—all in the same succession and sequence. . . . The eternal hour glass of existence is upended over and over and you with it, a dust grain of dust." Would you not throw yourself down . . . and curse the demon who spoke thus? Or did you once experience a tremendous moment when you would have answered him, "You are a god and never have I heard anything more godly." . . . How well disposed would you have to become to yourself and to life to *crave nothing more fervently* than this ultimate eternal confirmation and seal.[63]

The point of these passages is that Nietzsche's notion of eternal recurrence is not an "idea" in the Kantian sense of regulating our speculations, nor, of course, is it anything like a "theory," a relapse, so to speak, into the ancient time-concept with its cyclical motion. It is indeed a mere thought or, rather, a thought-experiment, and its poignancy resides in the intimate connection that binds the thought of Being and the thought of nothingness together. Here the need for confirmation arises not out of a Greek admiration for the invisible harmony and beauty that bind together the infinite diversity of particular beings, but out of the simple fact that nobody can think Being without at the same time thinking nothingness, or think Meaning without thinking futility, vanity, meaninglessness.

The way out of this perplexity seems to be indicated by the old argument that without an aboriginal confirmation of Being, there would be nothing to think about and nobody to do the thinking; in other words, the very activity of thinking no matter what kind of thought already presupposes existence. But such merely logical solutions are always treacherous; nobody who clings fast to the notion that "there is no truth" will ever be convinced if it is pointed out to him that the proposition is self-defeating. An existential, meta-logical solution of the perplexity can be found in Heidegger, who, as we saw, evinced something like the old Platonic wonder in reiterating the question Why is there anything at all rather than nothing? According to Heidegger, *to think* and *to thank* are essentially the same; the very words derive from the same etymological root. This, obviously, is closer to Plato's wondering admiration than any of the answers discussed. Its difficulty lies not in the etymological derivation and the lack of an argumentative demonstration. It is still the old difficulty inherent in Plato, of which Plato himself seems to have been well aware and which is discussed in the *Parmenides*.

Admiring wonder conceived as the starting-point of philosophy leaves no place for the factual existence of disharmony, of ugliness, and finally of evil. No Platonic dialogue deals with the question of evil, and only in the *Parmenides* does he show concern about the consequences that the undeniable existence of hideous things and ugly deeds is bound to have for his doctrine of ideas. If everything that appears partakes in an Idea visible only to the eye of the mind and derives from this Form whatever reality it may possess in the Cave of human affairs—the world of ordinary sense perception—then everything that appears at all, by no means only admirable things, owes its very appearingness to such a suprasensory entity to explain its presence in this world. So, asks Parmenides, what about utterly "trivial and undignified objects" such as "hair and mud and dirt," which have never aroused admiration in anybody? Plato, speaking through Socrates, does not use the later common justification of evil and ugliness as necessary parts of the whole that appear evil and ugly only to the limited perspective of men. Instead, Socrates replies that it would be simply absurd to ascribe ideas to such stuff—". . . in these cases, the things are just the things we see" —and suggests that it is better to retreat at this point "for fear of falling into a bottomless pit of nonsense." (Parmenides, however, an old man in the dialogue, points out: "That . . . is because you are still young, Socrates, and philosophy has not yet taken hold of you so firmly as I believe it will someday. You will not despise any of these things then, but at present your youth makes you still pay attention to what the world will think."[64] But the difficulty is not resolved and Plato never again raises the question.) We are not interested here in the doctrine of ideas, or only to the extent that one might be able to demonstrate that the notion of ideas occurred to Plato because of beautiful things and would never have occurred to him had he been surrounded by nothing but "trivial and undignified objects."

There is, of course, a decisive difference between Plato's and Parmenides' quest for divine matters and the seemingly more humble attempts of Solon and Socrates at defining the "unseen measures" that bind and determine human affairs, and the relevance of the difference for the history of philosophy, as distinguished from the history of thought, is very great. What matters in our context is that in both instances thought is concerned with invisible things that are pointed to, nevertheless, by appearances (the starry sky above us or the deeds and destinies of men), invisibles that are present in the visible world in much the same way as the Homeric gods, who were visible only to those whom they approached.

## 16   *The Roman answer*

In my attempt to isolate and examine one of the basic sources of non-cognitive thinking I have emphasized the elements of admiration, confirmation, and affirmation, which we encounter so powerfully in Greek philosophical and pre-philosophic thought and can trace throughout the centuries, not as a matter of influence but of often-repeated first-hand experience. I am not at all sure that what I have been describing runs counter to present-day experiences of thinking but I am quite sure that it runs counter to present-day opinion on the subject.

Common opinion on philosophy was formed by the Romans, who became the heirs of Greece, and it bears the stamp, not of the original Roman experience, which was exclusively political (and which we find in its purest form in Virgil), but of the last century of the Roman republic, when the *res publica*, the public thing, was already in the process of being lost, till finally, after Augustus' attempt at restoration, it became the private property of the imperial household. Philosophy, like the arts and letters, like poetry and historiography, had always been a Greek import; in Rome culture had been looked upon with some suspicion as long as the public thing was still intact, but it was also tolerated and even admired as a noble pastime for the educated and a means of beautification of the Eternal City. Only in the centuries of decline and fall, first of the republic and then of the empire, did these occupations become "serious," and did philosophy, for its part, Greek borrowings notwithstanding, develop into a "science," Cicero's *animi medicina*—the opposite of what it had been in Greece.[65] Its usefulness was to teach men how to cure their despairing minds by escaping from the world through thinking. Its famous watchword—which sounds almost as though it had been formulated in contradiction of the Platonic admiring wonder—became *nil admirari:* do not be surprised at anything, admire nothing.[66]

But it was not just the popular image of the figure of the philosopher, the wise man whom nothing can touch, that we owe to the Roman transmittal; Hegel's well-known saying about the relation of philosophy and reality ("the owl of Minerva begins its flight when dusk is falling")[67] bears the mark of the Roman rather than the Greek experience. For Hegel, Minerva's owl exemplified Plato and Aristotle rising, as it were, out of the disasters of the Peloponnesian war. Not philosophy, but the *political* philosophy of Plato and Aristotle grew out of the decline of the polis, "a shape of life grown old." And with respect to this political philosophy there is considerable evidence for the truth of Pascal's splendidly impertinent remark in the *Pensées:*

We can only think of Plato and Aristotle in grand academic robes. They were honest men, and like others laughing with their friends, and when they wanted to divert themselves, they wrote the *Laws* or the *Politics*, to amuse themselves. That part of their life was the least philosophic and the least serious. . . . If they wrote on politics, it was as if laying down rules for a lunatic asylum; if they presented the appearance of speaking of a great matter, it was because they knew that the madmen, to whom they spoke, thought they were kings and emperors. They entered into their principles in order to make their madness as little harmful as possible.[68]

In any event, the profound Roman influence on even so metaphysical a philosopher as Hegel is quite manifest in his first published book,[69] where he discusses the relation between philosophy and reality: "The need for philosophy arises when the unifying power has disappeared from the life of men, when the opposites have lost the living tension of their relatedness and their mutual interdependence and have become autonomous. Out of disunity, out of being torn apart, arises thought," namely, the need for reconciliation (*"Entzweiung ist der Quell des Bedürfnisses der Philosophie"*). What is Roman in the Hegelian notion of philosophy is that thinking does not arise out of reason's need but has an existential root in unhappiness—whose typically Roman character Hegel with his great sense of history recognized very clearly in his treatment of the "Roman World" in the late lecture course published as the *Philosophy of History*. "Stoicism, Epicureanism, and Scepticism ... although ... opposed to each other, had the same general purport, viz., rendering the soul absolutely indifferent to everything which the real world had to offer."[70] What he apparently did not recognize is the extent to which he himself had generalized the Roman experience: "The History of the World is not the theatre of happiness. Periods of happiness are blank pages in it, for they are periods of harmony."[71] Thinking then arises out of the disintegration of reality and the resulting *dis*unity of man and world, from which springs the need for another world, more harmonious and more meaningful.

And this sounds very plausible. How often indeed must the first thought-impulse have coincided with an impulse to escape a world that has become unbearable. It is improbable that this escape-impulse is less old than the admiring wonder. Yet we look in vain for its expression in conceptual language before the long centuries of decline that began when Lucretius and Cicero transformed Greek philosophy into something essentially Roman—which meant, among other things, something essentially practical.[72] And following these precursors with their mere foreboding of disaster—"everything is gradually decaying and nearing its end, worn out by old age," in the words of Lucretius[73]—it took over a hundred years before those thought-trains were developed into a sort of consistent philosophical system. That occurred with Epictetus, the Greek slave and the most acute mind, possibly, among the late Stoics. According to him, what must be learned to make life bearable is not really thinking, but "the correct use of imagination," the only thing we have entirely within our power. He still uses a deceptively familiar Greek vocabulary, but what he calls "the reasoning faculty" (*dynamis logikē*) has as little to do with Greek *logos* and *nous* as what he appeals to as "will" has to do with Aristotelian *proairesis*. He calls the faculty of thinking in itself "sterile" (*akarpa*);[74] for him the subject matter of philosophy is each man's own life, and what philosophy teaches man is an "art of living,"[75] how to deal with life, in the same fashion that carpentry teaches an apprentice how to deal with wood. What counts is not "theory" in the abstract but its use and application (*chrēsis tōn theōrēmatōn*); to think and to understand are a mere preparation for action; to "admire the mere power of exposition"—the *logos*, the reasoned argument and train of thought itself—is likely to turn man "into a grammarian instead of a philosopher."[76]

In other words, thinking has become a *technē*, a particular kind of craftsmanship, perhaps to be deemed the highest—certainly the most urgently needed, because its end product is the conduct of your own life. What was meant was not a way of life in the sense of a *bios theōrētikos* or *politikos*, a life devoted to some particular activity, but what Epictetus called "action"—an action in which you acted in unison with no one, which was supposed to change nothing but your self, and which could become manifest only in the *apatheia* and *ataraxia* of the "wise man," that is, in his refusal to react to whatever good or evil might befall him. "I must die, but must I also die sighing? I can't help being chained, but can't I help weeping? . . . You threaten to handcuff me. Man, what are you saying? You can't handcuff me; you manacle my hands. You are threatening to behead me; when did I say that my head could not be cut off?"[77]

Obviously, these are not just exercises in thinking but exercises in the power of the will. "Ask not that events should happen as you will, but let your will be that events should happen as they do, and you shall have peace" is the quintessence of this "wisdom"; for "it is impossible that what happens should be other than it is."[78]

This will be of considerable interest to us when we come to deal with the phenomenon of the will, an altogether different mental capacity, whose chief characteristic, compared with the ability to think, is that it neither speaks in the voice of reflection nor does it use arguments but only imperatives, even when it is commanding nothing more than thought or, rather, imagination. For in order to obtain the radical withdrawal from reality that Epictetus demands, the emphasis on thinking's ability to have present what is absent shifts from reflection to imagination, and this not in the sense of a utopian imagining of another, better, world; rather, the aim is to strengthen the original absent-mindedness of thought to such an extent that reality disappears altogether. If thinking is normally the faculty of making present what is absent, the Epictetian faculty of "dealing with impressions aright" consists in conjuring away and making absent what actually is present. All that existentially concerns you while living in the world of appearances is the "impressions" by which you are affected. Whether what affects you exists or is mere illusion depends on your decision whether or not you will recognize it as real.

Wherever philosophy is understood as the "science" that deals with the mind sheerly as consciousness—where therefore the question of reality can be left in suspense, bracketed out altogether—we encounter in fact the old Stoic position. Only missing is the original motive for making thought a mere instrument which does its business at the bidding of the will as master. In our context, the point is that this bracketing of reality is possible, and not because of the force of will power but because of the very nature of thinking. If one may count Epictetus among the philosophers, it is because he discovered that consciousness makes it possible for mental activities to recoil upon themselves.

If while perceiving an object outside myself I decide to

concentrate on my perception, on the act of seeing instead of the seen object, it is as if I lost the original object, because it loses its impact upon me. I have, so to speak, changed the subject—instead of the tree I now deal merely with the perceived tree, that is, with what Epictetus calls an "impression." This has the great advantage that I am no longer absorbed by the perceived object, something outside myself; the seen tree is inside me, invisible to the outside world as though it had never been a sense-object. The point here is that the "seen tree" is not a thought-thing but an "impression." It is not something absent that needed memory to store it up for the de-sensing process that prepares the mind's objects for thinking and is always preceded by experience in the world of appearances. The seen tree is "inside" me in its full sensory presence, the tree itself deprived only of its realness, an image and not an after-thought about trees. The trick discovered by Stoic philosophy is to use the mind in such a way that reality cannot touch its owner even when he has not withdrawn from it; instead of withdrawing mentally from everything that is present and close at hand, he has drawn every appearance inside himself, and his "consciousness" becomes a full substitute for the outside world presented as impression or image.

It is at this moment that consciousness indeed undergoes a decisive change: it is no longer the silent self-awareness that accompanies all my acts and thoughts and guarantees my identity, the simple I-am-I (nor is it a question here of the strange difference that inserts itself into the core of this identity, which we shall come to later, an insertion peculiar to mental activities because of their recoil upon themselves). Since I am no longer absorbed by an object given to my senses (even though this object, unchanged in its "essential" structure, remains present as an object of consciousness—what Husserl called the "intentional object"), I myself, as sheer consciousness, emerge as an entirely new entity. This new entity can exist in the world in complete independence and sovereignty and yet seemingly remain in possession of this world, namely, of its sheer "essence," stripped of its "existential" character, of its realness that could touch and threaten me in my own.

I have become I-for-myself in an emphatic way, finding in myself everything that was originally given as "alien" reality. It is not so much the mind as this monstrously enlarged consciousness that offers an ever-present, seemingly safe refuge from reality.

This bracketing of reality—getting rid of it by treating it as though it were nothing but a mere "impression"—has remained one of the great temptations of the "professional thinkers," till Hegel, one of the greatest of them, went even further and built his philosophy of the World Spirit on the experiences of the thinking ego: reinterpreting this ego on the model of consciousness, he carried the whole world into consciousness as though it were essentially nothing but a mental phenomenon.

The efficiency, for the philosopher, of turning away from the world into the self is beyond doubt. Existentially speaking, Parmenides was wrong when he said that only Being manifests itself in, and is the same as, thinking. Non-being is also thinkable if the will commands the mind. Its force of withdrawal is then perverted into an annihilating power, and nothingness becomes a full substitute for reality, because nothingness brings relief. The relief, of course, is unreal; it is merely psychological, a soothing of anxiety and fear. I still doubt that there ever was anybody who remained master of his "impressions" when roasted in the Phalarian Bull.

Epictetus, like Seneca, lived under the rule of Nero, that is, under rather desperate conditions, though he himself, unlike Seneca, was scarcely persecuted. But over a hundred years earlier, during the last century of the republic, Cicero, well versed in Greek philosophy, had discovered the thought-trains by which one could take one's way out of the world. He found that such thoughts, by no means as extreme or as carefully elaborated as in Epictetus, were likely to offer comfort and help in the world as it then was (and, of course, always is, more or less). Men who could teach this way of thinking were highly esteemed in Roman literary circles; Lucretius calls Epicurus—who more than two hundred years after his death finally got a pupil worthy of him—"a god" because "he was the first to invent a way of life which is now called wisdom and through his art rescued life from such storms and so much darkness."[79] For our purposes, however, Lucretius is not such a good example; he does not insist on thinking but on knowing. Knowledge acquired by reason will dispel ignorance and thus destroy the greatest evil—fear, whose source is superstition. A more appropriate example is Cicero's famous "Dream of Scipio."

To understand how extraordinary this concluding chapter of Cicero's *Republic* actually is and how strange its thoughts must have sounded to Roman ears, we must briefly recall the general background against which it was written. Philosophy had found a kind of foster home in Rome during the last century before Christ, and in that thoroughly political society it had first of all to prove that it was good for something. In the *Tusculan Disputations*, we find Cicero's first answer: it was a question of making Rome more beautiful and more civilized. Philosophy was a proper occupation for educated men when they had retired from public life and had no more important things to worry about. There was nothing essential about philosophizing. Nor did it have to do with the divine; to the Romans, founding and conserving political communities were the activities most closely resembling those of the gods. Nor had it any connection with immortality. Immortality was human as well as divine, but was not the property of individual men, "for whom death is not only necessary but frequently desirable." By contrast, it was definitely the potential property of human communities: "If a commonwealth (*civitas*) is destroyed and extinguished, it is as though—to compare small things with great—this whole world were to perish and collapse."[80] For communities, death is neither necessary nor ever desirable; it comes only as a punishment, "for a community ought to be so constituted that it be eternal."[81] All this is from the treatise that finishes with Scipio's Dream—hence, Cicero, though old now and disappointed, had clearly not changed his mind. As a matter of fact, nothing even in his *Republic* itself prepares us for the Dream of Scipio at the end—except the lamentations of Book 5: "Only in words and because of our vices, and for no other reasons, do we still retain and keep the public thing [the *res publica*, the subject matter of the treatise]; the thing itself we have lost long since."[82]

And then comes the dream.[83] Scipio Africanus, the victor of Carthage, relates a dream he had shortly before he destroyed the city. The dream showed him a hereafter where he met an ancestor who told him he would destroy Carthage and warned him that after the destruction of the city he would have to restore the public thing in Rome by assuming the supreme authority of Dictator, if only he could escape being assassinated—which, it turned out, he could not. (Cicero meant to say that Scipio might have been able to save the republic.) And in order to do the job properly, to summon up the necessary courage, he is told that he should hold (*sic habeto*) the following to be true: Men who have preserved the *patria* are certain to find their place in heaven and be blessed with eternal time. "For the highest god who governs the world likes nothing better than the assemblies and the intercourse of men which are called commonwealths; their governors and conservators return to heaven after having left this world. Their job on earth is to stand guard over the earth." This, of course, does not imply a Christian promise of resurrection in a hereafter; and although the citation of divine wishes is still in the vein of Roman traditions, there sounds an ominous note: it is as though, failing the promise of such a reward, men might no longer want to do what the public thing demands of them.

For—and this is essential—the rewards of this world, Scipio's ancestor informs him, are in no way sufficient to compensate you for your labors. They are insubstantial and unreal if you think about them from the right perspective: high up in heaven, Scipio is invited to look down on the earth, and the earth appears so small that "he was pained to see our empire as a mere dot." Whereupon he is told: if the earth appears small to you from here, then always look up to the sky so that you may be able to despise human matters.

For what kind of fame is it that you may be able to attain in the conversation of men or what kind of glory among them? Don't you see how narrow the space is in which glory and fame reside? And those who speak about us today, how long will they talk? And even if there were reason to place our trust in tradition and the memory of future generations, one day there will be natural catastrophes—

floods or fire—so that we cannot obtain a long-lasting fame, let alone an eternal one. If you raise your eyes you will see how futile all this is; fame was never eternal, and the oblivion of eternity extinguishes it.

I have given the gist of this passage at some length to make clear how much these proposed thought-trains stand in open contradiction to what Cicero, in common with other educated Romans, had always believed in *and* had expressed even in the same book. In our context, I wanted to offer an example (and an eminent one, perhaps the first recorded in intellectual history) of how certain trains of thought actually aim at thinking oneself out of the world, and by means of *relativization*. In relation to the universe, the earth is but a dot; what does it matter what happens on her? In relation to the immensity of time, centuries are but moments, and oblivion will finally cover everything and everybody; what does it matter what men do? In relation to death, the same for all, everything specific and distinguishing loses its weight; if there is no here-after—and life after death for Cicero is not an article of faith but a moral hypothesis—whatever you do or suffer does not matter. Here thinking means following a sequence of reasoning that will lift you to a viewpoint outside the world of appearances as well as outside your own life. Philosophy is called upon to compensate for the frustrations of politics and, more generally, of life itself.

This is the mere beginning of a tradition that culminated philosophically in Epictetus and reached a climax of intensity about five hundred years later, at the end of the Roman Empire. Boethius' *On the Consolation of Philosophy*, one of the most popular books throughout the Middle Ages and hardly read by anyone today, was written in a condition of extremity of which Cicero had no premonition. Boethius, a noble Roman, had fallen from the height of fortune, found himself in jail, and was awaiting his execution. Because of that setting, the book has been likened to the *Phaedo*—a rather strange analogy: Socrates in the midst of his friends after a trial in which he had been permitted to speak at length in his own defense, awaiting an easy, painless death, and Boethius jailed without a hearing, absolutely alone after the death sentence has been

pronounced in a mock trial at which he was not even present,
much less given the opportunity to defend himself, and now
waiting for execution by slow and abominable tortures. Although he is a Christian, it is Philosophy and neither God nor
Christ that comes to console him; and although, while still
in high office he had spent his "secret leisure" in studying and
translating Plato and Aristotle, he consoles himself with
typically Ciceronian and also Stoic thought-trains. Except that
what was mere relativization in Scipio's dream is now turned
into violent annihilation. The "immense spaces of eternity" to
which in duress you must direct your mind annihilate reality
as it exists for mortals; the ever-changing nature of Fortune
annihilates all pleasures, for even if you enjoy what Fortune
has given you (riches, honor, fame), you are in constant fear
of losing it. Fear annihilates all happiness. Everything you
unthinkingly believe to exist does not exist once you begin
to think about it—that is what Philosophy, the goddess of consolation, tells him. And here the question of evil, which is
hardly touched upon by Cicero, comes up. The thought-train
concerning evil, still rather primitive in Boethius, already contains all the elements we find later in a much more sophisticated and complex form throughout the Middle Ages. It runs
thus: God is the final cause of everything that is; God as the
"highest good" cannot be the cause of evil; everything that
is must have a cause; since there are only apparent causes of
evil but no ultimate cause, evil does not exist. The wicked
ones, he is told by Philosophy, not only are not powerful, they
*are not*. What you unthinkingly consider evil has its place in
the order of the universe, and insofar as it is, it is necessarily
good. Its bad aspects are an illusion of the senses which you
can get rid of by thinking. It is old Stoic advice: What you
negate by thought—and thought is in your power—cannot
affect you. Thinking makes it unreal. Immediately, of course,
we are reminded of Epictetus' glorification of what today
would be called will power; and undeniably there is an element of willing in this kind of thinking. To think along these
lines means to act upon yourself—the only action left when all
acting in the world has become futile.

What is so very striking about this thinking of late antiquity is that it is centered exclusively on the self. To that, John Adams, living in a world in his day not completely out of joint, had an answer: "A death bed, it is said, shows the emptiness of titles. That may be. [However] . . . shall laws and government, which regulate sublunary things, be neglected because they appear baubles at the hour of death?"[84]

I have dealt with two sources from which thinking as we know it historically has sprung, the one Greek, the other Roman, and they are different to the point of being opposites. On the one hand, admiring wonder at the spectacle into which man is born and for whose appreciation he is so well equipped in mind and body; on the other, the awful extremity of having been thrown into a world whose hostility is overwhelming, where fear is predominant and from which man tries his utmost to escape. There are numerous indications that this latter experience was by no means alien to the Greeks. Sophocles' "Not to be born surpasses every *logos;* second-best by far is to go as swiftly as possible whence we came"[85] seems to have been the poet's variation on a proverbial saying. The remarkable fact is that, so far as I know, this mood is nowhere mentioned as a source of Greek thought; perhaps even more remarkable, it has nowhere produced any great philosophy—unless one wants to count Schopenhauer among the great thinkers. But although the Greek and Roman mentalities were worlds apart and though the chief fault of textbook history of philosophy is smoothing out such sharp distinctions—till it sounds as if everybody somehow said vaguely the same thing—it is also true that the two mentalities do have things in common.

In both cases, thinking leaves the world of appearances. Only because thinking implies withdrawal can it be used as an instrument of escape. Moreover, as has already been emphasized, thinking implies an unawareness of the body and of the self and puts in their place the experience of sheer activity, more gratifying, according to Aristotle, than the satisfaction of all the other desires, since for every other pleasure we depend on something or somebody else.[86] Thinking is the only activity that needs nothing but itself for its exercise. "A generous man needs money to perform generous acts . . . and a man of self-control needs the opportunity of temptation."[87] Every other activity of high or low rank has something to overcome outside itself. This is true even of the performing arts, such as flute-playing, whose end and purpose is in the exercise itself—to say nothing of productive works, which are undertaken for their result and not for themselves and where happiness, the satisfaction of a job well done, comes after the activity itself has come to an end. The frugality of philosophers has always been proverbial, and Aristotle mentions this: "a man engaged in theoretical activity has no needs . . . and many things are only a hindrance to it. Only insofar as he is a human being . . . will he need such things for the business of being human [*anthrōpeuesthai*]"—having a body, living together with other men, and so on. In the same vein, Democritus recommends abstinence for thinking: it teaches how the *logos* derives its pleasures from itself (*auton ex heautou*).[88]

The unawareness of the body in the thinking experience combined with the sheer pleasure of the activity explains better than anything else not only the soothing, consoling effects certain thought-trains had on the men of late antiquity but also their curiously extreme theories of the power of mind over body—theories clearly refuted by common experience. Gibbon writes in his comments on Boethius: "Such topics of consolation, so obvious, so vague, or so abstruse, are ineffectual to subdue the feelings of human nature," and the final victory of Christianity, which offered these "topics" of philosophy as literal facts and sure promises, proves how right Gibbon was.[89] He added: "Yet the sense of misfortune may be diverted by the labour of thought," and he hinted at least at what actually is the case, namely, that fear for the body disappears as long as the "labour of thought" lasts, not because the contents of thought can overcome fear but because the thinking activity makes you unaware of having a body and can even overcome the sensations of minor discomforts. The inordinate strength of this experience may elucidate the otherwise rather strange historical fact that the ancient body-mind dichotomy with its strong hostility to the body could be adopted virtually intact by the Christian creed, which was based after all on the dogma of the incarnation (the Word become Flesh) and on belief in bodily resurrection, that is, on doctrines that should have spelled the end of the body-mind dichotomy and its unsolvable riddles.

Before turning to Socrates, I want to mention briefly the curious context in which the word "philosophize," the verb, not the noun, makes its first appearance. Herodotus tells us of Solon, who, having framed the laws for Athens, set out upon ten years of travel, partly for political reasons but also for sight-seeing—*theōrein*. He arrived at Sardis, where Croesus was at the height of his power. And Croesus, after having shown Solon all his riches, addressed him thus: "Stranger, great word has come to us about you, your wisdom and your wandering about, namely, that you have gone visiting many lands of the earth *philosophizing* with respect to the spectacles you saw. Therefore it occurred to me to ask you if you saw one whom you considered the happiest of all."[90] (The rest of the story is familiar: Croesus, expecting to be named the happiest man on earth, is told that no man, no matter how lucky he is, can be called happy before his death.) Croesus addresses Solon not because he has seen so many lands but because he is famous for philosophizing, reflecting upon what he sees; and Solon's answer, though based on experience, is clearly beyond experience. For the question, Who is the happiest of all?, he had substituted the question, What is happiness for mortals? And his answer to this question was a *philosophoumenon*, a reflection on human affairs (*anthrōpeiōn pragmatōn*) and on the length of human life, in which not one day is "like the other," so that "man is wholly chance." Under such conditions it is wise "to wait and mark the end,"[91] for man's life is a story and only the end of the story, when everything is completed, can tell you what it was all about. Human life, because it is marked by a beginning and an end, becomes whole, an entity in itself that can be subjected to judgment, only when it has ended in death; death not merely ends life, it also bestows upon it a silent completeness, snatched from the hazardous flux to which all things human are subject. This is the gist of what later became a proverbial *topos* throughout Greek and Latin antiquity—*nemo ante mortem beatus dici potest.*[92]

Solon himself was well aware of the difficult nature of such deceptively simple propositions. In a fragment that ties in very well with the story told by Herodotus, he is recorded as saying: "Most hard it is to perceive the hidden (*aphanes*) measure of judgment, which nevertheless [even though it does not appear] holds the limits of all things."[93] Here Solon sounds like a predecessor of Socrates, who also, as they said later, wanted to bring philosophy down from the sky to the earth and hence began to examine the invisible measures by which we judge human affairs. When asked who is the happiest among men, Solon responded by raising the question, And what if you please is happiness, how are you to measure it?—in the same way that Socrates was to raise the questions, What are courage, piety, friendship, *sōphrosynē*, knowledge, justice, and so on?

But Solon gives a kind of answer, and this answer, rightly understood in its implications, even contains what people today would call a whole philosophy in the sense of *Weltan-schauung:* the uncertainty of the future makes human life miserable, "danger is inherent in all works and deeds, nobody knows how a thing begun will turn out, one who does well fails to foresee what ill fortune may befall him, while a god gives good luck in everything to the evildoer."[94] Hence, the "No man can be called happy while he is still alive" actually means: "No man is happy; all mortals on whom the Sun gazes are wretches."[95] This is more than a reflection; it is already a kind of doctrine and as such un-Socratic. For Socrates, confronted with such questions, concludes virtually every strictly Socratic dialogue by saying: "I have failed utterly to discover what it is."[96] And this aporetic character of Socratic thinking means: admiring wonder at just or courageous deeds seen by the eyes of the body gives birth to such questions as What is courage? What is justice? The existence of courage or justice has been indicated to my senses by what I have seen, though they themselves are not present in sense perception, and hence not given as self-evident reality. The basic Socratic question—What do we *mean* when we use this class of words, later called "concepts"?—arises out of that experience. But the original wonder is not only not resolved in such questions, since they remain without answer, but even reinforced. What begins as wonder ends in perplexity and thence leads back to wonder: How marvelous that men can perform courageous or just deeds even though they do not know, can give no account of, what courage and justice are.

## 17   The answer of Socrates

To the question What makes us think? I have been giving (except in Solon's case) historically representative answers offered by professional philosophers. These answers are dubious for precisely that reason. The question, when asked by the professional, does not arise out of his own experiences while engaged in thinking. It is asked from outside—whether that outside is constituted by his professional interests as a thinker or by the common sense in himself that makes him question an activity that is out of order in ordinary living. And the answers we then receive are always too general and vague to have much sense for everyday living, in which thinking, after all, constantly occurs and constantly interrupts the ordinary processes of life—just as ordinary living constantly interrupts thinking. If we strip these answers of their doctrinal content, which of course varies enormously, all we get are confessions of a need: the need to concretize the implications of the Platonic wonder, the need (in Kant) of the reasoning faculty to transcend the limitations of the knowable, the need to become reconciled with what actually is and the course of the world—appearing in Hegel as "the need for philosophy," which can transform occurrences outside yourself into your own thoughts—or the need to search for the meaning of whatever is or occurs, as I have been saying here, no less generally, no less vaguely.

It is this helplessness of the thinking ego to give an account of itself that has made the philosophers, the professional thinkers, such a difficult tribe to deal with. For the trouble is that the thinking ego, as we have seen—in distinction from the self that, of course, exists in every thinker, too—has no urge to appear in the world of appearances. It is a slippery fellow, not only invisible to others but also, for the self, impalpable, impossible to grasp. This is partly because it is sheer activity, and partly because—as Hegel once said—"[as] an abstract ego it is liberated from the particularity of all other properties, dispositions, etc., and is active only with respect to the general, which is the same for all individuals."[97] In any case, seen from the world of appearances, from the marketplace, the thinking ego always lives in hiding, *lathē biōsas*. And our question, What makes us think?, is actually inquiring about ways and means to bring it out of hiding, to tease it, as it were, into manifestation.

The best, in fact the only, way I can think of to get hold of the question is to look for a model, an example of a thinker who was not a professional, who in his person unified two apparently contradictory passions, for thinking and acting—not in the sense of being eager to apply his thoughts or to establish theoretical standards for action but in the much more relevant sense of being equally at home in both spheres and able to move from one sphere to the other with the greatest apparent ease, very much as we ourselves constantly move back and forth between experiences in the world of appearances and the need for reflecting on them. Best suited for this role would be a man who counted himself neither among the many nor among the few (a distinction at least as old as Pythagoras), who had no aspiration to be a ruler of men, no claim even to be particularly well fitted by his superior wisdom to act in an advisory capacity to those in power, but not a man who submitted meekly to being ruled either; in brief, a thinker who always remained a man among men, who did not shun the marketplace, who was a citizen among citizens, doing nothing, claiming nothing except what in his opinion every citizen should be and have a right to. Such a man ought to be difficult to find: if he were able to represent for us the actual thinking activity, he would not have left a body of doctrine behind; he would not have cared to write down his thoughts even if, after he was through with thinking, there had been any residue tangible enough to set out in black and white. You will have guessed that I am thinking of Socrates. We would not know much about him, at least not enough to impress us greatly, if he had not made such an enormous impression on Plato, and we might not know anything about him, perhaps not even from Plato, if he had not decided to lay down his life, not for any specific belief or doctrine—he had none—but simply for the right to go about examining the opinions of other people, thinking about them and asking his interlocutors to do the same.

I hope the reader will not believe that I chose Socrates at random. But I must give a warning: there is a great deal of controversy about the historical Socrates, and though this is one of the more fascinating topics of learned contention, I shall ignore it[98] and only mention in passing what is likely to be the chief bone of contention—namely, my belief that there exists a sharp dividing line between what is authentically Socratic and the philosophy taught by Plato. The stumbling block here is the fact that Plato used Socrates as *the* philosopher, not only in the early and clearly "Socratic" dialogues but also later, when he often made him the spokesman for theories and doctrines that were entirely un-Socratic. In many instances, Plato himself clearly marked the differences, for example, in the *Symposium,* in Diotima's famous speech, which tells us expressly that Socrates does not know anything about the "greater mysteries" and may not be able to understand them. In other instances, however, the line is blurred, usually because Plato could still reckon on a reading public that would be aware of certain enormous inconsistencies—as when he lets Socrates say in the *Theaetetus*[99] that "great philosophers . . . from their youth up have never known the way to the marketplace," an anti-Socratic statement if ever there was one. And yet, to make matters worse, this by no means signifies that the same dialogue does not give fully authentic information about the real Socrates.[100]

No one, I think, will seriously dispute that my choice is historically justifiable. Less easily justifiable, perhaps, is the transformation of a historical figure into a model, for there is no doubt that some transformation is necessary if the figure in question is to perform the function we assign to it. Etienne Gilson, in his great book about Dante, wrote that in *The Divine Comedy* "a character . . . conserves . . . as much of its historical reality as the representative function that Dante assigns to it requires."[101] It seems easy enough to grant this kind of freedom to poets and to call it license—but worse when non-poets try their hand at it. Yet, justified or not, that is precisely what we do when we construct "ideal types"—not out of whole cloth, as in the allegories and personified abstractions so dear to the hearts of bad poets and some scholars, but out of the crowd of living beings past or present who seem to possess a representative significance. And Gilson hints at least at the true justification of this method (or technique) when he discusses the representative part assigned by Dante to Aquinas: the real Thomas, Gilson points out, would not have done what Dante made him do—eulogize Siger of Brabant—but the only reason that the real Thomas would have declined to pronounce such a eulogy would have been a certain human weakness, a defect of character, "the part of his make-up," as Gilson says, "which he had to leave at the gate of the *Paradiso* before he could enter."[102] There are a number of traits in the Xenophonian Socrates, whose historical credibility need not be doubted, that Socrates might have had to leave at the gate of Paradise.

The first thing that strikes us in Plato's Socratic dialogues is that they are all aporetic. The argument either leads nowhere or goes around in circles. In order to know what justice is, you must know what knowledge is, and in order to know that, you must have a previous, unexamined notion of knowledge.[103] Hence, "a man cannot try to discover either what he knows or what he does not know. If he knows, there is no need of inquiry; if he does not know . . . he does not even know what he is to look for."[104] Or, in the *Euthyphro:* in order to be pious you must know what piety is. The things that please the gods are pious; but are they pious because they please the gods or do they please the gods because they are pious?

None of the *logoi*, the arguments, ever stays put; they move around. And because Socrates, asking questions to which he does *not* know the answers, sets them in motion, once the statements have come full circle, it is usually Socrates who cheerfully proposes to start all over again and inquire what justice or piety or knowledge or happiness are.[105] For the topics of these early dialogues deal with very simple, everyday concepts, such as arise whenever people open their mouths and begin to talk. The introduction usually runs as follows: to be sure, there are happy people, just deeds, courageous men, beautiful things to see and admire, everybody knows about them; the trouble starts with our nouns, presumably derived from the adjectives we apply to particular cases as they *appear* to us (we *see* a happy man, *perceive* the courageous deed or the just decision). In short, the trouble arrives with such words as *happiness, courage, justice,* and so on, what we now call concepts—Solon's "non-appearing measure" (*aphanes metron*) "most difficult for the mind to comprehend, but nevertheless holding the limits of all things"[106]—and what Plato somewhat later called ideas perceivable only by the eyes of the mind. These words are part and parcel of our everyday speech, and still we can give no account of them; when we try to define them, they get slippery; when we talk about their meaning, nothing stays put any more, everything begins to move. So instead of repeating what we learned from Aristotle, that Socrates was the man who discovered the "concept," we shall ask what Socrates did when he discovered it. For surely these words were part of the Greek language before he tried to force the Athenians and himself to give an account of what they and he meant—in the firm belief, of course, that no speech would be possible without them.

Today that is no longer so certain. Our knowledge of the so-called primitive languages has taught us that the grouping together of many particulars under a name common to all of them is by no means a matter of course; these languages, whose vocabulary is often so remarkably rich, lack such abstract nouns even in relation to clearly visible objects. To simplify matters, let us take a noun which to us no longer sounds abstract at all. We can use the word "house" for a great number of objects—for the mud hut of a tribe, for the palace of a king, the country home of a city dweller, the cottage in the village, the apartment house in town—but we can hardly use it for the movable tents of some nomads. The house in and by itself, *auto kath'auto,* that which makes us use the word for all these particular and very different buildings, is never seen, either by the eyes of the body or by those of the mind; every imagined house, be it ever so abstract, having the bare minimum to make it recognizable, is already a particular house. This other, invisible, house, of which we must have a notion in order to recognize particular buildings as houses, has been explained in different ways and called by different names in the history of philosophy; with this we are not concerned here, although we might find it less hard to define than such words as "happiness" or "justice." The point here is that it implies something considerably less tangible than the structure perceived by our eyes. It implies "housing somebody" and being "dwelt in" as no tent, put up today and taken down tomorrow, could house or serve as a dwelling place. The word "house" is the "unseen measure," "holds the limits of all things" pertaining to dwelling; it is a word that could not exist unless one presupposed thinking about being housed, dwelling, having a home. As a word, "house" is shorthand for all these things, the kind of shorthand without which thinking and its characteristic swiftness would not be possible at all. *The word "house" is something like a frozen thought that thinking must unfreeze* whenever it wants to find out the original meaning. In medieval philosophy, this kind of thinking was called "meditation," and the word should be heard as different from, even opposed to, contemplation. At all events, this kind of pondering reflection does not produce definitions and in that sense is entirely without results, though somebody who had pondered the meaning of "house" might make his own look better.

Socrates, at any rate, is commonly said to have believed in the teachability of virtue, and he seems indeed to have held that talking and thinking about piety, justice, courage, and the rest were likely to make men more pious, more just, more courageous, despite the fact that neither definitions nor "values" were given them to direct their future conduct. What

Socrates actually believed in such matters can best be illustrated by the similes he applied to himself. He called himself a gadfly and a midwife; in Plato's account somebody else called him an "electric ray," a fish that paralyzes and numbs by contact, and Socrates recognized the likeness as apt, provided that his hearers understood that "the electric ray paralyzes others only through being paralyzed itself. . . . It isn't that, knowing the answers myself, I perplex other people. The truth is rather that I infect them also with the perplexity I feel myself."[107] Which, of course, sums up neatly the only way thinking can be taught—even though Socrates, as he repeatedly said, did not teach anything, for the simple reason that he had nothing to teach; he was "sterile" like the midwives in Greece, who were beyond the age of childbearing. (Since he had nothing to teach, no truth to hand out, he was accused of never revealing his own view [*gnōmē*]—as we learn from Xenophon, who defended him against the charge.)[108] It seems that he, unlike the professional philosophers, felt the urge to check with his fellow-men to learn whether his perplexities were shared by them—and this is quite different from the inclination to find solutions for riddles and then demonstrate them to others.

Let us look briefly at the three similes. First, Socrates is a gadfly: he knows how to sting the citizens who, without him, will "sleep on undisturbed for the rest of their lives" unless somebody comes along to arouse them. And what does he arouse them to? To thinking and examination, an activity without which life, in his view, was not only not worth much but was not fully alive. (On this subject, in the *Apology* as in other cases, Socrates is saying very nearly the opposite of what Plato made him say in the "improved apology" of the *Phaedo*. In the *Apology*, Socrates tells his fellow-citizens why he should live and also why, though life is "very dear" to him, he is not afraid of death; in the *Phaedo*, he explains to his friends how burdensome life is and why he is glad to die.)

Second, Socrates is a midwife: in the *Theaetetus*, he says that it is because he is sterile himself that he knows how to deliver others of their thoughts; moreover, thanks to his sterility, he has the expert knowledge of the midwife and can decide whether the child is a real child or a mere wind-egg of which the bearer must be cleansed. But in the dialogues, hardly anybody among Socrates' interlocutors has brought forth a thought that is not a wind-egg and that Socrates considered worth keeping alive. Rather, he did what Plato in the *Sophist*, certainly thinking of Socrates, said of the sophists: he purged people of their "opinions," that is, of those unexamined pre-judgments that would prevent them from thinking —helping them, as Plato said, to get rid of the bad in them, their opinions, yet without making them good, giving them truth.[109]

Third, Socrates, knowing that we do not know, and nevertheless unwilling to let it go at that, remains steadfast in his own perplexities and, like the electric ray, paralyzed himself, paralyzes anyone he comes into contact with. The electric ray, at first glance, seems to be the opposite of the gadfly; it paralyzes where the gadfly rouses. Yet what cannot fail to look like paralysis from the outside—from the standpoint of ordinary human affairs—is *felt* as the highest state of being active and alive. There exist, despite the scarcity of documentary evidence about the thinking experience, a number of utterances of thinkers throughout the centuries to bear this out.

Hence, Socrates, gadfly, midwife, electric ray, is not a philosopher (he teaches nothing and has nothing to teach) and he is not a sophist, for he does not claim to make men wise. He only points out to them that they are not wise, that nobody is—a "pursuit" keeping him so busy that he has no time for either public or private affairs.[110] And while he defends himself vigorously against the charge of corrupting the young, he nowhere pretends that he is improving them. Nevertheless, he claims that the appearance in Athens of thinking and examining represented in himself was the greatest good that ever befell the City.[111] Thus he was concerned with what thinking is good for, although, in this, as in all other respects, he did not give a clear-cut answer. We may be sure that a dialogue dealing with the question What is thinking good for? would have ended in the same perplexities as all the others.

If there had been a Socratic tradition in Western thought,

if, in Whitehead's words, the history of philosophy were a collection of footnotes not to Plato but to Socrates (which, of course, would have been impossible), we certainly would find in it no answer to our question, but at least a number of variations of it. Socrates himself, well aware that he was dealing with invisibles in his enterprise, used a metaphor to explain the thinking activity—the metaphor of the wind: "The winds themselves are invisible, yet what they do is manifest to us and we somehow feel their approach."[112] We find the same metaphor in Sophocles, who (in the *Antigone*)[113] counts "windswift thought" among the dubious, "awe-inspiring" (*deina*) things with which men are blessed or cursed. In our own time, Heidegger occasionally speaks of the "storm of thought," and he uses the metaphor explicitly at the only point in his work where he speaks directly of Socrates: "Throughout his life and up to his very death Socrates did nothing other than place himself in this draft, this current [of thinking], and maintain himself in it. This is why he is the purest of the West. This is why he wrote nothing. For anyone who begins, out of thinking, to write must inevitably be like those people who run for shelter from a wind too strong for them . . . all thinkers after Socrates, their greatness notwithstanding, were such refugees. Thinking became literature." In a later explanatory note he adds that to be the "purest" thinker does not mean to be the greatest.[114]

In the context in which Xenophon, always anxious to defend the master with his own vulgar arguments against vulgar accusations, mentions this metaphor, it does not make much sense. Still, even he indicates that the invisible wind of thought was manifest in the concepts, virtues, and "values" with which Socrates dealt in his examinations. The trouble is that this same wind, whenever it is roused, has the peculiarity of doing away with its own previous manifestations: this is why the same man can be understood and understand himself as gadfly as well as electric ray. It is in this invisible element's nature to undo, unfreeze, as it were, what language, the medium of thinking, has frozen into thought—words (concepts, sentences, definitions, doctrines) whose "weakness" and inflexibility Plato denounces so splendidly in the *Seventh Letter*. The conse-

quence is that thinking inevitably has a destructive, under-
mining effect on all established criteria, values, measurements
of good and evil, in short, on those customs and rules of conduct we treat of in morals and ethics. These frozen thoughts,
Socrates seems to say, come so handily that you can use them
in your sleep; but if the wind of thinking, which I shall now
stir in you, has shaken you from your sleep and made you
fully awake and alive, then you will see that you have nothing
in your grasp but perplexities, and the best we can do with
them is share them with each other.

Hence, the paralysis induced by thinking is twofold: it is
inherent in the *stop* and think, the interruption of all other
activities—psychologically, one may indeed define a "problem"
as a "situation which for some reason appreciably holds up
an organism in its effort to reach a goal"[115]—and it also may
have a dazing after-effect, when you come out of it, feeling
unsure of what seemed to you beyond doubt while you were
unthinkingly engaged in whatever you were doing. If what
you were doing consisted in applying general rules of conduct
to particular cases as they arise in ordinary life, you will find
yourself paralyzed because no such rules can withstand the
wind of thought. To take again the example of the frozen
thought inherent in the word "house," once you have thought
about its implied meaning—dwelling, having a home, being
housed—you are no longer as likely to accept for your own
home whatever the fashion of the time may prescribe; but this
by no means guarantees that you will be able to come up with
an acceptable solution to what has become "problematic."

This leads to the last and, perhaps, even greatest danger
of this dangerous and profitless enterprise. In the circle around
Socrates, there were men like Alcibiades and Critias—God
knows, by no means the worst among his so-called pupils—
who had turned out to be a real threat to the polis, and this
not because they had been paralyzed by the electric ray but,
on the contrary, because they had been aroused by the gadfly.
What they had been aroused to was license and cynicism.
Not content with being taught how to think without being
taught a doctrine, they changed the non-results of the Socratic
thinking examination into negative results: If we cannot define

what piety is, let us be impious—which is pretty much the opposite of what Socrates had hoped to achieve by talking about piety.

The quest for meaning, which relentlessly dissolves and examines anew all accepted doctrines and rules, can at any moment turn against itself, produce a reversal of the old values, and declare these contraries to be "new values." To a certain extent, this is what Nietzsche did when he reversed Platonism, forgetting that a reversed Plato is still Plato, or what Marx did when he turned Hegel upside down, producing a strictly Hegelian system of history in the process. Such negative results of thinking will then be used with the same unthinking routine as before; the moment they are applied to the realm of human affairs, it is as though they had never gone through the thinking process. What we commonly call "nihilism"—and are tempted to date historically, decry politically, and ascribe to thinkers who allegedly dared to think "dangerous thoughts"—is actually a danger inherent in the thinking activity itself. There are no dangerous thoughts; thinking itself is dangerous, but nihilism is not its product. Nihilism is but the other side of conventionalism; its creed consists of negations of the current so-called positive values, to which it remains bound. All critical examinations must go through a stage of at least hypothetically negating accepted opinions and "values" by searching out their implications and tacit assumptions, and in this sense nihilism may be seen as an ever-present danger of thinking.

But that danger does not arise out of the Socratic conviction that an unexamined life is not worth living, but, on the contrary, out of the desire to find results that would make further thinking unnecessary. Thinking is equally dangerous to all creeds and, by itself, does not bring forth any new creed. Its most dangerous aspect from the viewpoint of common sense is that what was meaningful while you were thinking dissolves the moment you want to apply it to everyday living. When common opinion gets hold of the "concepts," that is, the manifestations of thinking in everyday speech, and begins to handle them as though they were the results of cognition, the end can only be a clear demonstration that no man is wise. Practically, thinking means that each time you are confronted with some difficulty in life you have to make up your mind anew.

However, non-thinking, which seems so recommendable a state for political and moral affairs, also has its perils. By shielding people from the dangers of examination, it teaches them to hold fast to whatever the prescribed rules of conduct may be at a given time in a given society. What people then get used to is less the content of the rules, a close examination of which would always lead them into perplexity, than the *possession* of rules under which to subsume particulars. If somebody appears who, for whatever purposes, wishes to abolish the old "values" or virtues, he will find that easy enough, provided he offers a new code, and he will need relatively little force and no persuasion—i.e., proof that the new values are better than the old—to impose it. The more firmly men hold to the old code, the more eager will they be to assimilate themselves to the new one, which in practice means that the readiest to obey will be those who were the most respectable pillars of society, the least likely to indulge in thoughts, dangerous or otherwise, while those who to all appearances were the most unreliable elements of the old order will be the least tractable.

If ethical and moral matters really are what the etymology of the words indicates, it should be no more difficult to change the mores and habits of a people than it would be to change their table manners. The ease with which such a reversal can take place under certain conditions suggests indeed that everybody was fast asleep when it occurred. I am alluding, of course, to what happened in Nazi Germany and, to some extent, also in Stalinist Russia, when suddenly the basic commandments of Western morality were reversed: in one case, "Thou shalt not kill"; in the other, "Thou shalt not bear false witness against thy neighbor." And the sequel—the reversal of the reversal, the fact that it was so surprisingly easy "to re-educate" the Germans after the collapse of the Third

Reich, so easy indeed that it was as though re-education was automatic—should not console us either. It was actually the same phenomenon.

To come back to Socrates. The Athenians told him that thinking was subversive, that the wind of thought was a hurricane sweeping away all the established signs by which men orient themselves, bringing disorder into the cities and confusing the citizens. And though Socrates denies that thinking corrupts, he does not pretend that it improves anybody either. It rouses you from sleep, and this seems to him a great good for the City. Yet he does not say that he began his examining in order to become such a great benefactor. As far as he himself is concerned, there is nothing more to be said than that life deprived of thought would be meaningless, even though thought will never make men wise or give them the answers to thought's own questions. The meaning of what Socrates was doing lay in the activity itself. Or to put it differently: To think and to be fully alive are the same, and this implies that thinking must always begin afresh; it is an activity that accompanies living and is concerned with such concepts as justice, happiness, virtue, offered us by language itself as expressing the meaning of whatever happens in life and occurs to us while we are alive.

What I called the "quest" for meaning appears in Socrates' language as love, that is, love in its Greek significance of *Erōs*, not the Christian *agapē*. Love as Eros is primarily a need; it desires what it has not. Men love wisdom and therefore begin to philosophize because they are not wise, and they love beauty, and do beauty, as it were—*philokaloumen*, as Pericles called it in the Funeral Oration[116]—because they are not beautiful. Love is the only matter in which Socrates pretends to be an expert, and this skill guides him, too, in choosing his companions and friends: "While I may be worthless in all other matters, this talent I have been given: I can easily recognize a lover and a beloved."[117] By desiring what it has not, love establishes a relationship with what is not present. In order to bring this relationship into the open, make it appear, men want to speak about it—just as the lover wants to speak about the beloved. Because thought's quest is a kind of desirous love, the objects of thought can only be lovable things—beauty, wisdom, justice, and so on. Ugliness and evil are almost by definition excluded from the thinking concern. They may turn up as deficiencies, ugliness consisting in lack of beauty, evil, *kakia*, in lack of the good. As such, they have no roots of their own, no essence that thought could get hold of. If thinking dissolves positive concepts into their original meaning, then the same process must dissolve these "negative" concepts into their original meaninglessness, that is, into nothing for the thinking ego. That is why Socrates believed no one could do evil voluntarily—because of, as we would say, its ontological status: it consists in an absence, in something that is not. And that is also why Democritus, who thought of *logos*, speech, as following action in the same way that the shadow accompanies all real things, thus distinguishing them from mere semblances, counseled against speaking of evil deeds: ignoring evil, depriving it of any manifestation in speech, will turn it into a mere semblance, something that has no shadow.[118] We found the same exclusion of evil when we were following Plato's admiring, affirming wonder as it unfolds into thinking; it is found in almost all Occidental philosophers. It looks as though Socrates had nothing more to say about the connection between evil and lack of thought than that people who are not in love with beauty, justice, and wisdom are incapable of thought, just as, conversely, those who are in love with examining and thus "do philosophy" would be incapable of doing evil.

## 18 *The two-in-one*

Where does this leave us in regard to one of our chief problems—the possible interconnectedness of non-thought and evil? We are left with the conclusion that only people inspired by the Socratic *erōs*, the love of wisdom, beauty, and justice, are capable of thought and can be trusted. In other words, we are left with Plato's "noble natures," with the few of whom it may be true that none "does evil voluntarily." Yet the implied and dangerous conclusion, "Everybody wants to do good," is not true even in their case. (The sad truth of the matter is that most evil is done by people who never made up their minds to be or do either evil or good.) Socrates, who, unlike Plato, thought about all subjects and talked with everybody, cannot have believed that only the few are capable of thought and that only certain objects of thought, visible to the eyes of the well-trained mind but ineffable in discourse, bestow dignity and relevance on the thinking activity. If there is anything in thinking that can prevent men from doing evil, it must be some property inherent in the activity itself, regardless of its objects.

Socrates, that lover of perplexities, made very few positive statements. Among them are two propositions, closely interconnected, that deal with this subject. Both occur in the *Gorgias,* the dialogue about rhetoric, the art of addressing and convincing the many. The *Gorgias* does not belong among the early Socratic dialogues; it was written shortly before Plato became the head of the Academy. Moreover, its very subject matter is an art or form of discourse that would seemingly lose all sense if it were aporetic. And yet, this dialogue is still aporetic, except that Plato concludes it with one of his myths of a hereafter of rewards and punishments which apparently— that is, ironically—resolve all difficulties. The seriousness of these myths of his is purely political; it consists in their being addressed to the multitude. Yet the myths, certainly non-Socratic, of the *Gorgias* are of importance because they contain, albeit in a non-philosophical form, Plato's admission that men do commit evil acts voluntarily, and the additional implied admission that he, no more than Socrates, knew what to do philosophically with that disturbing fact. We may not know whether Socrates believed that ignorance causes evil and that virtue can be taught; but we do know that Plato thought it wiser to rely on threats.

The two positive Socratic propositions read as follows.

The first: "It is better to be wronged than to do wrong," to which Callicles, the interlocutor in the dialogue, replies as all Greece would have replied, "To suffer wrong is not the part of a man at all, but that of a slave for whom it is better to be dead than alive, as it is for anyone who is unable to come either to his own assistance when he is wronged or to that of anyone he cares about."[119] The second: "It would be better for me that my lyre or a chorus I directed should be out of tune and loud with discord, and that multitudes of men should disagree with me rather than that I, *being one,* should be out of harmony with myself and contradict me."[120] Which causes Callicles to tell Socrates that he is "going mad with eloquence," and that it would be better for him and everybody else if he would leave philosophy alone.[121]

And there he has a point. It was indeed philosophy, or, rather, the experience of thinking, that led Socrates to make these statements—although, of course, he did not start his enterprise in order to arrive at them, any more than other thinkers embarked upon theirs in order to be "happy."[122] (It would be a serious mistake, I believe, to understand these statements as the results of some cogitation about morality; they are insights, to be sure, but insights of experience, and as far as the thinking process itself is concerned they are at best incidental by-products.)

We have difficulty realizing how paradoxical the first statement must have sounded when it was made; after thousands of years of use and misuse, it reads like cheap moralizing. And the best demonstration of how difficult it is for modern readers to understand the thrust of the second is the fact that its key words, *"Being one"* (preceding "it would be worse for me to be at odds with myself than in disagreement with multitudes of men"), are frequently left out in translation. As to the first, it is a subjective statement; it means: it is better *for me* to suffer wrong than to do wrong. And in the dialogue where it occurs, it is simply countered by the opposite equally subjective statement, which, of course, sounds much more plausible. What becomes apparent is that Callicles and Socrates are talking about a different I: What is good for one is bad for the other.

If, on the other hand, we look at the proposition from the point of view of the world, as distinguished from those of the two speakers, we would have to say: What counts is that a wrong has been done; and for this, it is irrelevant who is better off, the wrong-doer or the wrong-sufferer. As citizens, we must prevent wrong-doing because the world in which we all live, wrong-doer, wrong-sufferer, and spectator, is at stake; the City has been wronged. Our law codes, with their distinction between crimes where indictment is mandatory and transgressions that pertain only to the private affairs of individuals who may or may not want to sue, take this into account. We could almost define a crime as that transgression of the law that demands punishment regardless of the one who has been wronged; the wronged one may feel like forgiving and forgetting, and there may be no danger for others if it can be assumed that the wrong-doer is altogether unlikely to do wrong again. Still, the law of the land permits no option because it is the community as a whole that has been violated.

In other words, Socrates is not talking here in the person of the citizen, who is supposed to be more concerned with the world than with his self; he talks as the man chiefly devoted to thinking. It is as though he said to Callicles: If you were like me, in love with wisdom and in need of thinking about everything and examining everything, you would know that if the world were as you depict it, divided into the strong and the weak, where "the strong do what they can and the weak suffer what they must" (Thucydides), so that no alternative exists but to either do or suffer wrong, then it is better to suffer than to do. But the presupposition is of course: *if you are in love with wisdom and philosophizing; if* you know what it means to examine.

To my knowledge there is only one other passage in Greek literature that, in almost the same words, says what Socrates said. "More unfortunate [*kakodaimonesteros*] than the wronged one is the wrong-doer,"[123] reads one of the fragments of Democritus, Parmenides' great adversary, who probably for this reason is never mentioned by Plato. The coincidence seems noteworthy because Democritus, as distinguished from Socrates, was not particularly interested in human affairs but he seems to have been quite interested in the experience of think-ing. It looks as though what we are tempted to understand as a purely moral proposition actually arose out of the thinking experience as such.

And this brings us to the second statement, which in fact is the prerequisite for the first one. It, too, is highly paradoxical. Socrates talks of being one and *therefore* not being able to risk getting out of harmony with himself. But nothing that is identical with itself, truly and absolutely *One*, as A is A, can be either in or out of harmony with itself; you always need at least two tones to produce a harmonious sound. Cer-tainly when I appear and am seen by others, I am one; otherwise I would be unrecognizable. And so long as I am together with others, barely conscious of myself, I am as I appear to others. We call *consciousness* (literally, as we have seen, "to know with myself") the curious fact that in a sense I also am for myself, though I hardly appear to me, which indicates that the Socratic "being one" is not so unproblematic as it seems; I am not only for others but for myself, and in this latter case, I clearly am not just one. A difference is inserted into my Oneness.

We know of this difference in other respects. Everything that exists among a plurality of things is not simply what it is, in its identity, but it is also different from others; this being different belongs to its very nature. When we try to get hold of it in thought, wanting to define it, we must take this otherness (*altereitas*) or difference into account. When we say what a thing is, we must say what it is *not* or we would speak in tautologies: every determination is negation, as Spinoza has it. Touching on this matter, the problem of identity and difference, there is a curious passage in Plato's *Sophist* that Heidegger has pointed to. The Stranger in the dialogue states that of two things—for instance, rest and motion—"each one is different [from the other], but itself *for itself* the same" (*hekaston heautō tauton*).[124] In interpreting the sentence, Heidegger puts the emphasis on the dative, *heautō*, for Plato does not say, as we would expect, *hekaston auto tauton,* "each one itself [taken out of context] is the same," in the sense of the tautological A is A, where difference arises out of the plurality of things. According to Heidegger, this dative means that "each thing itself is returned to itself, each itself is the same for itself [because it is] with itself. . . . Sameness implies the relation of 'with,' that is, a mediation, a connection, a synthesis: the unification into a unity."[125]

The passage Heidegger is examining occurs in the *Sophist's* final section about the *koinōnia,* the "community," the fitting and blending together, of the Ideas, and especially about the possible community of Difference and Identity, which seem to be contraries. "What is different is always so called with reference to other things" (*pros alla*),[126] but their opposites, things "that are what they are in themselves" (*kath' hauta*), partake in the "Idea" of difference insofar as they "refer back to themselves"—they are the same with or for themselves, so that each *eidos* is different from the rest, "not by virtue of its own nature, but because it partakes of the character of Difference,"[127] that is, not because it has a relation to something else from which it is different (*pros ti*), but because it exists among a plurality of Ideas, and "every entity qua entity harbors the possibility of being looked upon as different from something."[128] In our terms, wherever there is a plurality—of living beings, of things, of Ideas—there is difference, and this difference does not arise from the outside but is inherent in every entity in the form of duality, from which comes unity as unification.

This construction—Plato's implication as well as Heidegger's interpretation—seems to me erroneous. To take a mere thing out of its context with other things and to look on it only in its "relation" to itself (*kath' hauto*), that is, in its identity, reveals no difference, no otherness; along with its relation to something it is *not*, it loses its reality and acquires a curious kind of eeriness. In that way, it often appears in works of art, especially in Kafka's early prose pieces or in some paintings of van Gogh where a single object, a chair, a pair of shoes, is represented. But these art works are thought-things, and what gives them their meaning—as though they were not just themselves but *for* themselves—is precisely the transformation they have undergone when thinking took possession of them.

In other words, what is being transferred here is the experience of the thinking ego to things themselves. For nothing can be itself and at the same time for itself but the two-in-one that Socrates discovered as the essence of thought and Plato translated into conceptual language as the soundless dialogue *eme emautō*—between me and myself.[129] But, again, it is not the thinking activity that constitutes the unity, unifies the two-in-one; on the contrary, the two-in-one become One again when the outside world intrudes upon the thinker and cuts short the thinking process. Then, when he is called by his name back into the world of appearances, where he is always One, it is as though the two into which the thinking process had split him clapped together again. Thinking, existentially speaking, is a solitary but not a lonely business; solitude is that human situation in which I keep myself company. Loneliness comes about when I am alone without being able to split up into the two-in-one, without being able to keep myself company, when, as Jaspers used to say, "I am in default of myself" (*ich bleibe mir aus*), or, to put it differently, when I am one and without company.

Nothing perhaps indicates more strongly that man exists *essentially* in the plural than that his solitude actualizes his merely being conscious of himself, which we probably share with the higher animals, into a duality during the thinking activity. It is this *duality* of myself with myself that makes thinking a true activity, in which I am both the one who asks and the one who answers. Thinking can become dialectical and critical because it goes through this questioning and answering process, through the dialogue of *dialegesthai*, which actually is a "traveling through words," a *poreuesthai dia tōn logōn*,[130] whereby we constantly raise the basic Socratic question: *What do you mean when you say* . . . ? except that this *legein*, saying, is soundless and therefore so swift that its dialogical structure is somewhat difficult to detect.

The criterion of the mental dialogue is no longer truth, which would compel answers to the questions I raise with myself, either in the mode of Intuition, which compels with the force of sense evidence, or as necessary conclusions of reckoning with consequences in mathematical or logical reasoning, which rely on the structure of our brain and compel with its natural power. The only criterion of Socratic thinking is agreement, to be consistent with oneself, *homologein autos heautō*:[131] its opposite, to be in contradiction with oneself, *enantia legein autos heautō*,[132] actually means becoming one's own adversary. Hence Aristotle, in his earliest formulation of the famous axiom of contradiction, says explicitly that this is axiomatic: "we must necessarily believe it because . . . it is addressed not to the outward word [*exō logos,* that is, to the spoken word addressed to someone else, an interlocutor who may be either friend or adversary] but to the discourse *within the soul,* and though we can always raise objections to the outward word, to the *inward discourse* we cannot always object," because here the partner is oneself, and I cannot possibly want to become my own adversary.[133] (In this instance, we can watch how such an insight, won from the factual experience of the thinking ego, gets lost when it is generalized into a philosophical doctrine—"A cannot be both B and A under the same conditions and at the same time"—for we find the transformation being achieved by Aristotle himself when he discusses the same matter in his *Metaphysics*.[134])

A close reading of the *Organon,* the "Instrument," as the collection of Aristotle's early logical treatises has been called since the sixth century, clearly shows that what we now call "logic" was by no means originally meant as an "instrument of thought," of the inward discourse carried on "within the soul," but was designed as the science of correct talking and arguing when we are trying to convince others or give an account of what we state, always starting, as Socrates did, with premises most likely to be agreed on by most men or by most of those generally believed to be the wisest. In the early treatises, the axiom of non-contradiction, decisive only for the inward dialogue of thinking, has not yet been established as the most basic rule for discourse in general. Only after this special case had become the guiding example for all thought could Kant, who in his *Anthropology* had defined thinking as "talking with oneself . . . hence also inwardly listening,"[135] count the injunction "Always think consistently, in agreement with yourself" ("*Jederzeit mit sich selbst einstimmig denken*") among the maxims that must be regarded as "unchangeable commandments for the class of thinkers."[136]

In brief, the specifically human actualization of consciousness in the thinking dialogue between me and myself suggests that difference and otherness, which are such outstanding characteristics of the world of appearances as it is given to man for his habitat among a plurality of things, are the very conditions for the existence of man's mental ego as well, for this ego actually exists only in duality. And this ego—the I-am-I—experiences difference in identity precisely when it is not related to the things that appear but only related to itself. (This original duality, incidentally, explains the futility of the fashionable search for identity. Our modern identity crisis could be resolved only by never being alone and never trying to think.) Without that original split, Socrates' statement about harmony in a being that to all appearances is One would be meaningless.

Consciousness is not the same as thinking; acts of consciousness have in common with sense experience the fact that they are "intentional" and therefore *cognitive* acts, whereas the thinking ego does not think something but *about* something, and this act is dialectical: it proceeds in the form of a silent dialogue. Without consciousness in the sense of self-awareness, thinking would not be possible. What thinking actualizes in its unending process is difference, given as a mere raw fact (*factum brutum*) in consciousness; only in this humanized form does consciousness then become the outstanding characteristic of somebody who is a man and neither a god nor an animal. As the metaphor bridges the gap between the world of appearances and the mental activities going on within it, so the Socratic two-in-one heals the solitariness of thought; its inherent duality points to the infinite plurality which is the law of the earth.

To Socrates, the duality of the two-in-one meant no more than that if you want to think, you must see to it that the two who carry on the dialogue be in good shape, that the partners be *friends*. The partner who comes to life when you are alert and alone is the only one from whom you can never get away—except by ceasing to think. It is better to suffer wrong than to do wrong, because you can remain the friend of the sufferer; who would want to be the friend of and have to live together with a murderer? Not even another murderer. In the end, it is to this rather simple consideration of the importance of agreement between you and yourself that Kant's Categorical Imperative appeals. Underlying the imperative, "Act only on that maxim through which you can at the same time *will* that it should become a universal law,"[137] is the command "Do not contradict yourself." A murderer or a thief cannot will that "Thou shalt kill" and "Thou shalt steal" be general laws, since he naturally fears for his own life and property. If you make yourself an exception, you have contradicted yourself.

In one of the contested dialogues, the *Hippias Major*, which even if not by Plato may still give authentic testimony about Socrates, Socrates describes the situation simply and accurately. It is the end of the dialogue, the moment of going home. He tells Hippias, who has shown himself to be an especially thickheaded partner, how "blissfully fortunate" he is in comparison with poor Socrates, who at home is awaited by a very obnoxious fellow who always cross-examines him. "He is a close relative and lives in the same house." When he now will hear Socrates give utterance to Hippias' opinions, he will ask "whether he is not ashamed of talking about a beautiful way of life, when questioning makes it evident that he does not even know the meaning of the word 'beauty.' "[138] When Hippias goes home, he remains one, for, though he lives alone, he does not seek to keep himself company. He certainly does not lose consciousness; he is simply not in the habit of actualizing it. When Socrates goes home, he is not alone, he is *by* himself. Clearly, with this fellow who awaits him, Socrates has to come to some kind of agreement, because they live under the same roof. Better to be at odds with the whole world than be at odds with the only one you are forced to live together with when you have left company behind.

What Socrates discovered was that we can have intercourse with ourselves, as well as with others, and that the two kinds of intercourse are somehow interrelated. Aristotle, speaking about friendship, remarked: "The friend is another self"[139]—meaning: you can carry on the dialogue of thought with him just as well as with yourself. This is still in the Socratic tradition, except that Socrates would have said: The self, too, is a kind of friend. The guiding experience in these matters is, of course, friendship and not selfhood; I first talk with others before I talk with myself, examining whatever the joint talk may have been about, and then discover that I can conduct a dialogue not only with others but with myself as well. The common point, however, is that the dialogue of thought can be carried out only among friends, and its basic criterion, its supreme law, as it were, says: Do not contradict yourself.

It is characteristic of "base people" to be "at variance with themselves" (*diapherontai heautois*) and of wicked men to avoid their own company; their soul is in rebellion against itself (*stasiazei*).[140] What kind of dialogue can you conduct with yourself when your soul is not in harmony but at war with itself? Precisely the dialogue we overhear when Shakespeare's Richard III is alone:

> What do I fear? Myself? There's none else by:
> Richard loves Richard: that is, I am I.
> Is there a murderer here? No. Yes, I am:
> Then fly: what! from myself? Great reason why:
> Lest I revenge. What! myself upon myself?
> Alack! I love myself. Wherefore? For any good
> That I myself have done unto myself?
> O! no: alas! I rather hate myself
> For hateful deeds committed by myself.
> I am a villain. Yet I lie, I am not.
> Fool, of thyself speak well: fool, do not flatter.

Yet all this looks very different when midnight is past and Richard has escaped his own company to join that of his peers. Then:

> Conscience is but a word that cowards use,
> Devis'd at first to keep the strong in awe. . . .

Even Socrates, so much in love with the marketplace, has to go home, where he will be alone, in solitude, in order to meet the other fellow.

I have drawn attention to the passage in *Hippias Major* in its stark simplicity because it provides a metaphor that can help simplify—at the risk of over-simplification—matters that are difficult and therefore always in danger of over-complication. Later times have given the fellow who awaits Socrates in his home the name of "conscience." Before its tribunal, to adopt Kantian language, we have to appear and give account of ourselves. And I chose the passage in *Richard III*, because Shakespeare, though he uses the word "conscience," does not use it here in the accustomed way. It took language a long time to separate the word "consciousness" from "conscience," and in some languages, for instance, in French, such a separation never was made. Conscience, as we understand it in moral or legal matters, is supposedly always present within us, just like consciousness. And this conscience is also supposed to tell us what to do and what to repent; before it became the *lumen naturale* or Kant's practical reason, it was the voice of God.

Unlike this ever-present conscience, the fellow Socrates is talking about has been left at home; he fears him, as the murderers in *Richard III* fear conscience—as something that is absent. Here conscience appears as an after-thought, roused either by a crime, as in Richard's own case, or by unexamined opinions, as in the case of Socrates. Or it may be just the anticipated fear of such after-thoughts, as with Richard's hired murderers. This conscience, unlike the voice of God within us or the *lumen naturale,* gives no positive prescriptions (even the Socratic *daimōn,* his divine voice, only tells him what *not* to do); in Shakespeare's words "it fills a man full of obstacles." What causes a man to fear it is the anticipation of the presence of a witness who awaits him only *if* and when he goes home. Shakespeare's murderer says: "Every man that means to live well endeavors . . . to live without it," and success in that comes easy because all he has to do is never start the soundless solitary dialogue we call "thinking," never go home and examine things. This is not a matter of wickedness or goodness, as it is not a matter of intelligence or stupidity. A person who does not know that silent intercourse (in which we examine what we say and what we do) will not mind contradicting himself, and this means he will never be either able or willing to account for what he says or does; nor will he mind committing any crime, since he can count on its being forgotten the next moment. Bad people—Aristotle to the contrary notwithstanding—are *not* "full of regrets."

Thinking in its non-cognitive, non-specialized sense as a natural need of human life, the actualization of the difference given in consciousness, is not a prerogative of the few but an ever-present faculty in everybody; by the same token, inability to think is not a failing of the many who lack brain power but an ever-present possibility for everybody—scientists, scholars, and other specialists in mental enterprises not excluded. Everybody may come to shun that intercourse with oneself whose feasibility and importance Socrates first discovered. Thinking accompanies life and is itself the de-materialized quintessence of being alive; and since life is a process, its quintessence can only lie in the actual thinking process and not in any solid results or specific thoughts. A life without thinking is quite possible; it then fails to develop its own essence—it is not merely meaningless; it is not fully alive. Unthinking men are like sleepwalkers.

For the thinking ego and its experience, conscience that "fills a man full of obstacles" is a side effect. No matter what thought-trains the thinking ego thinks through, the self that we all are must take care not to do anything that would make it impossible for the two-in-one to be friends and live in harmony. This is what Spinoza meant by the term "acquiescence in one's self" (*acquiescentia in seipso*): "It can spring out of reason [reasoning], and this contentment is the greatest joy possible."[141] Its criterion for action will not be the usual rules, recognized by multitudes and agreed upon by society, but whether I shall be able to live with myself in peace when the time has come to think about my deeds and words. Conscience is the anticipation of the fellow who awaits you if and when you come home.

For the thinker himself this moral side effect is a marginal affair. And thinking as such does society little good, much less than the thirst for knowledge, which uses thinking as an instrument for other purposes. It does not create values; it will not find out, once and for all, what "the good" is; it does not confirm but, rather, dissolves accepted rules of conduct. And it has no political relevance unless special emergencies arise. That while I am alive I must be able to live with myself is a consideration that does not come up politically except in "boundary situations."

This term was coined by Jaspers for the general, unchanging human condition—"that I cannot live without struggling and suffering; that I cannot avoid guilt; that I must die"—to indicate an experience of "something immanent which already points to transcendence" and which, if we respond to it, will result in our *"becoming the Existenz we potentially are."*[142] In Jaspers, the term gets its suggestive plausibility less from specific experiences than from the simple fact that life itself, limited by birth and death, is a boundary affair in that my worldly existence always forces me to take account of a past when I was not yet and a future when I shall be no more. Here the point is that whenever I transcend the limits of my own life span and begin to reflect on this past, judging it, and this future, forming projects of the will, thinking ceases to be a politically marginal activity. And such reflections will inevitably arise in political emergencies.

When everybody is swept away unthinkingly by what everybody else does and believes in, those who think are drawn out of hiding because their refusal to join in is conspicuous and thereby becomes a kind of action. In such emergencies, it turns out that the purging component of thinking (Socrates' midwifery, which brings out the implications of unexamined opinions and thereby destroys them—values, doctrines, theories, and even convictions) is political by implication. For this destruction has a liberating effect on another faculty, the faculty of judgment, which one may call with some reason the most political of man's mental abilities. It is the faculty that judges *particulars* without subsuming them under general rules which can be taught and learned until they grow into habits that can be replaced by other habits and rules.

The faculty of judging particulars (as brought to light by Kant), the ability to say "this is wrong," "this is beautiful," and so on, is not the same as the faculty of thinking. Thinking deals with invisibles, with representations of things that are absent; judging always concerns particulars and things close at hand. But the two are interrelated, as are consciousness and conscience. If thinking—the two-in-one of the soundless dialogue—actualizes the difference within our identity as given in consciousness and thereby results in conscience as its by-product, then judging, the by-product of the liberating effect of thinking, realizes thinking, makes it manifest in the world of appearances, where I am never alone and always too busy to be able to think. The manifestation of the wind of thought is not knowledge; it is the ability to tell right from wrong, beautiful from ugly. And this, at the rare moments when the stakes are on the table, may indeed prevent catastrophes, at least for the self.

# Where Are We IV
# When We Think?

## 19 "Tantôt je pense et tantôt je suis" (*Valéry*): *the nowhere*

As I approach the end of these considerations, I hope that no reader expects a conclusive summary. For me to make such an attempt would stand in flagrant contradiction to what has been described here. If thinking is an activity that is its own end and if the only adequate metaphor for it, drawn from our ordinary sense experience, is the sensation of being alive, then it follows that all questions concerning the aim or purpose of thinking are as unanswerable as questions about the aim or purpose of life. I am putting the question— Where are we when we think?—at the end of our examination not because the answer could supply any conclusion but only because the question itself and the considerations it raises can make sense only in the context of this whole approach. Since what is to follow rests so heavily on my previous reflections, I shall briefly summarize them in what must appear (but are not meant) to be dogmatic propositions:

First, thinking is always out of order, interrupts all ordinary activities and is interrupted by them. The best illustration of this may still be—as the old story goes—Socrates' habit of suddenly "turning his mind to himself," breaking off all company, and taking up his position wherever he happened to be, "deaf to all entreaties" to continue with whatever he had been doing before.[1] Once, we are told by Xenophon, he remained in complete immobility for twenty-four hours in a military camp, deep in thought, as we would say.

Second, the manifestations of the thinking ego's authentic experiences are manifold: among them are the metaphysical fallacies, such as the two-world theory, and, more interestingly, the non-theoretical descriptions of thinking as a kind of dying or, conversely, the notion that while thinking we are members of another, noumenal, world—present to us by intimation even in the darkness of the actual here-and-now—or Aristotle's definition of the *bios theōrētikos* as a *bios xenikos*, the life of a stranger. The same experiences are reflected in the Cartesian doubt of the reality of the world, in Valéry's "At times I think, and at times I am" (as though to be real and to think were opposites), in Merleau-Ponty's "We are truly alone only on the condition that we do not know we are; it is this very ignorance which is our [the philosopher's] solitude."[2] And it is true that the thinking ego, whatever it may achieve, will never be able to reach reality qua reality or convince itself that anything actually exists and that life, human life, is more than a dream. (This suspicion that life is but a dream is, of course, among the most characteristic traits of Asian philosophy; examples from Indian philosophy are numerous. I shall give a Chinese example which is very telling because of its briefness. It reports a story told about the Taoist (i.e., anti-Confucian) philosopher Chuang Tzu. He "once dreamt he was a butterfly flitting and fluttering around, happy with himself and doing as he pleased. He didn't know he was Chuang Chou. Suddenly he woke up and there he was, solid and unmistakable Chuang Chou. But he didn't know if he was Chuang Chou who had dreamt he was a butterfly, or a butterfly dreaming it was Chuang Chou. Between Chuang Chou and a butterfly there must be *some* distinction!")[3]

The intensity of the thinking experience, on the other hand, manifests itself in the ease with which the opposition of thought and reality can be reversed, so that only thought seems to be real whereas all that merely is seems to be so transitory that it is as though it were not: "What is being *thought*, is; and what *is, is* only insofar as it is thought" (*Was gedacht ist, ist; und was* ist, ist *nur, insofern es Gedanke ist*).[4] The decisive point here, however, is that all such doubts disappear as soon as the thinker's solitude is broken in upon and the call of the world and our fellow-men changes the inner duality of the two-in-one into a One again. Hence the notion that everything that is might be a mere dream is either the nightmare that rises out of the thinking experience or the consoling thought to be summoned up, not when I have withdrawn from the world, but when the world has withdrawn from me and become unreal.

Third, these oddities of the thinking activity arise from the fact of withdrawal, inherent in all mental activities; thinking always deals with absences and removes itself from what is present and close at hand. This, of course, does not prove the existence of a world other than the one we are part of in ordinary life, but it means that reality and existence, which we can only conceive in terms of time and space, can be temporarily suspended, lose their weight and, together with this weight, their meaning for the thinking ego. What now, during the thinking activity, become meaningful are distillations, products of de-sensing, and such distillations are not mere abstract concepts; they were once called "essences."

Essences cannot be localized. Human thought that gets hold of them leaves the world of the particular and goes out in search of something generally *meaningful,* though not necessarily universally valid. Thinking always "generalizes," squeezes out of many particulars—which, thanks to the de-sensing process, it can pack together for swift manipulation—whatever meaning may inhere. Generalization is inherent in every thought, even though that thought is insisting on the universal primacy of the particular. In other words, the "essential" is what is applicable everywhere, and this "everywhere" that bestows on thought its specific weight is spatially speaking a "nowhere." The thinking ego, moving among universals, among invisible essences, is, strictly speaking, nowhere; it is homeless in an emphatic sense—which may explain the early rise of a cosmopolitan spirit among the philosophers.

The only great thinker I know of who was explicitly aware of this condition of homelessness as being natural to the thinking activity was Aristotle—perhaps because he knew so well and spelled out so clearly the difference between acting and thinking (the decisive distinction between the political and the philosophical way of life) and, drawing the obvious inference, refused to "share the fate" of Socrates and to let the Athenians "sin twice against philosophy." When a charge of impiety was brought against him, he left Athens and "withdrew to Chalcis, a stronghold of Macedonian influence."[5] He had counted homelessness among the great advantages of the philosopher's way of life in the *Protreptikos,* one of his early works, which was still well known in antiquity but has come down to us only in fragments. There he praises the *bios theōrētikos* because it needed "neither implements nor special places for [its] trade; wherever on earth somebody devotes himself to thinking, he will attain the truth everywhere as though it were present." Philosophers love this "nowhere" as though it were a country (*philochōrein*) and they desire to let all other activities go for the sake of *scholazein* (doing nothing, as we would say) because of the sweetness inherent in thinking or philosophizing itself.[6] The reason for this blessed independence is that philosophy (the cognition *kata logon*) is not concerned with particulars, with things given to the senses, but with universals (*kath' holou*), things that cannot be localized.[7] It would be a great mistake to look for such universals in practical-political matters, which always concern particulars; in this field, "general" statements, equally applicable everywhere, immediately degenerate into empty generalities. Action deals with particulars, and only particular statements can be valid in the field of ethics or politics.[8]

In other words, it may well be that we were posing a wrong, inappropriate question when we asked for the location of the thinking ego. Looked at from the perspective of the everyday world of appearances, the everywhere of the thinking ego—summoning into its presence whatever it pleases from any distance in time or space, which thought traverses with a velocity greater than light's—is a *nowhere.* And since this nowhere is by no means identical with the twofold nowhere from which we suddenly appear at birth and into which almost as suddenly we disappear in death, it might be conceived only as the Void. And the absolute void can be a limiting boundary concept; though not inconceivable, it is unthinkable. Obviously, if there is absolutely nothing, there can be nothing to think about. That we are in possession of these limiting boundary concepts enclosing our thought within unsurmountable walls—and the notion of an absolute beginning or an absolute end is among them—does not tell us more than that we are indeed *finite* beings. To assume that these limitations could serve to map out a place where the thinking ego could be localized would be just another variation of the two-world theory. Man's finitude, irrevocably given by virtue of his own short time span set in an infinity of time stretching into both past and future, constitutes the infrastructure, as it were, of all mental activities: it manifests itself as the only reality of which thinking qua thinking is aware, when the thinking ego has withdrawn from the world of appearances and lost the sense of realness inherent in the *sensus communis* by which we orient ourselves in this world.

In other words, Valéry's remark—when we think, we *are* not—would be right if our sense of realness were entirely determined by our spatial existence. The everywhere of thought is indeed a region of nowhere. But we are not only in space, we are also in time, remembering, collecting and recollecting what no longer is present out of "the belly of memory" (Augustine), anticipating and planning in the mode of willing what is not yet. Perhaps our question—Where are we when we think?—was wrong because by asking for the *topos* of this activity, we were exclusively spatially oriented—as though we had forgotten Kant's famous insight that "time is nothing but the form of inner sense, that is, of the intuition of ourselves and of our inner state." For Kant, that meant that time had nothing to do with appearances as such—"neither with shape nor position" as given to our senses—but only with appearances as affecting our "inner state," in which time determines "the relation of representation."[9] And these representations—by which we make present what is phenomenally absent —are, of course, thought-things, that is, experiences or notions that have gone through the de-materializing operation by which the mind prepares its own objects and by "generalizing" deprives them of their spatial properties as well.

Time determines the way these representations are related to each other by forcing them into the order of a sequence, and these sequences are what we usually call thought-trains. All thinking is discursive and, insofar as it follows a train of thought, it could by analogy be presented as "a line progressing to infinity," corresponding to the way we usually represent to ourselves the sequential nature of time. But in order to create such a line of thought we must transform the *juxtaposition* in which experiences are given to us into a *succession* of soundless words—the only medium in which we can think—which means we not only de-sense but de-spatialize the original experience.

## 20 *The gap between past and future:* *the* nunc stans

In the hope of finding out where the thinking ego is located in time and whether its relentless activity can be temporally determined, I shall turn to one of Kafka's parables, which, in my opinion, deals precisely with this matter. The parable is part of a collection of aphorisms entitled "HE."[10]

He has two antagonists; the first presses him from behind, from his origin. The second blocks the road in front of him. He gives battle to both. Actually, the first supports him in his fight with the second, for he wants to push him forward, and in the same way the second supports him in his fight with the first, since he drives him back. But it is only theoretically so. For it is not only the two antagonists who are there, but he himself as well, and who really knows his intentions? His dream, though, is that some time in an unguarded moment—and this, it must be admitted, would require a night darker than any night has ever been yet—he will jump out of the fighting line and be promoted, on account of his experience in fighting, to the position of umpire over his antagonists in their fight with each other.

For me, this parable describes the time sensation of the thinking ego. It analyzes poetically our "inner state" in regard to time, of which we are aware when we have withdrawn from the appearances and find our mental activities recoiling characteristically upon themselves—*cogito me cogitare, volo me velle,* and so on. The inner time sensation arises when we are not entirely absorbed by the absent non-visibles we are thinking about but begin to direct our attention onto the activity itself. In this situation past and future are equally present precisely because they are equally absent from our sense; thus the no-longer of the past is transformed by virtue of the spatial metaphor into something lying *behind* us and the not-yet of the future into something that *approaches* us from ahead (the German *Zukunft,* like the French *avenir,* means, literally What comes toward). In Kafka, this scene is a battleground where the forces of past and future clash with each other. Between them we find the man Kafka calls "He," who, if he wants to stand his ground at all, must give battle to both forces. The forces are "his" antagonists; they are not just opposites and would hardly fight with each other without "him" standing between them and making a stand against them; and even if such an antagonism were somehow inherent in the two and they could fight each other without "him," they would have long ago neutralized and destroyed each other, since as forces they clearly are equally powerful.

In other words, the time continuum, everlasting change, is broken up into the tenses past, present, future, whereby past and future are antagonistic to each other as the no-longer and the not-yet only because of the presence of man, who himself has an "origin," his birth, and an end, his death, and therefore stands at any given moment between them; this in-between is called the present. It is the insertion of man with his limited life span that transforms the continuously flowing stream of sheer change—which we can conceive of cyclically as well as in the form of rectilinear motion without ever being able to conceive of an absolute beginning or an absolute end—into time as we know it.

This parable in which two of time's tenses, the past and the future, are understood as antagonistic forces that crash into the present Now, sounds very strange to our ears, which-ever time concept we may happen to hold. The extreme parsimony of Kafka's language, in which for the sake of the fable's realism every actual reality that could have engendered the thought-world is eliminated, may cause it to sound stranger than the thought itself requires. I shall therefore use a curiously related story of Nietzsche's in the heavily allegorical style of *Thus Spake Zarathustra*. It is much easier to understand because it concerns, as its title says, merely a "Vision" or a "Riddle."[11] The allegory begins with Zarathustra's arrival at a gateway. The gateway, like every gateway, has an entrance and an exit, that is, can be seen as the meeting-place of two roads.

Two paths meet here; no one has yet followed either to its end. This long lane stretches back for an eternity. And the other long lane out there, that is another eternity. They contradict each other, these roads; they offend each other face to face—and it is here, at this gateway, that they come together. The name of the gateway is inscribed above: "Now" ["*Augenblick*"]. . . . Behold this Now! From this gateway Now, a long eternal lane leads *backward;* behind us lies an eternity [and another lane leads forward into an eternal future].

Heidegger, who interprets the passage in his *Nietzsche,*[12] observes that this view is not the view of the beholder but only that of the man who stands in the gateway; for the onlooker, time passes in the way we are used to think of it, in a succession of nows where one thing always succeeds another. There is no meeting-place; there are not two lanes or roads, there is only one. "The clash is produced only for the one who *himself is* the now. . . . Whoever stands in the Now is turning in both directions: for him Past and Future run against *each other*." And, summing up in the context of Nietzsche's doctrine of Eternal Recurrence, Heidegger says: "This is the authentic content of the doctrine of Eternal Recurrence, that Eternity *is* in the Now, that the Moment is not the futile Now which it is only for the onlooker, but the clash of Past and Future." (You have the same thought in Blake— "Hold infinity in the palm of your hand / And eternity in an hour.")

Returning to Kafka, we should remember that all these instances are dealing not with doctrines or theories but with thoughts related to the experiences of the thinking ego. Seen from the viewpoint of a continuously flowing everlasting stream, the insertion of man, fighting in both directions, produces a rupture which, by being defended in both directions, is extended to a gap, the present seen as the fighter's battleground. This battleground for Kafka is the metaphor for man's home on earth. Seen from the viewpoint of man, at each single moment inserted and caught in the middle between *his* past and *his* future, both aimed at the one who is creating his present, the battleground is an in-between, an extended Now on which he spends his life. The present, in ordinary life the most futile and slippery of the tenses—when I say "now" and point to it, it is already gone—is no more than the clash of a past, which is no more, with a future, which is approaching and not yet there. Man lives in this in-between, and what he calls the present is a life-long fight against the dead weight of the past, driving him forward with hope, and the fear of a future (whose only certainty is death), driving him backward toward "the quiet of the past" with nostalgia for and remembrance of the only reality he can be sure of.

It should not unduly alarm us that this time construct is totally different from the time sequence of ordinary life, where the three tenses smoothly follow each other and time itself can be understood in analogy to numerical sequences, fixed by the calendar, according to which the present is today, the past begins with yesterday, and the future begins tomorrow. Here, too, the present is surrounded by past and future inasmuch as it remains the fixed point from which we take our bearings, looking back or looking forward. That we can shape the everlasting stream of sheer change into a time continuum we owe not to time itself but to the continuity of our business and our activities in the world, in which *we continue* what we started yesterday and hope to finish tomorrow. In other words, the time continuum depends on the continuity of our everyday life, and the business of everyday life, in contrast to the activity of the thinking ego—always independent of the spatial circumstances surrounding it—is always spatially determined and conditioned. It is due to this thoroughgoing spatiality of our ordinary life that we can speak plausibly of time in spatial categories, that the past can appear to us as something lying "behind" us and the future as lying "ahead."

Kafka's time parable does not apply to man in his everyday occupations but only to the thinking ego, to the extent that it has withdrawn from the business of everyday life. The gap between past and future opens only in reflection, whose subject matter is what is absent—either what has already disappeared or what has not yet appeared. Reflection draws these absent "regions" into the mind's presence; from that perspective the activity of thinking can be understood as a fight against time itself. It is only because "he" thinks, and therefore is no longer carried along by the continuity of everyday life in a world of appearances, that past and future manifest themselves as pure entities, so that "he" can become aware of a no-longer that pushes him forward and a not-yet that drives him back.

Kafka's tale is, of course, couched in metaphorical language, and its images, drawn from everyday life, are meant as analogies, without which, as has already been indicated, mental phenomena cannot be described at all. And that always presents difficulties of interpretation. The specific difficulty here is that the reader must be aware that the thinking ego is not the self as it appears and moves in the world, remembering its own biographical past, as though "he" were *à la recherche du temps perdu* or planning his future. It is because the thinking ego is ageless and nowhere that past and future can become manifest to it as such, emptied, as it were, of their concrete content and liberated from all spatial categories. What the thinking ego senses as "his" dual antagonists are time itself, and the constant change it implies, the relentless motion that transforms all Being into Becoming, instead of letting it *be,* and thus incessantly destroys its being *present.* As such, time is the thinking ego's greatest enemy because—by virtue of the mind's incarnation in a body whose internal motions can never be immobilized—time inexorably and regularly interrupts the immobile quiet in which the mind is active without doing anything.

This final meaning of the parable comes to the fore in the

concluding sentence, when "he," situated in the time gap, which is an immovable present, a *nunc stans*, dreams of the unguarded moment when time will have exhausted its force; then quiet will settle down on the world, not an eternal quiet but just lasting long enough to give "him" the chance of jumping out of the fighting line to be promoted to the position of umpire, the spectator and judge outside the game of life, to whom the meaning of this time span between birth and death can be referred because "he" is not involved in it.

What are this dream and this region but the old dream Western metaphysics has dreamt from Parmenides to Hegel, of a timeless region, an eternal presence in complete quiet, lying beyond human clocks and calendars altogether, the region, precisely, of thought? And what is the "position of umpire," the desire for which prompts the dream, but the seat of Pythagoras' spectators, who are "the best" because they do not participate in the struggle for fame and gain, are disinterested, uncommitted, undisturbed, intent only on the spectacle itself? It is they who can find out its meaning and judge the performance.

Without doing too much violence to Kafka's magnificent story, one may perhaps go a step further. The trouble with Kafka's metaphor is that by jumping out of the fighting line "he" jumps out of this world altogether and judges from outside though not necessarily from above. Moreover, if it is the insertion of man that breaks up the indifferent flow of everlasting change by giving it an aim, namely, himself, the being who fights it, and if through that insertion the indifferent time stream is articulated into what is behind him, the past, what is ahead of him, the future, and himself, the fighting present, then it follows that man's presence causes the stream of time to deflect from whatever its original direction or (assuming a cyclical movement) ultimate non-direction may have been. The deflection seems inevitable because it is not just a passive object that is inserted into the stream, to be tossed about by its waves that go sweeping over his head, but a fighter who defends his own presence and thus defines what otherwise might be indifferent to him as "*his*" antagonists: the past, which he can fight with the help of the future; the future, which he fights supported by the past.

Without "him," there would be no difference between past and future, but only everlasting change. Or else these forces would clash head on and annihilate each other. But thanks to the insertion of a fighting presence, they meet at an angle, and the correct image would then have to be what the physicists call a parallelogram of forces. The advantage of this image is that the region of thought would no longer have to be situated beyond and above the world and human time; the fighter would no longer have to jump out of the fighting line in order to find the quiet and the stillness necessary for thinking. "He" would recognize that "his" fighting has not been in vain, since the battleground itself supplies the region where "he" can rest when "he" is exhausted. In other words, the location of the thinking ego in time would be the in-between of past and future, the present, this mysterious and slippery now, a mere gap in time, toward which nevertheless the more solid tenses of past and future are directed insofar as they denote that which *is* no more and that which *is* not yet. That they *are* at all, they obviously owe to man, who has inserted himself between them and established his presence there. Let me briefly follow the implications of the corrected image.

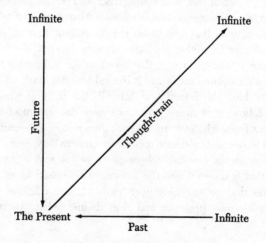

Ideally, the action of the two forces that form our parallelogram should result in a third force, the resultant diagonal whose origin would be the point at which the forces meet and upon which they act. The diagonal would remain on the same plane and not jump out of the dimension of the forces of time, but it would in one important respect differ from the forces whose result it is. The two antagonistic forces of past and future are both indefinite as to their origin; seen from the viewpoint of the present in the middle, the one comes from an infinite past and the other from an infinite future. But though they have no known beginning, they have a terminal ending, the point at which they meet and clash, which is the present. The diagonal force, on the contrary, has a definite origin, its starting-point being the clash of the two other forces, but it would be infinite with respect to its ending since it has resulted from the concerted action of two forces whose origin is infinity. This diagonal force, whose origin is known, whose direction is determined by past and future, but which exerts its force toward an undetermined end as though it could reach out into infinity, seems to me a perfect metaphor for the activity of thought.

If Kafka's "he" were able to walk along this diagonal, in perfect equidistance from the pressing forces of past and future, he would not, as the parable demands, have jumped out of the fighting line to be above and beyond the melee. For this diagonal, though pointing to some infinity, is limited, enclosed, as it were, by the forces of past and future, and thus protected against the void; it remains bound to and is rooted in the present—an entirely human present though it is fully actualized only in the thinking process and lasts no longer than this process lasts. It is the quiet of the Now in the time-pressed, time-tossed existence of man; it is somehow, to change the metaphor, the quiet in the center of a storm which, though totally unlike the storm, still belongs to it. In this gap between past and future, we find our place in time when we think, that is, when we are sufficiently removed from past and future to be relied on to find out their meaning, to assume the position of "umpire," of arbiter and judge over the manifold, never-ending affairs of human existence in the world, never arriving at a final solution to their riddles but ready with ever-new answers to the question of what it may be all about.

To avoid misunderstanding: the images I am using here to indicate, metaphorically and tentatively, the location of thought can be valid only within the realm of mental phenomena. Applied to historical or biographical time, these metaphors cannot possibly make sense; gaps in time do not occur there. Only insofar as he thinks, and that is insofar as he is *not*, according to Valéry, does man—a "He," as Kafka so rightly calls him, and not a "somebody"—in the full actuality of his concrete being, live in this gap between past and future, in this present which is timeless.

The gap, though we hear about it first as a *nunc stans*, the "standing now" in medieval philosophy, where it served, in the form of *nunc aeternitatis*, as model and metaphor for divine eternity,[13] is not a historical datum; it seems to be coeval with the existence of man on earth. Using a different metaphor, we call it the region of the spirit, but it is perhaps rather the path paved by thinking, the small inconspicuous track of non-time beaten by the activity of thought within the time-space given to natal and mortal men. Following that course, the thought-trains, remembrance and anticipation, save whatever they touch from the ruin of historical and biographical time. This small non-time space in the very heart of time, unlike the world and the culture into which we are born, cannot be inherited and handed down by tradition, although every great book of thought points to it somewhat cryptically— as we found Heraclitus saying of the notoriously cryptic and unreliable Delphic oracle: *"oute legei, oute kryptei alla sēmainei"* ("it does not say and it does not hide, it intimates").

Each new generation, every new human being, as he becomes conscious of being inserted between an infinite past and an infinite future, must discover and ploddingly pave anew the path of thought. And it is after all possible, and seems to me likely, that the strange survival of great works, their relative permanence throughout thousands of years, is due to their having been born in the small, inconspicuous track of non-time which their authors' thought had beaten between an infinite past and an infinite future by accepting past and future as directed, aimed, as it were, at themselves— as *their* predecessors and successors, *their* past and *their* future —thus establishing a present for themselves, a kind of timeless time in which men are able to create timeless works with which to transcend their own finiteness.

This timelessness, to be sure, is not eternity; it springs, as it were, from the clash of past and future, whereas eternity is the boundary concept that is unthinkable because it indicates the collapse of all temporal dimensions. The temporal dimension of the *nunc stans* experienced in the activity of thinking gathers the absent tenses, the not-yet and the no-more, together into its own presence. This is Kant's "land of pure intellect" (*Land des reinen Verstandes*), "an island, enclosed by nature itself within unalterable limits," and "surrounded by a wide and stormy ocean," the sea of everyday life.[14] And though I do not think that this is "the land of truth," it certainly is the only domain where the whole of one's life and its meaning—which remains ungraspable for mortal men (*nemo ante mortem beatus esse dici potest*), whose existence, in distinction from all other things which begin to *be* in the emphatic sense when they are completed, terminates when it *is* no more—where this ungraspable whole can manifest itself as the sheer continuity of the I-am, an enduring presence in the midst of the world's ever-changing transitoriness. It is because of this experience of the thinking ego that the primacy of the present, the most transitory of the tenses in the world of appearances, became an almost dogmatic tenet of philosophical speculation.

Let me now at the end of these long reflections draw attention, not to my "method," not to my "criteria" or, worse, my "values"—all of which in such an enterprise are mercifully hidden from its author though they may be or, rather, *seem* to be quite manifest to reader and listener—but to what in my opinion is the basic assumption of this investigation. I have spoken about the metaphysical "fallacies," which, as we found, do contain important hints of what this curious out-of-order activity called thinking may be all about. In other words,

I have clearly joined the ranks of those who for some time now have been attempting to dismantle metaphysics, and philosophy with all its categories, as we have known them from their beginning in Greece until today. Such dismantling is possible only on the assumption that the thread of tradition is broken and that we shall not be able to renew it. Historically speaking, what actually has broken down is the Roman trinity that for thousands of years united religion, authority, and tradition. The loss of this trinity does not destroy the past, and the dismantling process itself is not destructive; it only draws conclusions from a loss which is a fact and as such no longer a part of the "history of ideas" but of our political history, the history of our world.

What has been lost is the continuity of the past as it seemed to be handed down from generation to generation, developing in the process its own consistency. The dismantling process has its own technique, and I did not go into that here except peripherally. What you then are left with is still the past, but a *fragmented* past, which has lost its certainty of evaluation. About this, for brevity's sake, I shall quote a few lines which say it better and more densely than I could:

> Full fathom five thy father lies,
>   Of his bones are coral made,
> Those are pearls that were his eyes.
>   Nothing of him that doth fade
> But doth suffer a sea-change
>   Into something rich and strange.
>         *The Tempest*, Act I, Scene 2

It is with such fragments from the past, after their sea-change, that I have dealt here. That they could be used at all we owe to the timeless track that thinking beats into the world of space and time. If some of my listeners or readers should be tempted to try their luck at the technique of dismantling, let them be careful not to destroy the "rich and strange," the "coral" and the "pearls," which can probably be saved only as fragments.

> 'O plunge your hands in water,
>   Plunge them in up to the wrist;
> Stare, stare in the basin
>   And wonder what you've missed.

'The glacier knocks in the cupboard,
The desert sighs in the bed,
And the crack in the tea-cup opens
A lane to the land of the dead. . . .'
W. H. Auden[15]

Or to put the same in prose: "Some books are undeservedly forgotten, none are undeservedly remembered."[16]


## 21 Postscriptum

In the second volume of this work I shall deal with willing and judging, the two other mental activities. Looked at from the perspective of these time speculations, they concern matters that are absent either because they are not yet or because they are no more; but in contradistinction to the thinking activity, which deals with the invisibles in all experience and always tends to generalize, they always deal with particulars and in this respect are much closer to the world of appearances. If we wish to placate our common sense, so decisively offended by the need of reason to pursue its purposeless quest for meaning, it is tempting to justify this need solely on the grounds that thinking is an indispensable preparation for deciding what shall be and for evaluating what is no more. Since the past, being past, becomes subject to our judgment, judgment, in turn, would be a mere preparation for willing. This is undeniably the perspective, and, within limits, the legitimate perspective of man insofar as he is an acting being.

But this last attempt to defend the thinking activity against the reproach of being impractical and useless does not work. The decision the will arrives at can never be derived from the mechanics of desire or the deliberations of the intellect that may precede it. The will is either an organ of free spontaneity that interrupts all causal chains of motivation that would bind it or it is nothing but an illusion. In respect to desire, on one hand, and to reason, on the other, the will acts like "a kind of *coup d'état*," as Bergson once said, and this implies, of course, that "free acts are exceptional": "although we are free whenever we are willing to get back into ourselves, *it seldom happens that we are willing*" (italics added).[17] In other words, it is impossible to deal with the willing activity without touching on the problem of freedom.

I propose to take the internal evidence—in Bergson's terms, the "immediate datum of consciousness"—seriously and since I agree with many writers on this subject that this datum and all problems connected with it were unknown to Greek antiquity, I must accept that this faculty was "discovered," that we can date this discovery historically, and that we shall thereby find that it coincides with the discovery of human "inwardness" as a special region of our life. In brief, I shall analyze the faculty of the will in terms of its history.

I shall follow the experiences men have had with this paradoxical and self-contradictory faculty (every volition, since it speaks to itself in imperatives, produces its own counter-volition), starting from the Apostle Paul's early discovery of the will's impotence—"I do not do what I want, but I do the very thing I hate"[18]—and going on to examine the testimony left us by the Middle Ages, beginning with Augustine's insight that what are "at war" are not the spirit and the flesh but the mind, as will, with itself, man's "inmost self" with itself. I shall then proceed to the modern age, which, with the rise of the notion of progress, exchanged the old philosophical primacy of the present over the other tenses against the primacy of the future, a force that in Hegel's words "the Now cannot resist," so that thinking is understood "as essentially the negation of something being directly present" ("*in der Tat ist das Denken wesentlich die Negation eines unmittelbar Vorhandenen*").[19] Or in the words of Schelling: "In the final and highest instance there is no other Being than Will"[20]—an attitude that found its final climactic and self-defeating end in Nietzsche's "Will to Power."

At the same time I shall follow a parallel development in the history of the Will according to which volition is the inner capacity by which men decide about "whom" they are going to be, in what shape they wish to show themselves in the world of appearances. In other words, it is the will, whose subject matter is projects, not objects, which in a sense creates the *person* that can be blamed or praised and anyhow held responsible not merely for its actions but for its whole "Being," its *character*. The Marxian and existentialist notions, which play such a great role in twentieth-century thought and pretend that man is his own producer and maker, rest on these experiences, even though it is clear that nobody has "made" himself or "produced" his existence; this, I think, is the last of the metaphysical fallacies, corresponding to the modern age's emphasis on willing as a substitute for thinking.

I shall conclude the second volume with an analysis of the faculty of judgment, and here the chief difficulty will be the curious scarcity of sources providing authoritative testimony. Not till Kant's *Critique of Judgment* did this faculty become a major topic of a major thinker.

I shall show that my own main assumption in singling out judgment as a distinct capacity of our minds has been that judgments are not arrived at by either deduction or induction; in short, they have nothing in common with logical operations—as when we say: All men are mortal, Socrates is a man, hence, Socrates is mortal. We shall be in search of the "silent sense," which—when it was dealt with at all—has always, even in Kant, been thought of as "taste" and therefore as belonging to the realm of aesthetics. In practical and moral matters it was called "conscience," and conscience did not judge; it told you, as the divine voice of either God or reason, what to do, what not to do, and what to repent of. Whatever the voice of conscience may be, it cannot be said to be "silent," and its validity depends entirely upon an authority that is above and beyond all merely human laws and rules.

In Kant judgment emerges as "a peculiar talent which can be practised only and cannot be taught." Judgment deals with particulars, and when the thinking ego moving among generalities emerges from its withdrawal and returns to the world of particular appearances, it turns out that the mind needs a new "gift" to deal with them. "An obtuse or narrow-minded person," Kant believed, ". . . may indeed be trained through study, even to the extent of becoming learned. But as such people are commonly still lacking in judgment, it is not unusual to meet learned men who in the application of their scientific knowledge betray that original want, which can never be made good."[21] In Kant, it is reason with its "regulative ideas" that comes to the help of judgment, but if the faculty is separate from other faculties of the mind, then we shall have to ascribe to it its own *modus operandi*, its own way of proceeding.

And this is of some relevance to a whole set of problems by which modern thought is haunted, especially to the problem of theory and practice and to all attempts to arrive at a halfway plausible theory of ethics. Since Hegel and Marx, these questions have been treated in the perspective of History and on the assumption that there is such a thing as Progress of the human race. Finally we shall be left with the only alternative there is in these matters—we either can say with Hegel: *Die Weltgeschichte ist das Weltgericht,* leaving the ultimate judgment to Success, or we can maintain with Kant the autonomy of the minds of men and their possible independence of things as they are or as they have come into being.

Here we shall have to concern ourselves, not for the first time, with the concept of history, but we may be able to reflect on the oldest meaning of this word, which, like so many other terms in our political and philosophical language, is Greek in origin and derived from *historein*, to inquire in order to tell how it was—*legein ta eonta* in Herodotus. But the origin of this verb is again Homer (*Iliad* XVIII) where the noun *histor* ("historian," as it were) occurs, and that Homeric historian is the *judge.* If judgment is our faculty for dealing with the past, the historian is the inquiring man who by relating it sits in judgment over it. If that is so, we may reclaim our human dignity, win it back, as it were, from the pseudo-divinity named History of the modern age, without denying history's importance but denying its right to being the ultimate judge. Old Cato, with whom I started these reflections—"never am I less alone than when I am by myself, never am I more active than when I do nothing"—has left us a curious phrase which aptly sums up the political principle implied in the enterprise of reclamation. He said: *"Victrix causa deis placuit, sed victa Catoni"* ("The victorious cause pleased the gods, but the defeated one pleases Cato").

# Notes

## Introduction

1. *Critique of Pure Reason*, B871. For this and later citations, see Norman Kemp Smith's translation, *Immanuel Kant's Critique of Pure Reason*, New York, 1963, which the author frequently relied on.
2. *Eichmann in Jerusalem*, New York, 1963.
3. Notes on metaphysics, *Kant's handschriftlicher Nachlass*, vol. V, in *Kant's gesammelte Schriften*, Akademie Ausgabe, Berlin, Leipzig, 1928, vol. XVIII, 5636.
4. Hugh of St. Victor.
5. André Bridoux, *Descartes: Oeuvres et Lettres*, Pléiade ed., Paris, 1937, Introduction, p. viii. Cf. Galileo: *"les mathématiques sont la langue dans laquelle est écrit l'univers,"* p. xiii.
6. Nicholas Lobkowicz, *Theory and Practice: History of a Concept from Aristotle to Marx*, Notre Dame, 1967, p. 419.
7. *De Republica*, I, 17.
8. *The Phenomenology of Mind*, trans. J. B. Baillie (1910), New York, 1964, "Sense-Certainty," p. 159.
9. See the note to "Vom Wesen der Wahrheit," a lecture first given in 1930. Now in *Wegmarken*, Frankfurt, 1967, p. 97.
10. See "Glauben und Wissen" (1802), *Werke*, Frankfurt, 1970, vol. 2, p. 432.
11. 11th ed.
12. *Werke*, Darmstadt, 1963, vol. I, pp. 982, 621, 630, 968, 952, 959, 974.
13. Introduction to his *The Basic Works of Aristotle*, New York, 1941, p. xviii. In citations from Aristotle, McKeon's translation has occasionally been used.
14. *Critique of Pure Reason*, B878. The striking phrase occurs in the last section of the *Critique of Pure Reason*, where Kant

claims to have established metaphysics as a science the idea of which "is as old as speculative human reason; and what rational human being does not speculate, either in scholastic or in popular fashion?" (B871). This "science" . . . "has now fallen into general disrepute" because "more was expected from metaphysics than could reasonably be demanded" (B877). Cf. also sections 59 and 60 of *Prolegomena to Any Future Metaphysics*.

15. *The Gay Science*, bk. III, no. 125, "The madman."

16. "How the 'True World' finally became a fable," 6.

17. "Nietzsches Wort 'Gott ist tot,'" in *Holzwege*, Frankfurt, 1963, p. 193.

18. B125 and B9.

19. René Char, *Feuillets d'Hypnos*, Paris, 1946, no. 62.

20. *Symposium*, 212a.

21. *Kant's handschriftlicher Nachlass*, vol. VI, Akademie Ausgabe, vol. XVIII, 6900.

22. *Werke*, vol. I, p. 989.

23. "Prolegomena," *Werke*, vol. III, p. 245.

24. *Critique of Pure Reason*, Bxxx.

25. *Kant's handschriftlicher Nachlass*, vol. V, Akademie Ausgabe, vol. XVIII, 4849.

26. Trans. John Macquarrie and Edward Robinson, London, 1962, p. 1. Cf. pp. 151 and 324.

27. "Einleitung zu 'Was ist Metaphysik?'" in *Wegmarken*, p. 206.

28. Hegel, *The Phenomenology of Mind*, Baillie trans., Introduction, p. 131.

29. *Ibid.*, p. 144.

## Chapter I

1. The three ways of life are enumerated in *Nicomachean Ethics*, I, 5 and the *Eudemian Ethics*, 1215a35 ff. For the opposition of the beautiful to the necessary and the useful, see *Politics*, 1333a30 ff. It is interesting to compare the three Aristotelian ways of life with Plato's enumeration in the *Philebus*—the way of pleasure, the way of thinking (*phronēsis*), and a way of both mixed (22); to the way of pleasure Plato objects that pleasure in itself is unlimited in time as well as intensity: "it does not contain within itself and derive from itself either beginning or middle or end" (31a). And although

he "agrees with all sages (*sophoi*) . . . that *nous*, the faculty of thought and of truth, is for us king of heaven and earth" (28c), he also thinks that for mere mortals a life that "knows neither joy nor grief," though the most divine (33a-b), would be unbearable and that therefore "a mixture of the unlimited with what sets limits is the source of all beauty" (26b).

2. Thomas Langan, *Merleau-Ponty's Critique of Reason*, New Haven, London, 1966, p. 93.

3. Frag. 1.

4. *Republic*, VII, 514a–521b. *The Collected Dialogues of Plato*, eds. Edith Hamilton and Huntington Cairns, "Republic," trans. Paul Shorey, New York, 1961, has sometimes been drawn on, as has Francis MacDonald Cornford's *The Republic of Plato*, New York, London, 1941.

5. Kant, *Opus Postumum*, ed. Erich Adickes, Berlin, 1920, p. 44. Probable date of this remark is 1788.

6. *Critique of Pure Reason*, B565.

7. Maurice Merleau-Ponty, *The Visible and the Invisible*, Evanston, 1968, p. 17.

8. Maurice Merleau-Ponty, *Signs*, Evanston, 1964, Introduction, p. 20.

9. Hermann Diels and Walther Kranz, *Die Fragmente der Vorsokratiker*, Berlin, 1959, vol. II, B26.

10. *The Visible and the Invisible*, pp. 40–41.

11. *Das Tier als soziales Wesen*, Zürich, 1953, p. 252.

12. *Animal Forms and Patterns*, trans. Hella Czech, New York, 1967, p. 19.

13. *Ibid.*, p. 34.

14. *Das Tier als soziales Wesen*, p. 232.

15. *Ibid.*

16. *Ibid.*, p. 127.

17. *Animal Forms and Patterns*, pp. 112, 113.

18. *Das Tier als soziales Wesen*, p. 64.

19. *Biologie und Geist*, Zürich, 1956, p. 24.

20. *Of Human Understanding*, bk. III, chap. 1, no. 5.

21. Merleau-Ponty, *Signs*, Introduction, p. 17.

22. *The Visible and the Invisible*, p. 259.

23. *Signs*, p. 21.

24. *The Visible and the Invisible*, p. 259.

25. *De Anima*, 403a5–10.

26. *Ibid.*, 413b24 ff.

27. *De generatione animalium,* II, 3, 736b5–29, quoted from Lobkowicz, *op. cit.,* p. 24.

28. *De Interpretatione,* 16a3–13.

29. Mary McCarthy, "Hanging by a Thread," *The Writing on the Wall,* New York, 1970.

30. *Enarrationes in Psalmos, Patrologiae Latina,* J.-P. Migne, Paris, 1854–66, vol. 37, CXXXIV, 16.

31. Frag. 149.

32. Schelling, *Of Human Freedom* (1809), 414. Trans. James Gutmann, Chicago, 1936, p. 96.

33. Frag. 34.

34. *Critique of Pure Reason,* B354–B355.

35. *Ibid.,* A107. Cf. also B413: "In inner intuition there is nothing permanent," and B420: Nothing "permanent" is "given . . . in . . . intuition" "insofar as I think myself."

36. *The Visible and the Invisible,* pp. 18–19.

37. *Critique of Pure Reason,* A381.

38. *Critique of Pure Reason,* B565–B566. Kant writes here "transcendental" but means "transcendent." This is not the only passage in which he himself falls prey to the confusion that constitutes one of the pitfalls for the reader of his works. His clearest and simplest explanation of the use of the two words can be found in the *Prolegomena,* where he answers a critic, in the note on page 252 (*Werke,* vol. III), which reads as follows: "My place is the fruitful *bathos* of experience, and the word transcendental . . . does not signify something that transcends all experience, but what (*a priori*) precedes it in order to make it possible. If these concepts transcend experience I call their use transcendent." The object that determines appearances, as distinguished from experience, clearly transcends them as experiences.

39. *Critique of Pure Reason,* B566.

40. *Ibid.,* B197.

41. *Ibid.,* B724.

42. *Ibid.,* B429.

43. *The Philosopher and Theology,* New York, 1962, p. 7. In the same vein, Heidegger in the classroom used to tell the biography of Aristotle. "Aristotle," he said, "was born, worked [spent his life thinking], and died."

44. In his *Commentary* to I Corinthians 15.

45. *Critique of Pure Reason,* A381.

46. *Ibid.,* B157–B158.

47. *Ibid.,* B420.

48. The last and presumably best English translation, by John Manolesco, appeared under the title *Dreams of a Spirit Seer, and Other Writings,* New York, 1969. I have translated the passage myself from the German in *Werke,* vol. I, pp. 946–951.

49. "Allgemeine Naturgeschichte und Theorie des Himmels," *Werke,* vol. I, p. 384. English translation: *Universal Natural History and Theory of the Heavens,* trans. W. Hastie, Ann Arbor, 1969.

50. *The Bounds of Sense: An Essay on Kant's Critique of Pure Reason,* London, 1966, p. 249.

51. *The Visible and the Invisible,* pp. 28 ff.

52. *The Human Condition,* pp. 252 ff.

53. *Le Discours de la Méthode,* 3ème partie, in *Descartes: Oeuvres et Lettres,* pp. 111, 112; see, for first quotation, *The Philosophical Works of Descartes,* trans. Elizabeth S. Haldane and G. R. T. Ross, Cambridge, 1972, vol. I, p. 99.

54. Plato, *Philebus,* 67b, 52b.

55. *Ibid.,* 33b, 28c.

56. *Le Discours de la Méthode,* 4ème partie, in *Descartes: Oeuvres et Lettres,* p. 114; *The Philosophical Works,* vol. I, p. 101.

57. *The Visible and the Invisible,* pp. 36–37.

58. "Anthropologie," no. 24, *Werke,* vol. VI, p. 465.

59. Heidegger rightly points out: "Descartes himself stresses that the sentence [*cogito ergo sum*] is not a syllogism. The I-am is not a consequence of the I-think but, on the contrary, the *fundamentum,* the ground for it." Heidegger mentions the form the syllogism would have to take; it would read as follows: *Id quod cogitat est; cogito; ergo sum. Die Frage nach dem Ding,* Tübingen, 1962, p. 81.

60. *Tractatus,* 5.62; 6.431; 6.4311. Cf. *Notebooks 1914–1916,* New York, 1969, p. 75e.

61. Thomas Aquinas, *Summa Theologica,* pt. 1, qu. 1, 3 ad 2.

62. It seems that Gottsched was the first to speak of the common sense (*sensus communis*) as a "sixth sense." In *Versuch einer Kritischen Dichtkunst für die Deutschen,* 1730. Cf. Cicero, *De Oratore,* III, 50.

63. Quoted from Thomas Landon Thorson, *Biopolitics,* New York, 1970, p. 91.

64. *Summa Theologica,* pt. I, qu. 78, 4 ad 1.

65. *Op. cit., loc, cit.*

66. *Ibid.*
67. *Notebooks 1914–1916*, pp. 48, 48e.
68. *Politics*, 1324a16.
69. *The Visible and the Invisible*, p. 40.
70. *Philebus*, 25–26.
71. *Ibid.*, 31a.
72. Thomas S. Kuhn, *The Structure of Scientific Revolutions*, Chicago, 1962, p. 163.
73. *Critique of Pure Reason*, B367.
74. *De Interpretatione*, 17a1–4.
75. 980a22 ff.
76. *Monadology*, no. 33.
77. *Physics*, 188b30. Thomas Aquinas echoes the Aristotelian phrase: *"quasi ab ipsa veritate coacti"* (as though forced by truth itself), in his commentary on *De Anima*, I, 2, 43.
78. The *Dictionnaire de l'Académie* wrote in the same vein: *"La force de la vérité, pour dire le pouvoir que la vérité a sur l'esprit des hommes."*
79. W. H. Auden, "Talking to Myself," *Collected Poems*, New York, 1976, p. 653.
80. *Philosophie der Weltgeschichte*, Lasson ed., Leipzig, 1920, pt. I, pp. 61–62.
81. Notes on metaphysics, Akademie Ausgabe, vol. XVIII, 4849.
82. *Critique of Pure Reason*, A19, B33.
83. The only Kant interpretation I know of which could be quoted in support of my own understanding of Kant's distinction between reason and intellect is Eric Weil's consummate analysis of the *Critique of Pure Reason*, "Penser et Connaître, La Foi et la Chose-en-soi," in *Problèmes Kantiens*, 2nd ed., Paris, 1970. According to Weil, it is inevitable *"d'affirmer que Kant, qui dénie à la raison pure la possibilité de* connaître *et de développer une* science, *lui reconnaît, en revanche, celle d'acquérir un* savior *qui, au lieu de connaître,* pense" (p. 23). It must be admitted, however, that Weil's conclusions remain closer to Kant's own understanding of himself. Weil is chiefly interested in the interconnection of Pure and Practical reason and hence states that *"le fondement dernier de la philosophie kantienne doit être cherché dans sa théorie de l'homme, dans l'anthropologie philosophique, non dans une 'théorie de la connaissance'* . . ." (p. 33), whereas my chief reservations about Kant's philosophy concern precisely his moral philos-

ophy, that is, the *Critique of Practical Reason*, although I agree of course that those who read the *Critique of Pure Reason* as a kind of epistemology seem to ignore completely the concluding chapters of the book (p. 34).

The four essays of Weil's book, by far the most important items in the Kant literature of recent years, are all based on the simple but crucial insight that "*L'opposition* connaître . . . *et* penser . . . *est fondamentale pour la compréhension de la pensée kantienne*" (p. 112, n. 2).

84. *Critique of Pure Reason*, A314.
85. *Ibid.*, B868.
86. *Ibid.*, Bxxx.
87. *Ibid.*
88. *Ibid.*, B697.
89. *Ibid.*, B699.
90. *Ibid.*, B702.
91. *Ibid.*, B698.
92. *Ibid.*, B714.
93. *Ibid.*, B826.
94. *Ibid.*, B708.

## Chapter II

1. *De Veritate*, qu. XXII, art. 12.
2. *Critique of Pure Reason*, B171–B174.
3. *Critique of Judgment*, trans. J. H. Bernard, New York, 1951, Introduction, IV.
4. *Science of Logic*, Preface to the Second Edition.
5. *Philosophy of Right*, Preface.
6. Frag. 108.
7. Thucydides, II, 43.
8. *Critique of Pure Reason*, B400.
9. *Ibid.*, B275.
10. See Ernst Stadter, *Psychologie und Metaphysik der menschlichen Freiheit*, München, Paderborn, Wien, 1971, p. 195.
11. See the magnificent description of such a dream of "complete loneliness" in Kant's *Observations on the Feeling of the Beautiful and Sublime*, trans. John T. Goldthwait, Berkeley, Los Angeles, 1960, pp. 48–49.
12. *Critique of Pure Reason*, B157. Cf. chap. I of the present volume, pp. 43–45.
13. *Ibid.*, B158 n.

14. "Anthropologie," no. 28, *Werke,* vol. VI, p. 466.
15. *The Trinity,* bk. XI, chap. 3. English translation: *Fathers of the Church* series, Washington, D.C., 1963, vol. 45.
16. *Ibid.*
17. *Ibid.,* chap. 8.
18. *Ibid.,* chap. 10.
19. *An Introduction to Metaphysics,* trans. Ralph Manheim, New Haven, 1959, p. 12.
20. "Discours aux Chirurgiens," in *Variété,* Paris, 1957, vol. I, p. 916.
21. *Phaedo,* 64.
22. Diogenes Laertius, VII, 2.
23. *Sämmtliche Werke,* Leipzig, n.d., "Ueber den Tod," vol. II, p. 1240.
24. *Phaedo,* 64–67.
25. Cf. Valéry, *op. cit., loc. cit.*
26. See N. A. Greenberg's analysis, "Socrates' Choice in the *Crito,*" in *Harvard Studies in Classical Philology,* vol. 70, no. 1, 1965.
27. Heraclitus, frags. 104, 29.
28. *Republic,* 494a and 496d.
29. *Ibid.,* 496a ff. Cornford, *The Republic of Plato,* pp. 203–204.
30. *Philebus,* 62b.
31. *Laws,* 935: In disputes, "all are wont to indulge in ridicule of their opponent." It is impossible "to abuse without seeking to ridicule." Hence, "every writer of comedy or iambic or lyric song shall be strictly forbidden to ridicule any of the citizens . . . and if he disobeys he shall be banished from the country." For the passages in the *Republic,* however, in which the fear of ridicule plays hardly any role, see 394 ff. and 606 ff.
32. *Theaetetus,* 174a–d.
33. "Träume eines Geistersehers," *Werke,* vol. I, p. 951.
34. *Phaedo,* 64.
35. *Ibid.,* 66.
36. *Ibid.,* 65.
37. *Protreptikos,* B43, ed. Ingemar Düring, Frankfurt, 1969.
38. *Ibid.,* B110.
39. *Republic,* 500c.
40. Letter of March 1638, *Descartes: Oeuvres et Lettres,* p. 780.
41. Editor's note: we have been unable to find this reference.
42. Akademie Ausgabe, vol. XVIII, 5019 and 5036.

43. Plato, in the *Phaedo*, 84a, mentions Penelope's web but in the opposite sense. The "soul of the philosopher," set free from the bondage of pleasure and pain, will not act Penelope-like, undoing her own weaving. Once rid (through the *logismos*), of pleasure and pain that "nail" the soul to the body, the soul (Plato's thinking ego) changes its nature and no longer reasons (*logizesthai*) but looks upon (*theāsthai*) "the true and the divine" and abides there forever.

44. "Ueber das Wesen der Philosophischen Kritik," *Hegel Studienausgabe*, Frankfurt, 1968, vol. I, p. 103.

45. *Philosophie der Weltgeschichte*, Lasson ed, Leipzig, 1917, pt. II, pp. 4–5.

46. *Reason in History*, trans. Robert S. Hartman, Indianapolis, New York, 1953, p. 89.

47. *Reason in History*, p. 69. Author's translation.

48. Preface to *The Phenomenology of Mind*.

49. *Politics*, 1269a35, 1334a15; see bk. VII, chap. 15.

50. Paul Weiss, "A Philosophical Definition of Leisure," in *Leisure in America: Blessing or Curse*, ed. J. C. Charlesworth, Philadelphia, 1964, p. 21.

51. VIII, 8. I follow the translation given in Kirk and Raven, frag. 278.

52. *Timaeus*, 34b.

53. "Der Streit der Fakultäten," pt. II, 6 and 7, *Werke*, vol. VI, pp. 357–362.

54. "Ueber den Gemeinspruch," *Werke*, vol. VI, pp. 166–167.

55. Hegel, *Philosophie der Weltgeschichte*, Introduction.

56. *Sophist*, 254.

57. *Republic*, 517b, and *Phaedrus*, 247c.

58. *Sophist*, 254a–b.

59. See chap. I of the present volume, pp. 33–34. In the beginning of *De Interpretatione*, Aristotle refers to his *De Anima*, as having dealt with some of the same points, but nothing in *De Anima* seems to correspond to the points raised in *De Interpretatione*. If my reading of the text is correct, Aristotle might have thought of the passage used by me in chap. I, that is, *De Anima*, 403a5–10.

60. *De Interpretatione*, 16a4–17a9.

61. "Reflexionen zur Anthropologie," no. 897, Akademie Ausgabe, vol. XV, p. 392.

62. *Monologion*.

63. In what follows here, I have relied closely on the first chapter,

on "Language and Script," of Marcel Granet's great book *La
Pensée Chinoise,* Paris, 1934. I used the new German edition,
which has been brought up to date by Manfred Porkert: *Das
chinesische Denken—Inhalt, Form, Charakter,* München, 1971.

64. Kant, *Critique of Pure Reason,* B180.

65. B180–181.

66. *Tractatus,* 4.016 (*"Um das Wesen des Satzes zu verstehen,
denken wir an die Hieroglyphenschrift, welche die Tatsachen,
die sie beschreibt, abbildet. Und aus ihr wurde die Buchsta-
benschrift, ohne das Wesentliche der Abbildung zu ver-
lieren"*).

67. *A Defence of Poetry.*

68. *Poetics,* 1459a5.

69. *Ibid.,* 1457b17 ff.

70. *Critique of Judgment,* no. 59.

71. *Ibid.*

72. *Ibid.*

73. *Prolegomena to Every Future Metaphysics,* no. 58, trans. Carl
J. Friedrich, Modern Library, New York, n.d. Kant himself
had been aware of this peculiarity of philosophical language
in the pre-critical time: "Our higher rational concepts . . .
usually take on a physical garment in order to achieve clarity."
"Träume eines Geistersehers," p. 948.

74. No. 59. It would be interesting to examine Kant's notion of
"analogy" from the early writing to the *Opus Postumum,* for it
is striking how early it occurred to him that metaphorical
thinking—that is, thinking in analogies—could save speculative
thought from its peculiar unreality. Already in the *Allgemeine
Naturgeschichte und Theorie des Himmels,* published in 1755,
he writes with respect to the "probability" of God's existence:
"I am not so devoted to the consequences of my theory that
I should not be ready to acknowledge . . . its being undemonstrable. Nevertheless, I expect . . . that such a chart of
the infinite, comprehending as it does a subject which seems
. . . to be forever concealed from human understanding,
*will not on that account be at once regarded as a chimera,
especially when recourse is had to analogy.*" (Italics added.
English translation, by W. Hastie, quoted from *Kant's Cos-
mogony,* Glasgow, 1900, pp. 146–147.

75. See Francis MacDonald Cornford, *Plato's Theory of Knowledge,* New York, 1957, p. 275.

76. The essay, "The Chinese Written Character as a Medium for Poetry," edited by Ezra Pound, in *Instigations*, Freeport, N.Y., 1967, contains a curious plea for the Chinese script: "Its etymology is constantly visible." A phonetic word "does not bear its metaphor on its face. We forget that personality once meant, not the soul, but the soul's mask [through which the soul sounded, as it were—*per-sonare*]. This is the sort of thing one can not possibly forget in using the Chinese symbol. . . . With us, the poet is the one for whom the accumulated treasures of the race-words are real and active" (p. 25).

77. IX, 1–8.

78. Marshall Cohen's unfortunately unpublished manuscript "The Concept of Metaphor," which I was kindly permitted to consult, contains many examples, together with an excellent review of the literature on the subject.

79. *The Odyssey of Homer*, bk. XIX, ll. 203–209, trans. Richmond Lattimore, New York, 1967, p. 287.

80. "Das Homerische Gleichnis und der Anfang der Philosophie," in *Die Antike*, vol. XII, 1936.

81. Diels and Kranz, frag. B67.

82. *Aus der Erfahrung des Denkens*, Bern, 1947.

83. Bruno Snell, "From Myth to Logic: The Role of the Comparison," in *The Discovery of the Mind*, Harper Torchbooks, New York, Evanston, 1960, p. 201.

84. Hans Jonas, *The Phenomenon of Life*, New York, 1966, p. 135. His study of "The Nobility of Sight" is of unique help in the clarification of the history of Western thought.

85. Diels and Kranz, frag. 101a.

86. Aristotle seems to have thought along these lines in one of his scientific treatises: "Of these faculties, for the mere necessities of life and in itself, sight is the more important, but for the mind [*nous*] and indirectly [*kata symbebēkos*] hearing is the more important. . . . [It] makes the largest contribution to wisdom. For discourse, which is the cause of learning, is so because it is audible; but it is audible not in itself but indirectly, because speech is composed of words, and each word is a rational symbol. Consequently, of those who have been deprived of one sense or the other from birth, the blind are more intelligent than the deaf and the dumb." The point of the matter is that he seems never to have remembered this observation when he wrote philosophy. Aristotle, *On Sense and Sensible Objects*, 437a4–17.

87. *Op. cit.*, p. 152.

88. See Hans Jonas, chap. 3, on Philo of Alexandria, especially pp. 94–97, of *Von der Mythologie zur mystischen Philosophie*, Göttingen, 1954, which is the second part of *Gnosis und spätantiker Geist*, Göttingen, 1934.

89. *The Phenomenon of Life*, pp. 136–147. Cf. *Von der Mythologie*, pp. 138–152.

90. Bonn, 1960, pp. 200 f.

91. *Theaetetus*, 155d.

92. 982b11–22.

93. 983a14–20.

94. See, for instance, *Nicomachean Ethics*, VI, 8, where the *nous* is the mental perception (*aisthēsis*) of the "unchangeable primary or limiting terms" for which "there exists no *logos*" (1142a25–27). Cf. 1143b5.

95. *Seventh Letter*, 341b–343a, paraphrase.

96. On July 2, 1885.

97. No. 160.

98. *Nietzsche*, Pfullingen, 1961, vol. II, p. 484.

99. *Philosophical Investigations*, trans. G. E. M. Anscombe, New York, 1953, nos. 119, 19, 109.

100. *Phaedrus*, 274e–277c.

101. *Physics*, 209b15.

102. 286a, b.

103. 275d–277a.

104. *Philebus*, 38e–39b.

105. *Ibid.*, 39b–c.

106. 342.

107. *Ibid.*, 344b.

108. *Ibid.*, 343b.

109. *Ibid.*, 341e.

110. *Critique of Pure Reason*, B33. For: "*Nicht dadurch, dass ich bloss denke, erkenne ich irgend ein Objekt, sondern nur dadurch, dass ich eine gegebene Anschauung . . . bestimme, kann ich irgend einen Gegenstand erkennen*" ("I do not know an object merely in that I think, but only insofar as I determine a given intuition, can I know an object") (B406).

111. I am quoting from an early lecture-course of Heidegger's on Plato's *Sophist* (1924–25) according to a literal transcript, pp. 8, and 155, 160. See also Cornford's commentary on the *Sophist* in *Plato's Theory of Knowledge*, p. 189 and n. 1,

where *noein* is said to stand for the act of "intuition (*noēsis*) which *sees* directly, without . . . discursive reasoning."

112. 38 c–e.
113. P. 50 of chap. I of the present volume.
114. Aristotle, *Metaphysics*, 1003 a 21.
115. *Ibid.*, 984 b 10.
116. Thomas Aquinas, *De Veritate*, qu. I, art. 1.
117. *Critique of Pure Reason*, B82, B83.
118. *Sein und Zeit*, Tübingen, 1949, no. 44 (a), p. 217.
119. See Aristotle, *Posterior Analytics*, 100b5–17.
120. *An Introduction to Metaphysics* (1903), trans. T. E. Hulme, Indianapolis, New York, 1955, p. 45.
121. *Ibid.*
122. *Critique of Pure Reason*, B84 and B189–B191.
123. *An Introduction to Metaphysics*, p. 45.
124. *Protreptikos*, Düring ed., B87.
125. 1072b27.
126. 1072a21.
127. This mistranslation mars W. D. Ross's *Aristotle*, Meridian Books, New York, 1959, but is mercifully absent from his translation of the *Metaphysics* in Richard McKeon's *The Basic Works of Aristotle*.
128. *Philosophy of History*, Introduction, p. 9.
129. *Hegel's Philosophy of Right*, trans. T. M. Knox, London, Oxford, New York, 1967, addition to para. 2, p. 225.
130. *Wegmarken*, p. 19.
131. *Nicomachean Ethics*, 1175a12.
132. *Tractatus*, 401. It seems to me obvious that Wittgenstein's early language theory is solidly rooted in the old metaphysical axiom of truth as *adequatio rei et intellectus;* the trouble with this definition has always been that such an equation is possible only as intuition, namely, as an internal image that copies the sensorially given visible object. "The logical picture of a fact," which according to Wittgenstein is a "thought" (I am following Bertrand Russell's Introduction to the *Tractatus* in the bilingual edition, London, 1961, p. xii), is a contradiction in terms unless one takes "picture" as a metaphorical expression. There certainly exists a "relation which holds between language and the world," but whatever this relation may be, it is certainly not a "pictorial" one. If it were a pictorial relation, every proposition, unless it renders and repeats an accidental error in sensory perception (something looks like

a tree but turns out to be a man on closer inspection), would be true; however, I can make a great many propositions about a "fact" that say something quite meaningful without being necessarily true: "the sun turns about the earth" or "in September 1939 Poland invaded Germany"—the one being an error, the other being a lie. There are, on the other hand, propositions that are inherently unacceptable, as for instance "the triangle laughs," cited in the text, which is neither a true nor a false statement, but a meaningless one. The only internal linguistic criterion for propositions is sense or nonsense.

In view of these rather obvious difficulties and in view of the fact that Wittgenstein himself later rejected his "picture theory of propositions," it is rather interesting to find out how it occurred to him in the first place. There are, I think, two versions of this. He had been "reading a magazine in which there was a schematic picture depicting the possible sequence of events in an automobile accident. The picture there served as a proposition; that is, as a description of a possible state of affairs. It had this function owing to a correspondence between the parts of the picture and things in reality. It now occurred to Wittgenstein that one might reverse the analogy and say that a *proposition* serves as a *picture,* by virtue of a similar correspondence between *its* parts and the world. The way in which the parts of the proposition are combined—the *structure* of the proposition—depicts a possible combination of elements in reality." (See G. H. von Wright's "Biographical Sketch" in Norman Malcolm's *Ludwig Wittgenstein: A Memoir,* London, 1958, pp. 7–8.) What seems decisive here is that he did not take off from reality but from a *schematic reconstruction* of some event which itself had already been subjected to a process of thought, that is, he started from an illustration of a thought. In the *Philosophical Investigations* (663), there is an observation that reads like a refutation of this theory: "If I say 'I meant *him,*' very likely a picture comes to my mind . . . but the picture is only like an illustration to a story. From it alone it would mostly be impossible to conclude anything at all; only when one knows the story does one know the significance of the picture."

The second version of the origin of the "picture theory of propositions" is to be found in the *Tractatus* itself (4.0311) and sounds even more plausible. Wittgenstein, who replaced his earlier theory with the theory of language-games, seems to have been influenced by another game, frequently played in his time in society, the game of *tableaux vivants:* the rules demanded that somebody had to guess what proposition was expressed by the *tableau vivant* enacted by a number of persons. "One name stands for one thing, another for another thing, and they are combined with one another. In this way the whole group—like a tableau vivant—presents a state of affairs"; it actually is supposed to spell out a certain proposition.

I mention these things to indicate Wittgenstein's style of thinking. They may help explain "the puzzling thing about his later philosophy . . . that it is so piecemeal" and "has no master plan." (See the excellent presentation of David Pears, *Ludwig Wittgenstein,* New York, 1970, pp. 4 f.) The *Tractatus* also starts from a haphazard observation, from which, however, its author was able to develop a consistent theory that saved him from further haphazard observations and enabled him to write a continuous work. In spite of its frequent abruptness, the *Tractatus* is entirely consistent. The *Philosophical Investigations* shows how this ceaselessly active mind actually functioned, if it was not, almost accidentally, guided by a single assumption, for instance, by the thesis that "there must . . . be something in common between the structure of the sentence and the structure of the fact." (Russell, *op. cit.,* p. x, rightly calls this "the most fundamental thesis of Mr Wittgenstein's theory.") The most conspicuous property of the *Philosophical Investigations* is its breathlessness: it is as though somebody had actualized the *stop-and-think* inherent in thought to the point where it halted the whole thinking process and interrupted every thought-train by recoiling on itself. The English translation somehow mitigates this by rendering the ever-repeated *"Denk dir"* by a variety of words, such as "suppose," "imagine."

133. *Philosophical Investigations,* nos. 466–471.

## Chapter III

1. *Timaeus,* 90c (see n. 35 below).
2. See the very instructive *Theory and Practice,* by Nicholas Lobkowicz, p. 7n.

232

3. *Symposium*, 204a.
4. Pindar, *Nemea*, 6; *The Odes of Pindar,* trans. Richmond Lattimore, Chicago, 1947, p. 111.
5. I, 131.
6. *Sophist*, 219b.
7. *Republic*, 518c.
8. *The Discourses*, bk. II, Introduction.
9. Bruno Snell, "Pindar's Hymn to Zeus," *op. cit.*, pp. 77–79.
10. *Nemea*, 4, *Isthmia*, 4, both Lattimore trans.
11. *Isthmia*, 4, Lattimore trans.
12. Thucydides, II, 41.
13. *Protreptikos*, Düring ed., B19 and B110. Cf. *Eudemian Ethics*, 1216a11.
14. *Protreptikos*, Düring ed., B109.
15. *De Finibus Bonorum et Malorum*, II, 13.
16. Heraclitus, B29.
17. *Symposium*, 208c.
18. *Ibid.*, 208d.
19. Anaximander seems to have been the first to equate the divine with the *apeiron,* the Non-Limited, whose nature it was to be forever—ageless, immortal, and imperishable.
20. Frag. 8.
21. Charles H. Kahn, in his fascinating study "The Greek Verb 'to be' and the Concept of Being," examines "the pre-philosophical use of this verb which . . . serves to express the concept of Being in Greek" (p. 245). In *Foundations of Language,* vol. 2, 1966, p. 255.
22. B30.
23. Snell, *op. cit.*, p. 40.
24. Kahn, *op. cit.*, p. 260.
25. Frag. 3.
26. *Protreptikos*, Düring ed., B110.
27. *Philebus*, 28c.
28. *Symposium*, 212a.
29. *Nicomachean Ethics,* 1178b3, 1178b22, 1177b33 (the last from Martin Ostwald trans., Indianapolis, New York, 1962).
30. *Timaeus*, 90d, a.
31. Quoted from Jeremy Bernstein's "The Secrets of the Old One—II," *The New Yorker,* March 17, 1973.
32. Francis MacDonald Cornford, *Plato and Parmenides,* New York, 1957, Introduction, p. 27.
33. *Protreptikos*, Düring ed., B65.

34. Cornford, *Plato's Theory of Knowledge*, p. 189.
35. *Timaeus*, 90c.
36. *Philebus*, 59b, c.
37. "Philosophie der Weltgeschichte," *Hegel Studienausgabe*, vol. I, p. 291.
38. *De Rerum Natura*, bk. II, first lines; *On the Nature of the Universe*, trans. Ronald Latham, Penguin, Harmondsworth, 1951, p. 60.
39. I owe the quotations from Herder and Goethe to the interesting study of navigation, shipwreck, and spectator as "existential metaphors" in Hans Blumenberg, "Beobachtungen an Metaphern," in *Archiv für Begriffsgeschichte*, vol. XV, Heft 2, 1971, pp. 171 ff. For Voltaire, see his article "Curiosité" in his *Dictionnaire Philosophique*. For Herder, see also *Briefe zur Beförderung der Humanität*, 1792, 17th Letter; for Goethe, *Goethes Gespräche*, Artemis ed., Zürich, 1949, vol. 22, no. 725, p. 454.
40. 1177b27–33.
41. *Theaetetus*, 155d.
42. *Cratylus*, 408b.
43. B21a.
44. B54.
45. B123.
46. B93.
47. B107.
48. B32.
49. B108.
50. *The Friend*, III, 192, as quoted by Herbert Read in *Coleridge as Critic*, London, 1949, p. 30.
51. Now together with two later explications, an Introduction and an Epilogue, in *Wegmarken*, pp. 19 and 210.
52. 1714, no. 7.
53. *Critique of Pure Reason*, B641.
54. *Werke*, 6. Ergänzungsband, ed. M. Schröter, München, 1954, p. 242.
55. *Ibid.*, p. 7.
56. See the posthumously published *System der gesammten Philosophie* of 1804, in *Sämtliche Werke*, Abt. I, Stuttgart and Augsburg, 1860, vol. VI, p. 155.
57. *Sämtliche Werke*, Abt. I, vol. VII, p. 174.
58. *Ibid.*, Abt. II, vol. III, p. 163. Cf. also Karl Jaspers, *Schelling*, München, 1955, pp. 124–130.

59. Paris, 1958, pp. 161–171.

60. See the *Preisschrift* "Uber die Deutlichkeit der Grundsätze der natürlichen Theologie und der Moral" (1764), 4th Consideration, no. 1, *Werke*, vol. I, pp. 768–769.

61. "Uber den Optimismus," *Werke*, vol. I, p. 594.

62. *Ecce Homo*, "Thus Spoke Zarathustra," 1.

63. *The Gay Science*, bk. IV, no. 341.

64. 130d, e.

65. *Tusculanae Disputationes*, III, iii, 6.

66. *Ibid.*, III, xiv, 30. Cf. Horace, *Epistolae*, I, vi, 1. Plutarch (in his *De recta Ratione*, 13) mentions the Stoic maxim and ascribes it—in Greek translation, *mē thaumazein*—to Pythagoras. Democritus is supposed to have praised *athaumastia* and *athambia* as Stoic wisdom, but seems to have had no more in mind than the "wise man's" imperturbability and fearlessness.

67. *Hegel's Philosophy of Right*, p. 13.

68. *L'Oeuvre de Pascal*, Pléiade ed., Bruges, 1950, 294, p. 901.

69. *Differenz des Fichte'schen und Schelling'schen Systems der Philosophie* (1801), Meiner ed., 1962, pp. 12 ff.

70. Trans. J. Sibree, New York, 1956, p. 318.

71. *Ibid.*, p. 26.

72. This transformation is especially telling when the borrowing from Greek philosophy is most obvious, as when Cicero says man is destined *ad mundum contemplandum* and then immediately adds: *et imitandum* (*De Natura Deorum*, II, xiv, 37), which he understands in a strictly moral-political sense, and not scientifically as, centuries later, Francis Bacon would have understood it: "Nature to be commanded must be obeyed; and that which in contemplation is as the cause, in operation is as the rule . . ." (*Novum Organon*, Oxford ed., 1889, p. 192).

73. *De Rerum Natura*, bk. II, 1174; *On the Nature of the Universe*, Latham trans., p. 95.

74. *Discourses*, bk. I, chap. 17.

75. *Ibid.*, bk. I, chap. 15.

76. *The Manual*, 49; *The Stoic and Epicurean Philosophers*, ed. Whitney J. Oates, New York, 1940, p. 482.

77. *Discourses*, bk. I, chap. 1.

78. *The Manual*, 8, Oates ed., p. 470; *Fragments*, 8, Oates ed., p. 460.

79. *Op. cit.*, V, 7 ff. Author's translation.
80. *De Republica*, I, 7.
81. *Ibid.*, III, 23.
82. *Ibid.*, V, 1.
83. Modeled, of course, on the myth of Er that concludes Plato's *Republic*. For the important differences, see the analysis of Richard Harder, the late eminent German philologist, "Uber Ciceros Somnium Scipionis," in *Kleine Schriften*, München, 1960, pp. 354–395.
84. "Discourses on Davila," *The Works of John Adams*, ed. Charles Francis Adams, Boston, 1850–1856, vol. VI, p. 242.
85. *Oedipus at Colonnus.*
86. *Politics*, 1267a12.
87. *Nicomachean Ethics*, 1178a29–30.
88. Frag. 146.
89. *The Decline and Fall of the Roman Empire*, Modern Library, New York, n.d., vol. II, p. 471.
90. I, 30; my translation of *hōs philosopheōn gēn pollēn theōriēs heineken epelēlythas.*
91. I, 32.
92. The thought content of that saying was fully explicated only in Heidegger's death-analyses in *Being and Time*, which take their methodological cue from the fact that human life—as distinguished from "things," which start their worldly existence when they are complete and finished—is complete only when it *is* no more. Hence, only by anticipating its own death can it "appear" as a whole and be subjected to analysis.
93. E. Diehl, ed., *Anthologia Lyrica Graeca*, Leipzig, 1936, frag. 16.
94. *Ibid.*, frag. 13, ll. 63–70.
95. *Ibid.*, frag. 14.
96. *Charmides*, 175b.
97. Hegel's *Encyclopädie der philosophischen Wissenschaften*, Lasson ed., Leipzig, 1923, 23: *"Das Denken . . . sich als abstraktes Ich als von aller Partikularität sonstiger Eigenschaften, Zustände, usf. befreites verhält und nur das Allgemeine tut, in welchem es mit allen Individuen identisch ist."*
98. It is surprising, in examining the literature, often very learned, to see how very little all this erudition has been able to contribute to an understanding of the man. The only exception I have been able to unearth is a kind of inspired profile

by the classicist and philosopher Gregory Vlastos, "The Paradox of Socrates." See the Introduction to his carefully selected *The Philosophy of Socrates: A Collection of Critical Essays*, Anchor Books, New York, 1971.

99. 173d.

100. On the Socratic problem, see the short, reasonable account given by Laszlo Versényi as an Appendix to his *Socratic Humanism*, New Haven, London, 1963.

101. *Dante and Philosophy*, trans. David Moore, Harper Torchbooks, New York, Evanston, London, 1963, p. 267.

102. *Ibid.*, p. 273.

103. Thus in *Theaetetus* and *Charmides*.

104. *Meno*, 80e.

105. The frequent notion that Socrates tries to lead his interlocutor with his questions to certain results of which he is convinced in advance—like a clever professor with his students—seems to me entirely mistaken even if it is as ingeniously qualified as in Vlastos' essay mentioned above, in which he suggests (p. 13) that Socrates wanted the other "to find . . . out for himself," as in the *Meno*, which however is not aporetic. The most one could say is that Socrates wanted his partners in the dialogues to be as perplexed as he was. He was sincere when he said that he taught nothing. Thus he told Critias in the *Charmides*: "Critias, you act as though I professed to know the answers to the questions I ask you and could give them to you if I wished. It is not so. I inquire with you . . . because I don't myself have knowledge" (165b; cf. 166c–d).

106. Diehl, frag. 16.

107. *Meno*, 80c. Cf. the above-mentioned passage, n. 105.

108. *Memorabilia*, IV, vi, 15 and IV, iv, 9.

109. *Sophist*, 226–231.

110. *Apology*, 23b.

111. *Ibid.*, 30a.

112. Xenophon, *Memorabilia*, IV, iii, 14.

113. *Antigone*, 353.

114. The German text, from *Was Heisst Denken?*, Tübingen, 1954, p. 52, reads as follows: "*Sokrates hat zeit seines Lebens, bis in seinen Tod hinein, nichts anderes getan, als sich in den Zugwind dieses Zuges zu stellen und darin sich zu halten. Darum ist er der reinste Denker des Abendlandes. Deshalb hat er nichts geschrieben. Denn wer aus dem Denken zu schreiben*

beginnt, muss unweigerlich den Menschen gleichen, die vor allzu starkem Zugwind in den Windschatten flüchten. Es bleibt das Geheimnis einer noch verborgenen Geschichte, dass alle Denker des Abendlandes nach Sokrates, unbeschadet ihrer Grösse, solche Flüchtlinge sein mussten. Das Denken ging in die Literatur ein."

115. G. Humphrey, *Thinking: An Introduction to Its Experimental Psychology,* London and New York, 1951, p. 312.

116. Thucydides, II, 40.

117. *Lysis,* 204b–c.

118. Frags. 145, 190.

119. *Gorgias,* 474b, 483a, b.

120. *Ibid.,* 482c.

121. *Ibid.,* 482c, 484c, d.

122. Aristotle frequently insisted that thinking "produces" happiness, but if so, not in the way that medicine produces health but in the way that health makes a man healthy. *Nicomachean Ethics,* 1144a.

123. Diels and Kranz, B45.

124. 254d.

125. *Identity and Difference,* trans. Joan Stambaugh, New York, Evanston, London, 1969, pp. 24–25.

126. 255d.

127. *Sophist,* 255e; Cornford, *Plato's Theory of Knowledge,* p. 282.

128. Heidegger, *Sophist* lecture transcript, p. 382.

129. *Theaetetus,* 189e; *Sophist,* 263e.

130. *Sophist,* 253b.

131. *Protagoras,* 339c.

132. *Ibid.,* 339b, 340b.

133. *Posterior Analytics,* 76b22–25.

134. 1005b23–1008a2.

135. No. 36, *Werke,* vol. VI, p. 500.

136. No. 56, *ibid.,* p. 549.

137. "Grundlegung zur Metaphysik der Sitten," *Werke,* vol. 4, pp. 51–55.

138. 304d.

139. *Nicomachean Ethics,* 1166a30.

140. *Ibid.,* 1166b5–25.

141. *Ethics,* IV, 52; III, 25.

142. *Philosophy* (1932), trans. E. B. Ashton, Chicago, London, 1970, vol. 2, pp. 178–179.

238

## Chapter ·IV

1. *Symposium*, 174–175.
2. Merleau-Ponty, *Signs*, "The Philosopher and His Shadow," p. 174.
3. Quoted from Sebastian de Grazia, "About Chuang Tzu," *Dalhousie Review*, Summer 1974.
4. Hegel, *Encyclopädie der philosophischen Wissenschaften*, 465n.
5. Ross, *Aristotle*, p. 14.
6. *Protreptikos*, Düring ed., B56.
7. *Physics*, VI, viii, 189a5.
8. *Nicomachean Ethics*, 1141b24–1142a30. Cf. 1147a1–10.
9. *Critique of Pure Reason*, B49, B50.
10. *Gesammelte Schriften*, New York, 1946, vol. V, p. 287. English translation by Willa and Edwin Muir, *The Great Wall of China*, New York, 1946, p. 276–277.
11. Pt. III, "On the Vision and the Riddle," sect. 2.
12. Vol. I, pp. 311 f.
13. Duns Scotus, *Opus Oxoniense* I, dist. 40, q. 1, n. 3. Quoted from Walter Hoeres, *Der Wille als reine Vollkommenheit nach Duns Scotus*, München, 1962, p. 111, n. 72.
14. *Critique of Pure Reason*, B294 f.
15. "As I Walked Out One Evening," *Collected Poems*, p. 115.
16. W. H. Auden, *The Dyer's Hand and Other Essays*, Vintage Books, New York, 1968.
17. *Time and Free Will* (1910), trans. F. L. Pogson, Harper Torchbooks, New York, Evanston, 1960, pp. 158, 167, 240.
18. Romans 7:15.
19. *Encyclopädie*, 12.
20. *Of Human Freedom*, Gutmann trans., p. 8.
21. *Critique of Pure Reason*, B172–B173.

# Two / Willing

Introduction

The second volume of *The Life of the Mind* will be devoted to the faculty of the Will and, by implication, to the problem of Freedom, which, as Bergson said, "has been to the moderns what the paradoxes of the Eleatics were to the ancients." The phenomena we have to deal with are overlaid to an extraordinary extent by a coat of argumentative reasoning, by no means arbitrary and hence not to be neglected but which parts company with the actual experiences of the willing ego in favor of doctrines and theories that are not necessarily interested in "saving the phenomena."

One reason for these difficulties is very simple: the faculty of the Will was unknown to Greek antiquity and was discovered as a result of experiences about which we hear next to nothing before the first century of the Christian era. The problem for later centuries was to reconcile this faculty with the main tenets of Greek philosophy: men of thought were no longer willing to abandon philosophy altogether and say, with Paul, "we preach Christ crucified, a stumbling-block to Jews and folly to Gentiles," and let it go at that. This, as we shall see, only Paul himself was ever prepared to do.

But the end of the Christian era by no means spells the end of these difficulties. The main strictly Christian difficulty, viz., how to reconcile faith in an all-powerful and omniscient God with the claims of free will, survives in various ways deep into the modern age, where we often meet almost the same kind of argumentation as before. Either free will is found to clash with the law of causality or, later, it can hardly be reconciled with the laws of History, whose meaningfulness depends on progress or a *necessary* development of the World Spirit. These difficulties even persist when all strictly traditional—metaphysical or theological—interests have withered away. John

3

Stuart Mill, for instance, sums up an oft-repeated argument when he says: "Our *internal* consciousness tells us that we have a power, which the whole outward experience of the human race tells us that we never use." Or, to use the most extreme example, Nietzsche calls "the entire doctrine of the Will the most fateful *falsification* in psychology hitherto . . . essentially invented for the sake of punishment."

The greatest difficulty faced by every discussion of the Will is the simple fact that there is no other capacity of the mind whose very existence has been so consistently doubted and refuted by so eminent a series of philosophers. The latest is Gilbert Ryle, to whom the Will is an "artificial concept" corresponding to nothing that has ever existed and creating useless riddles like so many of the metaphysical fallacies. Unaware, apparently, of his distinguished predecessors, he sets out to refute "the doctrine that there exists a Faculty . . . of the 'Will,' and, accordingly, that there occur processes, or operations, corresponding to what it describes as volitions." He is aware of "the fact that Plato and Aristotle never mentioned [volitions] in their frequent and elaborate discussions of the nature of the soul and the springs of conduct," because they were still unacquainted with this "special hypothesis [of later times] the acceptance of which rests not on the discovery but on the postulation of [certain] ghostly thrusts."

It is in the nature of every critical examination of the faculty of the Will that it should be undertaken by "professional thinkers" (Kant's *Denker von Gewerbe*), and this gives rise to the suspicion that the denunciations of the Will as a mere illusion of consciousness and the refutations of its very existence, which we find supported by almost identical arguments in philosophers of widely differing assumptions, might be due to a basic conflict between the experiences of the thinking ego and those of the willing ego.

Although it is always the same mind that thinks and wills, as it is the same self that unites body, soul, and mind, it is by no means a matter of course that the thinking ego's evaluation can be trusted to remain unbiased and "objective" when it comes to other mental activities. For the truth of the matter is that the notion of free will serves not only as a necessary postulate of every ethics and every system of laws but is no less an "immediate datum of consciousness" (in the words of Bergson) than the I-think in Kant or the *cogito* in Descartes, whose existence was hardly ever doubted by traditional philosophy. To anticipate: what aroused the philosophers' distrust of this faculty was its inevitable connection with Freedom: "If I must necessarily will, why need I speak of will at all?" as Augustine put it. The touchstone of a free act is always our awareness that we could also have left undone what we actually did—something not at all true of mere desire or of the appetites, where bodily needs, the necessities of the life process, or the sheer force of wanting something close at hand may override any considerations of either Will or Reason. Willing, it appears, has an infinitely greater freedom than thinking, which even in its freest, most speculative form cannot escape the law of non-contradiction. This undeniable fact has never been felt to be an unmixed blessing. By men of thought, more often than not, it has been felt to be a curse.

In what follows, I shall take the internal evidence of an I-will as sufficient testimony to the reality of the phenomenon, and since I agree with Ryle—and many others—that this phenomenon and all the problems connected with it were unknown in Greek antiquity, I must accept what Ryle rejects, namely, that this faculty was indeed "discovered" and can be dated. In brief, I shall analyze the Will in terms of its history, and this in itself has its difficulties.

Are not the human faculties, as distinct from the conditions and circumstances of human life, coeval with the appearance of man on earth? If this were not the case, how could we ever understand the literature and thoughts of bygone ages? To be sure, there is a "history of ideas," and it would be rather easy to trace the idea of Freedom historically: how it changed from being a word indicating a political status—that of a free citizen and not a slave—and a physical fact—that of a healthy man, whose body was not paralyzed but able to obey his mind—into a word indicating an *inner* disposition by virtue of which a man could *feel* free when he actually was a slave or unable to move his limbs. Ideas are mental artifacts, and their history presupposes the unchanging identity of man the artificer. We shall return to this problem later. In any event, the fact is that prior to the rise of Christianity we nowhere find any notion of a mental faculty corresponding to the "idea" of Freedom, as the faculty of the Intellect corresponds to truth and the faculty of Reason to things beyond human knowledge, or, as we said here, to Meaning.

We shall begin our examination of the nature of the willing capability and its function in the life of the mind by investigating the post-classical and pre-modern literature testifying to the mental experiences that caused its discovery as well as to those that the discovery itself caused—a literature covering the period from Paul's Letter to the Romans to Duns Scotus' questioning of Thomas Aquinas' position. But first I shall deal briefly with Aristotle, partly because of "the philosopher" 's decisive influence on medieval thought, and partly because his notion of *proairesis,* in my opinion a kind of forerunner of the Will, can serve as a paradigmatic example of how certain problems of the soul were raised and answered before the discovery of the Will.

However, this section—embracing chapters II and III—will be preceded by a rather lengthy preliminary consideration of the arguments and theories which, since the revival of philosophy in the seventeenth century, have overlaid but also reinterpreted many of these authentic experiences. After all, it is with these theories, doctrines, and arguments in mind that we approach our subject.

The final section will begin with an examination of Nietzsche's and Heidegger's "conversion" to the philosophy of antiquity as a consequence of their re-evaluation and repudiation of the willing faculty. We then shall ask ourselves whether men of action were not perhaps in a better position to come to terms with the problems of the Will than the men of thought dealt with in the first volume of this study. What will be at stake here is the Will as the spring of action, that is, as a "power of *spontaneously* beginning a series of successive things or states" (Kant). No doubt every man, by virtue of his birth, is a new beginning, and his power of beginning may well correspond to this fact of the human condition. It is in line with these Augustinian reflections that the Will has sometimes, and not only by Augustine, been considered to be the actualization of the *principium individuationis*. The question is how this faculty of being able to bring about something new and hence to "change the world" can function in the world of appearances, namely, in an environment of factuality which is old by definition and which relentlessly transforms all the spontaneity of its newcomers into the "has been" of facts—*fieri; factus sum.*

# The Philosophers    I
and the Will

# 1   *Time and mental activities*

I concluded the first volume of *The Life of the Mind* with certain time speculations. This was an attempt to clarify a very old question, first raised by Plato but never answered by him: Where is the *topos noētos*, the region of the mind in which the philosopher dwells?[1] I reformulated it in the course of the inquiry as: Where are we when we think? To what do we withdraw when we withdraw from the world of appearances, stop all ordinary activities, and start what Parmenides, at the beginning of our philosophical tradition, had so emphatically urged on us: "Look at what, though absent [from the senses], is so reliably present to the mind."[2]

Framed in spatial terms, the question received a negative answer. Though known to us only in inseparable union with a body that is at home in the world of appearances by virtue of having arrived one day and knowing that one day it will depart, the invisible thinking ego is, strictly speaking, Nowhere. It has withdrawn from the world of appearances, including its own body, and therefore also from the self, of which it is no longer aware. This to the point that Plato can ironically call the philosopher a man in love with death, and Valéry can say *"Tantôt je pense et tantôt je suis,"* implying that the thinking ego loses all sense of reality and that the real, appearing self does not think. From this it follows that our question—Where are we when we think?—was asked outside the thinking experience, hence was inappropriate.

When we then decided to inquire into the time experience of the thinking ego, we found our question no longer out of place. Memory, the mind's power of having present what is irrevocably past and thus absent from the senses, has always been the most plausible paradigmatic example of the mind's power to make invisibles present. By virtue of this power, the

1. Notes are on pages 219–239.

mind seems to be even stronger than reality; it pits its strength against the inherent futility of everything that is subject to change; it collects and re-collects what otherwise would be doomed to ruin and oblivion. The time region in which this salvage takes place is the Present of the thinking ego, a kind of lasting "todayness" (*hodiernus*, "of this day," Augustine called God's eternity),[3] the "standing now" (*nunc stans*) of medieval meditation, an "enduring present" (Bergson's *présent qui dure*),[4] or "the gap between past and future," as we called it in explicating Kafka's time parable. But only if we accept the medieval interpretation of that time experience as an intimation of divine eternity are we forced to conclude that not just spatiality but also temporality is provisionally suspended in mental activities. Such an interpretation shrouds our whole mental life in an aura of mysticism and strangely overlooks the very ordinariness of the experience itself. The constitution of an "enduring present" is "the habitual, normal, banal act of our intellect,"[5] performed in every kind of reflection, whether its subject matter is ordinary day-to-day occurrences or whether the attention is focused on things forever invisible and outside the sphere of human power. The activity of the mind always creates for itself *un présent qui dure*, a "gap between past and future."

(Aristotle, it seems, was the first to mention this suspension of time's motion in an enduring present, and this, interestingly enough, in his discussion of pleasure, *hēdonē*, in the tenth book of the *Nicomachean Ethics*. "Pleasure," he says, "is not in time. For what takes place in a Now is a whole"—there is no motion. And since according to him the activity of thinking, "marvelous in purity and certainty," was the "most pleasant" of all activities, clearly he was talking about the motionless Now,[6] the later *nunc stans*. For him, the most sober of the great thinkers, this seems to have been no less a moment of rapture than it was for the medieval mystics except, of course, that Aristotle would have been the last to indulge in hysterical extravagances.)

I have said before that mental activities, and especially the activity of thinking, are always "out of order" when seen from the perspective of the unbroken continuity of our business in the world of appearances. There the chain of "nows" rolls on relentlessly, so that the present is understood as precariously binding past and future together: the moment we try to pin it down, it is either a "no more" or a "not yet." From that perspective, the enduring present looks like an extended "now"— a contradiction in terms—as though the thinking ego were capable of stretching the moment out and thus producing a kind of spatial habitat for itself. But this seeming spatiality of a temporal phenomenon is an error, caused by the metaphors we traditionally use in terminology dealing with the phenomenon of Time. As Bergson first discovered, they are all terms "borrowed from spatial language. If we want to reflect on time, it is space that responds." Thus "duration is always expressed as extension,"[7] and the past is understood as something lying behind us, the future as lying somewhere ahead of us. The reason for preferring the spatial metaphor is obvious: for our everyday business in the world, on which the thinking ego may reflect but in which it is not involved, we need time measurements, and we can measure time only by measuring spatial distances. Even the common distinction between spatial juxtaposition and temporal succession presupposes an extended space through which the succession must occur.

Such preliminary and by no means satisfactory considerations of the time concept seem to me necessary for our discussion of the willing ego because the Will, if it exists at all—and an uncomfortably large number of great philosophers who never doubted the existence of reason or mind held that the Will was nothing but an illusion—is as obviously our mental organ for the future as memory is our mental organ for the past. (The strange ambivalence of the English language, in which "will" as an auxiliary designates the future whereas the verb "to will" indicates volitions, properly speaking, testifies to our uncertainties in these matters.) In our context, the basic trouble with the Will is that it deals not merely with things that are absent from the senses and need to be made present through the mind's power of re-presentation, but with things, visibles and invisibles, that have never existed at all.

The moment we turn our mind to the future, we are no

longer concerned with "objects" but with *projects,* and it is not decisive whether they are formed spontaneously or as anticipated reactions to future circumstances. And just as the past always presents itself to the mind in the guise of certainty, the future's main characteristic is its basic uncertainty, no matter how high a degree of probability prediction may attain. In other words, we are dealing with matters that never were, that are not yet, and that may well never be. Our Last Will and Testament, providing for the only future of which we can be reasonably certain, namely our own death, shows that the Will's need to will is no less strong than Reason's need to think; in both instances the mind transcends its own natural limitations, either by asking unanswerable questions or by projecting itself into a future which, for the willing subject, will never be.

Aristotle laid the foundations for philosophy's attitude toward the Will, and throughout the centuries their resiliency has withstood the most momentous tests and challenges. According to Aristotle,[8] all matters that may be or may not be, that have happened but may not have happened, are by chance, *kata symbēbekos*—or, in the Latin translation, accidental or contingent—as distinguished from what necessarily is as it is, what *is* and cannot not be. This second, which he called the *"hypokeimenon,"* lies below what is added by chance, i.e., whatever does not belong to the very essence—as color is added to objects whose essence is independent of these "secondary qualities." Attributes that may or may not attach to what underlies them—their *substratum* or *substance* (the Latin translations of *hypokeimenon*)—are accidental.

There can hardly be anything more contingent than willed acts, which—on the assumption of free will—could all be defined as acts about which I know that I could as well have left them undone. A will that is not free is a contradiction in terms—unless one understands the faculty of volition as a mere auxiliary executive organ for whatever either desire or reason has proposed. In the framework of these categories, everything that happens in the realm of human affairs is accidental or contingent (*"prakton d'esti to endechomenon kai allōs echein,"* "what is brought into being by action is that which could also be otherwise"[9]): Aristotle's very words already indicate the realm's low ontological status—a status never seriously challenged till Hegel's discovery of Meaning and Necessity in History.

Within the sphere of human activities, Aristotle admitted one important exception to this rule, namely, making or fabrication—*poiein,* as distinct from *prattein,* acting or praxis. To use Aristotle's example, the craftsman who makes a "brazen sphere" joins together matter and form, brass and sphere, both of which existed before he began his work, and produces a *new* object to be added to a world consisting of man-made things and of things that have come into being independent of human doings. The human product, this "compound of matter and form"—for instance, a house made of wood according to a form pre-existing in the craftsman's mind (*nous*)—clearly was not made out of nothing, and so was understood by Aristotle to pre-exist "potentially" before it was actualized by human hands. This notion was derived from the mode of being peculiar to the nature of living things, where everything that appears grows out of something that contains the finished product potentially, as the oak exists potentially in the acorn and the animal in the semen.

The view that everything real must be preceded by a potentiality as one of its causes implicitly denies the future as an authentic tense: the future is nothing but a consequence of the past, and the difference between natural and man-made things is merely between those whose potentialities necessarily grow into actualities and those that may or may not be actualized. Under these circumstances, any notion of the Will as an organ for the future, as memory is an organ for the past, was entirely superfluous; Aristotle did not have to be aware of the Will's existence; the Greeks "do not even have a word for" what we consider to be "the mainspring of action." (*Thelein* means "to be ready, to be prepared for something," *boulesthai* is "to view something as [more] desirable," and Aristotle's own newly coined word, which comes closer than these to our notion of some mental state that must precede action, is *pro-airesis,* the "choice" between two possibilities, or, rather, the preference that makes me choose one action instead of another.)[10]

Authors well read in Greek literature have always been aware of this lacuna. Thus Gilson notices as a well-known fact "that Aristotle speaks neither of liberty nor of free will . . . the term itself is lacking,"[11] and Hobbes is already quite explicit on the point.[12] It is still somewhat difficult to spot, because the Greek language of course knows the distinction between intentional and unintentional acts, between the voluntary (*hekōn*) and the involuntary (*akōn*), that is, legally speaking, between murder and manslaughter, and Aristotle is careful to point out that only voluntary acts are subject to blame and praise,[13] but what he understands by voluntary means no more than that the act was not haphazard but was performed by the agent in full possession of his physical and mental strength—"the source of motion was in the agent"[14]—and the distinction covers no more than injuries committed in ignorance or as mishaps. An act in which I am under the threat of violence but am not physically coerced—as when I give my money, pulling it out with my own hands, to the man who threatens me with a gun—would have qualified as voluntary.

It is of some importance to note that this curious lacuna in Greek philosophy—"the fact that Plato and Aristotle never mentioned [volitions] in their frequent and elaborate discussions of the nature of the soul and the springs of conduct"[15] and that therefore it cannot be "seriously maintained that the problem of freedom ever became the subject of debate in the philosophy of Socrates, Plato, and Aristotle"[16]—is in perfect accord with the time concept of antiquity, which identified temporality with the circular movements of the heavenly bodies and with the no less cyclical nature of life on earth: the ever-repeated change of day and night, summer and winter, the constant renewal of animal species through birth and death. When Aristotle holds that "coming-into-being necessarily implies the pre-existence of something which is potentially but is not actually,"[17] he is applying the cyclical movement in which everything that is alive swings—where indeed every end is a beginning and every beginning an end, so that "coming-to-be continues though things are constantly being destroyed"[18]—to the realm of human affairs, and this to the point that he can say that not only events but even opinions (*doxai*) "as they occur among men, revolve not only once or a few times but infinitely often."[19] This strange view of human affairs was not peculiar to philosophic speculation. Thucydides' claim to leave to posterity a *ktēma es aei*—a sempiternally useful paradigm of how to inquire into the future by virtue of a clear knowledge of the greatest event yet known in history—rested implicitly on the same conviction of a recurrent movement of human affairs.

To us, who think in terms of a rectilinear time concept, with its emphasis on the uniqueness of the "historical moment," the Greek pre-philosophical praise of greatness and stress on the extraordinary, which, "whether for evil or for good" (Thucydides), beyond all moral considerations, deserves to be saved from oblivion, first by the bards and then by the historians, seems to be incompatible with their cyclical time concept. But until the philosophers discovered Being as everlasting, birthless as well as deathless, time and change in time constituted no problem. Homer's "circling years" provided no more than the background against which the noteworthy story had appeared and was being told. Traces of this earlier nonspeculative view can be found throughout Greek literature; thus Aristotle himself, in his discussion of *eudaimonia* (in the *Nicomachean Ethics*), is thinking in Homeric terms when he points to the ups and downs, the accidental circumstances (*tychai*) that "revolve many times in one person's lifetime," whereas his *eudaimonia* is more durable because it resides in certain activities (*energeiai kat' aretēn*) worth remembering because of their excellence and about which therefore "oblivion does not grow" (*genesthai*).[20]

No matter what historical origins and influences—Babylonian, Persian, Egyptian—we may be able to trace for the cyclical time concept, its emergence was logically almost inevitable once the philosophers had discovered an everlasting Being, birthless and deathless, within whose framework they then had to explain movement, change, the constant coming and going of living beings. Aristotle was quite explicit about the primacy of the assumption "that the whole heaven was not generated and cannot be destroyed, as some allege, but is single and forever, having no beginning and no end of its whole existence, containing and embracing in itself infinite time."[21] "That everything returns" is indeed, as Nietzsche observed, "the closest [possible] approximation of a world of Becoming to a world of Being."[22] Hence it is not surprising that the Greeks had no notion of the faculty of the Will, our mental organ for a future that in principle is indeterminable and therefore a possible harbinger of novelty. What is so very surprising is to find such a strong inclination to denounce the Will as an illusion or an entirely superfluous hypothesis after the Hebrew-Christian credo of a divine beginning—"In the beginning God created the heavens and the earth"—had become a dogmatic assumption of philosophy. Especially as this new creed also stated that man was the only creature made in God's own image, hence endowed with a like faculty of beginning. Yet of all the Christian thinkers, only Augustine, it seems, drew the consequence: "*[Initium] ut esset, creatus est homo*" ("That a beginning be made man was created").[23]

The reluctance to recognize the Will as a separate, autonomous mental faculty finally ceded during the long centuries of Christian philosophy, which we shall be examining later in greater detail. Whatever its indebtedness to Greek philosophy and especially to Aristotle, it was bound to break with the cyclical time concept of antiquity and its notion of everlasting recurrence. The story that begins with Adam's expulsion from Paradise and ends with Christ's death and resurrection is a story of unique, unrepeatable events: "Once Christ died for our sins; and rising from the dead, He dieth no more."[24] The story's sequence presupposes a rectilinear time concept; it has a definite beginning, a turning-point—the year One of our calendar[25]—and a definite end. And it was a story of supreme importance to the Christian, although it hardly touched the course of ordinary secular events: empires could be expected to rise and fall as in the past. Moreover, since the Christian's after-life was decided while he was still a "pilgrim on earth," he himself had a future beyond the determined, necessary end of his life, and it was in close connection with the preparation for a future life that the Will and its necessary Freedom in all their complexity were first discovered by Paul.

Hence one of the difficulties of our topic is that the problems we are dealing with have their "historical origin" in theology rather than in an unbroken tradition of philosophical thought.[26] For whatever may be the merits of post-antique assumptions about the location of human freedom in the I-will, it is certain that in the frame of pre-Christian thought freedom was localized in the I-can; freedom was an objective state of the body, not a datum of consciousness or of the mind. Freedom meant that one could do as one pleased, forced neither by the bidding of a master nor by some physical necessity that demanded laboring for wages in order to sustain the body nor by some somatic handicap such as ill health or the paralysis of one's members. According to Greek etymology, that is, according to Greek self-interpretation, the root of the word for freedom, *eleutheria,* is *eleuthein hopōs erō,* to go as I wish,[27] and there is no doubt that the basic freedom was understood as freedom of movement. A person was free who could move as he wished; the I-can, not the I-will, was the criterion.

## 2 The Will and the modern age

In the context of these preliminary considerations, we may be permitted to skip the complexities of the medieval era and try to have a brief look at the next important turning-point in our intellectual history, the rise of the modern age. Here we are entitled to expect an even stronger interest in a mental organ for the future than in the medieval period, because the modern age's main and entirely new concept, the notion of *Progress* as the ruling force in human history, placed an unprecedented emphasis on the future. Yet medieval speculations on the subject still exerted a strong influence at least in the sixteenth and seventeenth centuries. And, so strong was the suspicion of the willing faculty, so sharp the reluctance to grant human beings, unprotected by any divine Providence or guidance, absolute power over their own destinies and thus burden them with a formidable responsibility for things whose very existence would depend exclusively on themselves, so great, in Kant's words, was the embarrassment of "speculative reason in dealing with the question of the freedom of the will . . . [namely with] a power of *spontaneously* beginning a series of successive things or states"[28]—as distinguished from the faculty of choice between two or more given objects (the *liberum arbitrium*, strictly speaking)—that it was not till the last stage of the modern age that the Will began to be substituted for Reason as man's highest mental faculty. This coincided with the last era of authentic metaphysical thought; at the turn of the nineteenth century, still in the vein of the metaphysics that had started with Parmenides' equation of Being and Thinking (*to gar auto esti noein te kai einai*), suddenly, right after Kant, it became fashionable to equate Willing and Being.

Thus Schiller declared that "there is no other power in man but his Will," and Will as "the ground of reality has power over both, Reason and Sensuality," whose opposition—the opposition of two necessities, Truth and Passion—provides for the origin of freedom.[29] Thus Schopenhauer decided that the Kantian thing-in-itself, the Being behind the appearances, the world's "inmost nature," its "core," of which "the objective world . . . [is] merely the outward side," is Will,[30] while Schelling on a much higher level of speculation apodictically stated: "In the final and highest instance there is no other Being than Will."[31] This development, however, reached its culmination in Hegel's philosophy of history (which for that reason I prefer to treat separately) and came to a surprisingly rapid end at the close of the same century.

Nietzsche's philosophy, centered on the Will to Power, seems at first glance to constitute the climax of the Will's ascendancy in theoretical reflection. I think that this interpretation of Nietzsche is a misunderstanding caused partly by the rather unfortunate circumstances surrounding the first uncritical editions of his posthumously published writings. We owe to Nietzsche a number of decisive insights into the nature of the willing faculty and the willing ego, to which we shall return later, but most of the passages about the Will in his work testify to an outspoken hostility toward the "theory of 'freedom of the Will,' a hundred times refuted, [which] owes its permanence" precisely to its being "refutable": "Somebody always comes along who feels strong enough to refute it once more."[32]

Nietzsche's own final refutation is contained in his "thought of Eternal Return," the "basic concept of the *Zarathustra*," which expresses "the highest possible formula of affirmation."[33] As such, it stands historically in the series of "theodicies," those strange justifications of God or of Being which, ever since the seventeenth century, philosophers felt were needed to reconcile man's mind to the world in which he was to spend his life. The "thought of Eternal Return" implies an unconditional denial of the modern rectilinear time concept and its progressing course; it is nothing less than an explicit reversion to the cyclical time concept of antiquity. What makes it modern is the pathetic tone in which it is expressed, indicating the amount of willful intensity needed by modern man to regain the simple admiring and affirming wonder, *thaumazein,* which once, for Plato, was the beginning of philosophy. Modern philosophy, on the contrary, had originated in the Cartesian and Leibnizian doubt that Being—"Why is there something and not, rather, nothing?"—could be justified at all. Nietzsche speaks of Eternal Recurrence in the tone of a religious convert, and it *was* a conversion that brought him to it, though not a religious one. With this thought he tried to convert himself to the ancient concept of Being and deny the entire philosophical creed of the modern age, which he was the first to diagnose as the "Age of Suspicion." Ascribing his thought to an "inspiration," he does not doubt that "one must go back thousands of years to find somebody who would have the right to tell [him], 'this is also my experience.' "[34]

Although in the early decades of our century Nietzsche was read and misread by almost everybody in the European intellectual community, his influence on philosophy properly speaking was minimal; to this day, there are no Nietzscheans in the sense that there are still Kantians and Hegelians. His first recognition as a philosopher came with the very influential rebellion of thinkers against academic philosophy that, unhappily, goes under the name of "existentialism." No serious study of Nietzsche's thought existed before Jaspers' and Heidegger's books about him;[35] yet that does not mean that either Jaspers or Heidegger can be understood as a belated founder of a Nietzsche school. More important in the present context, neither Jaspers nor Heidegger in his own philosophy put the Will at the center of the human faculties.

For Jaspers, human freedom is guaranteed by our not having *the* truth; truth compels, and man can be free only because he does not know the answer to the ultimate questions: "I must will because I do *not* know. The Being which is inaccessible to knowledge can be revealed only to my volition. Not-knowing is the root of having to will."[36]

Heidegger in his early work had shared the modern age's emphasis on the future as the decisive temporal entity—"the future is the primary phenomenon of an original and authentic temporality"—and had introduced *Sorge* (a German word that appeared for the first time as a philosophical term in *Being and Time* and that means "a caring for," as well as "worry about the future") as the key existential fact of human existence. Ten years later he broke with the whole modern age's philosophy (in the second volume of his book about Nietzsche), precisely because he had discovered to what an extent the age itself, and not just its theoretical products, was based on the domination of the Will. He concluded his later philosophy with the seemingly paradoxical proposition of "willing not-to-will."[37]

To be sure, in his early philosophy Heidegger did not share the modern age's belief in Progress, and his proposition "to will not-to-will" has nothing in common with Nietzsche's overcoming of the Will by restricting it to willing that whatever happens shall happen again and again. But Heidegger's famous *Kehre*, the turning-about of his late philosophy, nevertheless somewhat resembles Nietzsche's conversion; in the first place, it *was* a kind of conversion, and secondly, it had the identical consequence of leading him back to the earliest Greek thinkers. It is as though at the very end, the thinkers of the modern age escaped into a "land of thought" (Kant)[38] where their own specifically modern preoccupations—with the future, with the Will as the mental organ for it, and with freedom as a problem—had been non-existent, where, in other words, there was no notion of a mental faculty that might correspond to freedom as the faculty of thinking corresponded to truth.

## 3   *The main objections to the Will in post-medieval philosophy*

The purpose of these preliminary remarks is to facilitate our approach to the complexities of the willing ego, and in our methodological concern we can hardly afford to overlook the simple fact that every philosophy of the Will is the product of the thinking rather than the willing ego. Though of course it is always the same mind that thinks and wills, we have seen that it cannot be taken for granted that the thinking ego's evaluation of the other mental activities will remain unbiased; and to find thinkers with widely different general philosophies raising identical arguments against the Will is bound to arouse our mistrust. I shall briefly outline the main objections as we find them in post-medieval philosophy before I enter into a discussion of Hegel's position.

There is, first, the ever-recurring disbelief in the very existence of the faculty. The Will is suspected of being a mere illusion, a phantasm of consciousness, a kind of delusion inherent in consciousness' very structure. "A wooden top," in Hobbes's words, ". . . lashed by the boys . . . sometimes spinning, sometimes hitting men on the shin, if it were sensible of its own motion, would think it proceeded from its own will, unless it felt what lashed it."[39] And Spinoza thought along the same lines: a stone set in motion by some external force "would believe itself to be completely free and would think that it continued in motion solely because of its own wish," provided that it was "conscious of its own endeavor" and "capable of thinking."[40] In other words, "men believe themselves to be free, simply because they are conscious of their actions, and unconscious of the causes whereby those actions are determined." Thus men are subjectively free, objectively necessitated. Spinoza's correspondents raise the obvious objection: "If this were granted, all wickedness would be excusable," which disturbs Spinoza not in the least. He answers: "Wicked men are not less to be feared, and not less harmful, when they are wicked from necessity."[41]

Hobbes and Spinoza admit the existence of the Will as a subjectively felt faculty and deny only its freedom: "I acknowledge this liberty, that I can do if I will; but to say I can will if I will, I take to be an absurd speech." For "Liberty or Freedom, signifieth properly the absence of . . . external impediments of motion. . . . But when the impediment of motion is in the constitution of the thing itself, we use not to say: it wants the liberty, but the power to move; as when a stone lieth still or a man is fastened to his bed by sickness." These reflections are entirely in accordance with the Greek position on the matter. What is no longer in line with classical philosophy is Hobbes's conclusion that "Liberty and necessity are consistent: as in the water, that hath not only liberty, but a necessity of descending by the channel; so likewise in the actions which men voluntarily do: which because they proceed from their will, proceed from liberty; and yet, because every act of man's will . . . proceedeth from some cause and that from another cause, in a continual chain . . . proceed from necessity. So that to him that could see the connection of those causes, the necessity of all men's voluntary actions would appear manifest."[42]

With both Hobbes and Spinoza the negation of the Will is firmly grounded in their respective philosophies. But we find virtually the same argument in Schopenhauer, whose general philosophy was very nearly the opposite and for whom consciousness or subjectivity was the very essence of Being: like Hobbes, he does not deny Will but denies that Will is free: there is an illusory feeling of freedom when I experience volition; when I deliberate about what to do next, and, rejecting a number of possibilities, finally come to some definite decision, it is "with just as free a will . . . as if water spoke to itself: 'I can make high waves . . . I can rush down hill . . . I can plunge down foaming and gushing . . . I can rise freely as a stream of water into the air (. . . in the fountain) . . . but I am doing none of these things now, and am voluntarily remaining quiet and clear water in the reflecting pond."[43] This kind of argument is best summed up by John Stuart Mill in the passage already quoted: "Our *internal* consciousness tells us that we have a power, which the whole outward experience of the human race tells us that we never use" (italics added).[44]

What is so striking in these objections raised against the very existence of the faculty is, first of all, that they are invariably raised in terms of the modern notion of consciousness—a notion just as unknown to ancient philosophy as the notion of the Will. The Greek *synesis*—that I can share knowledge with myself (*syniēmi*) about things to which no one else can testify —is the predecessor more of conscience than of consciousness,[45] as is seen when Plato mentions how the memory of the bloody deed haunts the homicide.[46]

Next, the same objections could easily be raised, but hardly ever were, against the existence of the faculty of thought. To be sure, Hobbes's reckoning with consequences, if that is to be understood as thinking, is not open to such suspicions, but this power of figuring and calculating ahead coincides, rather, with the willing ego's deliberations about means to an end or with the capacity used in solving riddles and mathematical problems. (Some such equation, clearly, is behind Ryle's refutation of "the doctrine that there exists a Faculty . . . of the 'Will' and, accordingly, that there occur processes, or operations, corresponding to what it describes as 'volitions.' " In Ryle's own words: "No one ever says such things as that . . . he performed five quick and easy volitions and two slow and difficult volitions between midday and lunch-time."[47] It cannot be seriously maintained that enduring thought-products, such as Kant's *Critique of Pure Reason* or Hegel's *Phenomenology of Mind,* could ever be understood in these terms.) The only philosophers I know of who dared doubt the existence of the faculty of thought were Nietzsche and Wittgenstein. The latter in his early thought-experiments held that the thinking ego (what he called the *"vorstellendes Subjekt,"* deriving his terminology from Schopenhauer) could "in the last resort be mere superstition," probably an "empty delusion, but the willing subject exists." In justification of his thesis Wittgenstein reiterates the arguments commonly raised in the seventeenth century against Spinoza's denial of the Will, to wit, "If the Will did not exist, neither would there be . . . the bearer of ethics."[48] As for Nietzsche, it must be said that he had his doubts about both willing and thinking.

The disturbing fact that even the so-called voluntarists among the philosophers, those entirely convinced, like Hobbes, of the *power* of the will, could so easily glide to doubting its very existence may be somewhat clarified by examining the second of our ever-recurring difficulties. What aroused the philosophers' distrust was precisely the inevitable connection with Freedom—to repeat, the notion of an unfree will is a contradiction in terms: "If I must necessarily will, why need I speak of will at all? . . . Our will would not be will unless it were in our power. Because it is in our power it is free."[49] To quote Descartes, whom one may count among the voluntarists: "No one, when he considers himself alone, fails to experience the fact that to will and to be free are the same thing."[50]

As I have said more than once, the touchstone of a free act—from the decision to get out of bed in the morning or take a walk in the afternoon to the highest resolutions by which we bind ourselves for the future—is always that we know that we could also have left undone what we actually did. Willing, it appears, is characterized by an infinitely greater freedom than thinking, and—again to repeat—this undeniable fact has never been felt to be an unmixed blessing. Thus we hear from Descartes: "I am conscious of a will so extended as to be subject to no limits. . . . It is free will alone . . . which I find to be so great in me that I can conceive no other idea to be more great; it is . . . this will that causes me to know that . . . I bear the image and similitude of God," and he immediately adds that this experience "consists solely in the fact that . . . we act in such a way that we are not in the least conscious that any outside force constrains us [in] the power of choosing to do a thing or choosing not to do it."[51]

In so saying, he leaves the door wide open on the one hand to the doubts of his successors and on the other to the attempts of his contemporaries "to make [God's] pre-ordinances harmonize with the freedom of our will."[52] Descartes himself, unwilling to become "involved in the great difficulties [that would ensue] if we undertook to reconcile God's foresight and omnipotence with human freedom," explicitly appeals to the beneficial limitations of "our thought [which] is finite" and therefore subject to certain rules, for instance, the axiom of non-contradiction, and the compelling "necessities" of self-evident truth.[53]

It is precisely the "lawless" freedom the will seems to enjoy that made even Kant occasionally talk of freedom as perhaps being no more than "a mere thought entity, a phantom of the brain."[54] Others, like Schopenhauer, found it easier to reconcile Freedom and Necessity and thus escape the dilemma inherent in the simple fact that man is at the same time a thinking and a willing being—a coincidence fraught with the most serious consequences—by simply declaring: "man does at all times only what he wills, and yet he does this necessarily. But this is due to the fact that he . . . *is* what he wills. . . . Subjectively . . . everyone feels that he always does only what he wills. But this merely means that his activity is a pure expression of his very own being. Every natural being, even the lowest, would feel the same, if it *could* feel."[55]

Our third difficulty is linked with that dilemma. In the eyes of philosophers who spoke in the name of the thinking ego, it had always been the curse of *contingency* that condemned the realm of merely human affairs to a rather low status in the ontological hierarchy. But before the modern age, there had existed—not many but a few—well-trodden escape routes, at least for philosophers. In antiquity, there was the *bios theōrētikos:* the thinker dwelt in the neighborhood of things necessary and everlasting, partaking in their Being to the extent that this is possible for mortals. In the era of Christian philosophy, there was the *vita contemplativa* of the monasteries and the universities, but also the consoling thought of divine Providence, joined to the expectation of an after-life when what had seemed contingent and meaningless in this world would become crystal clear, the soul seeing "face to face" instead of "though a glass, darkly," no longer knowing "in part"—for he shall "know even as also [he is] known." Without such hope for a Hereafter, even Kant still deemed human life too miserable, devoid of meaning, to be borne.

It is obvious that the advancing secularization, or, rather, de-Christianization, of the modern world, coupled, as it was, with an entirely new emphasis on the future, on progress, and therefore on things neither necessary nor sempiternal, would expose men of thought to the contingency of all things human more radically and more mercilessly than ever before. What had been ever since the end of antiquity the "problem of freedom" was now incorporated, as it were, in the haphazardness of history, "full of sound and fury," "a tale told by an idiot . . . signifying nothing," to which there corresponded the random character of personal decisions originating in a free will that was guided neither by reason nor by desire. And this old problem reappearing in the dress of the new age, the Age of Progress, which is reaching its end only now in our own time (as Progress rapidly nears the limits given by the human condition on earth), found its pseudo-solution in the nineteenth-century *philosophy of history*, whose greatest representative worked out an ingenious theory of a hidden Reason and Meaning in the course of world events, directing men's wills in all their contingency toward an ultimate goal they never intended. Once this story is complete—and Hegel seems to have believed that the beginning of the end of the story was coeval with the French Revolution—the backward-directed glance of the philosopher, through the sheer effort of the thinking ego, can internalize and recollect (*er-innern*) the meaningfulness and necessity of the unfolding movement, so that again he can dwell with what is and cannot not-be. Finally, in other words, the process of thinking coincides once more with authentic Being: thought has purified reality of the merely accidental.

## 4 *The problem of the new*

If we reconsider the objections raised by philosophers against the Will—against the faculty's existence, against the notion of human freedom implicit in it, and against the contingency adhering to free will, that is, to an act that by definition can also be left undone—it becomes obvious that they apply much less to what tradition knows as *liberum arbitrium,* the freedom of choice between two or more desirable objects or ways of conduct, than to the Will as an organ for the future and identical with the power of beginning something new. The *liberum arbitrium* decides between things equally possible and given to us, as it were, in *statu nascendi* as mere potentialities, whereas a power to begin something really new could not very well be preceded by any potentiality, which then would figure as one of the causes of the accomplished act.

I have previously mentioned Kant's embarrassment "in dealing with . . . a power of *spontaneously* beginning a series of successive things or states"—for instance, if "I at this moment arise from my chair . . . a new series . . . has its *absolute* beginning in this event, although [he adds] as regards time this event is only the continuation of a preceding series."[56] What is so very troublesome is the notion of an *absolute* beginning, for "a series occurring in the world can have only a relatively first beginning, being always preceded by some other state of things," and this is, of course, also true for the person of the thinker inasmuch as I who think never cease to be an appearance among appearances, no matter how successfully I may have withdrawn from them mentally. No doubt the very hypothesis of an absolute beginning goes back to the Biblical doctrine of Creation, as distinct from the Oriental theories of "emanation," according to which pre-existing forces developed and unfolded into a world. But this doctrine is a sufficient reason in our context only if one adds that God's creation is *ex nihilo,* and of such a creation the Hebrew Bible knows nothing; it is an addition of later speculations.[57]

These speculations arose when the Fathers of the Church had already begun to account for the Christian faith in terms of Greek philosophy, that is, when they were confronted with *Being,* for which the Hebrew language has no word. Logically speaking, it seems rather obvious that an equation of the universe with Being ought to imply "nothingness" as its opposite;

still, the transition from Nothing to Something is logically so difficult that one may tentatively suspect that it was the new willing ego which, regardless of doctrines and credos, found the idea of an absolute beginning appropriate to its experience of forming projects. For there is something fundamentally wrong with Kant's example. Only if he, arising from his chair, has something in mind he wishes to do, does this "event" start a "new series"; if this is not the case, if he habitually gets up at this time or if he gets up in order to fetch something he needs for his present occupation, this event is itself "the continuation of a preceding series."

But let us suppose that this was an oversight and that Kant had clearly in mind the "power of spontaneously beginning" and therefore was concerned about a possible reconciliation of a "new series of acts and states" with the time continuum that this "new series" interrupts: the traditional solution of the problem even at that date would still have been the Aristotelian distinction between potentiality and actuality, as saving the unity of the time concept by assuming that the "new series" was potentially contained in the "preceding series." But the insufficiency of the Aristotelian explanation is evident: Can anybody seriously maintain that the symphony produced by a composer was "possible before it was actual"?[58]—unless one means by "possible" no more than that it was clearly not impossible, which of course is entirely different from its having existed in a state of potentiality, waiting for some musician who would take the trouble to make it actual.

Yet, as Bergson very well knew, there is another side to the matter. In the perspective of memory, that is, looked at retrospectively, a freely performed act loses its air of contingency under the impact of now being an accomplished fact, of having become part and parcel of the reality in which we live. The impact of reality is overwhelming to the point that we are unable to "think it away"; the act appears to us now in the guise of necessity, a necessity that is by no means a mere delusion of consciousness or due only to our limited ability to imagine possible alternatives. This is most obvious in the realm of action, where no deed can be safely undone, but it is also true, though perhaps in a less compelling way, of the

countless new objects that human fabrication constantly adds
to the world and its civilization, art objects as well as use
objects; it is almost as impossible to think away the great art
works of our cultural inheritance as to think away the out-
break of the two World Wars or any other events that have
decided the very structure of our reality. In Bergson's own
words: "By virtue of its sheer factuality, reality throws its
shadow behind it into an infinitely distant past; thus it appears
to have existed in the mode of potentiality in advance of its
own actualization." (*"Par le seul fait de s'accomplir, la réalité
projette derrière son ombre dans le passé indéfiniment lointain;
elle paraît ainsi avoir préexisté, sous forme de possible à sa
propre réalisation."*)[59]

Seen in this perspective, which is the perspective of the
willing ego, it is not freedom but necessity that appears as a
delusion of consciousness. Bergson's insight seems to me both
elementary and highly significant, but may there not be significance, too, in the fact that this observation, despite its
simple plausibility, never played any role in the endless discussions of necessity versus freedom? As far as I know, the
point was made only once before Bergson. That was by Duns
Scotus, the lonely defender of the primacy of the Will over the
Intellect and—more than that—of the factor of contingency in
everything that is. If there is such a thing as Christian philosophy, then Duns Scotus would have to be recognized not only
as "the most important thinker of the Christian Middle Ages"[60]
but perhaps also as the unique one who did not seek a compromise between the Christian faith and Greek philosophy,
and who dared, therefore, to make it a badge of true "Christians [to say] that God acts contingently." "Those who deny
that some being is contingent," said Scotus, "should be exposed to torments until they concede that it is possible for them
not to be tormented."[61]

Whether contingency, for classical philosophy the ultimate
of meaninglessness, burst as a reality upon the early centuries
of the common era because of Biblical doctrine—which "pitted
contingency against necessity, particularity against universality, will against intellect," thus securing "a place for the 'con-

tingent' within philosophy against the latter's original bias"[62]— or whether the shattering political experiences of these early centuries had forced wide open the truisms and plausibilities of ancient thinking may be open to doubt. What is not open to doubt is that the original bias against contingency, particularity, and Will—and the predominance accorded to necessity, universality, and Intellect—survived the challenge deep into the modern age. Religious and medieval as well as secular and modern philosophy found many different ways of assimilating the Will, the organ of freedom and the future, to the older order of things. For however we may look at these matters, *factually* Bergson is quite right when he asserts: "Most philosophers . . . are unable . . . to conceive of radical novelty and unpredictability. . . . Even those very few who believed in the *liberum arbitrium* have reduced it to a simple 'choice' between two or several options, as though these options were 'possibilities' . . . and the Will was restricted to 'realizing' one of them. Hence, they still admitted . . . that everything is given. They seem never to have had the slightest notion of an entirely new activity. . . . And such an activity is after all free action."[63] No doubt, even today if we listen to a dispute between two philosophers one of whom argues for determinism and the other for freedom, "it will always be the determinist who appears to be right. . . . [The audience] will always agree that he is simple, clear, and true."[64]

Theoretically, the trouble has always been that free will— whether understood as freedom of choice or as the freedom to start something unpredictably new—seems utterly incompatible, not just with divine Providence, but with the law of causality; the Will's freedom can be assumed on the strength, or, rather, the weakness, of interior experience, but it cannot be proved. The implausibility of the assumption or Postulate of Freedom is due to our outward experiences in the world of appearances, where as a matter of fact, Kant notwithstanding, we seldom start a new series. Even Bergson, whose whole philosophy rests on the conviction that "each of us has the immediate knowledge . . . of his free spontaneity,"[65] admits that "although we are free whenever we are willing to get back into ourselves, it seldom happens that we are willing." And

"Free acts are exceptional."[66] (Most of our acts are taken care of by habits, just as many of our everyday judgments are taken care of by prejudices.)

The first to refuse consciously and deliberately to come to grips with the implausibility of free will was Descartes: "It would be absurd to doubt that of which we inwardly experience and perceive as existing within ourselves, just because we do not comprehend a matter which from its nature we know to be incomprehensible."[67] For "these matters are such that anyone ought to experience them in himself rather than be convinced by ratiocination; but you . . . appear not to pay heed to what the mind transacts within itself. Refuse then to be free, *if freedom does not please you*" (italics added).[68] To which one is tempted to reply that the Cartesian *Cogito* is certainly nothing but a "transaction of the mind within itself," but it never occurred either to Descartes or to those who objected to his philosophy to speak of thinking or *cogitare* as something assumed without proof, a mere datum of consciousness. What, then, is it that gives the *cogito me cogitare* its ascendancy over the *volo me velle*—even in Descartes, who was a "voluntarist"? *Could it be that professional thinkers, basing their speculations on the experience of the thinking ego, were less "pleased" with freedom than with necessity?* This suspicion appears inevitable when we consider the strange assembly of theories on record, theories trying either to deny outright the experience of freedom "within ourselves" or to weaken freedom by reconciling it with necessity by means of dialectical speculations that are entirely "speculative" in that they cannot appeal to any experience whatsoever. The suspicion is strengthened when one considers how closely all free-will theories are tied to the problem of evil. Thus Augustine begins his treatise *De libero arbitrio voluntatis* (*The Free Choice of the Will*) with the question: "Tell me, please, whether God is not the cause of evil?" It was a question first raised in all its complexity by Paul (in the Letter to the Romans) and then generalized into What is the cause of evil? with many variations concerning the existence both of physical harm caused by destructive nature and of deliberate malice caused by men.

The whole problem has haunted philosophers, and their

attempts at solving it have never been very successful; as a rule their arguments evade the issue in its stark simplicity. Evil is either denied true reality (it exists only as a deficient mode of the good) or is explained away as a kind of optical illusion (the fault is with our limited intellect, which fails to fit some particular properly into the encompassing whole that would justify it), all this on the unargued assumption that "only the whole is actually real" (*"nur das Ganze hat eigentliche Wirklichkeit"*), in the words of Hegel. Evil, not unlike freedom, seems to belong to those "things about which the most learned and ingenious men can know almost nothing."[69]

## 5   *The clash between thinking and willing: the tonality of mental activities*

If one looks at this record with eyes unclouded by theories and traditions, religious or secular, it is certainly hard to escape the conclusion that philosophers seem genetically unable to come to terms with certain phenomena of the mind and its position in the world, that we can no more trust men of thought to arrive at a fair estimate of the Will than we could trust them to arrive at a fair estimate of the body. But the philosophers' hostility to the body is well known and a matter of record ever since Plato at least. It is not motivated primarily by the unreliability of sense experience—for these errors can be corrected—or by the famous unruliness of the passions—for these can be tamed by reason—but by the simple and incorrigible nature of our bodily needs and wants. The body, as Plato rightly stresses, always "wants to be taken care of" and even under the best of circumstances—health and leisure on one hand, a well-regulated commonwealth on the other—it will interrupt with its ever-recurring claims the activity of the thinking ego; in terms of the Cave parable, it will compel the philosopher to return from the sky of Ideas to the Cave of human affairs. (It is usual to blame this hostility on the Christian antagonism toward the flesh. Not only is the hostility much older; one could even argue that one of the crucial Christian dogmas, the resurrection of the flesh, as distinguished from older speculations about the immortality of the soul, stood in sharp contrast not only to common gnostic beliefs but also to the common notions of classical philosophy.)

The antagonism of the thinking ego toward the Will is of course of a very different kind. The clash here is between two *mental* activities that seem unable to co-exist. When we form a volition, that is, when we focus our attention on some future project, we have no less withdrawn from the world of appearances than when we are following a train of thought. Thinking and willing are antagonists only insofar as they affect our psychic states; both, it is true, make present to our mind what is actually absent, but thinking draws into its enduring present what either is or at least has been, whereas willing, stretching out into the future, moves in a region where no such certainties exist. Our psychic apparatus—the soul as distinguished from the mind—is equipped to deal with what comes toward it from this region of the unknown by means of expectation, whose chief modes are hope and fear. The two modes of feeling are intimately connected in that each of them is prone to veer to its seeming opposite, and because of the uncertainties of the region these shiftings are almost automatic. Every hope carries within itself a fear, and every fear cures itself by turning to the corresponding hope. It is because of their shifting, unstable, and disquieting nature that classical antiquity counted both among the evil gifts of Pandora's box.

What the soul demands of the mind in this uncomfortable situation is not so much a prophetic gift that can foretell the future and thus confirm either hope or fear; far more soothing than the fraudulent games of the soothsayers—augurs, astrologists, and the like—is the no less fraudulent theory that claims to prove that whatever is or will be "was to be," in the felicitous phrase of Gilbert Ryle.[70] Fatalism, which indeed "no philosopher of the first or second rank has defended . . . or been at great pains to attack," has nevertheless had an astoundingly successful career in popular thinking throughout the centuries; "we do all have our fatalist moments," as Ryle says,[71] and the reason is that no other theory can lull so effectively any urge to act, any impulse to make a project, in short, any form of the I-will. These existential advantages of fatalism are clearly outlined in Cicero's treatise *On Fate,* still the classical argumentation of the case. For the proposition "Everything is foreordained," he uses the following example: When you get sick, "it is foreordained that you will recover or not recover, whether you call a doctor or do not call a doctor,"[72] and of course whether you call in a doctor or not would also be foreordained. Hence the argument leads into "infinite regress."[73] Under the name of "idle argument," it is rejected because it would obviously "lead to the entire abolition of action from life." Its great attraction is that through it "the mind is released from all necessity of motion."[74] In our context, the interest of the proposition lies in the fact that it succeeds in totally abolishing the future tense by assimilating it to the past. What *will* or may be *"was* to be," for "everything that will be, *if it will actually be,* cannot be conceived not to be" (*"quicquid futurum est, id intelligi non potest,* si futurum sit, *non futurum esse"*), as Leibniz put it.[75] The formula's soothing quality is borrowed from what Hegel called "the quiet of the past" (*"die Ruhe der Vergangenheit"*),[76] a quiet guaranteed by the fact that what is past cannot be undone and that the Will "cannot will backwards."[77]

It is not the future as such but the future as the Will's *project* that *negates* the given. In Hegel and Marx, the power of negation, whose motor drives History forward, is derived from the Will's ability to actualize a project: the project negates the now as well as the past and thus threatens the thinking ego's enduring present. Inasmuch as the mind, withdrawn from the world of appearances, draws the absent—what is no more as well as what is not yet—into its own presence, it looks as though past and future could be united under a common denominator and thus be saved together from the flux of time. But the *nunc stans,* the gap between past and future where we localized the thinking ego, while it can absorb what is no more without any disturbance from the outside world, cannot react with the same equanimity to projects formed by the will for the future. Every volition, although a mental activity, relates to the world of appearances in which its project is to be realized; in flagrant contrast to thinking, no willing is ever done for its own sake or finds its fulfillment in the act itself. Every volition not only concerns particulars but—and this is of great importance—looks forward to its own end, when willing-something will have changed into doing-it. In other words, the normal mood of the willing ego is impatience, disquiet, and worry (*Sorge*), not merely because of the soul's reacting to the future in fear and hope, but also because the will's project pre-supposes an I-can that is by no means guaranteed. The will's worrying disquiet can be stilled only by the I-can-and-I-do, that is, by a cessation of its own activity and release of the mind from its dominance.

In short, the will always wills to *do* something and thus implicitly holds in contempt sheer thinking, whose whole activity depends on "doing nothing." We shall see when we examine the history of the Will that no theologian or philosopher has ever praised the "sweetness" of the willing ego's experience, as philosophers were wont to praise that of the thinking ego. (There are two important exceptions: Duns Scotus and Nietzsche, both of whom understood the Will as a kind of power—"*voluntas est potentia quia ipsa aliquid potest.*" That is, the willing ego is delighted with itself—"*condelectari sibi*"—to the extent that the I-will anticipates an I-can; the I-will-*and*-I-can is the Will's delight.[78])

In this respect—let me call it the "tonality" of mental activities—the Will's ability to have present the not-yet is the very opposite of remembrance. Remembrance has a natural affinity to thought; all thoughts, as I have said, are after-thoughts. Thought-trains rise naturally, almost automatically, out of re-remembering, without any break. This is why *anamnēsis*, in Plato, could become such a plausible hypothesis for the human capacity for learning, and why Augustine could so very plausibly equate mind and *memoria*. Remembrance may affect the soul with longing for the past, but this nostalgia, while it may hold grief and sorrow, does not upset the mind's equanimity, because it concerns things which are beyond our power to change. On the contrary, the willing ego, looking forward and not backward, deals with things which are in our power but whose accomplishment is by no means certain. The resulting tension, unlike the rather stimulating excitement that may accompany problem-solving activities, causes a kind of disquiet in the soul easily bordering on turmoil, a mixture of fear and hope that becomes unbearable when it is discovered that, in Augustine's formula, to will and to be able to perform, *velle* and *posse*, are not the same. The tension can be overcome only by doing, that is, by giving up the mental activity altogether; a switch from willing to thinking produces no more than a temporary paralysis of the will, just as a switch from thinking to willing is felt by the thinking ego to be a temporary paralysis of the thinking activity.

Speaking in terms of tonality—that is, in terms of the way the mind affects the soul and produces its *moods,* regardless of outside events, thus creating a kind of *life* of the mind—the predominant mood of the thinking ego is *serenity,* the mere enjoyment of an activity that never has to overcome the resistance of matter. To the extent that this activity is closely connected with remembrance, its mood inclines to melancholy—according to Kant and Aristotle, the mood characteristic of the philosopher. The predominant mood of the Will is *tenseness,* which brings ruin to the "mind's tranquillity," Leibniz's "*animi tranquillitas,*" which, according to him, all "serious philosophers" insist on[79] and which he himself found in thought-trains proving that this is the "best of all possible worlds." In this perspective, the only task left for the Will is indeed to "will not to will," since every willed act can only interfere with the "universal harmony" of the world, in which "everything that is, looked at from the viewpoint of the Whole, is the best."[80]

Thus Leibniz, with admirable consistency, finds that the sin of Judas lies not in his betrayal of Jesus but in his suicide: in condemning himself, he implicitly condemned the whole of God's creation; by hating himself, he hated the Creator.[81] We find the same thought in its most radical version in one of Master Eckhart's condemned sentences: "Should a man have committed a thousand mortal sins, were he rightly dis-

posed he ought not to will not to have committed them"
(*"Wenn jemand tausend Todsünden begangen hätte, dürfte
er, wäre es recht um ihn bestellt, nicht wollen, sie nicht begangen zu haben"*).[82] We may be permitted to conjecture that
this startling rejection of repentance on the part of two Christian thinkers in Eckhart was motivated by a superabundance of
faith, which demanded, Jesus-like, that the sinner forgive himself as he was asked to forgive others, "seven times a day," because the alternative would be to declare that it would have
been better—not only for him but also for the whole of Creation
—never to be born ("that a millstone were hanged about his
neck, and he cast into the sea"), whereas in Leibniz we may
see it as an ultimate victory of the thinking ego over the willing ego, because of the latter's futile attempt at willing backward which, if successful, could only end in the annihilation of
everything that is.

## 6 *Hegel's solution: the philosophy of History*

No philosopher has described the willing ego in its clash
with the thinking ego with greater sympathy, insight, and consequence for the history of thought than Hegel. This is a
somewhat complex business, not only because of Hegel's eso-
teric and highly idiosyncratic terminology, but also because he
treats the whole problem in the course of his time speculations
and not in the rather meager though by no means insignificant
passages—in the *Phenomenology of Mind*, the *Philosophy
of Right*, the *Encyclopedia*, and the *Philosophy of History*—
that deal directly with the Will. These passages have been
assembled and interpreted by Alexandre Koyré in a little-
known and very important essay (published in 1934 under the
misleading title *Hegel à Iéna*),[83] devoted to Hegel's crucial
texts on Time—from the early *Jenenser Logik* and the *Jenenser Realphilosophie* to the *Phenomenology*, the *Encyclopedia*,
and the various manuscripts belonging to the *Philosophy of
History*. Koyré's translation and commentaries became "the

source and basis" of Alexandre Kojève's highly influential interpretation of the *Phenomenology*.[84] In the following I shall closely follow Koyré's argumentation.

His central thesis is that Hegel's "greatest originality" resides in his "insistence on the future, the primacy ascribed to the future over the past."[85] We would not find this surprising if it were not said about Hegel. Why should not a nineteenth-century thinker, sharing the confidence in Progress of his predecessors of the seventeenth and eighteenth centuries and of his contemporaries, too, draw the proper inference and ascribe to the future primacy over the past? After all, Hegel himself said that "everyone is the son of his own time, and therefore philosophy is *its time comprehended in thought*." But he also said in the same context that "to understand what exists is the task of philosophy, for what exists is reason," or "what is *thought* is, and what is exists only insofar as it is thought" (*"Was gedacht ist, ist; und was ist, ist nur, insofern es Gedanke ist"*).[86] And it is on this premise that Hegel's most important and most influential contribution to philosophy is based. For Hegel is, above all, the first thinker to conceive of a philosophy of history, that is, of the past: re-collected by the backward-directed glance of the thinking and remembering ego, it is "internalized" (*er-innert*), becomes part and parcel of the mind through "the effort of the concept" (*"die Anstrengung des Begriffs"*), and in this internalizing way achieves the *"reconciliation"* of Mind and World. Was there ever a greater triumph of the thinking ego than is represented in this scenario? In its withdrawal from the world of appearances, the thinking ego no longer has to pay the price of "absent-mindedness" and alienation from the world. According to Hegel, the mind, by sheer force of reflection, can assimilate to itself—suck into itself, as it were—not, to be sure, all the appearances but whatever has been meaningful in them, leaving aside everything not assimilable as irrelevant accident, without consequence for either the course of History or the train of discursive thought.

The primacy of the past, however—as Koyré discovered—disappears entirely when Hegel comes to discuss Time, for him, above all, "human time"[87] whose flux man first, as it were, unthinkingly experiences as sheer motion, until he happens to reflect on the meaning of outside events. It then turns out that the mind's attention is primarily directed toward the future, namely, toward the time that is in the process of coming toward us (indicated, as I have said, in the German *Zukunft*, from *zu kommen*, like the French *avenir* from *à venir*), and this anticipated future negates the mind's "enduring present," which it transforms into an anticipated "no-more." In this context, "the dominant dimension of time is the future, which takes priority over the past." "Time finds its truth in the future since it is the future that will finish and accomplish Being. But Being, finished and accomplished, belongs as such to the Past."[88] This reversal of the ordinary time sequence—past-present-future—is caused by man's denying his present: he "says *no* to his Now" and thus creates his own future.[89] Hegel himself does not mention the Will in this context, nor does Koyré, but it seems obvious that the faculty behind the Mind's negation is not thinking but willing, and that Hegel's description of experienced human time relates to the time sequence appropriate to the willing ego.

It is appropriate because the willing ego when it forms its projects does indeed live for the future. In Hegel's famous words, the reason "the present [the Now] cannot resist the future" is by no means the inexorability with which every today is followed by a tomorrow (for this tomorrow, if not projected and mastered by the Will, could just as well be a mere repetition of what went before—as indeed it frequently is); the today in its very essence is threatened only by the mind's interference, which negates it and, by virtue of the Will, summons up the absent not-yet, mentally canceling the present, or, rather, looking upon the present as that ephemeral time span whose essence is not to be: "The Now is empty . . . it fulfills itself in the future. The future is its reality."[90] From the perspective of the willing ego, "the future is directly within the present, for it is contained as its negative fact. The Now is just as much the being that disappears as it is also the non-being [that] . . . is converted into Being."[91]

To the extent that the self identifies itself with the willing ego—and we shall see that this identification is proposed by some of the voluntarists who derive the *principium individua-tionis* from the willing faculty—it exists "in a continual trans-formation of [its own] future into a Now, and it ceases to be the day when there is no future left, when there is nothing still outstanding [*le jour où il n'y a plus d'avenir, où rien n'est plus à venir*], when everything has arrived and when everything is 'accomplished.'"[92] Seen from the perspective of the Will, old age consists in the shrinkage of the future dimension, and man's death signifies less his disappearance from the world of appearances than his final loss of a future. This loss, however, coincides with the ultimate accomplishment of the individual's life, which at its end, having escaped the incessant change of time and the uncertainty of its own future, opens itself to the "tranquillity of the past" and thereby to inspection, reflection, and the backward glance of the thinking ego in its search for meaning. Hence, from the viewpoint of the thinking ego, old age, in Heidegger's words, is the time of meditation or, in the words of Sophocles, it is the time of "peace and freedom"[93]—release from bondage, not only to the passions of the body, but to the all-consuming passion the mind inflicts on the soul, the passion of the will called "ambition."

In other words, the past begins with disappearance of the future, and, in that tranquillity, the thinking ego asserts itself. But this happens only when everything has reached its end, when Becoming, in whose process Being unfolds and de-velops, has been arrested. For "restlessness is the ground of Being";[94] it is the price paid for Life, as death, or, rather, the anticipation of death, is the price paid for tranquillity. And the restlessness of the living does not come from contemplating either the cosmos or history; it is not the effect of external motion—the incessant movement of natural things or the in-cessant ups and downs of human destinies; it is localized in and engendered by the mind of man. What in later existential thought became the notion of the auto-production of man's mind we find in Hegel as the "auto-constitution of Time":[95] man is not just temporal; he *is* Time.

Without him there might be movement and motion, but there would not be Time. Nor could there be, if man's mind were equipped only for thinking, for reflecting on the given, on what is as it is and could not be otherwise; in that case man would live mentally in an everlasting present. He would be unable to realize that he himself once was not and that one day he will be no more, that is, he would be unable to understand what it means for him to exist. (It is because of Hegel's view that the human mind produces time that his other, more obvious, identification of logic and history comes about, and this identification is indeed, as Léon Brunschvicg pointed out long ago, "one of the essential pillars of his system."[96])

But in Hegel the mind produces time only by virtue of the will, its organ for the future, and the future in this perspective is also the source of the past, insofar as that is mentally engendered by the mind's anticipation of a second future, when the immediate I-shall-be will have become an I-shall-have-been. In this schema, the past is produced by the future, and thinking, which contemplates the past, is the result of the Will. For the will, in the last resort, anticipates the ultimate frustration of the will's projects, which is death; they too, one day, will have been. (It may be interesting to note that Heidegger, too, says *"Die Gewesenheit entspringt in gewisser Weise der Zukunft"*—the past, the "having-been," has its origin in a certain sense in the future.[97])

In Hegel, man is not distinguished from other animal species by being an *animal rationale* but by being the only living creature that knows about his own death. It is at this ultimate point of the willing ego's anticipation that the thinking ego constitutes itself. In the anticipation of death, the will's projects take on the appearance of an anticipated past and as such can become the object of reflection; and it is in this sense that Hegel maintains that only the mind that "does not ignore death" enables man to "dominate death," to "endure it and to maintain itself within it."[98] To put it in Koyré's words: at the moment in which the mind confronts its own end "the incessant motion of the temporal dialectics is arrested and time has 'fulfilled' itself; this 'fulfilled' time falls naturally and in its entirety into the past," which means that the "future has lost its power over it" and it has become ready for the enduring present of the thinking ego. Thus it turns out that "the [future's] true Being is to be the Now."[99] But in Hegel this *nunc stans* is no longer temporal; it is a *"nunc aeternitatis,"* as eternity for Hegel is also the quintessential nature of Time, the Platonic "image of eternity," seen as the "eternal movement of the mind."[100] Time itself is eternal in "the union of Present, Future and Past."[101]

To oversimplify: That there exists such a thing as the *Life* of the mind is due to the mind's organ for the future and its resulting "restlessness"; that there exists such a thing as the life of the *Mind* is due to death, which, foreseen as an absolute end, halts the will and transforms the future into an anticipated past, the will's projects into objects of thought, and the soul's expectation into an anticipated remembrance. Thus summarized and oversimplified, the doctrine of Hegel sounds so modern, the primacy of the future in its time speculations so well attuned to his century's dogmatic faith in Progress, and its shift from thinking to willing and back again to thinking so ingenious a solution of the modern philosopher's problem of how to come to terms with the tradition in a mode acceptable to the modern age, that one is inclined to dismiss the Hegelian construct as an authentic contribution to the problems of the willing ego. Yet in his time speculations Hegel has a strange predecessor to whom nothing could have been more alien than the notion of Progress nor anything of less interest than discovering a law that ruled over historical events.

That is Plotinus. He, too, holds that the human mind, man's "soul" (*psychē*), is the originator of time. Time is generated by the soul's "over-active" nature (*polypragmōn,* a term suggesting busybodiness); longing for its own future immortality, it "seeks for more than its present stage" and thus always "moves on to a 'next' and an 'after' and to what is not the same but is something else and then else again. So moving, we made a long stretch of our journey [toward our future eternity] and constructed time, the image of eternity." Thus, "time is the life of the soul"; since "the spreading out of life involves time," the soul "produces the succession [of time]

along with its activity" in the form of "discursive thought,"
whose discursiveness corresponds to the "soul's movement of
passing from one way of being to another"; hence time is "not
an accompaniment of Soul . . . but something which . . . is
in it and with it."[102] In other words, for Plotinus as for Hegel,
time is generated by the mind's innate restlessness, its stretching out to the future, its projects, and its negation of "the
present state." And in both cases the true fulfillment of time is
eternity, or, in secular terms, existentially speaking, the mind's
switch from willing to thinking.

However that may be, there are many passages in Hegel
that indicate that his philosophy is less inspired by the works
of his predecessors, less a reaction to their opinions, less an
attempt to "solve" problems of metaphysics, less bookish, in
brief, than the systems of almost all post-ancient philosophers,
not only those who came before him but those who came after,
too. In recent times this peculiarity has been often recognized.[103] It was Hegel who, by constructing a sequential history of philosophy that corresponded to factual, political
history—something quite unknown before him—actually
broke with the tradition, because he was the first great thinker
to take history seriously, that is, as yielding truth.

The realm of human affairs, in which everything that is has
been brought into being by man or men, had never been so
looked on by a philosopher. And the change was due to an
event—the French Revolution. "The revolution," Hegel admits,
"may have got its first impulse from philosophy," but its "world-
historical significance" consists in that, for the first time, man
dared to turn himself upside down, "to stand on his head and on
thought, and to build reality according to it." "Never since the
sun had stood in the firmament and the planets revolved
around him had it been perceived that man's existence centers
in his head, that is, in thought. . . . This was a glorious mental dawn. All thinking beings shared in the jubilation of this
epoch . . . a spiritual enthusiasm thrilled through the world,
as if the reconciliation between the Divine and the Secular was
now first accomplished."[104] What the event had shown
amounted to a new dignity of man; "making public the ideas

of how something ought to be [will cause] the lethargy of smugly sedate people [*die gesetzten Leute*], who always accept everything as it is, to disappear."[105]

Hegel never forgot that early experience. As late as 1829/30, he told his students: "In such times of political turnabout philosophy finds its place; this is when thought precedes and shapes reality. For when one form of the Spirit no longer gives satisfaction, philosophy sharply takes note of it in order to understand the dissatisfaction."[106] In short, he almost explicitly contradicted his famous statement about the owl of Minerva in the Preface to the *Philosophy of Right*. The "glorious mental dawn" of his youth inspired and informed all of his writing up to the end. In the French Revolution, principles and thoughts had been *realized;* a *reconciliation* had occurred between the "Divine," with which man spends his time while thinking, and the "secular," the affairs of men.

This reconciliation is at the center of the whole Hegelian system. If it was possible to understand *World History*—and not just the histories of particular epochs and nations—as a single succession of events whose eventual outcome would be the moment when the "Spiritual Kingdom . . . manifests itself in outward existence," becomes "embodied" in "secular life,"[107] then the course of history would no longer be haphazard and the realm of human affairs no longer devoid of meaning. The French Revolution had proved that "Truth in its living form [could be] exhibited in the affairs of the world."[108] Now one could indeed consider every moment in the world's historical sequence as an "it was to be" and assign to philosophy the task of "comprehending this plan" from its beginning, its "concealed fount" or "nascent principle . . . in the womb of time," up to its "phenomenal, present existence."[109] Hegel identifies this "Spiritual Kingdom" with the "Kingdom of the Will"[110] because the wills of men are necessary to bring the spiritual realm about, and for this reason he asserts that "the Freedom of the Will *per se* [that is, the freedom the Will necessarily wills] . . . is itself absolute . . . it is . . . that by which Man becomes Man, and is therefore the fundamental principle of the Mind."[111] As a matter of fact, the only guarantee—if such it is—that the ultimate goal of the unfolding of

the World Spirit in the world's affairs must be Freedom is implicit in the freedom that is implicit in the Will.

"The insight then to which . . . philosophy is to lead us,
is, that the real world is as it ought to be,"[112] and since for
Hegel philosophy is concerned with "what is true eternally,
neither with the Yesterday nor with the Tomorrow, but with
the Present as such, with the 'Now' in the sense of an absolute
presence,"[113] since the mind as perceived by the thinking ego
is "the Now as such," then philosophy has to reconcile the conflict between the thinking and the willing ego. It must unite
the time speculations belonging to the perspective of the Will
and its concentration on the future with Thinking and its perspective of an enduring present.

The attempt is far from being successful. As Koyré points
out in the concluding sentences of his essay, the Hegelian
notion of a "system" clashes with the primacy he accords to the
future. The latter demands that time shall never be terminated
so long as men exist on earth, whereas philosophy in the
Hegelian sense—the owl of Minerva that starts its flight at
dusk—demands an arrest in real time, not merely the suspension of time during the activity of the thinking ego. In other
words, Hegel's philosophy could claim objective truth only on
condition that history were factually at an end, that mankind
had no more future, that nothing could still occur that would
bring anything new. And Koyré adds: "It is possible that
Hegel believed this . . . even that he believed . . . that this
essential condition [for a philosophy of history] was *already* an
actuality . . . and that this had been the reason why he himself was able—had been able—to complete it."[114] (That in fact
is the conviction of Kojève, for whom the Hegelian system is
*the* truth and therefore the definite end of philosophy as well
as history.)

Hegel's ultimate failure to reconcile the two mental activities, thinking and willing, with their opposing time concepts,
seems to me evident, but he himself would have disagreed:
Speculative thought is precisely "the unity of thought and
*time*";[115] it does not deal with Being but with *Becoming*, and
the object of the thinking mind is not Being but an "intuited
Becoming."[116] The only motion that can be intuited is a

movement that swings in a circle forming "a cycle that returns into itself . . . that presupposes its beginning, and reaches its beginning only at the end." This cyclical time concept, as we saw, is in perfect accordance with Greek classical philosophy, while post-classical philosophy, following the discovery of the Will as the mental mainspring for action, demands a recti-linear time, without which Progress would be unthinkable. Hegel finds the solution to this problem, viz., how to transform the circles into a progressing line, by assuming that something exists behind all the individual members of the human species and that this something, named Mankind, is actually a kind of somebody that he called the "World Spirit," to him no mere thought-thing but a presence embodied (incarnated) in Man-kind as the mind of man is incarnated in the body. This World Spirit embodied in Mankind, as distinguished from individual men and particular nations, pursues a rectilinear movement inherent in the succession of the generations. Each new gen-eration forms a "new stage of existence, a new world" and thus has "to begin all over again," but *"it commences at a higher level"* because, being human and endowed with mind, namely Recollection, it "has conserved [the earlier] experience" (italics added).[117]

Such a movement, in which the cyclical and the rectilinear notions of time are reconciled or united by forming a *Spiral*, is grounded on the experiences of neither the thinking ego nor the willing ego; it is the non-experienced movement of the World Spirit that constitutes Hegel's *Geisterreich*, "the realm of spirits . . . assuming definite shape in existence, [by virtue of] a succession, where one detaches and sets loose the other and each takes over from the predecessor the empire of the spiritual world."[118] No doubt this is a most ingenious solution of the problem of the Will and its reconciliation with sheer thought, but it is won at the expense of both—the thinking ego's experience of an enduring present and the willing ego's insistence on the primacy of the future. In other words, it is no more than a hypothesis.

Moreover, the plausibility of the hypothesis depends en-tirely on the assumption of the existence of *one* World Mind ruling over the plurality of human wills and directing them toward a "meaningfulness" arising out of reason's need, that is, psychologically speaking, out of the very human wish to live in a world that *is* as it *ought* to be. We encounter a similar solution in Heidegger, whose insights into the nature of willing are incomparably more profound and whose lack of sympathy with that faculty is outspoken and constitutes the actual turning-about (*Kehre*) of the later Heidegger: not "the Human will is the origin of the will to will," but "man is willed by the Will to will without experiencing what this Will is about."[119]

A few technical remarks may be appropriate in view of the Hegel revival of the last decades in which some highly qualified thinkers have played a part. The ingenuity of the triadic dialectical movement—from Thesis to Antithesis to Synthesis—is especially impressive when applied to the modern notion of Progress. Although Hegel himself probably believed in an arrest in time, an end of History that would permit the Mind to intuit and conceptualize the whole cycle of Becoming, this dialectical movement seen in itself seems to guarantee an *infinite* progress, inasmuch as the first movement from Thesis to Antithesis results in a Synthesis, which immediately establishes itself as a new Thesis. Although the original movement is by no means progressive but swings back and returns upon itself, the motion from Thesis to Thesis establishes itself behind these cycles and constitutes a rectilinear line of progress. If we wish to visualize the kind of movement, the result would be the following figure:

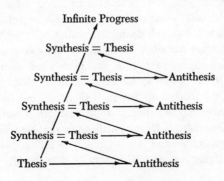

The advantage of the schema as a whole is that it assures progress and, without breaking up time's continuum, can still account for the undeniable historical fact of the rise and fall of civilizations. The advantage of the cyclical element in particular is that it permits us to look upon each end as a new beginning: Being and Nothingness "are the same thing, namely Becoming. . . . One direction is Passing Away: Being passes over into Nothing; but equally Nothing is its own opposite, a transition to Being, that is, Arising."[120] Moreover, the very infinity of the movement, though somehow in conflict with other Hegelian passages, is in perfect accord with the willing ego's time concept and the primacy it gives the future over the present and the past. The Will, untamed by Reason and its need to think, negates the present (and the past) even when the present confronts it with the actualization of its own project. Left to itself, man's Will "would rather will Nothingness than not will," as Nietzsche remarked,[121] and the notion of an infinite progress implicitly "denies every goal and admits ends only as means to outwit itself."[122] In other words, the famous power of negation inherent in the Will and conceived as the motor of History (not only in Marx but, by implication, already in Hegel) is an annihilating force that could just as well result in a process of permanent annihilation as of Infinite Progress.

The reason Hegel could construe the World-Historical movement in terms of an *ascending* line, traced by the "cunning of Reason" behind the backs of acting men, is to be found, in my opinion, in his never-questioned assumption that the dialectical process itself *starts* from Being, takes Being for granted (in contradistinction to a *Creatio ex nihilo*) in its march toward Not-Being and Becoming. The initial Being lends all further transitions their reality, their existential character, and prevents them from falling into the abyss of Not-Being. It is only because it follows on Being that "Not-Being contains [its] relation to Being; both Being and its negation are simultaneously asserted, and this assertion is Nothing as it exists in Becoming." Hegel justifies his starting-point by invoking Parmenides and the beginning of philosophy (that is, by "identifying logic and history"), thus tacitly rejecting

"Christian metaphysics," but one needs only to experiment with the thought of a dialectical movement starting from Not-Being in order to become aware that no Becoming could ever arise from it; the Not-Being at the beginning would annihilate everything generated. Hegel is quite aware of this; he knows that his apodictic proposition that "neither in heaven nor on earth is there anything not containing both Being and Nothing" rests on the solid assumption of the primacy of Being, which in turn simply corresponds to the *fact* that sheer nothingness, that is, a negation that does not negate something specific and particular, is unthinkable. All we can think is "a Nothing from which Something is to proceed; so that Being is already contained in the Beginning."[123]

*Quaestio mihi factus sum*

# The Discovery
of the
Inner Man

# II

## 7   The faculty of choice: proairesis, the forerunner of the Will

In my discussion of Thinking, I used the term "metaphysical fallacies," but without trying to refute them as though they were the simple result of logical or scientific error. Instead, I sought to demonstrate their authenticity by deriving them from the actual experiences of the thinking ego in its conflict with the world of appearances. As we saw, the thinking ego withdraws temporarily from that world without ever being able wholly to leave it, because of being incorporated in a bodily self, an appearance among appearances. The difficulties besetting any discussion of the Will have an obvious resemblance to what we found to be true of these fallacies, that is, they are likely to be caused by the nature of the faculty itself. However, while the discovery of reason and its peculiarities coincided with the discovery of the mind and the beginning of philosophy, the faculty of the Will became manifest much later. Our guiding question therefore will be: What experiences caused men to become aware of the fact that they were capable of forming volitions?

Tracing the history of a faculty can easily be mistaken for an effort to follow the history of an idea—as though here, for instance, we were concerned with the history of Freedom, or as though we mistook the Will for a mere "idea," which then indeed could turn out to be an "artificial concept" (Ryle) invented to solve artificial problems.[1] Ideas are thought-things, mental artifacts presupposing the identity of an artificer, and to assume that there is a history of the mind's faculties, as distinguished from the mind's products, seems like assuming that the human body, which is a toolmaker's and tool-user's body—the primordial tool being the human hand—is just as subject to change through the invention of new tools and implements as is the environment our hands continue to reshape. We know this is not the case. Could it be different with our mental faculties? Could the mind acquire new faculties in the course of history?

The fallacy underlying these questions rests on an almost matter-of-course identification of the mind with the brain. It is the mind that decides the existence of both use-objects and thought-things, and as the mind of the maker of use-objects is a toolmaker's mind, that is, the mind of a body endowed with hands, so the mind that originates thoughts and reifies them into thought-things or ideas is the mind of a creature endowed with a human brain and brain power. The brain, the tool of the mind, is indeed no more subject to change through the development of new mental faculties than the human hand is changed by the invention of new implements or by the enormous tangible change they effect in our environment. But the mind of man, its concerns and its faculties, is affected both by changes in the world, whose meaningfulness it examines, and, perhaps even more decisively, by its own activities. All of these are of a reflexive nature—none more so, as we shall see, than the activities of the willing ego—and yet they could never function properly without the never-changing tool of brain power, the most precious gift with which the body has endowed the human animal.

The problem we are confronted with is well known in art history, where it is called "the riddle of style," namely, the simple fact "that different ages and different nations have represented the visible world in such different ways." It is surprising that this could come about in the absence of any physical differences and perhaps even more surprising that we do not have the slightest difficulty in recognizing the realities they point to even when the "conventions" of representation adopted by us are altogether different.[2] In other words, what changes throughout the centuries is the human mind, and although these changes are very pronounced, so much so that we can date the products according to style and national origin with great precision, they are also strictly limited by the unchanging nature of the instruments with which the human body is endowed.

In the line of these reflections, we shall begin by asking

ourselves how Greek philosophy dealt with phenomena and data of human experience that our post-classical "conventions" have been accustomed to ascribe to the Will as the mainspring of action. For the purpose, we turn to Aristotle, and that for two reasons. There is, first, the simple historical fact of the decisive influence that the Aristotelian analyses of the soul exerted on all philosophies of the Will—except in the case of Paul, who, as we shall see, was content with sheer descriptions and refused to "philosophize" about his experiences. There is, second, the no less indubitable fact that no other Greek philosopher came so close to recognizing the strange lacuna we have spoken of in Greek language and thought and therefore can serve as a prime example of how certain psychological problems could be solved before the Will was discovered as a separate faculty of the mind.

The starting-point of Aristotle's reflections on the subject is the anti-Platonic insight that reason by itself does not move anything.[3] Hence the question guiding his examinations is: "What is it in the soul that originates movement?"[4] Aristotle admits the Platonic notion that reason gives commands (*keleuei*) because it knows what one should pursue and what one should avoid, but he denies that these commands are necessarily obeyed. The incontinent man (his paradigmatic example throughout these inquiries) follows his desires regardless of the commands of reason. On the other hand, at the recommendation of reason, these desires can be resisted. Hence they, too, have no obligatory force inherent in them: by themselves they do not originate movement. Here Aristotle is dealing with a phenomenon that later, after the discovery of the Will, appears as the distinction between will and inclination. The distinction becomes the cornerstone of Kantian ethics, but it makes its first appearance in medieval philosophy—for instance, in Master Eckhart's distinction between "the inclination to sin and the will to sin, the inclination being no sin," which leaves the question of the evil deed itself altogether out of account: "If I never did evil but had only the will to evil . . . it is as great a sin as though I had killed all men even though I had done nothing."[5]

Still, in Aristotle desire retains a priority in originating movement, which comes about through a playing together of reason and desire. It is desire for an absent object that stimulates reason to step in and calculate the best ways and means to obtain it. This calculating reason he calls *"nous praktikos,"* practical reason, as distinguished from *nous theōrētikos,* speculative or pure reason, the former being concerned only with what depends exclusively on men (*eph' hēmin*), with matters in their power and therefore contingent (they can be or not-be), while pure reason is concerned only with matters that are beyond human power to change.

Practical reason is needed to come to the aid of desire under certain conditions. "Desire is influenced by what is just at hand," thus easily obtainable—a suggestion carried by the very word used for appetite or desire, *orexis,* whose primary meaning, from *oregō,* indicates the stretching out of one's hand to reach for something nearby. Only when the fulfillment of a desire lies in the future and has to take the time factor into account is practical reason needed and stimulated by it. In the case of incontinence, it is the force of desire for what is close at hand that leads to incontinence, and here practical reason will intervene out of concern for future consequences. But men do not only desire what is close at hand; they are able to imagine objects of desire to secure which they need to calculate the appropriate means. It is this future imagined object of desire that stimulates practical reason; as far as the resulting motion, the act itself, is concerned, the desired object is the beginning, while for the calculating process the same object is the end of the movement.

It appears that Aristotle himself found this outline of the relation between reason and desire unsatisfactory as an adequate explication of human action. It still relies, though with modifications, on Plato's dichotomy of reason and desire. In his early *Protreptikos,* Aristotle had interpreted it thus: "One part of the soul is Reason. This is the natural ruler and judge of things concerning us. The nature of the other part is to follow it and submit to its rule."[6] We shall see later that to issue commands is among the chief characteristics of the Will. In Plato reason could take this function on itself because of the assumption that reason is concerned with truth, and truth indeed is compelling. But reason itself, while it leads to truth, is persuasive, not imperative, in the soundless thinking dialogue between me and myself; only those who are not capable of thinking need to be compelled.

Within man's soul, reason becomes a "ruling" and commanding principle only because of the desires, which are blind and devoid of reason and therefore supposed to obey blindly. This obedience is necessary for the mind's tranquillity, the undisturbed harmony between the Two-in-One that is guaranteed by the axiom of non-contradiction—do not contradict yourself, remain a friend of yourself: "all friendly feelings toward others are an extension of the friendly feelings a person has for himself."[7] In the event that the desires do not submit to the commands of reason, the result in Aristotle is the "base man," who contradicts himself and is "at variance with himself" (*diapherein*). Wicked men either "run away from life and do away with themselves," unable to bear their own company, or "seek the company of others with whom to spend their days; but they avoid their own company. For when they are by themselves they remember many events that make them uneasy . . . but when they are with others they can forget. . . . Their relations with themselves are not friendly . . . their soul is divided against itself . . . one part pulls in one direction and the other in another as if to tear the individual to pieces. . . . Bad people are full of regrets."[8]

This description of internal conflict, a conflict between reason and the appetites, may be adequate to explain conduct—in this case the conduct, or, rather, misconduct, of the incontinent man. It does not explain action, the subject matter of Aristotelian ethics, for action is not mere execution of the commands of reason; it is itself a reasonable activity, though an activity not of "theoretical reason" but of what in the treatise *On the Soul* is called "*nous praktikos*," practical reason. In the ethical treatises it is called *phronēsis*, a kind of insight and understanding of matters that are good or bad for men, a sort of sagacity—neither wisdom nor cleverness—needed for human affairs, which Sophocles, following common usage, ascribed to old age[9] and which Aristotle conceptualized. *Phronēsis* is required for any activity involving things within human power to achieve or not to achieve.

Such practical sense also guides production and the arts, but these have "an end other than themselves," whereas "action is itself an end."[10] (The distinction is the difference between the flute-player, for whom the playing is an end itself, and the flute-maker, whose activity is only a means and has come to an end when the flute is produced.) There is such a thing as *eupraxia*, action well done, and the doing of something well, regardless of its consequences, is then counted among the *aretai*, the Aristotelian excellences (or virtues). Actions of this sort are also moved not by reason but by desire, but the desire is not for an object, a "what" that I can grasp, seize, and use again as a means to another end; the desire is for a "how," a way of performing, excellence of appearance in the community—the proper realm of human affairs. Much later but quite in the Aristotelian spirit, Plotinus had this to say, as paraphrased by a recent interpreter: "What actually is in man's power in the sense that it depends entirely upon him . . . is the quality of his conduct, *to kalōs*"; man, if compelled to fight, is still free to fight bravely or in a cowardly way."[11]

Action in the sense of how men want to appear needs a deliberate planning ahead, for which Aristotle coins a new term, *proairesis*, choice in the sense of preference between alternatives—one rather than another. The *archai*, beginnings and principles, of this choice are desire *and* logos: logos provides us with the purpose for the sake of which we act; choice becomes the starting-point of the actions themselves.[12] Choice is a median faculty, inserted, as it were, into the earlier dichotomy of reason and desire, and its main function is to mediate between them.

The opposite of deliberate choice or preference is *pathos*, passion or emotion, as we would say, in the sense that we are motivated by something we suffer. (Thus a man may commit adultery out of passion and not because he has deliberately preferred adultery to chastity; he "may have stolen but not be a thief."[13]) The faculty of choice is necessary whenever men act for a purpose (*heneka tinos*), insofar as means have to be chosen, but the purpose itself, the ultimate end of the act for the sake of which it was embarked on in the first place, is not open to choice. The ultimate end of human acts is *eudaimonia*, happiness in the sense of "living well," which all men desire; all acts are but different means chosen to arrive at it. (The relationship between means and ends, whether in action or in fabrication, is that all means are equally justifiable by their ends; the specifically moral problem of the means-end relationship—whether all means can be justified by ends—is never even mentioned by Aristotle.) The element of reason in choice is called "deliberation," and we never deliberate about ends but about the means to attain them.[14] "No one chooses to be happy but to make money or run risks for the purpose of being happy."[15]

It is in the *Eudemian Ethics* that Aristotle explains in a more concrete way why he found it necessary to insert a new faculty into the old dichotomy and thus settle the old quarrel between reason and desire. He gives the example of incontinence: all men agree that incontinence is bad and not something to be desired; moderation or *sō-phrosynē*—that which saves (*sōzein*) practical reason (*phronēsis*)—is the naturally given criterion of all acts. If a man follows his desires, which are blind to future consequences, and thus indulges in incontinence, it is as though "the same man were to act at the same time both voluntarily [that is, intentionally] and involuntarily [that is, contrary to his intentions]," and this, Aristotle remarks, "is impossible."[16]

*Proairesis* is the way out of the contradiction. If reason and desire remained without mediation, in their crude natural antagonism, we would have to conclude that man, beset by the conflicting urges of both faculties, "forces himself away from his desire" when he remains continent and "forces himself away from his reason" when desire overwhelms him. But no such being-forced occurs in either case; both acts are done intentionally, and "when the principle is from within, there is no force."[17] What actually happens is that, reason and desire being in conflict, the decision between them is a matter of "preference," of deliberate choice. What intervenes is reason, not *nous*, which is concerned with things that are forever and cannot be otherwise than they are, but *dianoia* or *phronēsis*, which deal with things in our power, as distinguished from desires and imaginations that may stretch out to things we can never achieve, as when we wish to be gods or immortal.

*Proairesis*, the faculty of choice, one is tempted to conclude, is the precursor of the Will. It opens up a first, small restricted space for the human mind, which without it was delivered to two opposed compelling forces: the force of self-evident truth, with which we are not free to agree or disagree, on one side; on the other, the force of passions and appetites, in which it is as though nature overwhelms us unless reason "forces" us away. But the space left to freedom is very small. We deliberate only about *means* to an end that we take for granted, that we cannot choose. Nobody deliberates and chooses health or happiness as his aim, though we may think about them; ends are inherent in human nature and the same for all.[18] As to the means, "sometimes we have to find what [they] are, and sometimes how they are to be used or through whom they can be acquired."[19] Hence, the means, too, not just the ends, are given, and our free choice concerns only a "rational" selection between them; *proairesis* is the arbiter between several possibilities.

In Latin, Aristotle's faculty of choice is *liberum arbitrium*. Whenever we come upon it in medieval discussions of the Will, we are not dealing with a spontaneous power of beginning something new, nor with an autonomous faculty, determined by its own nature and obeying its own laws. The most grotesque example of it is Buridan's ass: the poor beast would have starved to death between two equidistant, equally nice-smelling bundles of hay, as no deliberation would give him a reason for preferring one to the other, and he only survived because he was smart enough to forgo free choice, trust his desire, and grasp what lay within reach.

The *liberum arbitrium* is neither spontaneous nor autonomous; we find the last vestiges of an arbiter between reason and desire still surviving in Kant, whose "good will" finds itself in a strange predicament: it is either "good without qualifications," in which case it enjoys complete autonomy but has no choice, or it receives its law—the categorical imperative—from "practical reason," which tells the will what to do and adds: Don't make an exception of yourself, obey the axiom of non-contradiction, which, since Socrates, has ruled the soundless dialogue of thought. The Will in Kant is in fact "practical reason"[20] much in the sense of Aristotle's *nous praktikos;* it borrows its obligatory power from the compulsion exerted on the mind by self-evident truth or logical reasoning. This is why Kant asserted time and again that every "Thou-shalt" that does not come from outside but rises up in the mind itself implies a "Thou-canst." What is at stake is clearly the conviction that whatever depends on us and concerns only ourselves is within our power, and this conviction is what Aristotle and Kant basically have in common, although their estimation of the importance of the realm of human affairs is greatly at variance. Freedom becomes a problem, and the Will as an independent autonomous faculty is discovered, only when men begin to doubt the coincidence of the Thou-shalt and the I-can, when the question arises: *Are things that concern only me within my power?*

## 8   The Apostle Paul and the impotence of the Will

The first and fundamental answer to the question I raised at the beginning of this chapter—what experiences caused men to become aware of their capability of forming volitions?—is that these experiences, Hebrew in origin, were not political and did not relate to the world, either to the world of appearances and man's position within it or to the realm of human affairs, whose existence depends upon deeds and actions, but were exclusively located within man himself. When we deal with experiences relevant to the Will, we are dealing with experiences that men have not only with themselves, but also *inside* themselves.

Such experiences were by no means unknown to Greek antiquity. In the previous volume, I spoke at some length of the Socratic discovery of the two-in-one, which we today would call "consciousness" and which originally had the function of what we today call "conscience." We saw how this two-in-one as a sheer fact of consciousness was actualized and articulated in the "soundless dialogue" that since Plato we have called "thinking." This thinking dialogue between me and myself takes place only in solitude, in a withdrawal from the world of appearances, where ordinarily we are together with others and appear as one to ourselves as well as to them. But the inwardness of the thinking dialogue that makes of philosophy Hegel's "solitary business" (although it is aware of itself—Descartes' *cogito me cogitare,* Kant's *Ich denke,* silently accompanying everything I do) is not thematically concerned with the Self but, on the contrary, with the experiences and questions that this Self, an appearance among appearances, feels are in need of examination. This meditating examination of everything given can be disturbed by the necessities of life, by the presence of others, by all kinds of urgent business. But none of the factors interfering with the mind's activity rises out of the mind itself, for the two-in-one are friends and partners, and to keep intact this "harmony" is the thinking ego's foremost concern.

The Apostle Paul's discovery, which he describes in great detail in the Letter to the Romans (written between A.D. 54 and 58), again concerns a two-in-one, but these two are not friends or partners; they are in constant struggle with each other. Precisely when he "wants to do right (*to kalon*)," he finds that "evil lies close at hand" (7:21), for "if the law had not said, 'You shall not covet,' " he "should not have known what it is to covet." Hence, it is the command of the law that occasioned "all kinds of covetousness. Apart from the law sin lies dead" (7:7, 8).

The function of the law is equivocal: it is "good, in order that sin might be shown to be sin" (7:13), but since it speaks in the voice of command, it "arouses the passions" and "revives sin." "The very commandment which promised life proved to

be death to me" (7:9–10). The result is that "I do not understand my own actions. ["I have become a question to myself."] For I do not do what I want, but I do the very thing I
hate" (7:15). And the point of the matter is that this inner conflict can never be settled in favor of either obedience to the law
or submission to sin; this inner "wretchedness," according to
Paul, can be healed only through grace, gratuitously. It was
this insight that "flashed about" the man of Tarsus named
Saul, who had been, as he said, an "extremely zealous" Pharisee
(Galatians 1:14), belonging to the "strictest party of our religion" (Acts 26:4). What he wanted was "righteousness"
(*dikaiosynē*), but righteousness, namely, to "abide by all things
written in the book of the law, and do them" (Galatians 3:10),
is impossible; this is the "curse of the law," and "if righteousness were through the law, then Christ died to no purpose"
(Galatians 2:21).

That, however, is only one side of the matter. Paul became
the founder of the Christian religion not only because, by his
own declaration, he was "entrusted with the gospel to the
uncircumcised" (Galatians 2:7), but also because wherever he
went he preached the "resurrection of the dead" (Acts 24:21).
The center of his concern, in sharp and obvious distinction
from that of the gospels, is not Jesus of Nazareth, his preaching and his deeds, but Christ, crucified and resurrected.
From this source he derived his new doctrine that became "a
stumbling-block to Jews and folly to Gentiles" (I Corinthians
1:23).

It is the concern with eternal life, ubiquitous in the Roman
Empire at the time, that separates the new era so sharply from
antiquity and becomes the common bond that syncretistically
united the many new Oriental cults. Not that Paul's concern
with individual resurrection was Jewish in origin; to the He-
brews, immortality was felt to be necessary only for the people
and granted only to them; the individual was content to survive in his progeny, content also to die old and "sated with
years." And in the ancient world, Roman or Greek, the only
immortality asked for or striven for was the non-oblivion of
the great name and the great deed, and therefore of the institu-
tions—the *polis* or *civitas*—which could guarantee a continuity

of remembrance. (When Paul said that "the wages of sin is death" [Romans 6:23], he might have been recalling the words of Cicero, who had said that although men must die, communities [*civitates*] are meant to be eternal and perish only as a consequence of their sins.) Lying behind the many new beliefs is clearly the common experience of a declining, perhaps a dying, world; and the "good news" of Christianity in its eschatological aspects said clearly enough: You who have believed that men die but that the world is everlasting need only turn about, to a faith that the world comes to an end but that you yourself will have everlasting life. Then, of course, the question of "righteousness," namely, of being worthy of this eternal life, takes on an altogether new, personal importance.

Concern with personal, individual immortality appears in the gospels, too, all of them written during the last third of the first century. Jesus is commonly asked, "What shall I do to inherit eternal life?" (e.g., Luke 10:25), but Jesus seems not to have preached resurrection. Instead, he said that if people would do as he told them—"go and do likewise" or "follow me"—then "the kingdom of God is in the midst of you" (Luke 17:21) or "has come upon you" (Matthew 12:28). If people pressed him further, his answer was always the same: Fulfill the law as you know it *and* "sell all that you have and distribute it to the poor" (Luke 18:22). The thrust of Jesus' teaching is contained in this "and," which drove the well-known and accepted law to its inherent extreme. This is what he must have meant when he said, "I have come not to abolish [the law] but to fulfill [it]" (Matthew 5:17). Hence, not "Love your neighbors," but "Love your enemies"; "to him who strikes you on the cheek, offer the other also"; "from him who takes away your cloak do not withhold your coat as well." In short, not "What you don't want to be done to you, don't do to others," but "As you wish that men would do to you, do so to them" (Luke 6:27–31)—certainly the most radical possible version of "Love your neighbor *as yourself*."

Paul was certainly aware of the radical turn the old demand to fulfill the law had taken in the teaching of Jesus of Nazareth. And he may well have suddenly understood that in this lay the law's only true fulfillment, and then have found out that such fulfillment was beyond human power: it led to an I-will-but-can*not*, even though Jesus himself seems never to have told any of his followers that they could not do what they willed to do. Still, in Jesus, there is already a new stress on the inner life. He would not have gone so far as Eckhart, more than a thousand years later, and asserted that having the will to do was enough to "earn eternal life," for "before God to will to do according to my capacity and to have done are the same." Yet Jesus' stress on the "Thou shall not covet," the only one of the Ten Commandments that relates to an inner life, points in that direction—"every one who looks at a woman lustfully has already committed adultery . . . in his heart" (Matthew 5:28). Similarly, in Eckhart, a man who has the will to kill without ever killing anybody has committed no less a sin than were he to have murdered the whole human race.[21]

Of perhaps even greater relevance are Jesus' preachings against hypocrisy as the sin of the Pharisees and his suspicion of appearances: "Why do you see the speck that is in your brother's eye but do not notice the log that is in your own eye?" (Luke 6:41). And they "like to go about in long robes, and love salutations in the market places" (Luke 20:46), which poses a problem that must have been familiar to men of the Law. The trouble is that whatever good you do, by the very fact of its appearing either to others or to yourself becomes subject to self-doubt.[22] Jesus knew about that: "Do not let your left hand know what your right hand is doing" (Matthew 6:3), that is, live in hiding, in hiding even from yourself, and do not bother to *be* good—"No one is good but God alone" (Luke 18:19). Yet this lovely carelessness could hardly be maintained when to do good *and to be good* had become the requirement for overcoming death and being granted eternal life.

Hence, when we come to Paul, the accent shifts entirely from doing to believing, from the outward man living in a world of appearances (himself an appearance among appearances and therefore subject to semblance and illusion) to an inwardness which by definition never unequivocally manifests itself and can be scrutinized only by a God who also never appears unequivocally. The ways of this God are inscrutable. For the Gentiles, His chief property is His invisibility; for Paul himself, what is the most inscrutable is that "Sin indeed was in the world before the law was given but sin is not counted where there is no law" (Romans 5:13), so that it is entirely possible "that Gentiles who did not pursue righteousness have attained it . . . but that Israel who pursued the righteousness which is based on the law did not succeed in fulfilling that law" (Romans 9:30–31). That the law cannot be fulfilled, that the will to fulfill the law activates another will, the will to sin, and that the one will is never without the other—that is the subject Paul deals with in the Letter to the Romans.

Paul, it is true, does not discuss it in terms of two wills but in terms of two laws—the law of the mind that lets him delight in the law of God "in his inmost self" and the law of his "members" that tells him to do what in his inmost self he hates. Law itself is understood as the voice of a master demanding obedience; the Thou-shalt of the law demands and expects a voluntary act of submission, an I-will of agreement. The Old Law said: thou shalt do; the New Law says: thou shalt *will*. It was the experience of an imperative demanding *voluntary* submission that led to the discovery of the Will, and inherent in this experience was the wondrous fact of a freedom that none of the ancient peoples—Greek, Roman, or Hebrew— had been aware of, namely, that there is a faculty in man by virtue of which, regardless of necessity and compulsion, he can say "Yes" or "No," agree or disagree with what is factually given, including his own self and his existence, and that this faculty may determine what he is going to do.

But this faculty is of a curiously paradoxical nature. It is actualized by an imperative that says not merely "Thou shalt" —as when the mind speaks to the body and, as Augustine put it later, the body immediately and, as it were, mindlessly obeys—but says "Thou *shalt will*," and this already implies that, whatever I may in fact eventually do, I can answer: I will, or I will not. The very commandment, the Thou-shalt, puts me before a choice between an I-will and an I-will-not, that is, theologically speaking, between obedience and disobedience. (Disobedience, it will be remembered, later becomes the mortal sin *par excellence*, and obedience, the very foundation of Christian ethics, the "virtue above all virtues" [Eckhart], and one, incidentally, that, unlike poverty and chastity, can hardly be derived from the teaching and preaching of Jesus of Nazareth.) If the will did not have the choice of saying "No," it would no longer be a will; and if there were not a *counter-will* within me that is aroused by the very commandment of the Thou-shalt, if, to speak in Paul's terms, "sin" did not dwell "within me" (Romans 7:20), I would not need a will at all.

I have spoken earlier of the reflexive nature of mental activities: the *cogito me cogitare,* the *volo me velle* (even judgment, the least reflexive of the three, recoils, acts back upon itself). Later we shall be seeing that this reflexivity is nowhere stronger than in the willing ego; the point is that every I-will arises out of a natural inclination toward freedom, that is, out of the natural revulsion of free men toward being at someone's bidding. The will always addresses itself to itself; when the command says, Thou shalt, the will replies, Thou shalt *will* as the command says—and not mindlessly execute orders. That is the moment when the internal contest begins, for the aroused counter-will has a like power of command. Hence, the reason "all who rely on works of the law are under a curse" (Galatians 3:10) is not only the I-will-and-can*not* but also the fact that the I-will inevitably is countered by an I-nill, so that even if the law is obeyed and fulfilled, there remains this inner resistance.

In the fight between the I-will and the I-nill, the outcome can depend only on an act—if works no longer count, the Will is helpless. And since the conflict is between *velle* and *nolle,* persuasion nowhere enters, as it did in the old conflict between reason and the appetites. For the phenomenon itself, that "I do not do the good I want, but the evil I do not want is what I do" (Romans 7:19), is of course not new. We find almost the same words in Ovid: "I see what is better and approve of it; I follow what is worse,"[23] and this is probably a translation of the famous passage in Euripides' *Medea* (lines 1078–80): "I know indeed what evil I intend to do; but stronger than my deliberations [*bouleumata*] is my *thymos* [what makes me move], which is the cause of the greatest evils among mortals." Euripides and Ovid might have deplored the weakness of reason when confronted with the passionate drive of the desires, and Aristotle might have gone a step farther and detected a self-contradiction in the choosing of the worse, an act that provided him with his definition of the "base man," but none of them would have ascribed the phenomenon to a free choice of the Will.

The Will, split and automatically producing its own counter-will, is in need of being healed, of becoming one again. Like thinking, willing has split the one into a two-in-one, but for the thinking ego a "healing" of the split would be the worst thing that could happen; it would put an end to thinking altogether. Well, it would be very tempting to conclude that divine mercy, Paul's solution for the wretchedness of the Will, actually abolishes the Will by miraculously depriving it of its counter-will. But this is no longer a matter of volitions, since mercy cannot be striven for; salvation "depends not upon man's will or exertion, but upon God's mercy," and He "has mercy upon whomever he wills, and he hardens the heart of whomever he wills" (Romans 9:16, 18). Moreover, just as "the law came in" not merely to make sin identifiable but to "increase the trespass," so grace "abounded" where "sin increased"—*felix culpa* indeed, for how could men know the glory if they were unacquainted with wretchedness; how would we know what day was if there were no night?

In brief, the will is impotent not because of something outside that prevents willing from succeeding, but because the will hinders itself. And wherever, as in Jesus, it does not hinder itself, it does not yet exist. For Paul, the explanation is relatively simple: the conflict is between flesh and spirit, and the trouble is that men are both, carnal and spiritual. The flesh will die, and therefore to live according to the flesh means certain death. The chief task of the spirit is not just to rule over the appetites and make the flesh obey but to bring about its mortification—to crucify it "with its passions and desires" (Galatians 5:24), which in fact is beyond human power. We saw that from the perspective of the thinking ego a certain suspicion of the body was only natural. Man's carnality, though not necessarily the source of sin, interrupts the mind's thinking activity and offers a resistance to the soundless, swift dialogue of the mind's exchange with itself, an exchange whose very "sweetness" consists in a spirituality in which no material factor intervenes. This is a far cry from the aggressive hostility to the body that we find in Paul, a hostility, moreover, that, quite apart from prejudices against the flesh, arises out of the very essence of the Will. Its mental origin notwithstanding, the will grows aware of itself only by overcoming resistance, and "flesh" in Paul's reasoning (as in the later disguise of "inclination") becomes the metaphor for an internal resistance. Thus, even in this simplistic scheme, the discovery of the Will has already opened a veritable Pandora's box of unanswerable questions, of which Paul himself was by no means unaware and which from then on were to plague with absurdities any strictly Christian philosophy.

Paul knew how easy it would be to infer from his presentation that we are "to continue in sin that grace may abound" (Romans 6:1) ("why not do evil that good may come?—as some people slanderously charge us with saying" [Romans 3:8]) although he hardly foresaw how much discipline and rigidity of dogma would be required to protect the Church against the *pecca fortiter*. He was also quite aware of the greatest stumbling-block for a Christian *philosophy:* the obvious contradiction between an all-knowing, all-powerful God and what Augustine later called the "monstrosity" of the Will. How can God permit this human wretchedness? Above all, how can He "still find fault," since no one "can resist his will" (Romans 9:19)? Paul was a Roman citizen, spoke and wrote koine Greek, and was obviously well informed about Roman law and Greek thought. Yet the founder of the Christian religion (if not of the Church) remained a Jew, and there could perhaps be no more forceful proof of it than his answer to the unanswerable questions his new faith and the new discoveries of his own inwardness had raised.

It is almost word for word the answer Job gave when he was led to question the inscrutable ways of the Hebrew God. Like Job's, Paul's reply is very simple and entirely unphilosophical: "But, who are you, a man, to answer back to God? Will what is molded say to its molder, 'Why have you made me thus?' Has the potter no right over the clay, to make out of the same lump one vessel for beauty and another for menial use? What if God, desiring . . . to make known his power, has endured . . . the vessels of wrath made for destruction, in order to make known the riches of his glory for the vessels of mercy, which he has prepared beforehand for glory . . . ?" (Romans 9:20–23; Job 10). In the same vein, God, cutting off all interrogation, had spoken to Job, who had dared to question *Him:* "I will question you and you shall declare to me. Where were you when I laid the foundations of the earth? . . . Shall a fault-finder contend with the Almighty?" And to this there exists indeed only Job's answer: "I have uttered what I did not understand, things too wonderful for me, which I did not know" (Job 42:3).

Unlike his doctrine of the resurrection of the dead, Paul's *argumentum ad hominem,* as it were, cutting short all questions with a Who-are-you-to-ask? failed to survive the early stages of the Christian faith. Historically speaking, that is, since of course we cannot know how many Christians in the long centuries of an *imitatio Christi* remained untouched by the ever-repeated attempts to reconcile absolute Hebrew faith in the Creator-God with Greek philosophy. The Jewish communities, at any rate, were warned against any kind of speculation; the Talmud, provoked by Gnosticism, told them: "It were better for the man never to be born who thinks about four matters: what is above and what is below, what was before and what will be afterward."[24]

Like a faint echo of this faithful awe before the mystery of all Being, centuries later we hear Augustine repeating what must have been a well-known joke at the time: "I answer the man who says: What did God do before He made heaven and earth? . . . : He was preparing Hell for those who pry into such deep matters." But Augustine did not let the matter rest at that. Several chapters further on (in the *Confessions*), after denouncing unjokingly those who ask such questions as men attacked "by a criminal disease that makes them thirst for more than they can hold," gives the logically correct and existentially unsatisfactory answer that, since the Creator-God is eternal, He must have created time when He created Heaven and Earth, so that there could be no "before" prior to the Creation. "Let them see that there could be no time without a created being."[25]

## 9  *Epictetus and the omnipotence of the Will*

In the Letter to the Romans, Paul describes an inner experience, the experience of the I-will-and-I-can*not*. This experience, followed by the experience of God's mercy, is overwhelming. He explains what happened to him and tells us how and why the two occurrences are interconnected. In the course of the explanation he develops the first comprehensive theory of history, of what history is all about, and he lays the foundations of Christian doctrine. But he does so in terms of facts; he does not *argue,* and this is what distinguishes him most sharply from Epictetus, with whom otherwise he had much in common.

They were just about contemporaries, came from roughly the same region in the Near East, lived in the Hellenized Roman Empire, and spoke the same language (the Koine), though one was a Roman citizen and the other a freedman, a former slave, one was a Jew and the other a Stoic. They also have in common a certain moral rigidity which sets them apart from their surroundings. They both declare that to covet your neighbor's wife means to have committed adultery. They denounce in almost the same words the intellectual establishment of their time—the Pharisees in Paul's case, the philosophers (Stoics and Academicians) in Epictetus'—as hypocrites who do not conduct themselves in accordance with their teaching. "Show me a Stoic if you can!" exclaims Epictetus. "Show me one who is sick and yet happy, in peril and yet happy, dying and yet happy, in exile and happy, in disgrace and happy. . . . By the gods I would fain see a Stoic."[26] This scorn is more outspoken and plays an even greater role in Epictetus than in Paul. Finally, they share an almost instinctive contempt for the body—this "bag," in Epictetus' words, which day by day

I stuff, and then empty: "what could be more tiresome?"[27]—and insist on the distinction between an "inmost self" (Paul) and "outward things."[28]

In each, the actual content of inwardness is described exclusively in terms of the promptings of the Will, which Paul believed to be impotent and Epictetus declared to be almighty: "Where lies the good? In the will. Where lies evil? In the will. Where lies neither? In what is not within the will's control."[29] At first glance, this is old Stoic doctrine but without any of the old Stoa's philosophical underpinnings; from Epictetus, we do not hear about the intrinsic goodness of nature according to which (*kata physin*) men ought to live and think—think away, that is, all apparent evil as a necessary component of an all-comprehensive good. In our context the interest of Epictetus lies precisely in the absence of such metaphysical doctrines from his teaching.

He was primarily a teacher and, since he taught and did not write,[30] he apparently thought of himself as a follower of Socrates, forgetting, like most of Socrates' so-called followers, that Socrates had nothing to teach. Anyhow, Epictetus considered himself a philosopher and he defined philosophy's subject matter as "the art of living one's life."[31] This art consisted mainly in having an argument ready for every emergency, for every situation of acute misery. His starting-point was the ancient *omnes homines beati esse volunt,* all men wish to be happy, and the only question for philosophy was to find out how to arrive at this matter-of-course goal. Except that Epictetus, in agreement with the mood of the time and in contrast to the pre-Christian era, was convinced that life, as it is given on earth, with the inevitable ending in death, and hence beset by fear and trembling, was incapable of giving real happiness without a special effort of man's will. Thus "happiness" changed its meaning; it was no longer understood as *eudaimonia,* the *activity* of *eu zēn,* living well, but as *euroia biou,* a Stoic metaphor indicating a free-flowing life, undisturbed by storms, tempests, or obstacles. Its characteristics were serenity, *galēnē,* the stillness after the storm, and tranquillity, *eudia,* fair weather[32]—metaphors unknown to classical antiquity. They all relate to a mood of the soul that is best described in

negative terms (like *ataraxia*) and indeed consists in something wholly negative: to be "happy" now meant primarily
"not to be miserable." Philosophy could teach "the processes of
reason," the arguments, "like weapons bright and ready for
use,"[33] to be directed against the wretchedness of real life.

Reason discovers that what makes you miserable is not
death threatening from the outside but the fear of death
within you, not pain but the fear of pain—"it is not death or
pain which is a fearful thing, but the fear of pain or death."[34]
Hence the only thing to be rightly afraid of is fear itself, and
while men cannot escape death or pain, they can argue themselves out of the fear within themselves by eliminating the
impressions fearful things have imprinted on their minds: "if
we kept our fear not for death or exile, but for fear itself, then
we should practice to avoid what we think evil."[35] (We need
only recall the many instances that testify to the role played in
the household of the soul by an overwhelming fear of being
afraid, or imagine how reckless human courage would be if
experienced pain left no memory behind—Epictetus' "impression"—in order to realize the down-to-earth psychological
value of these apparently far-fetched theories.)

Once reason has discovered this inward region where man
is confronted only by the "impressions" outward things make
on his mind rather than by their factual existence, its task has
been accomplished. The philosopher is no longer the thinker
examining whatever may come his way but the man who has
trained himself never to "turn to outward things," no matter
where he happens to be. Epictetus gives an illuminating example of the attitude. He lets his philosopher go to the games
like everybody else; but unlike the "vulgar" crowd of other
spectators, he is "concerned" there only with himself and his
own "happiness"; hence, he forces himself to "wish only that to
happen which does happen, and only him to win who does
win."[36] This turning away from reality while still in the midst
of it, in contrast to the withdrawal of the thinking ego into the
solitude of the soundless dialogue between me and myself,
where every thought is an after-thought by definition, has the
most far-reaching consequences. It means, for instance, that
when one is going somewhere one pays *no* attention to one's

goal but is interested only in one's "own activity" of walking, "or when deliberating is interested [only] in the act of deliberation, and not in getting that for which he is planning."[37] In terms of the game parable, it is as though these spectators, looking with blinded eyes, were mere ghostlike apparitions in the world of appearances.

It may be helpful to compare this attitude with that of the philosopher in the old Pythagorean parable about the Olympic Games; the best were those who did not participate in the struggle for fame or gain but were mere spectators, interested in the games for their own sake. Not a trace of such disinterested interest is left here. Only the self is of interest, and the self's unchallengeable ruler is argumentative reason, not the old *nous,* the inner organ for truth, the invisible eye of the mind directed toward the invisible in the visible world, but a *dynamis logikē,* whose greatest distinction is that it takes "cognizance of itself and of all things else" and "has the power to approve or disapprove its own action."[38] At first glance this may look like the Socratic two-in-one actualized in the thinking process but in reality it is much closer to what we today would call consciousness.

Epictetus' discovery was that the mind, because it could retain outward "impressions" (*phantasiai*), was able to deal with all "outside things" as mere "data of consciousness," as we would say. The *dynamis logikē* examines both itself and the "impressions" imprinted on the mind. Philosophy teaches us how to "deal with impressions aright"; it tests them and "distinguishes them and makes use of none which is untested." Looking at a table does not enable us to decide whether the table is good or bad; vision does not tell us, nor do any of our other senses. Only the mind, which deals not with real tables but with impressions of tables, can tell us. ("What tells us that gold is a goodly thing? For the gold does not tell us. Clearly it is the faculty that deals with impressions."[39]) The point is that you don't have to go outside yourself if your concern is wholly for that self. Only insofar as the mind can draw things into itself are they of any value.

Once the mind has withdrawn from outside things into the

inwardness of its own impressions, it discovers that in one respect it is entirely independent of all outside influences: "Can anyone prevent you from agreeing to what is true? No one. Can anyone compel you to accept the false? No one. Do you see that in this sphere your faculty is free from let and hindrance and constraint and compulsion?"[40] That it is in the nature of truth to "necessitate" the mind is an old insight: "*hōsper hyp' autēs tēs alētheias anagkasthentes,*" "necessitated as it were by truth itself," as Aristotle says when talking of self-evident theories standing in need of no special reasoning.[41] But in Epictetus this truth and its *dynamis logikē* have nothing at all to do with knowledge or cognition, for which "the processes of logic are unfruitful"[42]—literally good for nothing (*akarpa*). Knowledge and cognition concern "outside things," independent of man and beyond his power; hence, they are not, or should not be, of concern to him.

The beginning of philosophy is "an awareness [*synaisthē-sis*] of one's own weakness in regard to necessary things." We have no "innate conception" of things we ought to know, such as "a right-angled triangle," but we can be taught by people who know, and those who do not yet know *know* that they don't know. It is quite different with things which actually concern us and on which the kind of life we lead depends. In this sphere everybody is born with an it-seems-to-me, *dokei moi,* an opinion, and there our difficulty begins: "in the discovery of conflict in men's minds with one another" and the "attempt to discover a standard, just as we discover the balance to deal with weights and the rule to deal with things straight and crooked. This is the beginning of philosophy."[43]

Philosophy, then, sets the standards and norms and teaches man how to *use* his sensory faculties, how "to deal with impressions aright," and how "to test them and calculate the value of each." The criterion of every philosophy is therefore its usefulness in the business of leading a life free from pain. More specifically, it teaches certain lines of thought that can defeat the innate impotence of men. In this general philosophical framework it ought to be reason, argumentative reasoning, that is given primacy over all the mental faculties; but this is not the case. In his violent denunciation of men who were "philosophers only with their lips," Epictetus points to the appalling gap between a man's teachings and his actual conduct, and by implication hints at the old insight that reason by itself neither moves nor achieves anything. The great achiever is not reason but the Will. "Consider who you are" is an exhortation addressed to reason, it seems, but what is then discovered is that "man . . . has nothing more sovereign [*kyriōteros*] than will [*proairesis*] . . . all else [is] subject to this, and will itself is free from slavery and subjection." Reason (*logos*), it is true, distinguishes man from the animals, which therefore are "marked for service," while man is "fitted for command";[44] yet the organ capable of command is not reason but Will. If philosophy deals with the "art of living your own life" and if its supreme criterion is usefulness in these terms, then "philosophy means very little else but this— to search how it is practicable to exercise the will to get and the will to avoid without hindrance."[45]

The first thing reason can teach the will is the distinction between things that depend on man, those that are in his power (the Aristotelian *eph' hēmin*), and those that are not. The power of the will rests on its sovereign decision to concern itself only with things within man's power, and these reside exclusively in human inwardness.[46] Hence, the will's first decision is not-to-will what it cannot get and to cease nilling what it cannot avoid—in short, not to concern itself with anything over which it has no power. ("What matters it whether the world is composed of atoms or of infinite parts or of fire and earth? Is it not enough to know . . . the limits of the will to get and the will to avoid . . . and to dismiss those things that are beyond us?"[47]) And since "it is impossible that what happens should be other than it is,"[48] since man, in other words, is entirely powerless in the real world, he has been given the miraculous faculties of reason and will that permit him to reproduce the outside—complete but deprived of its reality—inside his mind, where he is undisputed lord and master. There he rules over himself and over the objects of his concern, for the will can be hindered only by itself. Everything that seems to be real, the world of appearances, actually needs my consent in order to be real *for me*. And this consent cannot be forced on me: if I withhold it, then the reality of the world disappears as though it were a mere apparition.

This faculty of turning away from the outside toward an invincible inside obviously needs "training" (*gymnazein*) and constant arguing, for not only does man live his ordinary life in the world as it is; but his inside itself, so long as he is alive, is located within some outside, a body that is not in his power but belongs to the "outside things." The constant question is whether your will is strong enough not merely to distract your attention from external, threatening things but to fasten your imagination on different "impressions" in the actual presence of pain and misfortune. To withhold consent, or bracket out reality, is by no means an exercise in sheer thinking; it has to prove itself in actual fact. "I must die. I must be imprisoned. I must suffer exile. But: must I die groaning? Must I whine as well? Can anyone hinder me from going into exile with a smile?" The master threatens to chain me: "What say you? Chain me? My leg you will chain—yes, but not my will—no, not even Zeus can conquer that."[49]

Epictetus gives many examples, which we do not need to enumerate here; they make tedious reading, like exercises in a schoolbook. The upshot is always the same. What bothers men is not what actually happens to them but their own "judgment" (*dogma*, in the sense of belief or opinion): "You will be harmed only when you think you are harmed. No one can harm you without your consent."[50] "For instance, what does it mean to be slandered? Stand by a stone and slander it: what effect will you produce?"[51] Be stonelike and you will be invulnerable. *Ataraxia*, invulnerability, is all you need in order to *feel* free once you have discovered that reality itself depends on your consent to recognize it as such.

Like almost all Stoics, Epictetus recognized that the body's vulnerability puts certain limits on this inner freedom. Unable to deny that it is not mere wishes or desires that make us unfree, but the "fetters attached to us in the shape of the body,"[52] they therefore had to prove that these fetters are not unbreakable. An answer to the question What restrains us from suicide? becomes a necessary topic of these writings. Epictetus, at any rate, seems to have quite clearly realized that this kind of unlimited inner freedom actually presupposes that "one must remember and hold fast to this, that *the door is open*."⁵³ For a philosophy of total world-alienation, there is much truth in the remarkable sentence with which Camus began his first book: "*Il n'y a qu'un problème philosophique vraiment sérieux: c'est le suicide*."⁵⁴

At first glance, this doctrine of invulnerability and apathy (*apatheia*)—how to shield yourself against reality, how to lose your ability to be affected by it, for better or worse, in joy or in sorrow—seems so obviously open to refutation that the enormous argumentative as well as emotional influence of Stoicism on some of the best minds of Western mankind seems well-nigh incomprehensible. In Augustine, we find such a refutation in its shortest and most plausible form. The Stoics, he says, have found the trick of how to pretend to be happy: "Since a man cannot get what he wants, he wants what he can get" ("*Ideo igitur id vult quod potest, quoniam quod vult non potest*").⁵⁵ Moreover, he goes on, the Stoics assume that "all men by nature wish to be happy" but they do not believe in immortality, at least not in bodily resurrection, that is, not in a future deathless *life*, and this is a contradiction in terms. For "if all men really will to be happy they must necessarily also will to be immortal. . . . In order to *live* happily you must first be alive" ("*Cum ergo beati esse omnes homines velint, si vere volunt, profecto et esse immortales volunt. . . . Ut enim homo beate vivat, oportet ut vivat*").⁵⁶ In other words, mortal men cannot be happy, and the Stoics' insistence on the fear of death as the main source of unhappiness testifies to this; the most they can achieve is to become "apathetic," to be unaffected by either life or death.

This refutation, however, so plausible on this level of argument, misses a number of rather important points. There is first the question of why a will should be necessary in order *not* to will, why it should not be possible simply to lose the faculty under the sway of the superior insights of right reasoning. After all, don't we all know how relatively easy it has always been to lose at least the habit, if not the faculty, of thinking? Nothing more is needed than to live in constant distraction and never leave the company of others. It may be argued that it is harder to break men of the habit of wanting what is beyond their power than of the habit of thinking, but for a sufficiently "trained" man, it ought not to be necessary to repeat the not-willing over and over—since the *mē thele,* the "do not will" where you cannot prevent, is at least as important to this schooling as the mere appeal to will power.

Closely connected with the foregoing, and even more puzzling, is the fact that Epictetus is by no means content with the will's power *not*-to-will. He does not just preach indifference to everything that is not within our power; he insistently demands that man will what happens anyhow. I have already cited the game parable in which the man whose sole concern is with the feeling-well of the self is admonished to wish "only that to happen which does happen, and only him to win who does win." In a different context Epictetus goes much farther and praises (unnamed) "philosophers" who said "that 'if the good man knew coming events beforehand he would help on nature, even if it meant working with disease, and death and maiming.' "[57] To be sure, in his argument he falls back on the old Stoic notion of *heimarmenē,* the doctrine of fate which holds that everything happens in harmony with the nature of the universe and that every particular thing, man or animal, plant or stone, has its task allotted to it by the whole and is justified by it. But not only is Epictetus very explicitly uninterested in any question relating to nature or the universe; but also nothing in the old doctrine indicates that man's will, totally ineffectual by definition, would be of avail in the "ordering of the universe." Epictetus is interested in what happens to him: "I will a thing and it does not happen; what is there more wretched than I? I will it not and it happens; what is more wretched than I?"[58] In short, in order "to live well" it is not enough to "ask *not* that events should happen as you will"; you must "let your will be that events should happen as they do."[59]

It is only when will power has reached this climactic point, where it can will what *is* and thus never be "at odds with outward things," that it can be said to be omnipotent. Underlying all the arguments for such omnipotence is the matter-of-course assumption that reality *for me* gets its realness from my consent; and underlying that assumption, guaranteeing its practical effectiveness, is the simple fact that I can commit suicide when I truly find life unbearable—"the door is always open." And here this solution does not imply, as it does, for instance, in Camus, a kind of cosmic rebellion against the human condition; to Epictetus, such a rebellion would be entirely pointless, since "it is impossible that what happens should be other than it is."[60] It is unthinkable because even an absolute negation depends on the sheer inexplicable thereness of all that is, including myself, and Epictetus nowhere demands an explanation or justification of the inexplicable. Hence, as Augustine will later argue,[61] those who believe they choose non-being when they commit suicide are in error; they choose a form of being that will come about one day anyhow and they choose peace, which of course is only a form of being.

The sole force that can hinder this basic, active consent given by the will is the will itself. Hence the criterion for right conduct is: "Will to be pleased, you with yourself" (*"theléson aresai autos seautó"*). And Epictetus adds: "Will to appear noble to the god" (*"theléson kalos phanēnai tō theō"*),[62] but the addendum is actually redundant, for Epictetus does not believe in a transcendent God but holds that the soul is godlike and that the god is "within you, you are a fragment of him."[63] The willing ego, it turns out, is no less split in two than the Socratic two-in-one of Plato's dialogue of thought. But, as we saw with Paul, the two in the willing ego are far from enjoying a friendly, harmonious intercourse with each other, although in Epictetus their frankly antagonistic relationship does not subject the self to the extremes of despair that we hear so much of in Paul's lamentation. Epictetus characterizes their relation as an ongoing "struggle" (*agōn*), an Olympic contest demanding an ever-attentive suspicion of myself by myself: "In one word, [the philosopher, who always looks to himself for benefit and harm] keeps watch and guard on himself *as his own* enemy [*hōs echthron heautou*], lying in wait for him."[64] We need only remind ourselves of Aristotle's insight ("all friendly feelings toward others are an extension of the friendly feelings a person has for himself") to gauge the distance the human mind has traveled since antiquity.

The philosopher's self, ruled by the willing ego that tells him that nothing can hinder or constrain it but the will itself, is engaged in a never-ending fight with the counter-will, engendered, precisely, by his own will. The price paid for the Will's omnipotence is very high; the worst that, from the viewpoint of the thinking ego, could happen to the two-in-one, namely, to be "at variance with yourself," has become part and parcel of the human condition. And the fact that this fate is no longer assigned to Aristotle's "base man" but, on the contrary, to the good and wise man who has learned the art of conducting his own life in no matter what external circumstances may well cause one to wonder whether this "cure" of human misery was not worse than the disease.

Still, in this lamentable business there is one decisive discovery that no argument can eliminate and that at least explains why the feeling of omnipotence as well as of human freedom could come out of the experiences of the willing ego. A point we touched on marginally in our discussion of Paul, namely, that all obedience presumes the power to disobey, is at the very center of Epictetus' considerations. There the heart of the matter is the Will's power to assent or dissent, say Yes or No insofar, at any rate, as I myself am concerned. This is why things that in their pure existence—i.e., "impressions" of outside things—depend only on me are also in my power; not only can I will to change the world (though the proposition is of doubtful interest to an individual subject totally alienated from the world in which it finds itself), I can also deny reality to anything and everything by virtue of an I-will-not. This power must have had something awful, truly overpowering, for the human mind, for there has never been a philosopher or theologian who, after having paid due attention to the implied No in every Yes, did not squarely turn around and demand an emphatic consent, advising man, as Seneca did in a sentence quoted with great approbation by Master Eckhart, "to accept all occurrences as though he himself had desired them and asked for them." To be sure, if in this universal agreement one sees no more than the willing ego's last and deepest resentment of its existential impotence in the world as it factually is, he will also see only another argument here for the illusionary character of the faculty, an ultimate confirmation of its being an "artificial concept." Man in that case would have been given a truly "monstrous" faculty (Augustine), compelled by its nature to demand a power it is able to exercise only in the illusion-ridden region of sheer phantasy—the inwardness of a mind that has successfully separated itself from all outward appearance in its relentless quest for absolute tranquillity. And as the last and ironic reward for so much effort, it will have obtained an uncomfortably intimate acquaintance with the "painful storehouse and treasure of evils," in the words of Democritus, or with the "abyss" which, according to Augustine, lies hidden "in the good heart and in the evil heart."[65]

## 10  *Augustine, the first philosopher of the Will*

> If it is due to Scripture that there is
> a philosophy which is Christian,
> it is due to the Greek tradition that
> Christianity possesses a philosophy.
> Etienne Gilson

Augustine, the first Christian philosopher and, one is tempted to add, the only philosopher the Romans ever had,[66] was also the first man of thought who turned to religion because of philosophical perplexities. Like many educated people of the time, he had been brought up as a Christian; yet what he himself eventually described as a conversion—the subject matter of his *Confessions*—was utterly different from the experience that changed the extremely zealous Pharisee Saul into Paul, the Christian Apostle and follower of Jesus of Nazareth.

In the *Confessions*, Augustine tells how his heart had first been set "on fire" by Cicero's *Hortensius,* a book (now lost) that contained an exhortation to philosophy. Augustine kept quoting from it till the end of his life. He became the first Christian philosopher because throughout his life he held fast to philosophy. His treatise *On the Trinity,* a defense of the crucial dogma of the Christian Church, is at the same time the most profound and the most articulated development of his own very original philosophical position. But its starting-point remained the Roman and Stoic quest for happiness—"Certain it is, said Cicero, that we all want to be happy."[67] In his youth he had turned to philosophy out of inner wretchedness and as a man he turned to religion because philosophy had failed him. This pragmatic attitude, the demand that philosophy be "life's leader" (Cicero),[68] is typically Roman; it had a more lasting influence on the formation of Augustine's thought than did Plotinus and the Neoplatonists, to whom he owed whatever he knew of Greek philosophy. Not that the general human wish to be happy had escaped the attention of the Greeks —the Roman proverb seems to have been a translation from the Greek—but this desire was not what made them do philosophy. Only the Romans were convinced that "there is no reason for man to philosophize unless in order to be happy."[69]

We find this pragmatic concern for private happiness throughout the Middle Ages; it underlies the hope for eternal salvation and the fear of eternal damnation and clarifies many otherwise rather abstruse speculations whose Roman origins are difficult to detect. That the Roman Catholic Church, despite the decisive influx of Greek philosophy, remained so profoundly Roman was due in no small measure to the strange coincidence that her first and most influential philosopher should also have been the first man of thought to draw his deepest inspiration from Latin sources and experiences. In Augustine, the striving for eternal life as the *summum bonum* and the interpretation of eternal death as the *summum malum* reached the highest level of articulation because he combined them with the new era's discovery of an *inward* life. He understood that the exclusive interest in this inner self meant that "I have become a question for myself" (*"quaestio mihi factus sum"*)—a question that philosophy as it was then taught and learned neither raised nor answered.[70] The famous analyses of the concept of Time in the eleventh book of the *Confessions* are a paradigmatic illustration of the challenge of the new and problematic: time is something utterly familiar and ordinary so long as no one asks What is Time?—at which moment it turns into an "intricate riddle" whose challenge is that it is both entirely ordinary and entirely "hidden."[71]

There is no doubt that Augustine belongs among the great and original thinkers, but he was not a "systematic thinker," and it is true that the main body of his work is "littered with lines of thought that are not worked through to their conclusion and with abandoned literary enterprises"[72]—besides being shot through with repetitions. What is remarkable under the cirmcumstances is the continuity of the chief topics that finally, at the end of his life, he subjected to a searching examination titled *Retractationes,* or "Recantations," as though the Bishop and Prince of the Church were his own Inquisitor. Perhaps the most crucial of these ever-recurring topics was the "Free Choice of the Will" (the *Liberum arbitrium voluntatis*), as a faculty distinct from desire and reason, although he devoted but one whole treatise to it under that title. This was an early work, whose first part is still entirely in the vein of his other early philosophical writings despite its having been written after the dramatic event of his conversion and baptism.

It rather speaks, I think, for the quality of the man and the thinker that it took him ten years to write down in minute detail what to him was the most momentous event of his life—and this not just for remembrance's or piety's sake but for the sake of its mental implications. As his most recent biographer, Peter Brown, puts it a bit simplistically, "he was very definitely not a *type croyant,* such as had been common among educated men in the Latin world before his time";[73] for Augustine, it was not a matter of abandoning the uncertainties of philosophy in favor of revealed Truth but of finding the philosophical implications of his new faith. In that tremendous effort he relied first of all on the Letters of the Apostle Paul, and the measure of his success can perhaps best be gauged by the fact that his authority throughout the subsequent centuries of Christian philosophy became equal to that of Aristotle—for the Middle Ages "the philosopher."

Let us start with Augustine's early interest in the faculty of the Will as expounded in the first part of the early treatise (the two concluding parts were written almost ten years later,

roughly at the same time as the *Confessions*). Its leading
question is an inquiry into the cause of evil: "for evil could not
have come into being without a cause" and God cannot be the
cause of evil because "God is good." The question, current
even then, had "disturbed [him] exceedingly since his youth
. . . and indeed driven [him] into heresy," namely, into adhering to the teachings of Mani.[74] What follows is strictly
argumentative reasoning (though in dialogue form) as we found
it in Epictetus, and the telling points at this late time sound
like a summing up for educational purposes until we reach
the conclusion, where the disciple is made to say: "I question
whether free will . . . ought to have been given to us by Him
who made us. For it seems that we would not have been able
to sin, if we did not have free will. And it is to be feared that
in this way God may appear to be the cause of our evil deeds."
At this point Augustine reassures the questioner and post-
pones the discussion.[75] Thirty years later, in a different way,
in the *City of God,* he takes up the question of the "purpose of
the Will" as the "purpose of Man."

The question whose answer he postponed for so many
years is the starting-point for Augustine's own philosophy of
the Will. But a close interpretation of Paul's Letter to the Romans was the original occasion of his framing it. In the *Confessions,* as well as in the last two sections of *On Free Choice
of the Will,* he draws the philosophical inferences and articu-
lates the consequences of the strange phenomenon (that it is
possible to will and, in the absence of any outside hindrance,
still be unable to perform) which Paul had described in terms
of antagonistic laws. But Augustine does not speak of two
laws but of "*two wills,* one new and the other old, one carnal
and the other spiritual," and describes in detail, like Paul, how
these wills struggled "within" him and how their "discord
undid [his] soul."[76] In other words, he is careful to avoid his
own earlier Manichaean heresy, which taught that two antagonistic principles rule the world, one good and one evil, one
carnal and one spiritual. For him now, there is only one law,
and the first insight therefore is the most obvious but also the
most startling one: "*Non hoc est velle quod posse,*" "to will
and to be able are not the same."[77]

It is startling because the two faculties, willing and per-forming, are so closely connected: "Will must be present for power to be operative"; and power, needless to say, must be present for the will to draw on. "If you act . . . it can never be without willing" even if "you do a thing unwillingly, under compulsion." "When you do not act" it may be that "will is lacking" or that "the power is lacking."[78] This is all the more surprising as Augustine agrees with the Stoics' main argument for the predominance of the Will, namely, that "nothing is so much in our power as the will itself, for there is no interval, the moment we will—there it is,"[79] except that he does not believe that the Will is enough. "The law would not command if there were no will, nor would grace help if will were enough." The point here is that the Law does not address itself to the mind, in which case it would simply reveal and not command; it addresses itself to the Will because "the mind is not moved until it wills to be moved." And this is why only the Will, and neither reason nor the appetites and desires, is "in our power; it is free."[80]

This proof of the freedom of the Will draws exclusively on an inner power of affirmation or negation that has nothing to do with any actual *posse* or *potestas*—the faculty needed to perform the Will's commands. The proof obtains its plausibility from a comparison of willing with reason, on the one hand, and with the desires, on the other, neither of which can be said to be free. (We saw that Aristotle introduced his *proairesis* to avoid the dilemma of saying either that the "good man" *forces* himself away from his appetites or that the "base man" *forces* himself away from his reason.) Whatever reason tells me is compelling as far as reason is concerned. I may be able to say "No" to a truth disclosed to me, but I cannot possibly do this on rational grounds. The appetites rise in my body automatically, and my desires are aroused by objects outside myself; I may say "No" to them on the advice given by reason or the law of God, but reason itself does not move me to resistance. (Duns Scotus, very much influenced by Augustine, later elaborates on the argument. To be sure, carnal man, in the sense Paul understood him, cannot be free; but spiritual man is not free either. Whatever power the intellect may have over the mind is a necessitating power; what the intellect can never prove to the mind is that it should not merely subject itself to it but also will to do so.[81])

The faculty of Choice, so decisive for the *liberum arbitrium,* here applies not to the deliberative selection of means toward an end but primarily—and, in Augustine, exclusively—to the choice between *velle* and *nolle,* between willing and nilling. This *nolle* has nothing to do with the will-not-to-will, and it cannot be translated as I-will-not because this suggests an absence of will. *Nolle* is no less actively transitive than *velle,* no less a faculty of will: if I will what I do not desire, I nill my desires; and in the same way I can nill what reason tells me is right. In every act of the will, there is an I-will *and I-nill* involved. These are the two wills whose "discord" Augustine said "undid [his] soul." To be sure, "he who wills, wills something," and this something is presented to him "either from without through the body's senses or comes into the mind in hidden ways," but the point is that none of these objects determine the will.[82]

What is it then that causes the will to will? What sets the will in motion? The question is inevitable, but the answer turns out to lead into an infinite regress. For if the question were to be answered, "will you not inquire again for the cause of that cause if you find it?" Will you not wish to know "the cause of the will prior to the will"? Could it not be inherent in the Will to have no cause in this sense? "For either the will is its own cause or it is not a will."[83] The Will is a fact which in its sheer contingent factuality cannot be explained in terms of causality. Or—to anticipate a late suggestion of Heidegger's—since the will experiences itself as *causing* things to happen which otherwise would not have happened, could it not be that it is neither the intellect nor our thirst for knowledge (which could be stilled by straightforward information), but precisely the will that lurks behind our quest for causes—as though behind every Why there existed a latent wish not just to learn and to know but to learn the know-how?

Finally, still tracing the difficulties that are described but not explained in the Letter to the Romans, Augustine comes to interpret the scandalous side of Paul's doctrine of grace: "Law came in to increase the trespass; but where sin increased, grace abounded all the more." From that it is indeed difficult not to conclude: "Let us do evil that good may come." Or, to put it more mildly, that it is worthwhile to have been incapable of doing good because of the overwhelming joy of grace—as Augustine himself once said.[84] His answer in the *Confessions* points to the strange ways of the soul even in default of any specifically religious experiences. The soul is "more delighted at finding or recovering the things it loves, than if it had always had them. . . . The victorious commander triumphs . . . and the greater the peril in battle, the greater joy in triumph. . . . A friend is sick . . . he is restored, and though he walks not with his former strength, there is such joy, as there had not been when he was able to walk strongly and soundly." And so it is with all things; human life is "full of witnesses" to it. "The greatest joy is ushered in by the greatest painfulness"—this is the "allotted mode of being" of all living things, from "the angel to the worm." Even God, since He is a living god, "doth joy more over one sinner that repenteth than over ninety and nine persons that need no repentance."[85] This mode of being (*modus*) is equally valid for base and for noble things, for mortal things and things divine.

This is certainly the quintessence of what Paul had to say, but expressed in a non-descriptive, conceptual way: without appealing to any purely theological interpretation, it effaces the edge of Paul's lamentations and latent accusations, from which only the *argumentum ad hominem*, the Job-like question "Who are *you* to ask such questions and to raise such objections?" could save him.

In Augustine's refutation of Stoicism, we can see a similar transformation and solidification brought about by means of conceptual thought. What was actually scandalous in that doctrine was not that man could will to say "No" to reality but that this No was not enough; in order to find tranquillity, man was told, he had to train his will to say "Yes" and to "let your will be that events should happen as they do." Augustine understands that this willed submissiveness presupposes a severe limitation of the willing capacity itself. Although in his view every *velle* is accompanied by a *nolle*, the freedom of the faculty is limited because no created being can will against creation, for this would be—even in the case of suicide—a will directed not only against a counter-will but against the very existence of the willing or nilling subject. The will, the faculty of a living being, cannot say "I'd rather not *be*," or "I would prefer nothingness as such." Anybody who says "I'd rather not exist than be unhappy" cannot be trusted, since while he is saying it he is still alive.

Yet this may be so only because being alive always implies a wish to go on being; therefore most people prefer "to be unhappy than to be nothing at all." But what about those who say "If I had been consulted before I existed, I'd have preferred not to exist rather than be unhappy"? They have not considered that even this proposition is stated on the firm ground of Being; if they would consider the matter properly, they would find that their very unhappiness makes them, as it were, exist less than they wish; it takes some existence from them. "The degree of their unhappiness is commensurate with the distance from that which *is* in the highest degree [*quod summe est*]" and therefore outside the temporal order, which is shot through with non-existence—"for temporal things have no existence before they exist; while they exist, they are passing away; once they have passed away, they will never exist again." All men fear death, and this feeling is "truer" than any opinion that may lead you "to think that you ought to will not to exist," for the fact is that "beginning to exist is the same as proceeding toward non-existence." In short, "all things by the very fact that they *are* are good," evil and sin included; and this not only because of their divine origin and because of a belief in a Creator-God, but also because your own existence prevents you from either thinking or willing absolute non-existence. In this context it should be noted that Augustine (although most of what I have been quoting is drawn from the last part of his *De libero arbitrio voluntatis*) nowhere demands, as Eckhart later does, that "A good man ought to conform his will to the divine will, so that he will what God wills: hence, if God has willed me to sin, I should not will not to have committed my sin; this is my true repentance."[86]

What Augustine infers from this theory of Being is not Will but Praise: "Give thanks that you are"; "praise all things for the very fact that they are." Avoid saying not only " 'It would be better if [sinners] had not existed,' but also 'They ought to have been made differently.' " And the same is true for everything, since "all things have been created in their proper order," and if you "dare to find fault with a desert," do so only because you can compare it "with what is better." It is "as if a man who grasped by his reason perfect roundness became disgusted" because he could not find it in nature. He should be grateful for having the idea of roundness.[87]

In the previous volume, I spoke of the ancient Greek notion that all appearances, inasmuch as they *appear*, not only imply the presence of sentient creatures capable of perceiving them but also demand recognition and *praise*. This notion was a kind of philosophical justification of poetry and the arts; world-alienation, which preceded the rise of Stoic and Christian thought, succeeded in obliterating it from our tradition of philosophy—though never entirely from the reflections of poets. (You can still find it, very emphatically expressed, in W. H. Auden—who speaks of "That singular command / I do not understand, / *Bless what there is for being,* / Which has to be obeyed, for / What else am I made for, / Agreeing or disagreeing?"[88]—in the Russian poet Osip Mandelstam, and, of course, in the poetry of Rainer Maria Rilke.) Where we find it in a strictly Christian context, it already has an uncomfortably argumentative flavor, as though it were simply a necessary inference from the unquestioned faith in a Creator-God, as though Christians were duty-bound to repeat God's words after the Creation—"And God saw everything . . . and . . . it was very good." In any event, Augustine's observations on the impossibility of nilling absolutely because you cannot nill your own existence while you are nilling—hence cannot nill absolutely even by committing suicide—are an effective refutation of the mental tricks Stoic philosophers had recommended to enable men to withdraw from the world while still living in it.

. . . . . .

We return to the question of the Will in the *Confessions*, which are almost entirely non-argumentative and rich in what we today would call "phenomenological" descriptions. For although Augustine starts by conceptualizing Paul's position, he goes far beyond that, also far beyond his own first conceptual conclusions—that "to will and to be able to perform are not the same," that "the law would not command if there were no will, nor would grace help if will were enough," that it is our mind's allotted mode of being to perceive only through the succession of opposites, of day becoming night and night becoming day, and we learn about justice only by experiencing injustice, about courage only through cowardice, and so on. Reflecting on what had actually happened during the "hot contention wherein he had engaged with himself" before his conversion, he discovered that Paul's interpretation of a struggle between flesh and spirit was wrong. For "more easily did my body obey the weakest willing of my soul, in moving its limbs at its nod, than my soul had obeyed itself in carrying out this great will that could be done in the will alone."[89] Hence the trouble was not the dual nature of man, half carnal and half spiritual; it was to be found in the faculty of the Will itself.

"Whence is this monstrosity? and why is it? . . . The mind commands the body, and is obeyed instantly; the mind commands itself and is resisted?" (*"Unde hoc monstrum, et quare istud? Imperat animus corpori, et paretur statim; imperat animus sibi et resistitur?"*) The body has no will of its own and is obedient to the mind although that is different from the body. But the moment "the mind commands the mind to will, and the mind is not something different, yet it does not [will]. Whence is this monstrosity and why? I say it commands that itself would will a thing, and would not give that command unless it willed, and it does not that which is commanded." Perhaps, he continues, this can be explained by a weakness in the will, a lack of commitment: The mind perhaps "willeth not entirely, and therefore does not command entirely . . . and therefore what it commands *is* not." But who does the commanding here, the mind or the will? Does the mind (*animus*) command the will, and does it hesitate, so that the will does not receive an unequivocal command? The answer is no, for it is "the will [that] commandeth that there be a will, not another will [as would be the case if the *mind* were divided between conflicting wills], but the same will itself."[90]

The split occurs in the will itself; the conflict arises neither out of a split between mind and will nor out of a split between flesh and mind. This is attested by the very fact that the Will always speaks in imperatives: "Thou shalt will," says the Will to itself. Only the Will itself has the power to issue such commands, and "if the will were 'entire,' it would not command itself to be." It is in the Will's nature to double itself, and in this sense, wherever there is a will, there are always "two wills neither of which is entire [*tota*], and what is present to one of them is absent from the other." For this reason you always need two antagonistic wills to will at all; it is "not monstrous therefore partly to will and partly to nill" (*"Et ideo sunt duae voluntates, quia una earum tota non est. . . . Non igitur monstrum partim velle, partim nolle"*). The trouble is that it is the same willing ego that simultaneously wills and nills: "It was I who willed, I who nilled, I, I myself; I neither willed totally nor nilled entirely"—and this does not mean that I was of "two minds, one good, the other evil," but that the uproar of two wills in one and the same mind "rent me asunder."[91]

The Manicheans explained the conflict by the assumption of two contrary natures, one good and the other evil. But "if there were as many contrary natures as there are wills that resist themselves, there would not be two natures only but many." For we find the same conflict of wills where no choice between good and evil is at stake, where both wills must be called evil or both good. Whenever a man tries to come to a decision in such matters, "you find one soul fluctuating between various wills." Suppose somebody tries to make up his mind between "going to the circus or the theatre, if both be open the same day; or, thirdly, to rob another's house . . . or, fourthly, to commit adultery . . . all these meeting together in the same junction of time, and all being equally desired, which cannot at one time be acted." Here we have four wills, all bad and all conflicting with each other and "rending" the willing ego. And the same is true for "wills that are good."[92]

Augustine does not say here how these conflicts are resolved except that he admits that at a certain moment a goal is chosen "whither the one entire will may be borne which before was divided into many." But the healing of the will, and this is decisive, does not come about through divine grace. At the end of the *Confessions* he returns once more to the problem and relying on certain very different considerations that are explicitly argued in the treatise *On the Trinity* (which he was to spend fifteen years writing, from 400 to 416), he diagnoses the ultimate unifying will that eventually decides a man's conduct as *Love*.

Love is the "weight of the soul," its law of gravitation, that which brings the soul's movement to its rest. Somewhat influenced by Aristotelian physics, he holds that the end of all movement is rest, and now he understands the emotions—the motions of the soul—in analogy to the movements of the physical world. For "nothing else do bodies desire by their weight than what souls desire by their love." Hence, in the *Confessions:* "My weight is my love; by it I am borne whithersoever I am borne."[93] The soul's gravity, the essence of who somebody is, and which as such is inscrutable to human eyes, becomes manifest in this love.

Let us retain the following. First: The split within the Will is a conflict, and not a dialogue, and it is independent of the content that is willed. A bad will is no less split than a good one and vice versa. Second: The will as the commander of the body is no more than an executive organ of the mind and as such quite unproblematic. The body obeys the mind because it is possessed of no organ that would make disobedience possible. The will, addressing itself to itself, arouses the counter-will because the exchange is entirely mental; a contest is possible only between equals. A will that would be "entire," without a counter-will, could no longer be a will properly speaking. Third: Since it is in the nature of the will to command and demand obedience, it is also in the nature of the will to be resisted. Finally: Within the framework of the *Confessions,* no solution to the riddle of this "monstrous" faculty is given; how the will, divided against itself, finally reaches the moment when it becomes "entire" remains a mystery. If this is the way the will functions, how does it ever arrive at moving me to act—to prefer, for instance, robbery to adultery? For Augustine's "fluctuations of the soul" between many equally desirable ends are quite unlike Aristotle's deliberations, which concern not ends but means to an end that is given by human nature. No such ultimate arbiter appears in Augustine's main analyses except at the very end of the *Confessions,* when he suddenly begins to speak of the Will as a kind of Love, "the weight of our soul," but without giving any account of this strange equation.

Some such solution is evidently required, since we know that these conflicts of the willing ego are finally resolved. Actually, as I shall show later, what looks like a *deus ex machina* in the *Confessions* is derived from a different theory of the Will. But before we turn to *On the Trinity,* it may be useful to stop to see how the same problem is treated in terms of consciousness by a modern thinker.

John Stuart Mill, examining the question of free will, suggests that "the confusion of ideas" current in this philosophical area "must . . . be very natural to the human mind," and he describes—less vividly and also less precisely but in words strangely similar to those we have just been hearing—the conflicts the willing ego is subject to. It is wrong, he insists, to describe them as "taking place between me and some foreign power, which I conquer or by which I am overcome. [For] it is obvious that 'I' am both parties in the contest; the conflict is between me and myself. . . . What causes Me, or, if you please, my Will, to be identified with one side rather than with the other, is that one of the Me's represents a more *permanent* state of my feelings than the other does."

Mill needed this "permanence" because he "disputed altogether that we are conscious of being able to act in opposition to the strongest desire or aversion"; he therefore had to explain the phenomenon of regret. What he then discovered was that "after the temptation has been yielded to [that is, the strongest desire at the moment], the desiring 'I' will come to an end, but the conscience-stricken 'I' may *endure* to the end of life." Though this enduring, conscience-stricken "I" plays no role in Mill's later considerations, here it suggests the intervention of something, called "conscience" or "character," that survives all single, temporally limited, volitions or desires. According to Mill, the "enduring I," which manifests itself only after volition has come to its end, should be similar to whatever prevented Buridan's ass from starving between two equally nice-smelling hay bundles: "From mere lassitude . . . combined with the sensation of hunger" the animal "would cease thinking of the rival objects at all." But this Mill could hardly admit, as the "enduring I" is of course one of the "parties in the contest," and when he says "the object of moral education is to educate the will," he is assuming that it is possible to teach one of the parties to win. Education enters here as a *deus ex machina:* Mill's proposition rests on an unexamined assumption—such as moral philosophers often adopt with great confidence and which actually can be neither proved nor disproved.[94]

That strange confidence cannot be expected from Augustine; it arose much later in order to neutralize, at least in the sphere of ethics and, as it were, by fiat the universal doubt that characterizes the modern age—which Nietzsche, rightly, I think, called the "era of suspicion." When men could no longer *praise,* they turned their greatest conceptual efforts to *justifying* God and His Creation in theodicies. But of course Augustine, too, needed some means of redemption for the Will. Divine grace would not help once he had discovered that the brokenness of the Will was the same for the evil and for the good will; it is rather difficult to imagine God's gratuitous grace deciding whether I should go to the theater or commit adultery. Augustine finds his solution in an entirely new approach to the problem. He now undertakes to investigate the Will not in isolation from other mental faculties but in its interconnectedness with them; the leading question now is: What function has the will in the life of the mind as a whole? Yet the phenomenal datum that suggested the answer even before it was found and duly outlined is curiously like Mill's "enduring I." In Augustine's words, it is "that there is One within me who is more myself than my self."[95]

The dominant insight of the treatise *On the Trinity* is derived from the mystery of the Christian trinity. Father, Son, and Holy Ghost, three substances when each is related to itself, can at the same time form a One, thus insuring that the dogma does not signify a break with monotheism. The unity comes about because all three substances are "mutually predicated relatively" to each other without thereby losing their existence "in their own substance." (This is not the case, for instance, when color and the colored object are "mutually predicated" in their relation to each other, for color has "not any proper substance in itself, since colored body is a substance but color is *in* a substance."[96])

The paradigm for a mutually predicated relationship of independent "substances" is *friendship:* two men who are friends can be said to be "independent substances" insofar as they are related to themselves; they are friends only relatively to each other. A pair of friends forms a unity, a One, insofar and as long as they are friends; the moment the friendship ceases they are again two "substances," independent of each other. This demonstrates that somebody or something can be a One when related only to itself and still be so related to another, so intimately *bound* together with it, that the two can appear as a One without changing their "substance," losing their substantial independence and identity. This is the way of the Holy Trinity: God remains One while related only to Himself but He is three in the unity with Son and Holy Ghost.

The point here is that such a mutually predicated relationship can occur only among "equals"; hence one cannot apply it to the relationship of body and soul, of carnal man and spiritual man, even though they always appear together, because here the soul is obviously the ruling principle. However, for Augustine the mysterious three-in-one must be found somewhere in human nature since God created man in His own image; and since it is precisely man's mind that distinguishes him from all other creatures, the three-in-one is likely to be found in the structure of the mind.

We find the first inklings of this new line of investigation at the end of the *Confessions,* the work that most closely precedes *On the Trinity.* There for the first time it occurs to him to use the theological dogma of the three-in-one as a general philosophical principle. He asks the reader to "consider these three things that are in themselves . . . [and] are far other than the Trinity . . . the three things I speak of are, to Be, to Know, and to Will. [The three are interconnected.] For I Am, and I Know, and I Will; I Am Knowing and Willing; and I know myself to Be and to Will; and I Will to Be and to Know. In these three let him discern who can, how inseparable is one life, one mind, one essence; finally, how inseparable a distinction there is, and yet there is a distinction."[97] The analogy of course does not mean that Being is an analogy of the Father, Knowing an analogy of the Son, and Willing of the Holy Ghost. What interests Augustine is merely that the mental "I" contains three altogether different things that are inseparable and yet distinct.

This triad of Being, Willing, and Knowing occurs only in the rather tentative formula of the *Confessions:* obviously Being does not belong here, since it is not a faculty of the mind. In *On the Trinity,* the most important mental triad is Memory, Intellect, and Will. These three faculties are "not three minds but one mind. . . . They are mutually referred to each other . . . and each one is comprehended by" the other two and relates back to itself: "I remember that I have memory, understanding, and will; and I understand that I understand, will, and remember; and I will that I will, remember, and understand."[98] These three faculties are equal in rank, but their Oneness is due to the Will.

The Will tells the memory what to retain and what to forget; it tells the intellect what to choose for its understanding. Memory and Intellect are both contemplative and, as such, passive; it is the Will that makes them function and eventually "binds them together." And only when by virtue of one of them, namely, the Will, the three are "forced into one do we speak of *thought"—cogitatio,* which Augustine, playing with etymology, derives from *cogere (coactum),* to force together, to unite forcefully. *("Atque ita fit illa trinitas ex memoria, et interna visione, et quae utrumque copulat voluntate. Quia tria [in unum] coguntur, ab ipso coactu cogitatio dicitur."*[99])

The Will's binding force functions not only in purely mental activity; it is manifest also in sense perception. This element of the mind is what makes sensation meaningful: In every act of vision, says Augustine, we must "distinguish the following three things . . . the object which we see . . . and this can naturally exist before it is seen; secondly, the vision which was not there before we perceived the object . . . and thirdly the power that fixes the sense of sight on the object . . . namely, the attention of the mind." Without the latter, a function of the Will, we have only sensory "impressions" without any actual perceiving of them; an object is *seen* only when we concentrate our mind on the perception. We can see without perceiving, and hear without listening, as frequently happens when we are absent-minded. The "attention of the mind" is needed to transform sensation into perception; the Will that "fixes the sense on that thing which we see and binds both together" is essentially different from the seeing eye and the visible object; it is mind and not body.[100]

Moreover, by fixing our mind on what we see or hear, we tell our memory what to remember and our intellect what to understand, what objects to go after in search of knowledge. Memory and intellect have withdrawn from outside appearances and deal not with these themselves (the real tree) but with images (the seen tree), and these images clearly are inside us. In other words, the Will, by virtue of *attention,* first unites our sense organs with the real world in a meaningful way, and then drags, as it were, this outside world into ourselves and prepares it for further mental operations: to be remembered, to be understood, to be asserted or denied. For the inner images are by no means mere illusions. "Concentrating exclusively on the inner phantasies and turning the mind's eye completely away from the bodies which surround our senses," we come "upon so striking a likeness of the bodily species expressed from memory" that it is hard to tell whether we are seeing or merely imagining. "So great is the power of the mind over its body" that sheer imagination "can arouse the genital organs."[101] And this *power* of the mind is due not to the Intellect and not to Memory but only to the Will that unites the mind's inwardness with the outward world. Man's privileged position within the Creation, in the outward world, is due to the mind which "imagines within, yet imagines things that are from without. For no one could use these things [of the outward world] . . . unless the images of sensible things were retained in the memory, and unless . . . the same will [were] adapted both to bodies without and to their images within."[102]

This Will as the unifying force binding man's sensory apparatus to the outside world and then joining together man's different mental faculties has two characteristics that were entirely absent from the various descriptions we have had of the Will up to now. This Will could indeed be understood as "the spring of action"; by directing the senses' attention, presiding over the images impressed on memory, and providing the intellect with material for understanding, the Will prepares the ground on which action can take place. This Will, one is tempted to say, is so busy preparing action that it hardly has time to get caught in the controversy with its own counter-will. "And just as in man and woman there is one flesh of two, so the one nature of the mind [the Will] embraces our intellect and action, or our council and execution . . . so as it was said of those: 'They shall be two in one flesh,' so it can be said of these [the inward and the outward man]: 'Two in one mind.' "[103]

Here is a first intimation of certain consequences that Duns Scotus much later will draw from Augustinian voluntarism: the Will's redemption cannot be mental and does not come by divine intervention either; redemption comes from the act which—often like a *"coup d'état,"* in Bergson's felicitous phrase—interrupts the conflict between *velle* and *nolle*. And the price of the redemption is, as we shall see, *freedom*. As Duns Scotus expressed it (in the summary of a modern commentator), "It is possible for me to be writing at this moment, just as it is possible for me not to be writing." I am still entirely free, and I pay for this freedom by the curious fact that the Will always wills and nills at the same time: the mental activity in its case does not exclude its opposite. "Yet my *act* of writing excludes its opposite. By one act of the will I can determine myself to write, and by another I can decide not to write, but I cannot be simultaneously in act in regard to both things together."[104] In other words, the Will is redeemed by ceasing to will and starting to act, and the cessation cannot originate in an act of the will-not-to-will because this would be but another volition.

In Augustine, as well as later in Duns Scotus, the solution of the Will's inner conflict comes about through a transformation of the Will itself, its transformation into *Love*. The Will— seen in its functional operative aspect as a coupling, binding agent—can also be defined as Love (*voluntas: amor seu dilectio*[105]), for Love is obviously the most successful coupling agent. In Love, there are again "three things: he that loves, and that which is loved, and Love. . . . [Love] is a certain life which couples . . . together two things, namely, him that loves and that which is loved."[106] In the same way, Will qua attention was needed to effect perception by coupling together the one with eyes to see and that which is visible; it is only that the uniting force of love is stronger. For what love unites is "marvelously glued together" so that there is a cohesion between lover and the beloved—"*cohaerunt enim mirabiliter glutino amoris.*"[107] The great advantage of the transformation is not only Love's greater force in uniting what remains separate—when the Will uniting "the form of the body that is seen and its image which arises in the sense, that is, the vision . . . is so violent that [it keeps the sense *fixed* on the vision once it has been formed], it can be called love, or desire, or passion"[108]—but also that love, as distinguished from will and desire, is not extinguished when it reaches its goal but enables the mind "to remain *steadfast* in order to *enjoy*" it.

What the will is not able to accomplish is this steadfast enjoyment; will is given as a mental faculty because the mind "is not sufficient to itself" and "through its need and want, it becomes excessively intent upon its own actions."[109] The will decides how to *use* memory and intellect, that is, it "refers them to something else," but it does not know how "to use with the joy, not of hope, but of the actual thing."[110] That is the reason the will is never satisfied, for "satisfaction means that the will is at rest,"[111] and nothing—certainly not hope— can still the will's restlessness "save endurance," the quiet and lasting enjoyment of something present; only "the force of love is so great that the mind draws in with itself those things upon which it has long reflected with love."[112] The whole mind "is in those things upon which it thinks with love," and these are the things "without which it cannot think of itself."[113]

The emphasis here is on the mind *thinking* of itself, and the love that stills the will's turmoil and restlessness is not a love of tangible things but of the "footprints" "sensible things" have left on the inwardness of the mind. (Throughout the treatise, Augustine is careful to distinguish between thinking and knowing, or between wisdom and knowledge. "It is one thing not to know oneself, and another thing not to think of oneself."[114]) In the case of Love, the lasting "footprint" that the mind has transformed into an intelligible thing would be neither the one who loves nor his beloved but the third element, namely, Love itself, the love with which the lovers love each other.

The difficulty with such "intelligible things" is that although they are as "present to the gaze of the mind as . . . tangible things are present . . . to the senses of the body," a man "who arrives [at them] does not abide in them . . . and thus a transitory thought is formed of a thing that is not transitory. And this transitory thought is committed to the memory . . . so that there may be a place to which the thought may again return." (The example he gives of lastingness in the midst of human transience is drawn from music. It is as if "one were to grasp [a melody] passing through intervals of time while it stands apart from time in a kind of secret and sublime silence"; without memory to record the sequence of sounds, one could never even "conceive of the melody as long as that singing could be heard."[115]) What Love brings about is lastingness, a perdurance of which the mind otherwise seems incapable. Augustine has conceptualized Paul's words in the Letter to the Corinthians: "Love never ends"; of the three that "abide"—Faith, Hope, Love—"the greatest [the most durable, as it were] is love" (I Corinthians 13:8).

To summarize: this Will of Augustine's, which is not understood as a separate faculty but in its function within the mind as a whole, where all single faculties—memory, intellect, and will—are "mutually referred to each other,"[116] finds its redemption in being transformed into Love. Love as a kind of enduring and conflictless Will has an obvious resemblance to Mill's "enduring I," which finally prevails in the will's decisions. Augustine's Love exerts its influence through the "weight"—"the will resembles a weight"[117]—it adds to the soul, thus arresting its fluctuations. Men do not become just by knowing what is just but by loving justice. Love is the soul's gravity, or the other way round: "the specific gravity of bodies is, as it were, their love."[118] What is saved, moreover, in this transformation of his earlier conception is the Will's power of assertion and denial; there is no greater assertion of something or somebody than to love it, that is, to say: I will that you be—*Amo: Volo ut sis.*

Thus far, we have left to one side all strictly theological questions and with them the chief problem free will presents to all strictly Christian philosophy. In the first centuries after Christ, the existence of the universe could be explained as emanation, the outflow of divine and anti-divine forces, requiring no personal God behind it. Or, following the Hebrew tradition, it could be explained as creation having a divine person for its author. The divine author created the world of His own free will and out of nothingness. And He created man after His image, that is, endowed, too, with a free will. From then on, the theories of emanation corresponded to the fatalist or determinist theories of necessity; the creation theories had to deal theologically with the Free Will of God, Who decided to create the world, and to reconcile this Freedom with the freedom of the creature, man. Insofar as God is omnipotent (He can overrule man's will), and has foreknowledge, human freedom seems to be doubly canceled out. The standard argument, then, is: God only foreknows; He does not compel. You find the argument in Augustine, too, but at his best he proposes a very different line of thought.

Earlier, we took up the basic arguments put forward for determinism and fatalism because of their great importance to the mentality of the ancient world, especially Roman antiquity. And we saw, following Cicero, how this reasoning always ended in contradictions and paradoxes. You remember the so-called idle argument—When you were sick, whether you would recover or not recover was predestined, hence why have called a doctor; but whether you called a doctor or did not call him was also predetermined, and so on. In other words, all your faculties become *idle* once you think along these lines without cheating. The reasoning relies on antecedent causes; that is, it relies on the past. But what you actually are interested in is of course the future. You want the future to be predictable—"it was to be"—but the moment you start arguing along these lines, you are up against another paradox: "If I can foresee that I am going to be killed tomorrow in an airplane crash, then I will not get out of bed tomorrow. But then I will not be so killed. But then I will not have correctly foreseen the future."[119] The flaw in the two arguments, the one relating to the past, the other to the future, is the same: the first extrapolates the present into the past, the second extrapolates it into the future, and both assume that the extrapolator stands outside the sphere in which the real event takes place and that he, the outside observer, has no power at all to act—he himself is not a cause. In other words, since man is himself part and parcel of the temporal process, a being with a past and a special faculty for the past, called "memory," since he lives in the present and looks forward to the future, he cannot jump out of the temporal order.

I pointed out earlier that the argument of determinism receives its actual poignancy only if a Foreknower is introduced who stands outside the temporal order and looks on what is happening from the perspective of eternity. By introducing such a Foreknower, Augustine was able to arrive at the most dubious and also most terrible of his teachings, the doctrine of predestination. We are not interested here in this doctrine, a perverse radicalization of Paul's teaching that salvation lies not in works but in faith and is given by God's grace—so that not even faith is within man's power. You find it in one of the last treatises, *On Grace and Free Will*, written against the Pelagians, who, referring precisely to Augustine's earlier doctrines of the Will, had emphasized "the merits of the antecedent good will" for the reception of grace, which was given wholly gratuitously only in the forgiveness of sins.[120]

The philosophical arguments, not for predestination but for the possible co-existence of God's omniscience and man's free will, occur in a discussion of Plato's *Timaeus*. Human knowledge is of "various kinds"; men know

> in different ways things which as yet are not, things which are, and things which have been. [But] not in our fashion does He look forward to what is future, nor does He look at what is present nor look back at what is past, but in a manner far and profoundly different from the way of our thoughts. For He does not pass from this to that [following in thought what has changed from past to present to future], but he sees altogether unchangeably; so that all things which [for us] emerge temporally—the future which is not yet as well as the present that already is and the past which is no more— are comprehended by Him in a stable and sempiternal presence: nor does He see differently with the eyes of the body and differently with the mind, for He is not composed of mind and body: nor [does He see] in different fashion the now, the before, the later; for His knowledge, unlike ours, is not a knowledge of three different times, present, past, and future through whose variations our knowledge is affected. . . . Nor is there any intention that passes from thought to thought in Whose bodyless intuition all things which He knows are present together at once. For He knows all times with no temporal notions, just as He moves all temporal things with no temporal movements.[121]

In this context, one can no longer speak of God's *Fore*knowledge; for Him, past and future do not exist. Eternity, understood in human terms, is an everlasting present. "If the present were always present . . . it would no longer be time but eternity."[122]

I have quoted this argument at some length because if one can assume that there is a *person* for whom the temporal order does not exist, the co-existence of God's omniscience and man's free will ceases to be an insoluble problem. At the very least it can be approached as part of the problem of man's temporality, that is, in a consideration of all our faculties as related to time. This new view, explicated in the *City of God,* is prepared for in the famous eleventh book of the *Confessions,* to which we now briefly turn.

Regarded in temporal categories, "the present of things past is in memory, the present of things present is in a mental intuition [*contuitus*—a gaze that gathers things together and "pays attention" to them], and the present of things future is in expectation."[123] But these threefold presents of the mind do not in themselves constitute time; they constitute time only because they pass into each other "from the future through the present by which it passes to the past"; and the present is the least lasting of them, since it has no "space" of its own. Hence time passes "from that which does not yet exist, by that which has no space, into that which no longer exists."[124] Time, therefore, cannot possibly be constituted by "the movements of the heavenly bodies"; the movements of bodies are "in time" only insofar as they have a beginning and an end; and time that can be measured is in the mind itself, namely, "from the time I began to see until I cease to see." For "we measure in fact the interval from some beginning up to some kind of end," and this is possible only because the mind retains in its own present the expectation of that which is not yet, which it then "pays attention to and remembers when it passes through."

The mind performs this temporalizing action in each everyday act: "I am about to recite a psalm. . . . The life of this action of mine is distended into memory in respect to the part I have already recited and into expectation in respect to the part I am about to recite. Attention is present, through which what was future is conveyed over [*traiiciatur*], that it may become past." Attention, as we have seen, is one of the major functions of the Will, the great unifier, which here, in what Augustine calls the "distention of the mind," binds together the tenses of time into the mind's present. "Attention abides and through it what will be present proceeds to become something absent," namely, the past. And "the same holds for the whole of man's life," which without the mind's distention would never be a whole; "the same [also] for the whole era of the children of men, of which all the lives of men are parts," namely, insofar as this era can be recounted as a coherent continuous story.[125]

From the perspective, then, of the temporality of the human faculties, Augustine in the last of the great treatises, the *City of God*, returns once more to the problem of the Will.[126] He states the main difficulty: God, "though Himself eternal, and *without beginning*, caused time to have a beginning; and man, whom He had not made previously, He made in time."[127] The creation of the world and of time coincide—"the world was made *not* in time, but simultaneously with time"—not only because creation itself implies a beginning but also because living creatures were made before the making of man. "Where there is no creature whose changing movement admits of succession, there cannot be time at all . . . time being impossible without the creature."[128] But what, then, was God's purpose in creating man, asks Augustine; why did He "will to make him in time," him "whom He had never made before"? He calls this question "a depth indeed" and speaks of "the unsearchable depth of this purpose" of creating *"temporal man [hominem temporalem]* who has never before been," that is, a creature that does not just live "in time" but is essentially temporal, is, as it were, time's essence.[129]

To answer "this very difficult question of the eternal God creating new things," Augustine first finds it necessary to refute the philosophers' cyclical time concepts, inasmuch as novelty could not occur in cycles. He then gives a very surprising answer to the question of why it was necessary to create Man, apart from and above all other living things. In order, he says, that there may be novelty, a *beginning* must exist; "and this beginning never before existed," that is, not before Man's creation. Hence, that such a beginning "might be, man was created before whom nobody was" (*"quod initium eo modo antea nunquam fuit. Hoc ergo ut esset, creatus est homo, ante quem nullus fuit"*).[130] And Augustine distinguishes this from the beginning of the creation by using the word *"initium"* for the creation of Man but *"principium"* for the creation of the heaven and the earth.[131] As for the living creatures, made before Man, they were created "in numbers," as species beings, unlike Man, who was created in the singular and continued to be "propagated from individuals."[132]

It is Man's character of individuality that explains Augustine's saying that there was "nobody" before him, namely, nobody whom one could call a "person"; this individuality manifests itself in the Will. Augustine proposes the case of identical twins, both "of a like temperament of body and soul." How can we tell them apart? The only endowment by which they are distinguished from each other is their will—"if both are tempted equally and one yields and consents to the temptation while the other remains unmoved . . . what causes this but their own wills in cases . . . where the temperament is identical?"[133]

In other words, and somehow elaborating on these speculations: Man is put into a world of change and movement as a new beginning because he knows that he has a beginning and will have an end; he even knows that his beginning is the beginning of his end—"our whole life is nothing but a race toward death."[134] In this sense, no animal, no species being, has a beginning or an end. With man, created in God's own image, a being came into the world that, because it was a beginning running toward an end, could be endowed with the capacity of willing and nilling.

In this respect, he was the image of a Creator-God; but since he was temporal and not eternal, the capacity was entirely directed toward the future. (Wherever Augustine speaks of the three tenses, he stresses the primacy of the future—like Hegel, as we saw; the primacy of the Will among the mental faculties necessitates the primacy of the future in time speculations.) Every man, being created in the singular, is a new beginning by virtue of his birth; if Augustine had drawn the consequences of these speculations, he would have defined men, not, like the Greeks, as mortals, but as "natals," and he would have defined the freedom of the Will not as the *liberum arbitrium*, the free choice between willing and nilling, but as the freedom of which Kant speaks in the *Critique of Pure Reason.*

His "faculty of spontaneously beginning a series in time," which "occurring in the world can have only a relatively first beginning" and still is "an absolutely first beginning not in time but in causality" must once again be invoked here. "If, for instance, I at this moment arise from my chair in complete freedom . . . a new series, with all its natural consequences *in infinitum,* has its absolute beginning in this event."[135] The distinction between an "absolute" and a "relative" beginning points to the same phenomenon we find in Augustine's distinction between the *principium* of the Heaven and the Earth and the *initium* of Man. And had Kant known of Augustine's philosophy of natality he might have agreed that the freedom of a *relatively* absolute spontaneity is no more embarrassing to human reason than the fact that men are *born*—newcomers again and again in a world that preceded them in time. The freedom of spontaneity is part and parcel of the human condition. Its mental organ is the Will.

# Will and Intellect

III

## 11  Thomas Aquinas and the primacy of Intellect

More than forty years ago, Etienne Gilson, the great reviver of Christian philosophy, speaking at Aberdeen as the Gifford Lecturer, addressed himself to the magnificent revival of Greek thought in the thirteenth century; the result was a classical and, I think, lasting statement—*The Spirit of Medieval Philosophy*—on "the basic principle of all medieval speculation." He was referring to the *fides quaerens intellectum*, Anselm's "faith asking the intellect for help" and thereby making philosophy *ancilla theologiae*, the handmaid of faith. There was always the danger that the handmaid might become the "mistress," as Pope Gregory IX warned the University of Paris, anticipating Luther's fulminant attacks on this *stultitia*, this folly, by more than two hundred years. I mention Gilson's name, certainly not to invite comparisons—which would be fatal to myself—but, rather, out of a feeling of gratitude and also in order to explain why, in what follows, I shall avoid discussing matters that were dealt with long ago in such a masterly way and whose result is available—even in paperback.

Eight hundred years separate Thomas from Augustine, time enough not just to make a saint and Father of the Church out of the Bishop of Hippo but to confer on him an authority equal to that of Aristotle and almost equal to that of the Apostle Paul. In the Middle Ages such authority was of the utmost importance; nothing could be more damaging to a new doctrine than a frank avowal that it was new; never was what Gilson called "ipsedixitism" more dominant. Even when Thomas expressly disagrees with an opinion, he needs an authoritative quote to establish the doctrine against which he will then argue. To be sure, this had something to do with the absolute authority of God's word, recorded in books, the Old and the New Testament, but the point here is that almost *every* author that was known—Christian, Jewish, Moslem—was quoted as an "authority," either for the truth or for some important untruth.

In other words, when we study these medieval works we must remember that their authors lived in monasteries—without which such a thing as a "history of ideas" in the Western world would not exist—and that means that these writings came out of a world of books. But Augustine's reflections, by contrast, had been intimately connected with his experiences; it was important to him to describe them in detail, and even when he treated such speculative matters as the origin of evil (in the early dialogue *On Free Choice of the Will*), it scarcely occurred to him to quote the opinions of a host of erudite and worthy men on the subject.

The Scholastic authors use experience only to give an example supporting their argument; experience itself does not inspire the argument. What actually arises from the examples is a curious kind of casuistry, a technique of bringing general principles to bear on particular cases. The last author still to write clearly of the perplexities of his mind or soul, entirely undisturbed by bookish concerns, was Anselm of Canterbury, and that was two hundred years before Thomas. This, of course, is not to say that the Scholastic authors were unconcerned with the actual issues and merely inspired by arguments, but to say that we are now entering an "age of commentators" (Gilson), whose thoughts were always guided by some written authority, and it would be a grave error to believe that this authority was necessarily or even primarily ecclesiastical or scriptural. Yet Gilson, whose mentality was so admirably attuned to the requirements of his great subject, and who recognized that "it is due to scripture that there is a philosophy which is Christian, [as] it is due to the Greek tradition that Christianity possesses a philosophy," could seriously suggest that the reason Plato and Aristotle failed to penetrate to the ultimate truth was to be found in the unfortunate fact that they had not "the advantage of reading the first lines of Genesis . . . had they done so the whole history of philosophy might have been different."[1]

Thomas' great unfinished masterwork, the *Summa Theo-*

*logica,* was originally intended for pedagogical purposes, as a textbook for the new universities. It enumerates in a strictly systematic manner all possible questions, all possible arguments, and presumes to give final answers to each of them. No later system I know of can rival this codification of presumably established truths, the *sum* of coherent knowledge. Every philosophical system aims at offering the restless mind a kind of mental habitat, a secure home, but none has ever succeeded so well, and none, I think, was so free of contradictions. Anyone willing to make the considerable mental effort to enter that home was rewarded by the assurance that in its many mansions he would never find himself perplexed or estranged.

To read Thomas is to learn how such domiciles are built. First, the Questions are raised in the most abstract but non-speculative manner; then, the points of inquiry for each question are sorted out, followed by the Objections that can be made to every possible answer; whereupon an "On the contrary" introduces the opposite position; only when this whole ground has been laid does Thomas' own answer follow, complete with specific replies to the Objections. This schematic order never alters, and the reader patient enough to follow the sequence of question upon question, answer upon answer, taking account of each objection and each contrary position, will find himself spellbound by the immensity of an intellect that seems to know it all. In every instance, an appeal is made to some authority, and this is particularly striking when arguments that are being refuted have first been brought forward backed by an authoritative quotation.

Not that the citation of authority is the only or even the dominant way of argumentation. It is always accompanied by a kind of sheer rational demonstration, usually iron-clad. No rhetoric, no kind of persuasion is ever used; the reader is compelled as only truth can compel. The trust in compelling truth, so general in medieval philosophy, is boundless in Thomas. He distinguishes three kinds of necessity: absolute necessity, which is rational—for instance, that three angles of a triangle are equal to two right angles; relative necessity, which is that of utility—for instance, food is necessary for life or a horse is necessary for a journey; and coercion imposed by an outside agent. And of these only the last is "repugnant to the will."[2] Truth compels; it does not command as the will commands, and it does not coerce. It is what Scotus later called the *dictamen rationis*, the "dictate of reason," that is, a power which prescribes in the form of speech (*dicere*) and whose force has its limits in the limitations of rational intercourse.

With unsurpassed clarity, Thomas distinguishes between two "apprehensive" faculties, intellect and reason; these have their corresponding intellectually appetitive faculties, will and *liberum arbitrium* or free choice. Intellect and reason deal with truth. Intellect, also called "universal reason," deals with mathematical or self-evident truth, first principles needing no demonstration to be assented to, whereas reason, or particular reason, is the faculty by which we draw particular conclusions from universal propositions as in syllogisms. Universal reason is by nature contemplative, while the task of particular reason is "to come from one thing to the knowledge of another, and so . . . we reason about conclusions, that are known from the principles."[3] This discursive reasoning process dominates all his writings. (The Age of Enlightenment has been called the Age of Reason—which may or may not be an apt description; these centuries of the Middle Ages are certainly best called the Age of Reasoning.) The distinction would be that truth, perceived by the intellect only, is revealed to and compels the mind without any activity on the mind's part, whereas in the discursive reasoning process the mind compels itself.

The argumentative reasoning process is set in motion by the faith of a rational creature whose intellect naturally turns to its Creator for help in seeking out "such knowledge of the true being" that He is "as may lie within the power of my natural reason."[4] What was revealed to faith in Scripture was not subject to doubt, any more than the self-evidence of first principles was doubted by Greek philosophy. Truth is compelling. What distinguishes this power of compulsion in Thomas from the necessitation of Greek *alētheia* is not that the decisive revelation comes from without but that "to the truth promulgated from without by revelation, responded the light of reason from within. Faith, *ex auditu* [for instance, Moses listening to the divine voice], at once awoke an answering chord."[5]

If one comes to Thomas and Duns Scotus from Augustine, the most striking change is that neither is interested in the problematic structure of the Will, seen as an isolated faculty; what is at stake for them is the relation between Will and Reason or Intellect, and the dominant question is which of these mental faculties is "nobler" and therefore entitled to primacy over the other. It may be of even greater significance, especially in view of Augustine's enormous influence on both thinkers, that, of Augustine's three mental faculties—Memory, Intellect, and Will—one has been lost, namely, Memory, the most specifically Roman one, binding men back to the past. And this loss turned out to be final; nowhere in our philosophical tradition does Memory again attain the same rank as Intellect and Will. Quite apart from the consequences of this loss for all strictly political philosophy,[6] it is obvious that what went out with memory—*sedes animi est in memoria*—was a sense of the thoroughly temporal character of human nature and human existence, manifest in Augustine's *homo temporalis*.[7]

The Intellect, which in Augustine related to whatever was present in the mind, in Thomas relates back to *first principles,* that is, to what comes logically before anything else; it is from them that the reasoning process that deals with particulars takes off.[8] The proper object of the Will is the end, yet this end is no more the future than the "first principle" is the past; principle and end are logical, not temporal, categories. So far as the Will is concerned, Thomas, closely following the *Nicomachean Ethics,* insists chiefly on the means-end category, and as in Aristotle, the end, though the Will's object, is given to the Will by the apprehensive faculties, that is, by the Intellect. Hence, the proper "order of action" is this: "First there is the apprehension of the end . . . then counsel [deliberation] about the means; and finally desire for the means."[9] At each step, the apprehensive power precedes, and has primacy over, the appetitive movement.

The conceptual foundation of all these distinctions is that

"goodness and Being" differ only in thought; they are "the same *realiter*," and this to the point where they can be said to be "convertible": "As much as [a man] has of Being, so much has he of goodness, while so far as something is lacking in the fullness of [his] Being, so far does this fall short of goodness and is said to be evil."[10] No being, insofar as it *is*, can be said to be evil, "but only insofar as it lacks Being." All this of course is no more than an elaboration of Augustine's position, but the position is enlarged and conceptually sharpened. From the perspective of the apprehensive faculties, Being appears under the aspect of truth; from the perspective of the Will, where the end is the good, it appears "under the aspect of desirableness, which Being does not express." Evil is not a principle, because it is sheer *absence*, and absence can be stated "in a privative and in a negative sense. Absence of good, taken negatively, is not evil . . . for instance, if a man lacks the swiftness of the horse; evil is an absence where something is *deprived* of a good that belongs to it essentially—for instance, the blind man, who is deprived of sight."[11] Because of its privative character, absolute or radical evil cannot exist. No evil exists in which one can detect "the total absence of good." For "*if the wholly evil could be, it would destroy itself.*"[12]

Thomas was not the first to regard evil as nothing but "privation," a kind of optical illusion that comes about if the whole, of which evil is only a part, is not taken into account. Already Aristotle had had the notion of a universe "wherein every part has its own perfectly ordered place" so that the inherent goodness of fire "causes evil to water" by accident.[13] And it remains the most resilient, and ever-repeated traditional argument against the real existence of evil; even Kant, who coined the concept of "radical evil," by no means believed that one who "cannot prove a lover" may on that account be "determined to prove a villain," that, to use Augustine's language, *velle* and *nolle* are interconnected and that the true choice of the Will is between willing and nilling. Still, it is true that this old *topos* of philosophy makes more sense in Thomas than in most other systems because the center of Thomas' system, its "first principle," is Being. In the context of his philosophy, "to say that God created not only the world but the evil in it, would be to say that God created nothingness," as Gilson pointed out.[14]

All created things, whose main distinction is that they *are*, aspire "to Being [each] after its own manner," but only the Intellect has "knowledge" of Being as a whole; the senses "do not know Being except under the conditions of *here* and *now*."[15] The Intellect "apprehends Being absolutely, and for all time," and man, insofar as he is endowed with this faculty, cannot but desire "always to exist." This is the "natural inclination" of the Will, whose ultimate goal is as "necessary" to it as truth is compelling to the Intellect. The Will is free, properly speaking, only with respect to "particular goods," by which it is not "necessarily moved," although the appetites may be moved by them. The ultimate goal, the Intellect's desire to exist forever, keeps the appetites under control so that the concrete distinction between men and animals manifests itself in the fact that man "is not moved at once [by his appetites, which he shares with all other living things] . . . but *awaits* the command of the Will, which is the superior appetite . . . and so the lower appetite is not sufficient to cause movement unless the higher appetite consents."[16]

It is obvious that Being, Thomas' first principle, is simply a conceptualization of Life and the life instinct—the fact that every living thing instinctively preserves life and shuns death. This, too, is an elaboration of thoughts we found expressed in more tentative formulae by Augustine, but its inherent consequence, an equation of the Will with the life instinct—without any relation to a possible eternal life—is commonly drawn only in the nineteenth century. In Schopenhauer it is explicitly stated; and in Nietzsche's will to power, truth itself is understood as a function of the life process: what we call truth is those propositions without which we could not go on living. Not reason but our will to live makes truth compelling.

We now turn to the question of which of the two mental powers, if compared with one another, is "absolutely higher and nobler." At first sight the question seems not to make much sense, since the ultimate object is the same; it is Being that appears good and desirable to the Will and true to the Intellect. And Thomas agrees: these two powers "include one another in their acts, because the Intellect understands that the Will wills, and the Will wills the Intellect to understand."[17] Even if we distinguish between the "good" and the "true" as corresponding to different faculties of the mind, it turns out that they are very similar because both are *universal* in scope. As the Intellect is "apprehensive of universal being and truth," so the Will is "appetitive of universal good," and, just as the Intellect has reasoning as its subordinate power for dealing with the particulars, so the Will has the faculty of free choice (*liberum arbitrium*) as its subservient helper in sorting out the appropriate particular means to a universal end. Moreover, since both faculties have Being as their ultimate objective—in the guise of the True or of the Good—they seem to be equals, each of them attended by its proper servant to handle mere particulars.

Hence, the really distinctive line separating higher and lower faculties seems to be the line dividing "superior" and "subservient" faculties, and that distinction is never questioned. For Thomas—as for nearly all his successors in philosophy, of whom there are more than avowed Thomists—it was a matter of course, actually the very touchstone of philosophy as a separate discipline, that the universal is "nobler and higher in rank" than the particular, and the only proof this needed was and remained the old Aristotelian statement that the whole is always greater than the sum of its parts.

The great and rather lonely distinction of John Duns Scotus is to have questioned and challenged that assumption: Being in its universality is but a thought, what it lacks is *reality;* only particular things (*res*), which are characterized by "thisness" (*haecceity*) can be said to be real for man. Hence Scotus sharply contrasted "intuitive cognition, whose proper object is the existing singular perceived as existing, and abstractive cognition, whose proper object is the *quiddity* or essence of the known thing."[18] Therefore—and this is decisive—the mental image (the seen tree), because it has lost its actual existence, is of less ontological stature than the actual tree, although no knowledge of what a thing is would be possible without mental images. The consequence of this reversal is that *this* particular man, for instance, in his living existence is higher in rank than, and precedes, the species or the mere thought of mankind. (Kierkegaard later raised a very similar argument against Hegel.)

The reversal seems a rather obvious consequence for a philosophy that drew its main inspiration from the Bible, that is, from a Creator-God, who certainly was a person, who created men in His own image, that is, necessarily as persons. And Thomas is enough of a Christian to hold that *"persona significat id quod est perfectissimum in tota natura"* ("the person signifies what is most perfect in the whole of nature").[19] The Biblical basis, as Augustine showed, is in Genesis, where all natural species were created in the plural—*"plura simul iussit exsistere"* ("He commanded them to be many at once"). Only man was created as a singular, so that the human species (taken as an animal species) multiplied out of a One: *"ex uno . . . multiplicavit genus humanum."*[20] In Augustine and in Scotus, but not in Aquinas, the Will is the mental organ that actualizes this singularity; it is the *principium individuationis.*

To return to Thomas, he insists: "If Intellect and Will be compared with one another according to the universality of their respective objects then . . . the Intellect is absolutely higher and nobler than the Will." And this proposition is all the more significant because it does not follow from his general philosophy of Being. This is admitted in a way by Thomas himself. For him the primacy of the Intellect over the Will does not lie so much in the primacy of their respective objects—Truth over the Good—as in the way the two faculties "concur" within the human mind: "Every movement of the will [is] . . . preceded by apprehension"—no one can will what he does not know—"whereas . . . apprehension is not preceded by an act of the will."[21] (Here, of course, he parts company with Augustine, who maintained the primacy of the Will qua attention even for acts of sense perception.) This precedence shows itself in every volition. In "free choice," for instance, in which the means to an end are "elected," the two powers concur in the election: "cognitive power . . . by which we judge one thing to be preferred to another . . . and appetitive power [whereby] it is required that the appetite should accept the judgment of counsel."[22]

If we look upon the Augustinian and the Thomistic positions in purely psychological terms, as their authors frequently used to argue them, we have to admit that their opposition is somewhat spurious because they are equally plausible. Who would deny that no one can will what he does not somehow know or, on the contrary, that some volition precedes, and decides upon, the direction we want our knowledge or our search for knowledge to go? Thomas' true reason for maintaining the primacy of the Intellect—like Augustine's final reason for electing the primacy of the Will—lies in the undemonstrable answer to the ultimate question of all medieval thinkers: In what does "man's last end and happiness consist?"[23] We know that Augustine's answer was love; he intended to spend his after-life in an undesiring, never-to-be-sundered union of the creature with its creator. Whereas Thomas, obviously replying (though without mentioning them) to Augustine and the Augustinians, answers: Although someone might think that man's last end and happiness consists "not in knowing God, but in loving Him, or in some other act of will toward Him," he, Thomas, maintains that "it is one thing to possess the good which is our end, and another to love it; for love was imperfect before we possessed the end, and perfect after we obtained possession." For him, a love without desire is unthinkable and therefore the answer is categorical: "Man's ultimate happiness is essentially to know God by the Intellect; it is not an act of the Will." Here Thomas is following his teacher, Albertus Magnus, who had declared that "the supreme bliss comes to pass when the Intellect finds itself in the state of contemplation."[24] It is noteworthy to see Dante in full agreement:

> Hence may be seen how the celestial bliss
> Is founded on the act that seeth God,
> Not that which loves, which comes after this.[25]

At the start of these considerations I tried to stress the distinction between Will and desire, and by implication distinguish the concept of Love in Augustine's philosophy of the

Will from the Platonic *eros* in the *Symposium,* where it indicates a deficiency in the lover and a longing for the possession
of whatever he may be lacking. What I have just quoted from
Thomas shows, I think, to what an extent his concept of the
appetitive faculties is still indebted to the notion of a desire to
*possess* in a hereafter whatever may be lacking in earthly life.
For the Will, basically understood as desire, stops when the
desired object is brought into its possession, and the notion
that "the Will is blessed when it is in possession of what it
wills"[26] is simply not true—this is precisely the moment when
the Will ceases to will. The Intellect, which, according to
Thomas, is "a passive power,"[27] is assured of its primacy over
the Will not only because it "presents an object to the appetite," and hence is prior to it, but also because it survives the
Will, which is extinguished, as it were, when the object has
been attained. The transformation of Will into Love—in
Augustine as well as in Duns Scotus—was at least partly inspired by a more radical separation of the Will from appetites
and desires as well as by a different notion of "man's last end
and happiness." Even in the hereafter man still remains man,
and his "ultimate happiness" cannot be sheer "passivity." Love
could be invoked to redeem the Will because it is still active,
though without restlessness, neither pursuing an end nor
afraid of losing it.

That there could be an *activity* that has its end in itself and
therefore can be understood outside the means-end category
never enters Thomas' considerations. For him, "every agent
acts for an end . . . the principle of this motion lies in the end.
Hence it is that the art, which is concerned with the end, by its
command moves the art which is concerned with the means;
just as the *art of sailing commands the art of shipbuilding.*"[28]
To be sure, this comes right out of the *Nicomachean Ethics,*
except that in Aristotle it is true of only one kind of activity,
namely, *poiēsis,* the productive arts, as distinguished from the
performing arts, where the end lies in the activity itself—flute-
playing, compared with flute-making, or just going for a
walk, compared with walking in order to reach a predetermined destination. In Aristotle it is quite clear that *praxis* must
be understood in analogy to the performing arts and cannot be

understood in terms of the means-end category; and it is quite
striking that Thomas, who depended so heavily on the Philosopher's teachings and especially on the *Nicomachean Ethics,*
should have neglected the distinction between *poiēsis* and
*praxis.*

Whatever the advantages of this distinction may be—and I
think they are crucial for any theory of action—they are of
little relevance to Thomas' notion of ultimate happiness. He
opposes Contemplation to any kind of doing, and here he is
quite in agreement with Aristotle, for whom the *energeia
tou theou* is contemplative, since action as well as production
would be "petty and unworthy of the gods." ("If we take away
action from a living being, to say nothing of production, what
is left but contemplation?") Hence, humanly speaking, contemplation is "not-doing-anything," being blessed by sheer
intuition, blissfully at rest. Happiness, says Aristotle, "depends
on leisure, for our purpose in being busy [either acting or
making] is to have leisure, and we wage war in order to have
peace."[29] For Thomas, only this last end—the bliss of contemplation—"moves the will" necessarily; "the will cannot not-
will it." Hence "the Will moves the Intellect to be active in
the way an agent is said to move; but the Intellect moves the
Will in the way the end moves"[30]—that is, in the way Aristotle's
"unmoved mover" was supposed to move, and how could that
move except by virtue of "being loved," as the lover is moved
by the beloved?[31]

What in Aristotle was the "most continuous of all pleasures" is now hoped for as eternal bliss, not the pleasure that
may attend volitions but a delight that puts the will to rest, so
that the ultimate end of the Will, seen in reference to itself, is
to cease willing—in short, to attain its own non-being. And in
the context of Thomas' thought, this implies that every activity, since its end is never reached while it is still active, ultimately aims at its own self-destruction; the means disappear
when the end is reached. (It is as though, while writing a
book, one were constantly driven by the desire to have it
finished and be rid of writing.) To what extremes Thomas, in
his single-minded predilection for contemplation as sheer seeing and not-doing, was prepared to go becomes manifest in a

rather casual side remark he lets drop when interpreting a Pauline text dealing with human love between two persons. Could the "enjoyment" of loving somebody, he asks, signify that the Will's ultimate "end" has been placed in man? The answer is "No," for, according to Thomas, what Paul said in effect was that "he enjoyed his brother as a *means* toward the enjoyment of God"[32]—and God, as we have seen, cannot be reached by Man's Will or Love but only by his Intellect.

This is of course a far cry from Augustine's Love, which loves the love of the beloved, and it is also rather offensive to the ears of those who, schooled by Kant, are pretty well convinced that we ought to "treat humanity, whether in [our] own person or in that of any other . . . as an end withal, never as means only."[33]

## 12 *Duns Scotus and the primacy of the Will*

When we now come to Duns Scotus, no leap over the centuries, with the inevitable discontinuities and discords that make the historian suspicious, will be involved. He was not more than a generation younger than Thomas Aquinas, almost his contemporary. We are still in the midst of Scholasticism. In the texts you will find the same curious mixture of ancient quotations—treated as authorities—and argumentative reason. Although Scotus did not write a *Summa,* he proceeds in the same way as Aquinas: first, the Question states what is being inquired about (for instance, monotheism: "I ask whether there is but one God"); then the Pros and Contras, based on authoritative quotations, are discussed; next the arguments of other thinkers are given; finally, under *Respondeo,* Scotus states his own opinions, the *viae,* "Ways," as he calls them, for thought-trains, along with correct arguments, to travel.[34] No doubt at first glance it looks as though the only point of difference with Thomistic scholasticism were the question of the primacy of the Will, which is "proved" by Scotus with no less argumentative plausibility than Thomas had deployed in proving the primacy of the Intellect, and with scarcely fewer quo-

tations from Aristotle. To put the opposing arguments in a nutshell: If Thomas had argued that the Will is an executive
organ, necessary to execute the insights of the Intellect, a
merely "subservient" faculty, Duns Scotus holds that "*Intellectus . . . est causa subserviens voluntatis.*" The Intellect serves
the Will by providing it with its objects as well as with the
necessary knowledge; i.e., the Intellect in its turn becomes a
merely subservient faculty. It needs the Will to direct its attention and can function properly only when its object is "confirmed" by the Will. Without this confirmation the Intellect
ceases to function.[35]

It would be somewhat pointless here to enter the old controversy as to whether Scotus was an "Aristotelian" or an
"Augustinian"—scholars have gone so far as to maintain that
"Duns Scotus is as much a disciple of Aristotle as St. Thomas
is"[36]—because Scotus actually was neither. But to the extent
that the debate makes sense, that is, so to speak, biograph-
ically, it seems that Bettoni, the Italian Scotus scholar, is
right: "Duns Scotus remains an Augustinian who profited to
the utmost degree from the Aristotelian method in the exposition of the thoughts and doctrines that form his metaphysical
vision of reality."[37]

These and similar evaluations are surface reactions, but
unhappily they have succeeded in obliterating to a large degree the originality of the man and the significance of his
thought, as though the *Doctor subtilis'* chief claim to our attention *were* subtlety, the unique complexity and intricacy of
his presentation. Scotus was a Franciscan, and Franciscan
literature was always greatly affected by the fact that
Thomas, a Dominican, despite early difficulties, was recognized as a saint by the Church and his *Summa Theologica,*
first used, and finally prescribed, as *the* textbook for the study
of philosophy and theology in all Catholic schools. In other
words, Franciscan literature is apologetic, usually cautiously
defensive, even though Scotus' own polemics are directed at
Henry of Ghent rather than turned on Thomas.[38]

A closer reading of the texts will soon disabuse one of those
first impressions; the difference and distinction of the man
show most clearly when he seems to be in complete conformity

with the rules of Scholasticism. Thus, in a lengthy interpretive rendering of Aristotle, he suddenly proposes to "reinforce the Philosopher's reasoning" and, in discussing Anselm of Canterbury's "proof" of the existence of God, he will almost casually yield to the inclination to "touch it up" a bit, indeed quite considerably. The point is that he insisted on "establishing by reason" arguments derived from authority.[39]

Standing at the turning-point—the early fourteenth century—when the Middle Ages were changing into the Renaissance, he could indeed have said what Pico della Mirandola said at the end of the fifteenth century, in the middle of the Renaissance: "Pledged to the doctrine of no man, I have ranged through all the masters of philosophy, investigated all books, and come to know all schools."[40] Except that Scotus would not have shared the naïve trust of later philosophers in reason's persuasive power. At the heart of his reflection, as well as at the heart of his piety, is the firm conviction that, touching the questions that "pertain to our end and to our sempiternal perpetuity, the most learned and most ingenious men could know almost nothing by natural reason."[41] For "to those who have no faith, right reason, as it seems to itself, shows that the condition of its nature is to be mortal both in body and soul."[42]

It is his close attention to opinions to which he remained uncommitted, but whose examination and interpretation make up the body of his work, that is likely to lead the reader astray. Scotus certainly was not a skeptic—ancient or modern—but he had a critical turn of mind, something that is, and always has been, very rare. From this perspective, large portions of his writings read like a relentless attempt to *prove* by sheer argumentation what he suspected could not be proved; how could he be sure of being right against almost everybody else unless he followed all the arguments and subjected them to what Petrus Johannis Olivi had called an *"experimentum suitatis,"* an experiment of the mind with itself? That was why he found it necessary to "reinforce" the old arguments or "touch them up" a bit. He knew very well what he was doing. As he said: "I wish to give the most reasonable interpretation to [other thinkers'] words that I possibly can."[43] Only in this essentially non-polemical way could the inherent weakness of the argumentation be demonstrated.

In Scotus' own mature thought, this manifest weakness of natural reason can never be used as an argument for the superiority of irrational faculties; he was no mystic, and the notion that "man is irrational" was to him "unthinkable" (*"incogitabile"*).[44] What we are dealing with, according to him, is the natural limitation of an essentially *limited* creature whose finitude is absolute, "prior to any reference it may have to another essence." "For, just as a body is first limited in itself by its own proper boundaries before it is limited in respect to anything else . . . so the finite form is first limited in itself before it is limited with respect to matter."[45] This finitude of the human intellect—very much like that of Augustine's *homo temporalis*—is due to the simple fact that man qua man has not created himself, though he is able to multiply like other animal species. Hence for Scotus the question is never how to derive (draw down, deduce) finitude from divine infinity or how to ascend from human finitude to divine infinity, but how to explain that an absolutely finite being can conceive of something infinite and call it "God." "Why is it that the intellect . . . does not find the notion of something infinite repugnant?"[46]

To put it differently: What is it in the human mind that makes it capable of transcending its own limitations, its absolute finitude? And the answer to this question in Scotus, as distinguished from Thomas, is the Will. To be sure, no philosophy can ever be a substitute for divine revelation, which the Christian accepts on the strength of testimony in which he has faith. Creation and resurrection are articles of faith; they cannot be proved or refuted by natural reason. As such they are *contingent,* factual truths whose opposite is not inconceivable; they relate to events that might not have happened. For those brought up in the Christian faith they have the same validity as other events of which we know only because we trust the testimony of witnesses—for instance, the fact that the world existed before we were born or that there are places on the earth where we have never been, or even that certain persons are our parents.[47]

A radical doubt that rejects the testimony of witnesses and relies on reason alone is impossible for men; it is a mere rhetorical device of solipsism, constantly refuted by the doubter's own existence. All men live together on the solid foundation of a *fides acquisita,* an acquired faith they have in common. The test for the countless facts whose trustworthiness we constantly take for granted is that they must make sense for men as they are constituted. And in this respect, the dogma of resurrection makes much more sense than the philosophers' notion of the soul's immortality: a creature endowed with body and soul can find sense only in an after-life in which he is resurrected from death as he is and knows himself to be. The philosophers' "proofs" of the soul's immortality, even if they were logically correct, would be irrelevant. To be existentially relevant for the *"viator,"* the wayfarer or pilgrim on earth, the after-life must be a "second life," not an entirely different mode of being as a disembodied entity.

Yet while it seems obvious to Scotus that the philosophers' natural reason never attained the "truths" proclaimed by divine revelation, it remains undeniable that the notion of divinity antedated any Christian revelation, and that means that there must be a mental capacity in man by which he can transcend whatever is given to him, transcend, that is, the very factuality of Being. He seems to be able to transcend himself. For man, according to Scotus, was created together with Being, as part and parcel of it—just as man, according to Augustine, was created not in time but together with time. His intellect is attuned to this Being as his sense organs are fitted for the perception of appearances; his intellect is "natural," *"cadit sub natura"*;[48] whatever the intellect proposes to him, man is *forced* to accept, compelled by the evidence of the object: *"Non habet in potestate sua intelligere et non intelligere."*[49]

It is different with the Will. The Will may find it difficult not to accept what reason dictates, *but the thing is not impossible,* just as it is not impossible for the Will to resist strong natural appetites: *"Difficile est, voluntatem non inclinari ad id, quod est dictatum a ratione practica ultimatim, non tamen est impossibile, sicut voluntas naturaliter inclinatur, sibi dismissa, ad condelectandum appetitui sensitivo, non tamen impossibile, ut frequenter resistat, ut patet in virtuosis et sanctis.*"[50] It is the possibility of resistance to the needs of desire, on the one hand, and the dictates of intellect and reason, on the other, that constitutes human freedom.

The Will's autonomy, its complete independence of things as they are, which the schoolmen call "indifference"—by which they mean that the will is "undetermined" (*indeterminata*) by any object presented to it—has only one limitation: it cannot deny Being altogether. Man's limitation is nowhere more manifest than in the fact that his mind, the willing faculty included, can hold as an article of faith that God created Being *ex nihilo*, out of nothingness, and yet be unable to conceive "nothingness." Hence the Will's indifference relates to contradictories—*voluntas autem sola habet indifferentiam ad contradictoria;* only the willing ego knows that "a decision actually taken need not have been taken and a choice other than the one actually made might have been made."[51]

This is the test by which freedom is demonstrated, and neither desire nor the intellect can measure up to it: an object presented to desire can only attract or repel, and an issue presented to the intellect can only be affirmed or negated. But it is the basic quality of our will that we may will or nill the object presented by reason or desire: *"in potestate voluntatis nostrae est habere nolle et velle, quae sunt contraria, respectu unius obiecti"* ("It is in the power of our will to will and to nill, which are contraries, with respect to the same object").[52] In saying this, Scotus, of course, does not deny that two successive volitions are necessary to will and nill the same object; but he does maintain that the willing ego in performing one of them is aware of being free to perform its contrary also: "The essential characteristic of our volitional acts is . . . the power to choose between opposite things *and to revoke the choice once it has been made*" (italics added).[53] Precisely this freedom, which is manifest only as a mental activity—the power to revoke disappears once the volition has been executed—is what we spoke of earlier in terms of a brokenness of the will.

Besides being open to contraries, the Will can *suspend* itself, and while such suspension can only be the result of another volition—in contradistinction to the Nietzschean and

Heideggerian Will-not-to-will, which we shall discuss later—this second volition, in which "indifference" is directly chosen, is an important testimony to human freedom, to the mind's ability to avoid all coercive determination from the outside. It is because of their freedom that men, though part and parcel of created Being, can praise God's creation, for if such praise derived from their reason it would be no more than a natural reaction caused by our given harmony with all the other parts of the universe. But by the same token they can also abstain from such praise and even "hate God and find satisfaction in such hatred" or at least refuse to love Him.

This refusal, which Scotus does not mention in his discussion of the possible hatred of God, is posited in analogy to his objection to the old "all men will to be happy." He admits that of course all men by nature wish to be happy (although no agreement about happiness exists), but the Will—and here is the crucial point—can transcend nature, in this case suspend it: there is a difference between man's natural inclination to happiness and happiness as the deliberately chosen goal of one's life; it is by no means impossible for man to discount happiness altogether in making his willed projects. As far as natural inclination is concerned, and the limitation nature sets on the power of the Will, all that can be affirmed is that no man can "will to be miserable."[54] Scotus avoids giving a clear answer to the question of whether hatred of God is possible or not, because of the close relation of that question to the question of evil. In line with all his predecessors and successors, he, too, denies that man can will evil as evil, "but not without raising some doubts as to the possibility of the opposite view."[55]

The Will's autonomy—"nothing else but the will is the total cause of volition" ("*nihil aliud a voluntate est causa totalis volitionis in voluntate*")[56]—decisively limits the power of reason, whose dictate is not absolute, but it does not limit the power of nature, be it the nature of the inner man, called "inclinations," or that of exterior circumstances. The will is by no means omnipotent in its actual effectiveness: its force consists solely in that it cannot be coerced to will. To illustrate this mental freedom, Scotus gives the example of a man "who hurls himself from a high place."[57] Does not this act terminate his freedom since he now necessarily falls? According to Scotus, it does not. While the man is necessarily falling, compelled by the law of gravity, he remains free to continue "to will to fall," and can also of course change his mind, in which case he would be unable to undo what he started voluntarily and would find himself in the hands of necessity. We remember Spinoza's example of the rolling stone which, if endowed with consciousness, would necessarily be prey to the illusion that it had hurled itself and was now rolling of its own free will. Such comparisons are useful in order to realize to what an extent such propositions and their illustrations, disguised in the form of plausible arguments, depend on preliminary assumptions about necessity or freedom as self-evident facts. To stay with the present illustration—no law of gravity can have power over the freedom guaranteed in interior experience; no interior experience has any direct validity in the world as it really and necessarily is according to outer experience and the correct reasoning of the intellect.

Duns Scotus distinguishes between two kinds of will: "natural will" (*ut natura*), which follows the natural inclinations, and may be inspired by reason as well as by desire, and "free will" (*ut libera*) properly speaking.[58] He agrees with nearly every other philosopher that it is in human nature to incline toward the good and explains the evil will as human weakness, the blemish of a creature that has come from nothingness (*"creatio ex nihilo"*) and has therefore a certain inclination to sink back into nothingness (*"omnis creatura potest tendere in nihil et in non esse, eo quod de nihilo est"*).[59] Natural will works like "gravity in bodies," and he calls it *"affectio commodi,"* our being affected by what is proper and expedient. If man had only his natural will, he would at best be a *bonum animal,* a kind of enlightened brute, whose very rationality would help him to choose appropriate means to ends given by human nature. Free will—as distinguished from the *liberum arbitrium,* which is only free to select the means to a pre-designed end—freely designs ends that are pursued *for their own sake,* and of this pursuance only the Will is capable: "[*voluntas*] *enim est productiva actum,*" "for the Will produces its own act."[60] The trouble is that Scotus does not seem to say anywhere what this freely designed end actually is, although he seems to have understood the activity of free designing as the Will's actual perfection.[61]

It is with great regret that I admit that this cannot be the place (and that I would not be qualified if it were the place) to do justice to Duns Scotus' originality of thought, especially to the "passion for constructive thinking that pervades all of [his] genuine work,"[62] which he had neither the time—he died too young, too young for a philosopher—nor perhaps the inclination to present systematically. It is hard to think of any great philosopher, any one of the great thinkers—of whom there are not many—who still "needs [so much] to be discovered and helped by our attention and understanding."[63]

Such help will be all the more welcome and all the more difficult to provide, for the very good reason that finding a comfortable niche for him between predecessors and successors in the history of ideas will not be possible. Avoiding the textbook cliché of the "systematic opponent of St. Thomas" will not be enough, and in his insistence on the Will as the nobler faculty compared with the Intellect he had many predecessors among the schoolmen—the most important was Petrus Johannis Olivi.[64] Nor will it be enough to clarify and bring out in detail his undoubtedly great influence on Leibniz and Descartes, even though it is still true, as Windelband said more than seventy years ago, that their links with "the greatest of the scholastics . . . have unfortunately not found the consideration or treatment that they deserve."[65] Certainly the intimate presence of the Augustinian inheritance in his work is too patent to escape notice—there is no one who read Augustine with greater sympathy and deeper understanding—and his indebtedness to Aristotle was perhaps even greater than that of Aquinas. Still the simple truth is that for his quintessential thought—contingency, the price gladly paid for freedom—he had neither predecessors nor successors. Nor for his method: a careful elaboration of Olivi's *experimentum suitatis* in

thought-experiments, which were framed as the ultimate test
of the mind's critical examination in the course of its transac-
tions with and within itself (*experimur in nobis, experientia
interna*[66]).

In the following I shall try to summarize those strikingly
original and highly relevant thought-trains—or thought-
experiments—which clearly go against the grain of our philosophical and theological traditions but are easily overlooked
because they are presented in the manner of the schoolmen
and easily lost in the intricacies of Scotian argumentations. I
have already mentioned some of the striking insights: first, his
objection to the old cliché that "all men will to be happy" (of
which nothing more was left than "no man can will to be
miserable"); second, his no less surprising proof of the existence
of contingency ("let all those who deny contingency be tortured until they admit that it would be possible *not* to be
tortured"[67]). Stumbling on such down-to-earth remarks in their
erudite surroundings, one is tempted to read them as mere
witticisms. Their validity, according to Scotus, depends on the
*experientia interna,* an experience of the mind whose evidence
can be denied only by those who lack the experience, as a
blind man would deny the experience of color. The dry,
tindery quality of such remarks could suggest flashes of insight
rather than thought-trains, but these abrupt flashes usually
occur only in the thought-thing, a single pithy sentence that is
the result of long previous critical examinations. It is characteristic of Scotus that, despite his "passion for constructive
thinking," he was no system builder; his most surprising insights often appear casually and, as it were, out of context; he
must have known of the disadvantages of this, for he warns us
explicitly against entering into disputes with "contentious" op-
ponents who, lacking "internal experience," are likely to win an
argument and lose the issue at stake.[68]

Let us start with Contingency as the price to be paid for
freedom. Scotus is the only thinker for whom the word "contingent" has no derogatory association: "I say that contingency
is not merely a privation or defect of Being like the deformity
. . . which is sin. Rather, contingency is a positive mode of

Being, just as necessity is another mode."[69] This position seems to him unavoidable, a matter of intellectual integrity, if one wishes to save freedom. The primacy of the Intellect over the Will must be rejected "because it cannot save freedom in any way"—*"quia hoc nullo modo salvat libertatem."*[70] For him the main distinction between Christians and pagans lies in the Biblical notion of the origin of the universe: the universe of Genesis did not come into being through the emanation of predetermined necessary forces, so that its existence would also be necessary, but was created *ex nihilo* by the decision of a Creator-God Who, we must suppose, was entirely free to create a different world in which neither our mathematical truths nor our moral precepts would be valid. From this it follows that everything that is might possibly not have been—save God Himself. His existence is necessary from the perspective of a non-necessary world which He freely "designed," but not necessary in the sense that there had ever been a necessity that coerced or inspired Him in His creation; such a necessity working through Him would be in clear contradiction to God's omnipotence as well as to His supremacy.

Men are part and parcel of this Creation, and all their natural capabilities, including their intellect, naturally follow the laws laid down by divine Fiat. Yet Man, in contradistinction to all other parts of Creation, was not freely designed; he was created in God's own image—as though God needed not only angels in some supranatural world, but some creatures after His likeness in the midst of worldly nature to keep Him company. The hallmark of this creature, obviously closer to God than any other, is by no means creativity; in that case the creature would indeed have been something like a "mortal god" (and to my mind this is very likely the reason that Scotus did not follow up his notion of a "freely designed goal of the Will" even though he seems to have thought of such a "content-less ability to design freely" as "true perfection"[71]). Rather, God's creature is distinguished by the mental capacity to affirm or negate freely, uncoerced by either desire or reasoning. It is as though Being, having come into existence, needed God's final judgment for its fulfillment—"And God saw everything that He had made, and behold, it was very good"—and this judgment was elicited also from the mortal that had been created in His likeness.

At any rate the price of the Will's freedom is to be free vis-à-vis every object; man can "hate God and find satisfaction in such hatred," because some pleasure (*delectatio*) attends every volition.[72] The Will's freedom does not consist in the selection of means for a predetermined end—*eudaimonia* or *beatitudo* or *blessedness*—precisely because this end is already *given* by human nature; it consists in freely affirming or negating or hating whatever confronts it. It is this freedom of the will mentally to *take a position* that sets man apart from the rest of creation; without it he would be an enlightened animal (*bonum animal*) at best, or, as Olivi had said earlier, a *bestia intellectualis,* an intellectual beast.[73] The miracle of the human mind is that by virtue of the Will it can transcend everything ("*voluntas transcendit omne creatum,*" as Olivi said[74]), and this is the sign of man's being created in God's image. The Biblical notion that God showed him His preference by giving him dominion over all the works of His hands (Psalm 8) would only make him the highest of all created things; it would not set him absolutely apart from them. The willing ego, when it says in its highest manifestation, "*Amo: Volo ut sis,*" "I love you; I want you to be"—and not "I want to have you" or "I want to rule you"—shows itself capable of the same love with which supposedly God loves men, whom He created only because He willed them to exist and whom He *loves without desiring them.*

That is how the matter presented itself to the Christian; it is why "Christians . . . say that God acts contingently . . . freely and contingently."[75] But it is also possible, according to Scotus, to arrive at the same evaluation of contingency by way of philosophy. After all, it was the Philosopher who had defined the contingent and the accidental (*to symbēbekos*) as that which "could as well not be" (*endechomenon mē einai*),[76] and what was the willing ego more aware of in every volition than that it could also not will (*experitur enim qui vult se posse non velle*[77])? How would man ever have been capable of distinguishing a free act of will from an overwhelming desire without that infallible internal test?

What apparently spoke against the Will's freedom to will or to nill was the law of causality, which Scotus also knew in the Aristotelian version: a chain of causation that would make movement intelligible and ultimately lead to an unmoved source of all motion, "the unmoved mover," a cause that itself is not caused. The strength of the argument, or, rather, its explicatory force, lies in the assumption that no more than one cause is sufficient to explain why something should be rather than not-be, that is, to explain motion and change. Scotus challenges the whole notion of a chain of causality leading in an unbroken line through a succession of sufficient and necessary causes and having to arrive finally at a First uncaused Cause in order to avoid an infinite regress.

He starts the discussion by asking "whether the act of the will is caused in the will by the object moving it or by the will moving itself" and rejects the answer that the will is moved by an object outside itself, since in no way can that save freedom (*"quia hoc nullo modo salvat libertatem"*). The opposite answer, that the Will is omnipotent, he rejects because it cannot account for all the consequences that follow a volition (*"quia tunc non possunt salvari omnes conditiones quae consequuntur actum volendi"*). Thus he arrives at his "median position," actually the only position that saves both phenomena—freedom and necessity. Presented in this form, it sounds like one of the usual Scholastic logical exercises, a rather empty play with abstract concepts. Scotus, however, at once pursues the inquiry further and arrives at a theory of "partial causes . . . [which] may concur on an equal basis and independently of one another."

Taking as his prime example procreation, where two independent substances, male and female, must come together to bring forth the child, he reaches the theory that all change occurs because a plurality of causes happens to coincide, and the coincidence engenders the texture of reality in human affairs.[78] Therefore the crux of the matter is not simply to insist on God's original freedom in creating the world, and

hence on the possibility that He might have created a totally
different one, but to show that change and motion as such, the
phenomena that originally, in Aristotle, had led to the Law of
Causality, the *aitiai* as well as the *archai*, are ruled by Contingency.

"By 'contingent,' " said Scotus, "I do not mean something
that is not necessary or which was not always in existence, but
something whose opposite could have occurred at the time
that this actually did. That is why I do not say that something
is contingent, but that something is *caused contingently*."[79] In
other words, it is precisely the causative element in human
affairs that condemns them to contingency and unpredictability. Nothing indeed could be in greater contradiction to every
philosophical tradition than this insistence on the contingent
character of processes. (We need only think of the libraries
that have been produced to explain the necessity of the out-
breaks of the last two wars, each theory picking out a different
single cause—when in truth nothing seems more plausible
than that it was a coincidence of causes, perhaps finally set in
motion by one more additional one, that "contingently caused"
the two conflagrations.)

Although this notion of contingency corresponds to the experience of the willing ego, which in the act of volition knows
itself to be free, uncoerced by its aims to act or not to act in
their pursuit, at the same time it is in apparently unsolvable
opposition to another, equally valid experience of the mind
and of common sense telling us that actually we live in a
factual world of *necessity*. A thing may have happened quite
at random, but, once it has come into existence and assumed
reality, it loses its aspect of contingency and presents itself
to us in the guise of necessity. And even if the event is of our
own making, or at least we are one of its contributing causes
—as in contracting marriage or committing a crime—the
simple existential fact that it now is as it has become (for
whatever reasons) is likely to withstand all reflections on its
original randomness. Once the contingent has happened, we
can no longer unravel the strands that entangled it until it
became an *event*—as though it could still be or not be.[80]

The reason for this strange switch of perspective, which is

at the root of many of the paradoxes connected with the problem of freedom, is that there is no substitute, real or imagined, for existence as such. To be sure, the flux of time and change may dissolve facts and events; but each of these dissolutions, even the most radical change, already presupposes the reality that preceded it. In Scotus' words, *"everything that is past is absolutely necessary."*[81] It has *become* the necessary condition for my own existence, and I cannot, mentally or otherwise, conceive of my own non-existence since, being part and parcel of Being, I am unable to conceive of nothingness, just as I conceive of God as the Creator of Being but not of a God prior to the *creatio ex nihilo*.

In other words, the Aristotelian understanding of actuality as necessarily growing out of a preceding potentiality would be verifiable only if it were possible to revolve the process back from actuality into potentiality, at least mentally; but this cannot be done. All we can say about the actual is that it obviously was *not* impossible; we can never prove that it was necessary just because it now turns out to be impossible for us to imagine a state of affairs in which it had not happened.

This is what made John Stuart Mill say that "our internal consciousness tells us that we have a power [i.e., freedom], which the whole outward experience of the human race tells us that we never use"; for what does this "outward experience of the human race" consist of but the record of historians, whose backward-directed glance looks toward what *has been* —*factum est*—and has therefore already become necessary? At this moment "outward experience" displaces the certainties of "internal consciousness" without, however, destroying them, and the result is that for a mind wanting to co-ordinate and keep in balance both "internal consciousness" and "outward experience," it looks as though the ground of necessity itself depends on a contingency.

If, on the other hand, the mind, in its uneasiness about the apparent contradiction it faces, decides to take its bearings exclusively from its own inwardness and enters into a state of reflection on the past, it will find that here, too, factually, as the result of Becoming, has already re-arranged and eliminated the randomness of the processes into a pattern of necessity. That is the necessary condition of the existential presence of the thinking ego pondering on the meaning of what has become and now *is*. Without an a priori assumption of some unilinear sequence of events having been caused necessarily and not contingently, no explanation of any coherence would be possible. The obvious, even the only possible, way to prepare and tell a story is to eliminate from the real happening the "accidental" elements, a faithful enumeration of which may be impossible anyhow, even for a computerized brain.

Scotus is reported to have cheerfully admitted that "there is no real answer to the question as to the way in which freedom and necessity can be reconciled."[82] He was still unacquainted with Hegelian dialectics in which the process of necessity can produce freedom. But to his way of thinking, no such reconciliation was needed, for freedom and necessity were two altogether different dimensions of the mind; if there was a conflict at all, it would amount to an intramural conflict between the willing and the thinking ego, a conflict in which the will directs the intellect and makes man ask the question: Why? The reason for this is simple: the will, as Nietzsche was later to discover, is incapable of "willing backwards"; hence, let the intellect try to find out what went wrong. The question Why?—what is the *cause?*—is suggested by the will because the will experiences itself as a causative agent.

It is this aspect of the Will we stress when we say that "the Will is the spring of action"; or, in the language of the schoolmen, that "our will . . . is productive of acts, and is that by which its possessor operates in formally willing."[83] Speaking in terms of causality, the will first causes volitions, and these volitions then cause certain effects which no will can undo. The intellect, trying to provide the will with an explicatory cause to quiet its resentment at its own helplessness, will fabricate a story to make the data fall into place. Without an assumption of necessity, the story would lack all coherence.

In other words, the past, precisely because it is the "absolutely necessary," is beyond the reach of the Will. For Scotus himself, the matter presented itself more simply: the decisive opposites are not freedom and necessity, but freedom and nature—Will *ut natura* and Will *ut libera*.[84] Like the Intellect, the Will is *naturally* inclined to necessity, except that the Will, unlike the Intellect, can successfully resist the inclination.

Closely connected with this doctrine of contingency is Scotus' surprisingly simple solution to the age-old problem of freedom insofar as the problem arises out of the willing faculty itself. We discussed at some length the curious brokenness of the will, the fact that the two-in-one division, characteristic of all processes of the mind and first discovered—by Socrates and Plato—in the thinking process, turns into a deadly struggle between an I-will and I-nill (between *velle* and *nolle*) which must both be present in order to guarantee freedom: *"Experitur enim qui vult se posse non velle,"* "One who experiences a volition also has the experience of being able not to will."[85] The schoolmen, following the Apostle Paul and Augustine's philosophy of the Will, were in accord that divine grace was necessary to heal the Will's misery. Scotus, perhaps the most pious among them, disagreed. No divine intervention is necessary to redeem the willing ego.

It knows very well how to heal itself of the consequences of the priceless and yet highly questionable gift of human freedom, questionable because the fact that the will is free, undetermined and unlimited by either an exterior or an internally given object, does not signify that man qua man enjoys unlimited freedom. Man's normal way of escaping from his freedom is simply to *act* on the propositions of the will: "For example, it is possible for me to be writing at this moment, just as it is possible for me not to be writing; yet, my act of writing excludes its opposite. By one act of the will I can determine myself to write, and by another act I can decide not to write, but I cannot be simultaneously in act in regard to both things together."[86] In other words, the human will is indetermined, open to contraries, and hence broken only so long as its sole activity consists in forming volitions; the moment it stops willing and starts to act on one of the will's propositions, it loses its freedom—and man, the possessor of the willing ego, is as happy over the loss as Buridan's ass was happy to resolve the problem of choosing between two bundles of hay by following his instinct: stop choosing and start eating.

Underlying this solution, which seems simplistic at first

glance, there is a distinction Scotus made—probably under Aristotle's influence—between *activum* and *factivum*. It is between sheer activity, the Aristotelian *energeia*, which has its end and *ergon* within itself, and fabrication, *facere*, which consists in "producing or fashioning some external object," and this implies "that the operation is transient, that is, has a term outside the agent. Man's artifacts are produced by a transient activity."[87] Mental activities, such as thinking or willing, are activities of the first kind, and these, Scotus considered, though they are resultless in the real world, are of higher "perfection" because essentially they are not transient. They cease, not because they have reached their own end but only because man as a limited and conditioned creature is unable to continue them indefinitely.

Scotus likens these mental activities to the "activity" of light, which "is permanently renewed from its source and thus conserves its inner constancy and simply abides."[88] Because the gift of free will was bestowed upon an *ens creatum*, this being in order to save itself is forced to switch from the *activum* to the *factivum*, from sheer activity to the fashioning of something that finds its term naturally with the emergence of the product. The switch is possible because there is an I-can inherent in every I-will, and this I-can sets limitations on the I-will that are not outside the willing activity itself. *"Voluntas est potentia quia ipsa aliquid potest,"* "the Will is a power because it *can* achieve something," and this potency, inherent in the Will, is indeed the "opposite of the *potentia passiva* of the Aristotelians. It is an active . . . powerful I-can . . . which the ego experiences."[89]

With this experience of the Will as a mental potency whose power does not consist, as in Epictetus, in shielding the mind against reality but on the contrary, inspires it and endows it with self-confidence, it is as though we have reached the end of a history whose beginning was the Apostle Paul's discovery that *velle* and *posse* do not coincide—a coincidence taken for granted in pre-Christian antiquity. Scotus' last word about the Will as a mental faculty relates to the same phenomenon that was elucidated more fully many centuries later in Nietzsche's and Heidegger's equation of Will and Power—except that

Scotus was still unaware of the annihilating (nihilistic) aspect of the phenomenon, that is, of the power generated by negation. He does not yet look upon the future as an anticipated negation of the present—or only perhaps in the general sense of perceiving the inherent futility of all merely worldly events (as Augustine said: *"quod futurum est, transiturum expectatur,"* "what is in the future is expected as something that will have been"[90]).

Man is capable of transcending the world of Being together with which he was created and which remains his habitat until death; yet even his mental activities are never unrelated to the world given to the senses. Thus the intellect is "bound up with the senses," and "its innate function is to understand sensory data"; in a similar way, the Will is "bound up with the sensory appetite" and its innate function is "to enjoy itself." *"Voluntas conjuncta appetitui sensitivo nata est condelectari sibi, sicut intellectus conjunctus sensui natus est intelligere sensibilia."*[91] The decisive words here are the *condelectari sibi*, a delight inherent in the willing activity itself as distinct from the delight of desire in having the desired object, which is transient—possession extinguishes the desire and the delight. The *condelectatio sibi* borrows its delight from its closeness to desire, and Scotus said explicitly that no mental delight can compete with the delight arising from the fulfillment of sensual desire, except that this delight is almost as transient as the desire itself.[92] Hence, he distinguishes sharply between will and desire because only the will is not transient. An inherent delight of the will in itself is as natural to the will as understanding and knowing are to the intellect, and can be detected even in hatred; but its innate perfection, the final peace between the two-in-one, can come about only when the will is transformed into *love*. If the will were mere desire to possess, it would cease to be once the object is possessed: I do not desire what I have.

To the extent that Scotus speculates about an after-life—that is, an "ideal" existence for man qua man—this hoped-for transformation of the will into love with its inherent *delectatio* is decisive. The transformation of willing into loving does not signify that loving ceases to be an activity whose end is within itself; hence future blessedness, the beatitude enjoyed in an after-life, cannot possibly consist in rest and contemplation. Contemplation of the *summum bonum,* of the highest "thing," ergo, God, would be the ideal of the intellect, which is always grounded in intuition, the grasping of a thing in its "thisness," *haecceitas,* which in this life is imperfect not only because here the highest remains unknown but also because intuition of thisness is imperfect: "the intellect . . . has recourse to universal concepts, precisely because it is incapable of grasping the haecceity."[93] The notion of "eternal peace," or of Rest, arises out of the experience of restlessness, of the desires and appetites of a needy being that can transcend them in mental activities without ever being capable of escaping them altogether. What the will in a state of blessedness, that is, in an after-life, no longer needs or is no longer capable of, is *rejection* and hatred, but this does not mean that man in a state of blessedness has lost the faculty of saying "Yes."

That unconditional acceptance is called "Love" by Scotus: *"Amo: volo ut sis."* "Beatitude is therefore the act by which the will comes in contact with the object presented to it by the intellect and loves it, thus fully satisfying its natural desire for it."[94] Here again love is understood as an activity but no longer a mental one, as its object is no longer absent from the senses and no longer imperfectly known to the intellect. For "beatitude . . . consists in the full and perfect attainment of the object as it is in itself, and not merely as it is in the mind."[95] The mind, transcending the existential conditions of the "wayfarer," or pilgrim on earth, has an intimation of such future blessedness in its experience of sheer activity, that is, in a transformation of willing into *loving.* Falling back on the Augustinian distinction of *uti* and *frui,* using something for the sake of something else and enjoying it for its own sake, Scotus says that the essence of beatitude consists in *"fruitio,"* the "perfect love of God for God's sake . . . thus distinct from the love of God for one's own sake." Even if the latter is love for the sake of one's soul's salvation, it is still *amor concupiscentiae,* desirous love.[96] Already in Augustine we find the transformation of willing into loving, and it is more than likely that the reflections of both thinkers were guided by Paul's words about the "love that never ends," not even when "that which is perfect comes" and all else has "passed away" (I Corinthians 13:8–13). In Augustine the transformation comes about because of the binding force of the will; there is no stronger binding force than the love with which the lovers love each other ("marvelously glued together").[97] But for Scotus the experiential ground of love's everlastingness is that he conceives of a love that is not only, as it were, emptied, purified of desires and needs, but in which the very *faculty* of the Will is transformed into sheer activity.

If in this life it is the miracle of the human mind that man at least mentally and provisionally can transcend his earthly conditions and enjoy the sheer actuality of an exercise that has its end in itself, then it is the hoped-for miracle of an after-life that man in his whole existence will be spiritualized. Scotus speaks of a "Glorified body,"[98] no longer dependent on "faculties" whose activities are interrupted either by the *factivum*, the making and fashioning of objects, or by the desires of a needy creature—both of which render transient every activity in this life, the mental ones not excluded. Transformed into love, the restlessness of the will is stilled but not extinguished; love's abiding power is felt not as the arrest of motion—as the end of the fury of war is felt as the quiet of peace—but as the serenity of a self-contained, self-fulfilling, everlasting movement. Here are not the quiet and delight that follow upon a perfect operation, but the stillness of an act resting in its end. In this life we know of such acts in our *experientia interna*, and, according to Scotus, we should be able to understand them as intimations of an uncertain future when they would last forever. Then "the operating faculty will find itself calmed in its object through the perfect act [love] by which it attains it."[99]

The idea that there could be an activity that finds its rest within itself is as surprisingly original—without precedent or sequel in the history of Western thought—as Scotus' ontological preference of the contingent over the necessary and of the existent particular over the universal. I have tried to show that in Scotus we meet not simple conceptual reversals but genuine new insights, all of which could probably be explicated as the speculative conditions for a philosophy of freedom. As far as I can see, in the history of philosophy only Kant can equal Duns Scotus in his unconditional commitment to freedom. And yet certainly Kant had no knowledge of him. I shall therefore end with an odd passage from the *Critique of Pure Reason* that at least deals with the same problem though without any mention of Freedom or the Will:

There is something very strange in the fact, that once we assume something to exist we cannot avoid inferring that something exists necessarily. . . . On the other hand, if I take the concept of anything, no matter what, I find that the existence of this thing can never be represented by me as absolutely necessary, and that, whatever it may be that exists, nothing prevents me from thinking its non-existence. Thus while I may indeed be obliged to assume something necessary as a condition of the existent in general, I cannot think any particular thing as in itself necessary. In other words, I can never *complete* the regress to the conditions of existence save by assuming a necessary being, and yet am never in a position to *begin* with such a being. [And concluding this deliberation a few pages later] . . . there is nothing which absolutely binds reason to accept such an existence; on the contrary it can always annihilate it in thought, without contradiction; absolute necessity is a necessity that is to be found in thought alone.[100]

To which, taught by Scotus, one may add that absolute nothingness cannot be found in thought. We shall have occasion later to come back to this idea when we discuss the uncertain destinies of the willing faculty at the close of the modern age.

# Conclusions IV

## 13. *German Idealism and the*
## *"rainbow-bridge of concepts"*

Before we come to the final part of these considerations I shall try to justify the last and largest leap over the centuries in this sketchy and fragmentary presentation that I had the presumption to announce as a history of the Will. I have already mentioned my doubts as to whether there can legitimately be a "history of ideas," a *Geistesgeschichte* that rests on the assumption that ideas follow and generate one another in a temporal succession. The assumption makes sense only in the system of Hegel's dialectics. But, apart from any theories, a record does exist of the thoughts of great thinkers whose place in factual history is unchallengeable and whose testimony affirming or negating the Will we have touched on here only in passing—Descartes and Leibniz on one side of the argument, Hobbes and Spinoza on the other.

The only great thinker in these centuries who would be truly irrelevant to our context is Kant. His Will is not a *special* mental capability distinct from thinking, but practical reason, a *Vernunftwille* not unlike Aristotle's *nous praktikos;* the statement that "pure reason can be practical is the chief thesis of the Kantian moral philosophy"[1] is perfectly right. Kant's Will is neither freedom of choice (*liberum arbitrium*) nor its own cause; for Kant, sheer spontaneity, which he often called "absolute spontaneity," exists only in thinking. Kant's Will is delegated by reason to be its executive organ in all matters of conduct.

Much more embarrassing, and thus in need of justification, is the omission from our considerations of the development of German idealism after Kant, the leap we have made over Fichte, Schelling, and Hegel, who in their speculative way summed up the centuries of the modern age. For the rise and decline of the modern age is not a figment of the "history of ideas" but a factual event that can be dated: the discovery of the whole earth and of part of the universe, the rise of modern science and its technology, followed by the decline of the Church's authority, by secularization and enlightenment.

This momentous factual break occurring in our past has been characterized and interpreted from many different and legitimate viewpoints; in our context, the most decisive development that took place during these centuries was the subjectivization of cognitive as well as metaphysical thought. Only during these centuries did man become the center of concern to science as well as to philosophy. It had not happened in earlier times, even though, as we saw, the discovery of the Will coincided with the discovery of the "interior man" at a moment when man had become a "question for himself." Only when science had proved not merely that human senses were subject to error—which could be corrected in the light of new evidence in order to reveal "truth"—but that his sensory apparatus was forever incapable of self-evident certainties, did man's mind, now entirely thrown back upon itself, begin, with Descartes, to look for a "certainty" that would be a pure datum of consciousness. When Nietzsche called the modern age the "school of suspicion," he meant that, starting at least with Descartes, man was no longer sure of anything, not even of being real; he needed proof, not only of God's existence but also of his own. The certainty of the I-am is what Descartes found in his *cogito me cogitare;* that is, in a mental experience for which none of the senses, which give us the reality of ourselves and of an exterior world, is necessary.

To be sure, this certainty is very questionable. Already Pascal, himself influenced by Descartes, objected that this consciousness would hardly be sufficient to distinguish between dream and reality: a poor artisan dreaming for twelve hours every night that he was king would have the same life (and enjoy the same amount of "happiness") as a king who dreamed every night that he was nothing but a poor artisan. Moreover, since "one frequently dreams that he is dreaming," nothing can guarantee that what we call our life is not wholly a dream from which we shall awaken in death. To doubt everything (*"de omnibus dubitandum est"*) and find certainty in the very activity of doubting demanded by the "new Philosophy [that] calls all in doubt" (Donne) does not help, for is the doubter not obliged to doubt that he doubts? True, no one went that far, but that only means that "no one was ever a perfect skeptic [*pyrrhonien*, in Pascal]," though not because reason fortified him; he was restrained by "nature, [which] helped impotent reason"; and so Cartesianism was "something like the story of Don Quixote."[2]

Centuries later, Nietzsche, still thinking in the same vein, suspected that it was our Cartesian "belief in the [thinking] 'ego' . . . as the sole reality [that made us] . . . ascribe reality to things in general."[3] Indeed, nothing became more characteristic of the last stages of metaphysics than this kind of turning-of-the-tables, of which Nietzsche, with his mercilessly honest thought-experiments, was the greatest master. But that game—still a thought-game rather than a language-game—did not become possible until, with the rise of German idealism, all bridges had been broken "except the rainbow-bridges of concepts,"[4] or, to put it less poetically, until it dawned on the philosophers that "the novelty of our contemporary position in philosophy lies in the conviction, which no era had before us, that we do not possess the truth. All previous generations 'possessed the truth,' even the skeptics."[5]

Nietzsche and Heidegger are wrong, I think, in their dating of that modern conviction; actually it had accompanied the rise of modern science and then was attenuated by the Cartesian "certainty" as a substitute for truth; this in its turn was destroyed by Kant along with the remnants of Scholasticism, which in the form of logical exercises and the dogmatism of the "schools" had led a rather brittle existence of sheer erudition. But only at the end of the nineteenth century (here Heidegger is right) did the conviction of not possessing the truth become the common opinion of the educated classes and establish itself as something like the Spirit of the Age, of which Nietzsche was probably the most fearless representative.

However, the mighty factor that delayed this reaction for centuries itself sprang up with the rise of the sciences as the natural response of every thinking man to the enormous and enormously rapid advance in human knowledge, an advance that was bound to make the previous centuries since antiquity appear as sheer stagnation by comparison. The concept of *Progress* as a vast co-operative drive in the interest of knowledge for its own sake, "in which all scientists of the past, the present and the future have a part . . . appeared for the first time fully developed in the works of Francis Bacon."[6] With it there came about, at first almost automatically, an important shift in the understanding of Time, the emergence of the Future to the rank formerly occupied by the Present or the Past. The notion that each subsequent generation would necessarily know more than its predecessor and that this progressing would never be completed—a conviction that only in our time has found challengers—was important enough; but for our context, even more important is the simple, matter-of-fact perception that "scientific knowledge" has been and can be attained only "step by step through contributions of *generations* of explorers building upon and gradually amending the findings of their predecessors."

The rise of science had begun with the new discoveries of the astronomers, scientists who not only had "used most systematically" the findings of their predecessors, but who, without the records of past generations, and reliable records at that, would have been unable to make any "progress" at all, since the life-span of one man, or one generation of men, is evidently too short to verify findings and validate scientific hypotheses. But "the astronomers composed star catalogues to be used by future scientists," i.e., they had laid a basis for scientific advances. (Astronomy, of course, was not wholly alone in initiating progress. Thomas Aquinas was conscious of an "increase in scientific knowledge"—"*augmentum factum est*"—which he explained by "the defects of knowledge of those who first invented the sciences." Craftsmen, too, used to the method of trial and error, were keenly aware of certain improvements in their crafts. Yet the guilds themselves "stressed the continuity rather than the progress of craftsmanship," and "the only passage in the extant literature which clearly expresses the idea of the gradual progress of knowledge, or better, technological skill, occurs in a treatise on artillery."[7]) Still, the decisive breakthrough that gave modern science its impetus occurred in astronomy, and the idea of Progress, which from then on dominated every other science till it finally became the dominant notion of the equally modern concept of History, was originally based on the pooling of data, the exchange of knowledge, and the slow accumulation of records that were the requisites of astronomical advance. It was only after the world-shaking discoveries of the sixteenth and seventeenth centuries that what had been going on in that field came to the attention of those who were concerned with the general human condition.

Thus, while the "new philosophy" proving the inadequacy of our senses had "called all in doubt" and given rise to suspicion and despair, the equally manifest forward movement of knowledge gave rise to an immense optimism as to what man can know and learn. Except that this optimism did not apply to men in the singular, not even to the relatively small community of scientists; it applied only to the succession of generations, that is, to Mankind as a whole. In the words of Pascal, who was the first to detect that the idea of Progress was a necessary complement to the idea of Mankind, it was the "particularly [human] prerogative [distinguishing man from animal] that not only each human being can daily advance in knowledge, but that all men together progress continually while the universe grows older . . . so that the whole succession of men throughout the centuries should be *considered as one and the same man who lives forever* and continually learns" (italics added).[8]

What is decisive in this formulation is that the notion of "all men together," which is of course a thought, not a reality, was immediately construed on the model of "man," of a "subject" that could serve as a noun for all kinds of activities expressed in verbs. This concept was not a metaphor, properly speaking; it was a full-fledged *personification* such as we find in the allegories of Renaissance narratives. In other words, *Progress became the project of Mankind,* acting behind the backs of real men—a personified force that we find somewhat later in Adam Smith's "invisible hand," in Kant's "ruse of nature," Hegel's "cunning of Reason," and Marx's "dialectical materialism." To be sure, the historian of ideas will see in these notions nothing more than the secularization of divine Providence, an interpretation that is all the more questionable since we find the personification of Mankind in Pascal, who would certainly have been the last to desire a secular replacement for God as the true ruler of the world.

However that may be, the interconnected ideas of Mankind and Progress came to the foreground of philosophical speculations only after the French Revolution had demonstrated to the minds of its most thoughtful spectators the possible actualization of such invisibles as *liberté, fraternité, égalité,* and thus seemed to constitute a tangible refutation of the oldest conviction of thinking men, to wit, that the ups and downs of history and the ever-changing affairs of men are not worth serious consideration. (To contemporary ears Plato's famous dictum in the *Laws* that a serious man keeps his seriousness for serious things and "does not waste it on trifles"[9] such as human affairs may sound extreme; in fact, it was never challenged before Vico, and Vico had no influence or echo till the nineteenth century.) The event of the French Revolution, the climax in many respects of the modern age, changed "the pale cast of thought" for almost a century; philosophers, a notoriously melancholy tribe of men, became cheerful and optimistic. They now believed in the Future and left the age-old lamentations over the course of the world to the historians. What centuries of scientific advances, fully grasped only by the participants in the great enterprise yet by no means beyond the general comprehension of the philosopher, had been unable to achieve was now brought about in a matter of a few decades: philosophers were converted to a faith in the progress not only of knowledge but also of human affairs generally.

And while they began to reflect, with a commitment never before witnessed, on the course of *History,* they could not help becoming aware almost immediately of the greatest riddle presented to them by their new subject matter. That was the simple fact that no action ever attains its intended goal and that Progress—or any other fixed meaningfulness in the historical process—arises out of a senseless "mixture of error and violence" (Goethe), out of a "melancholy haphazardness" in the "meaningless course of human affairs" (Kant). What sense there is can be detected only by the wisdom of hindsight, when men no longer act but begin to tell the story of what has happened; then it seems as though men, while pursuing their aims at cross-purposes, without rhyme and reason, had been led by an "intention of nature," by the "guiding thread of reason."[10] I have quoted Kant and Goethe, both of whom, as it were, stopped at the threshold of the new generation, that of the German Idealists for whom the events of the French Revolution were the decisive experiences of their lives. But that "the facts of known history" taken by themselves "possess neither a common basis nor continuity nor coherence" was already known to Vico, and Hegel, long after, was still insisting that "passions, private aims, and the satisfaction of selfish desires, are . . . the most effective springs of action." Hence, not the record of past events but only the story makes sense, and what is so striking in Kant's remarks at the end of his life is that he immediately understood that the subject of History's action would have to be Mankind, rather than man or any verifiable human community. Striking, too, is the fact that he was able to realize the great flaw in History's project: "It will always remain bewildering that the earlier generations seem to carry on their burdensome business only for the sake of the later . . . and that only the last should have the good fortune to dwell in the [completed] building."[11]

Probably it was sheer coincidence that the generation that grew to maturity under the impact of the eighteenth-century revolutions was also mentally formed by Kant's liberation of thought, by his resolution of the old dilemma between dogmatism and skepticism through the introduction of a self-critique of Reason. And as the revolution encouraged them to transfer the notion of Progress from scientific advancement to the realm of human affairs and understand it as the progress of History, it was only natural that their attention should be directed toward the Will as the spring of action and the organ of the Future. The result was that "the thought of making freedom the sum and substance of philosophy emancipated the human spirit in all its relationships," emancipated the thinking ego for free speculation in thought-trains whose ultimate goal was to "prove . . . that not only is the Ego all, but contrariwise too, all is Ego."[12]

What had appeared in a restrictive, tentative way in Pascal's personified concept of Mankind now began to proliferate to an incredible degree. The activities of men, whether thinking or acting, were all transformed into activities of personified concepts—which made philosophy both infinitely more difficult (the chief difficulty in Hegel's philosophy is its abstractness, its only occasional hints at the actual data and phenomena he has in mind) and incredibly more alive. It was a veritable orgy of sheer speculation, which, in sharp contrast with Kant's critical reason, was brimful of historical data in a disguised state of radical abstraction. Since the personified concept itself is supposed to act, it looks as though (in Schelling's words) philosophy has "raised itself to a higher standpoint," to a "higher realism" in which mere thought-things, Kant's *noumena,* dematerialized products of the thinking ego's reflection on actual data—historical data in Hegel, mythological or religious in Schelling—begin their curious disembodied ghostly dance whose steps and rhythms are neither regulated nor limited by any idea of reason.

It was in this region of pure speculation that the Will appeared during the short period of German Idealism. "In the final and highest instance," declared Schelling, "there is no other Being than Will. Will is primordial Being, and all predicates apply to it alone—groundlessness, eternity, independence of time, self-affirmation! All philosophy strives only to find this highest expression."[13] And quoting this passage in his *What Is Called Thinking?,* Heidegger at once adds: "The predicates, then, which metaphysical thought has since antiquity attributed to Being, Schelling finds in their final, highest . . . most perfected form in willing. *The Will in this willing does not mean here a capacity of the human soul,* however; the word 'willing' here designates the Being of beings as a whole" (italics added).[14] No doubt Heidegger is right; Schelling's Will is a metaphysical entity but, unlike the more common and older metaphysical fallacies, it is personified. In a different context and more precisely, Heidegger himself sums up the meaning of this personified Concept: the *false* "opinion [easily] arises that the human will is the origin of the will-to-will, while on the contrary, man is being willed by the Will-to-will without even experiencing the essence of such willing."[15]

With these words Heidegger resolutely turns against the subjectivism of the modern age as well as against phenomenological analyses, whose chief aim has always been to "save the phenomena" as given in consciousness. And what he turns to while entering on the "rainbow bridge of concepts" is German Idealism and its ingenuous exclusion of man and man's faculties in favor of personified concepts.

Nietzsche diagnosed the inspiration behind this post-Kantian German philosophy with unsurpassed clarity; he knew that philosophy only too well and finally went a similar, perhaps even more extreme way himself.

[German philosophy, said Nietzsche] is the most fundamental form of . . . homesickness there has ever been: the longing for the best that has ever existed. One is no longer at home anywhere; at last one longs back for that place in which alone one can be at home: the *Greek* world! But it is in precisely that direction that all bridges are broken—except the rainbow-bridges of concepts. . . . To be sure, one must be very light, very subtle, very thin to step across these bridges! But what happiness there is already in this will to spirituality, to ghostliness [*Geisterhaftigkeit*] almost! . . . One wants to go *back*, through the Church Fathers to the Greeks. . . . German philosophy is a piece of . . . will to Renaissance, will to go on with the discovery of antiquity, the digging up of ancient philosophy, above all of the pre-Socratics—the most deeply buried of all Greek temples! A few centuries hence, perhaps, one will judge that all German philosophy derives its real dignity from being a gradual reclamation of the soil of antiquity . . . we are growing more Greek by the day; at first, as is only fair, in concepts and evaluations, as Hellenizing ghosts, as it were. . . .[16]

No doubt the personified concept had its root in verifiable experience, but the pseudo-kingdom of disembodied spirits working behind men's backs was built out of homesickness for another world, in which man's spirit could feel at home.

This, then, is my justification for having omitted from our considerations that body of thought, German Idealism, in which sheer speculation in the realm of metaphysics perhaps reached its climax together with its end. I did not want to cross the "rainbow-bridge of concepts," perhaps because I am not homesick enough, in any event because I do not believe in a world, be it a past world or a future world, in which man's mind, equipped for withdrawing from the world of appearances, could or should ever be comfortably at home. Moreover, at least in the cases of Nietzsche and Heidegger, it was precisely a confrontation with the Will as a human faculty and not as an ontological category that prompted them first to repudiate the faculty and *then* turn about to put their confidence in this ghostly home of personified concepts which so obviously was "built" and decorated by the thinking, as opposed to the willing, ego.

## 14  Nietzsche's repudiation of the Will

In my discussion of the Will I have repeatedly mentioned two altogether different ways of understanding the faculty: as a faculty of *choice* between objects or goals, the *liberum arbitrium*, which acts as arbiter between given ends and deliberates freely about means to reach them; and, on the other hand, as our "faculty for beginning spontaneously a series in time" (Kant)[17] or Augustine's *"initium ut esset homo creatus est,"* man's capacity for beginning because he himself is a beginning. With the modern age's concept of Progress and its inherent shift from understanding the future as that which approaches us to that which we determine by the Will's projects, the instigating power of the Will was bound to come to the foreground. And so indeed it did, as far as we can tell from the common opinion of the time.

On the other hand, nothing is more characteristic of the beginnings of what we now call "existentialism" than the absence of any such optimistic overtones. According to Nietzsche, only "lack of historical sense," a lack that for him is "the original error of all philosophers,"[18] can explain that optimism: "Let us not be deceived! Time marches forward; we'd like to believe that everything that is in it also marches forward—that the development is one that moves forward." And as to Progress' correlate, the idea of mankind: " 'Mankind' does not advance; it does not even exist."[19]

In other words, though the universal suspicion at the beginning of the modern age had been powerfully neutralized, held in check, first by the very notion of Progress and then by its seeming embodiment and apogee in the French Revolution, this had proved to be only a delaying action, whose force eventually exhausted itself. If one wants to look on this development historically, one can only say that Nietzsche's thought-experiments—"such an experimental philosophy as I live anticipates experimentally even the possibilities of the most fundamental nihilism"[20]—at last completed what had begun with Descartes and Pascal in the seventeenth century.

Men, forever tempted to lift the veil of the future—with the aid of computers or horoscopes or the intestines of sacrificial animals—have a worse record to show in these "sciences" than in almost any other scientific endeavor. Still, if it were a matter of honest competition between futurologists in respect to our own time, the prize might well go to John Donne, a poet without any scientific ambitions, who in 1611 wrote in immediate reaction to what he knew was going on in the sciences (which for a long time would still be operating under the name of "natural philosophy"). He did not have to wait for Descartes, or Pascal, to draw all the conclusions from what he perceived.

> And new Philosophy calls all in doubt,
> The Element of fire is quite put out;
> The Sun is lost and th'earth, and no mans wit
> Can well direct him where to looke for it. . . .
> 'Tis all in pieces, all cohaerence gone;
> All just supply, and all Relation:
> Prince, Subject, Father, Sonne, are things forgot. . . .

And he ends with lamentations that needed roughly three hundred years to be heard again: "when thou knowst this, Thou knowst how ugly a monster . . . how wan a Ghost . . . how drie a Cinder this world is."[21]

It is against this historical background that we shall have

to consider the last two thinkers still close enough to the West's philosophical heritage to recognize in the Will one of the mind's important faculties. We start with Nietzsche and remember that he never wrote any book with the title "Will to Power," that the collection of fragments, notes, and aphorisms bearing this title was published posthumously, selected from a chaos of unconnected and often contradictory sayings. Each one of them is what all Nietzsche's mature writings actually are, namely, a thought-experiment, a literary genre surprisingly rare in our recorded history. The most obvious analogy is Pascal's *Pensées*, which share with Nietzsche's *Will to Power* a haphazardness of arrangement that has led later editors to try to *re*arrange them, with the rather annoying result that the reader has a good deal of trouble identifying and dating them.

We shall consider first a number of simple descriptive statements without metaphysical or general philosophical connotations. Most of them will sound rather familiar, but it will be better not to jump to the conclusion that we may be confronted here with bookish influences. To draw such inferences is especially tempting in the case of Heidegger because of his profound knowledge of medieval philosophy, on the one hand, and his insistence on the primacy of the future tense in *Being and Time* (which I have already spoken of), on the other. It is all the more noteworthy that in his discussion of the Will, which chiefly takes the form of an interpretation of Nietzsche, he nowhere mentions Augustine's discoveries in the *Confessions*. Hence what will sound familiar in the following is best ascribed to the peculiar characteristics of the willing faculty; even Schopenhauer's influence on the young Nietzsche we may disregard without great scruples. Nietzsche knew that "Schopenhauer spoke of the 'will'; but nothing is more characteristic of his philosophy than the absence of all genuine willing,"[22] and he saw correctly that the reason for this lay in a "basic misunderstanding of the *will* (as if craving, instinct, drive were the *essence* of the will)" whereas "the will is precisely that which treats cravings as their master and appoints to them their way and measure."[23]

For "to will is not the same as to desire, to strive for, to want: from all these it is distinguished through the element of

Command. . . . That something is commanded, this is inherent in willing."[24] Heidegger comments: "No characteristic phrase occurs more frequently in Nietzsche than . . . to will is to command; inherent in Will is the commanding thought."[25] It is no less characteristic that this commanding thought is directed only very rarely toward dominating others: command and obedience both occur in the mind—in a fashion strangely similar to Augustine's conception, of which Nietzsche certainly knew nothing.

He explains at some length in *Beyond Good and Evil:*

Somebody who wills gives orders to something *in* him that obeys. . . . The strangest aspect of this multiple phenomenon we call 'Will' is that we have but one word for it, and especially only one word for the fact that *we are in every given case at the same time those who issue the orders and those who obey them;* insofar as we obey, we experience the feelings of coercion, urging, pressing, resisting, which usually begin to manifest themselves immediately after the act of willing; insofar however . . . as we are in command . . . we experience a sensation of pleasure, and this all the more strongly as we are used to overcoming the dichotomy through the notion of the I, the Ego, and this in such a way that we take the obedience in ourselves for granted and therefore identify willing and performing, willing and acting [italics added].

This willing operation existing only in our minds overcomes the mental duality of the two-in-one that has become a battle between one who commands and one who is supposed to obey by identifying the "I" as a whole with the commanding part and anticipating that the other, the resisting part, will obey and do as it is told. "What is called 'freedom of the will' is essentially a passionate superiority toward a someone who must obey. 'I am free; "he" must obey'—the consciousness of this is the very willing."[26]

We would not expect Nietzsche to believe in divine grace as the healing power for the Will's duality. What *is* unexpected in the above description is that he detected in the "consciousness" of the struggle a kind of trick of the "I" that enables it to escape the conflict by identifying itself with the commanding part and to overlook, as it were, the unpleasant, paralyzing sentiments of being coerced and hence always on the point of resisting. Nietzsche often denounces this feeling of superiority as an illusion, albeit a wholesome one. In other passages, he accounts for the "strangeness" of the whole phenomenon by calling it an "oscillation [of the will] between yes and no," but he sticks to the feeling of the "I" 's superiority by identifying the oscillation with a kind of swinging from pleasure to pain. The pleasure, different in this as in other respects from Scotus' *delectatio,* is clearly the anticipated joy of the I-can inherent in the willing act itself, independent of performance, of the triumphal feeling we all know when we perform well, regardless of praise or audience. In Nietzsche, the point is that he numbers the negative slave-feelings of being coerced and of resisting or resenting among the necessary obstacles without which the Will would not even know its own power. Only by surmounting an inner resistance does the Will become aware of its genesis: it did not spring up to obtain power; power is its very source. Again in *Beyond Good and Evil*: " 'Freedom of the will' is the word for that manifold pleasurable condition of the willer *who is in command and at the same time* considers himself as one with the executor of the command—as such enjoying the triumph over the resistance, but possessed of the judgment that it is his will itself that is overcoming the resistance. In this fashion the willer adds the pleasurable feelings of executing . . . to his pleasurable feeling as Commander."[27]

This description, which takes the two-in-one of the Will, the resisting "I" and the triumphant "I," to be the source of the Will's power, owes its plausibility to the unexpected introduction of the pain-pleasure principle into the discussion: "to posit pleasure and displeasure as cardinal facts."[28] Just as the mere absence of pain can never cause pleasure, so the Will, if it did not have to overcome resistance, could never achieve power. Here, unwittingly following the ancient hedonist philosophies rather than the contemporary pleasure-pain calculus, Nietzsche relies in his description on the experience of *release* from pain—not on the mere absence of pain or the mere presence of pleasure. The intensity of the sensation of release is only matched by the intensity of the sensation of pain and is always greater than any pleasure unrelated to pain. The pleasure of drinking the most exquisite wine cannot be compared in intensity with the pleasure felt by a desperately thirsty man who obtains his first drink of water. In this sense there is a clear distinction between joy, independent of and unrelated to needs and desires, and pleasure, the sensuous lust of a creature whose body is alive to the extent that it is in need of something it does not have.

Joy, it seems, can only be experienced if one is wholly free of pain and desire; that is, it stands outside the pain-pleasure calculus, which Nietzsche despised because of its inbred utilitarianism. Joy—what Nietzsche called the Dionysian principle —comes from *abundance,* and it is true that all joy is a kind of luxury; it overcomes us, and we can indulge in it only after the needs of life have been satisfied. But this is not to deny the sensuous element in joy as well; abundance is still *life's* abundance, and the Dionysian principle in its sensuous lust turns to destruction precisely because abundance can afford destruction. In this respect is not the Will in the closest possible affinity with the life-principle, which constantly produces and destroys? Hence Nietzsche defines the Dionysian as "temporary identification with the principle of life (including the voluptuousness of the martyr)," as "Joy in the destruction . . . and at the sight of its progressive ruin . . . Joy in what is coming and lies in the future, which triumphs over existing things, however good."[29]

The Nietzschean shift from the I-will to the anticipated I-can, which negates the Paulinian I-will-and-I-can*not* and thereby all Christian ethics, is based on an unqualified Yes to Life, that is, on an elevation of Life as experienced outside all mental activities to the rank of supreme value by which everything else is to be evaluated. This is possible and plausible because there is indeed an I-can inherent in every I-will, as we saw in our discussion of Duns Scotus: *"Voluntas est potentia quia ipsa alquid potest"* ("The Will is a power because it *can* achieve something").[30] The Nietzschean Will, however, is not limited by its own inherent I-can; for instance, it can will eternity, and Nietzsche looks forward to a future that will produce the "superman," that is, a new human species strong enough to live in the thought of an "eternal recurrence." "We produced the weightiest thought—*now let us produce the being* to whom it will be easy and blessed! . . . To celebrate the future, not the past. To sing [*dichten*] the myth of the future."[31]

Life as the highest value cannot, of course, be demonstrated; it is a mere hypothesis, the assumption made by common sense that the will is free because without that assumption—as has been said over and over—no precept of a moral, religious, or juridical nature could possibly make sense. It is contradicted by the "scientific hypothesis" according to which—as Kant, notably, pointed out—every act, the moment it enters the world, falls into a network of causes, and thus appears in a sequence of occurrences explicable only in the context of causality. For Nietzsche, it is decisive that the common-sense hypothesis constitutes a "dominant sentiment from which we cannot liberate ourselves even if the scientific hypothesis were demonstrated."[32] But the identification of willing with living, the notion that our urge to live and our will to will are ultimately the same, has other and perhaps more serious consequences for Nietzsche's concept of power.

This may become clear when we turn to two leading metaphors in *The Gay Science*, one having to do with life and the other introducing the theme of "Eternal Recurrence"—the "basic idea of Zarathustra," as he called it in *Ecce Homo*, and the basic idea also of the posthumous aphorisms collected under the misleading, non-Nietzschean title *The Will to Power*. The first appears under the title "Will and Wave" (*Wille und Welle*):

How greedily this wave approaches, as if it were after something! How it crawls with terrifying haste into the inmost nooks of this labyrinthine cliff! . . . it seems that something of value, high value, must be hidden there.—And now it comes back, a little more slowly but still quite white with excitement; is it disappointed? Has it found what it looked for? Does it pretend to be disappointed?—But already another wave is approaching, still more greedily and savagely than the first, and its soul, too, seems to be full of secrets and the lust to dig up treasures. *Thus live waves—thus live we who will.* . . . Carry on as you like, roaring with

overweening pleasure and malice—or dive again . . . and throw
your infinite white mane of foam and spray over them: Everything
suits me, for everything suits you so well, and *I am so well disposed
toward you* for everything. . . . For . . . I know you and your
secret, I know your kind! You and I—are we not of one kind?—You
and I—do we not have one secret? [Italics added.]³³

Here at first it seems as though we were dealing with a
perfect metaphor, a "perfect resemblance of two relations between totally dissimilar things."³⁴ The relation of the waves to
the sea from which they erupt without intent or aim, creating
a tremendous purposeless excitement, resembles and therefore
illuminates the turmoil the Will excites in the household of the
soul—always seemingly in quest of something till it quiets
down, yet never extinguished, always ready for a new assault.
The Will enjoys willing as the sea enjoys waves, for "rather
than not will, man even wills *nothingness*."³⁵ Upon closer examination, however, it appears that something quite decisive
has happened here to what was originally a typically Homeric
metaphor. Those metaphors, we saw, were always irreversible:
Looking upon the storms of the sea, you were reminded of
your inward emotions; but those emotions did not tell you
anything about the sea. In the Nietzschean metaphor, the two
dissimilar things the metaphor is bringing together not only
resemble each other, for Nietzsche they are identical; and·the
"secret" of which he is so proud is precisely his knowledge of
this identity. Will and Wave are the same, and one is even
tempted to assume that the experiences of the willing ego had
made Nietzsche discover the turmoil of the sea.

In other words, the appearances of the world have become
a mere *symbol* for inward experiences, with the consequence
that the metaphor, originally designed to bridge the rift between the thinking or willing ego and the world of appearances, collapses. The collapse has come about not because of a
superior weight given to the "objects" that confront human life
but, rather, because of a partisanship for man's soul apparatus,
whose experiences are understood to have absolute primacy.
There are many passages in Nietzsche that point to this fundamental anthropomorphism. To cite only one example: "All the
presuppositions of mechanistic theory [in Nietzsche identical

with the "scientific hypothesis"]—matter, atom, gravity, pressure and stress—are not 'facts-in-themselves' but interpretations with the aid of psychical fictions."[36] Modern science has come to strangely similar suspicions in its speculative reflections on its own results: today's "astrophysicists . . . must reckon with . . . the possibility that their outer world is only our inner world turned inside out" (Lewis Mumford).

We now turn to our second story, which is actually not a metaphor or a symbol but a *parable*, the story of a thought-experiment that Nietzsche entitled *"Das grösste Schwergewicht,"* the thought that would weigh most heavily on you.

What, if some day or night a demon were to steal after you into your loneliest loneliness and say to you: "This life as you now live it, you will have to live once more and innumerable times more; and there will be nothing new in it, but every pain and every joy and every thought and sigh and everything unutterably small or great in your life will have to return to you, all in the same succession and sequence—even this spider and this moonlight between the trees, and even this moment and I myself. The eternal hourglass of existence is turned upside down again and again, and you with it, speck of dust!"

Would you not throw yourself down and gnash your teeth and curse the demon who spoke thus? Or have you once experienced a tremendous moment when you would have answered him: "You are a god and never have I heard anything more divine." If this thought gained possession of you, it would change you as you are or perhaps crush you. The question in each and every thing, "Do you desire this once more and innumerable times more?" would lie upon your actions as the greatest weight. Or *how well disposed would you have to become to yourself and to life to crave nothing more fervently* than this ultimate eternal confirmation and seal? [Italics added.][37]

No later version of the eternal-recurrence notion displays so unequivocally its main characteristic, namely, that it is not a theory, not a doctrine, not even a hypothesis, but a mere thought-experiment. As such, since it implies an experimental return to the ancient cyclical time concept, it seems to be in flagrant contradiction with any possible notion of the Will, whose projects always assume rectilinear time and a future that is unknown and therefore open to change. In the context of Nietzsche's own statements on the Will, and the shift he postulated from the I-will to an anticipated I-can, the only affinity between the two stories would seem to lie in the "tremendous moment" of overflowing "benevolence"—the being "well disposed to" Life—that obviously gave birth in each case to the thought.

If we see it in terms of his notion of the Will, this would be the moment when the I-can feeling is at its peak and spreads a general "feeling of strength" (*Kraftgefühl*). That emotion, as Nietzsche observes, often arises in us "even before the deed, occasioned by the idea of what is to be done (as at the sight of an enemy or an obstacle to which we feel ourselves equal)." To the operating will this emotion is of little consequence; it is "always an accompanying feeling," to which we wrongly ascribe the "force of action," the quality of a causative agent. "Our belief in causality is belief in force and effect; a transference from our experience [in which] we identify force and the feeling of force."[38] Hume's famous discovery that the relation between cause and effect rests on belief engendered by custom and association, and not on knowledge, was made afresh, and in many variations, by Nietzsche, who was unaware of having had a predecessor.

His own examination is more searching and more critical because, in the place of Hume's utility calculus and his "moral sentiment," he puts the experience of an I-will which is followed by an effect, that is, he uses the fact that man is conscious of himself as a causative agent even before he has done anything. But Nietzsche does not believe that this renders the Will less irrelevant; for Nietzsche as well as for Hume, free will is an illusion inherent in human nature, an illusion which philosophy, a critical examination of our faculties, will cure us of. Except that for Nietzsche the moral consequences of the cure are decidedly more serious.

If we can no longer ascribe "the value of an action . . . to the *intention*, the purpose for the sake of which one has acted or lived . . . [if] the absence of intention and purpose in events comes more and more to the foreground of consciousness," the conclusion seems inevitable that "Nothing has any meaning," for "this melancholy sentence means 'All meaning lies in intention, and if intention is altogether lacking, then meaning is altogether lacking too.' " Hence: "Why could 'a purpose' not be an epiphenomenon in the series of changes of effective forces that bring forth purposive action—a pale image in our consciousness . . . a symptom of occurrences, *not* their cause?—But with this we have criticized the *will itself:* is it not an illusion to take for a cause that which rises to consciousness as an act of will?" ( Italics added.)[39]

The fact that this passage is contemporaneous with the passages about "Eternal Recurrence" justifies us in asking whether and how these two thoughts can be, if not reconciled, at any rate conceived in such a way that they will not clash head on with each other. Let us first comment very briefly on the few important non-speculative but, rather, descriptive statements made by Nietzsche on the Will.

There is, first—what seems obvious but had never been pointed out before—that "the Will cannot will backward"; it cannot stop the wheel of time. This is Nietzsche's version of the I-will-and-I-can*not*, for it is precisely this willing-backward that the Will wills and intends. From that impotence Nietzsche derives all human evil—resentment, the thirst for vengeance (we punish because we cannot undo what has been done), the thirst for the power to dominate others. To this "genealogy of morals," we could add that the Will's impotence persuades men to prefer looking backward, remembering and thinking, because, to the backward glance, everything that is *appears* to be necessary. The repudiation of willing liberates man from a responsibility that would be unbearable if nothing that was done could be undone. In any case, it was probably the Will's clash with the past that made Nietzsche experiment with Eternal Recurrence.

Second, the concept "will-to-power" is redundant: the Will generates power by willing, hence the will whose objective is humility is no less powerful than the will to rule over others. The willing act itself is already an act of potency, an indication of strength (the "feeling of strength," *Kraftgefühl*) that goes beyond what is required to meet the needs and demands of everyday life. If there is a simple contradiction in Nietzsche's thought-experiments, it is the contradiction between the Will's factual impotence—it wills but cannot will backward—and this feeling of strength.

Third, the Will—whether it wills backward and senses its impotence or wills forward and senses its strength—transcends the sheer givenness of the world. This transcendence is gratuitous and corresponds to the overwhelming superabundance of Life. Hence the Will's authentic goal is abundance: "By the words 'freedom of the Will' we signify this feeling of a surplus of strength," and the feeling is more than a mere illusion of consciousness because it does correspond with the superabundance of life itself. Hence one could understand all of Life as a Will-to-power. "Only where there is life is there also will: not will to life but . . . will to power."[40] For one could very well explain "nourishment" as the "consequence of insatiable appropriation, of the will to power, [and] 'procreation' [as] the crumbling that supervenes when the ruling cells are incapable of organizing that which has been appropriated."[41]

This transcending, which is inherent in willing, Nietzsche calls "Overcoming." It is possible because of abundance: the activity itself is seen as creativity, and the "virtue" that corresponds to this whole complex of ideas is Generosity—the overcoming of the thirst for vengeance. It is the extravagance and "recklessness [*Übermut*] of an overflowing, spendthrift will" that opens up a future beyond all past and present. *Surplus*, according to Nietzsche as well as to Marx (the sheer fact of a surplus of labor force left over after the requirements for the preservation of individual life and of species survival have been met), constitutes the *conditio-per-quam* of all culture. The so-called superman is man insofar as he is able to transcend, "overcome," himself. But this overcoming, we should not forget, is a merely mental exercise: to "recreate all 'it was' into a 'thus I willed it'—that alone should I call redemption."[42] For "Man seeks . . . a world that is not self-contradictory, not deceptive, does not change, a *true* world. . . ." Man, as he is now when he is honest, is a nihilist, namely, "a man who judges of the world as it is that it ought *not* to be, and of the world as it ought to be that it does not exist. . . . [To overcome nihilism one needs] the strength to reverse values and to deify . . . the apparent world as the only world, and to call them good."[43]

Clearly, what is needful is not to change the world or men but to change their way of "evaluating" it, their way, in other words, of thinking and reflecting about it. In Nietzsche's words, what must be overcome are the philosophers, those whose "life is an experiment of cognition";[44] they must be taught how to cope. Had Nietzsche developed these thoughts into a systematic philosophy, he would have fashioned a kind of greatly enriched Epictetian doctrine, teaching once more the "art of living one's own life," whose psychologically powerful trick consists in *willing* that to happen which happens anyhow.[45]

But the point is that Nietzsche, who knew and estimated Epictetus very highly, did not stop with the discovery of the Will's mental omnipotence. He embarked on a construction of the given world that would make sense, be a fitting abode for a creature whose "strength of will [is great enough] to do without meaning in things . . . [who] can endure to live in a meaningless world."[46] "Eternal Recurrence" is the term for this final redeeming thought inasmuch as it proclaims the "*Innocence* of all Becoming" (*die Unschuld des Werdens*) and with that its inherent aimlessness and purposelessness, its freedom from guilt and responsibility.

"Innocence of Becoming" and "Eternal Recurrence" are not drawn from a mental faculty; they are rooted in the indisputable *fact* that we indeed are "thrown" into the world (Heidegger), that no one has asked us if we wished to be here or wished to be as we are. For all we know or can ever know, "no one is responsible for man's being there at all, for his being such-and-such, or for his being in these circumstances or in this environment." Hence, the basic insight into the essence of Being is "that *there are no moral facts at all*," an insight Nietzsche, as he said, "was the first to formulate." Its consequences are very great, not only because Christianity and its concept of a " 'moral world-order' infects the innocence of becoming by means of 'punishment' and 'guilt' [and therefore can be seen as] a metaphysics of the hangman," but because, with the elimination of intent and purpose, of somebody who can "be held responsible," causality itself is eliminated; nothing can be "traced back" to a cause once the *"causa prima"* is eliminated.[47]

With the elimination of cause and effect, there is no longer any sense in the rectilinear structure of Time whose past is always understood as the cause of the present, whose present is the tense of intention and preparation of our projects for the future, and whose future is the outcome of both. Besides, that time construct crumbles under the weight of the no less factual insight that "Everything passes," that the future brings only what *will have been*, and therefore that everything that is "deserves to pass away."[48] Just as every I-will, in its identification with the commanding part of the two-in-one, triumphantly anticipates an I-can, so expectation, the mood with which the Will affects the soul, contains within itself the melancholy of an and-this-too-*will-have-been*, the foreseeing of the future's past, which reasserts the Past as the dominant tense of Time. The only redemption from this all-devouring Past is the thought that everything that passes returns, that is, a cyclical time construct that makes Being swing within itself.

And is not Life itself construed so, does not one day follow upon the next, season succeed season by repeating itself in eternal sameness? Is not this world view much "truer" to reality as we know it than the world view of the philosophers? "If the motion of the world aimed at a final state, that state would have been reached. The sole fundamental fact, however, is that it does not aim at a final state; and every philosophy and scientific hypothesis . . . which necessitates such a final state is *refuted* by this fundamental fact. I seek a conception of the world that takes this fact into account. Becoming must be explained without recourse to final intentions; Becoming must appear justified at every moment (or incapable of being evaluated; which amounts to the same thing); the present must absolutely not be justified by reference to a future, nor the past by reference to the present. . . ." Nietzsche then summarizes: "1. Becoming does not aim at a *final state*, does not flow into 'being.' 2. Becoming is not a merely *apparent state;* perhaps the world of beings is mere appearance. 3. Becoming is of [equal value at] every moment . . . in other words, it has no value at all, for anything against which to measure it . . . is lacking. *The total value of the world cannot be evaluated.*"⁴⁹

In the turmoil of aphorisms, remarks, and thought-experiments that constitute the posthumous collection entitled *The Will to Power* the importance of this last passage, which I have quoted at some length, is difficult to spot. Judging by internal evidence, I am inclined to think of it as Nietzsche's last word on the subject; and this last word clearly spells a repudiation of the Will and the willing ego, whose internal experiences have misled thinking men into assuming that there are such things as cause and effect, intention and goal, in reality. The superman is one who has overcome these fallacies, whose insights are strong enough either to resist the promptings of the Will or to turn his own will around, redeem it from all oscillations, quiet it to that stillness where "looking away" is "the only negation,"⁵⁰ because nothing is left but the "wish to be a Yes-sayer," to bless everything there is for being, "to bless and say Amen."⁵¹

## 15 *Heidegger's Will-not-to-will*

Neither the word "willing" nor the word "thinking" occurs in Heidegger's early work before the so-called reversal (*Kehre*) or "turn-about" that took place in the mid-thirties; and Nietzsche's name is nowhere mentioned in *Being and Time.*⁵² Hence Heidegger's position on the faculty of the Will, culminating in his passionate insistence on willing *"not to will"*— which of course has nothing to do with the Will's oscillation between *velle* and *nolle,* willing and nilling—arises directly from his extremely careful investigation of Nietzsche's work, to which, after 1940, he returns time and again. Still, the two volumes of his *Nietzsche,* which were published in 1961, are in certain respects the most telling; they contain lecture courses from the years 1936 to 1940, that is, the very years when the "reversal" actually occurred and therefore had not yet been subjected to Heidegger's own interpretations. If in reading these two volumes one ignores Heidegger's later re-interpretation (which came out before the *Nietzsche*), one is tempted to date the "reversal" as a concrete autobiographical event precisely between volume I and volume II; for, to put it bluntly, the first volume explicates Nietzsche by going along with him, while the second is written in a subdued but unmistakable polemical tone. This important change of mood has been observed, as far as I know, only by J. L. Mehta, in his excellent book on *The Philosophy of Martin Heidegger*,[53] and less decisively by Walter Schulz. The relevance of this dating seems evident: what the reversal originally turns against is primarily the will-to-power. In Heidegger's understanding, the will to rule and to dominate is a kind of original sin, of which he found himself guilty when he tried to come to terms with his brief past in the Nazi movement.

When he later announced publicly—for the first time in the *Letter on Humanism* (1949)[54]—that there had been a "reversal," for years in fact, in a larger sense, he had been recasting his views on the whole of history from the Greeks to the present and focusing primarily not on the Will but on the relation between Being and Man. Originally during those years, the "reversal" had been a turning against the self-assertion of man (as proclaimed in the famous speech delivered when he became rector of Freiburg University in 1933[55]), symbolically incarnated in Prometheus, "the first philosopher," a figure nowhere else mentioned in his work. Now it turned against the alleged subjectivism of *Being and Time* and the book's primary concern with man's existence, his mode of being.

To put the matter in a rough and oversimplified way: while Heidegger had always been concerned with "the question of the meaning of Being," his first, "provisional," goal had been to analyze the being of man as the only entity that can ask the question because it touches his own being; hence, when man raises the question What is Being?, he is thrown back upon himself. But when, thrown back upon himself, he raises the question Who is Man?, it is Being, on the contrary, that moves into the foreground; it is Being, as now emerges, that bids man to think. ("Heidegger was forced to move away from the original approach of *Being and Time;* instead of seeking to approach Being through the openness and transcendence inherent in man, he now tries to define man in terms of Being."[56]) And the first demand Being makes of man is to think out the "ontological difference," that is, the difference between the sheer isness of beings and the Being of this isness itself, the Being of Being. As Heidegger himself states it in the *Letter on Humanism:* "To put it simply, thinking is thinking of Being, where the 'of' has a double meaning. Thinking is of Being, insofar as, being brought to pass by Being, it belongs to Being. At the same time it is thinking of Being insofar as, belonging to Being, it listens to Being."[57] Man's listening transforms the silent claim of Being into speech, and "language is the language of Being as the clouds are the clouds of the sky."[58]

The "reversal" in this sense has two important consequences that have hardly anything to do with the repudiation of the Will. First, Thinking is no longer "subjective." To be sure, without being thought by man, Being would never become manifest; it depends upon man, who offers it an abode: "language is the abode of Being." But what man thinks does not arise from his own spontaneity or creativity; it is the obedient response to the command of Being. Second, the entities in which the world of appearances is given to man distract man from Being, which hides behind them—very much as the trees hide the forest that nevertheless, seen from outside, is constituted by them.

In other words, "Oblivion of Being" (*Seinsvergessenheit*) belongs to the very nature of the relation between Man and Being. Heidegger now is no longer content to eliminate the willing ego in favor of the thinking ego—maintaining, for instance, as he still does in the *Nietzsche,* that the Will's insistence on the future forces man into *oblivion* of the past, that it robs thinking of its foremost activity, which is *an-denken,* remembrance: "The Will has never owned the beginning, has left and abandoned it essentially through forgetting."[59] Now he desubjectivizes thinking itself, robs it of its Subject, man as a thinking being, and transforms it into a function of Being, in which all "efficacy rests . . . flowing from there towards the essent [*das Seiende*]," thereby determining the actual course of the world. "Thinking, in turn, lets itself be claimed by Being [that is the actual meaning of what happens through the essents], in order to give utterance to the truth of Being."[60] This re-interpretation of the "reversal," rather than the reversal itself, determines the entire development of Heidegger's late philosophy. Contained in a nutshell in the *Brief über den Humanismus,* which interprets *Being and Time* as a necessary anticipation of and preparation for the "reversal," it centers on the notion that to think, namely, "to say the unspoken word of Being," is the only authentic "doing" (*Tun*) of man; in it, the "History of Being" (*Seinsgeschichte*), transcending all mere human acts and superior to them, actually comes to pass. This thinking reminisces insofar as it hears the voice of Being in the utterances of the great philosophers of the past; but the past comes to it from the opposite direction, so that the "descent" (*Abstieg*) into the past coincides with the patient, thoughtful expectation of the arrival of the future, the *"avenant."*[61]

We start with the original reversal. Even in the first *Nietzsche* volume, where Heidegger carefully follows Nietzsche's descriptive characterizations of the Will, he uses what later appears as the "ontological difference": the distinction between the Being of Being and the isness (*Seiendheit*) of entities. According to this interpretation, the will-to-power signifies the isness, the chief mode in which everything that is actually *is*. In this aspect, the Will is understood as a mere function of the life process—"world comes into being through the carrying out of the life process"[62]—whereas "Eternal Recurrence" is seen as Nietzsche's term for the Being of Being, through which time's transient nature is eliminated and Becoming, the medium of the will-to-power's purposiveness, receives the seal of Being. "Eternal Recurrence" is the most affirmative thought because it is the negation of the negation. In that perspective, the will-to-power is no more than a biological urge that keeps the wheel rolling and is transcended by a Will that goes beyond the mere life instinct in saying "Yes" to Life. In Nietzsche's view, as we saw, "Becoming has no goal; it does not end in 'Being.' . . . Becoming is of equal value at every moment:

. . . in other words, it has no value, for there is nothing by which value could be measured and in respect to which the word 'value' would make sense."[63]

As Heidegger sees it, the real contradiction in Nietzsche is not due to the seeming opposition between the will-to-power, which, being goal-directed, presupposes a rectilinear time concept, and Eternal Recurrence, with its cyclical time concept. It lies, rather, in Nietzsche's "transvaluation of values," which, according to Nietzsche himself, could make sense only in the framework of the will-to-power but which he nevertheless saw as the ultimate consequence of the "Eternal Recurrence" thought. In other words, in the last analysis, it was the will-to-power, "in itself value-positing," that determined Nietzsche's philosophy of the Will. The will-to-power finally "evaluates" an eternally recurring Becoming as the sole way out of the meaninglessness of life and world, and this transposition is not only a return to "the subjectivity of which the distinctive mark is evaluative thinking,"[64] but also suffers from the same lack of radicalism characteristic of Nietzsche's inverted Platonism, which, by putting things upside down or downside up, still keeps intact the categorical framework in which such reversals can operate.

Heidegger's strictly phenomenological analyses of the Will in volume I of his *Nietzsche* closely follow his early analyses of the self in *Being and Time,* except that the Will takes the place ascribed to Care in the earlier work. We read: "Self-observation and self-examination never bring the self to light or show how we are ourselves. But by willing, and also by nilling, we do just that; we appear in a light that itself is lighted by the act of willing. To will always means: to bring oneself to one's self. . . . Willing, we encounter ourselves as who we are authentically. . . ."[65] Hence, "to will is essentially to will one's own self, but not a merely given self that is as it is, but the self that wants to become what it is. . . . The will to get away from one's self is actually an act of nilling."[66] We shall see later that this return to the concept of the self of *Being and Time* is not without importance for the "reversal," or "change of mood," manifest in the second volume.

In the second volume, the emphasis shifts decisively from

the thought of "Eternal Recurrence" to an interpretation of the Will as almost exclusively will-to-power, in the specific sense of a will to rule and dominate rather than as an expression of the life instinct. The notion of volume I, that every act of willing, by virtue of being a command, generates a counter-will (*Widerwillen*)—that is, the notion of a necessary obstacle in every act of willing, which first must overcome a non-willing —is now generalized into an inherent characteristic of every act of making. For a carpenter, for instance, the wood constitutes the obstacle "against which" he works when he forces it to become a table.[67] This again is generalized: every object by virtue of being an "object"—and not merely a thing, independent of human evaluation, calculation, and making—is there to be overcome by a subject. The will-to-power is the culmination of the modern age's subjectivization; all of man's faculties stand under the Will's command. "The Will is to will to be master. . . . [It is] fundamentally and exclusively: Command. . . . In the command the one who issues the command obeys . . . himself. Thus the commanding [self] is its own superior."[68]

Here the concept of the Will indeed loses the biological characteristics that play such an important role in Nietzsche's understanding of the Will as a mere symptom of the life instinct. It is in the nature of power—and no longer in the nature of life's superabundance and surplus—to spread and expand: "Power exists only insofar as its power increases and insofar as [the will-to-power] commands this increase." The Will urges itself on by issuing orders; not life but "the will-to-power is the essence of power. This essence, and never a [limited] amount of power, remains the goal of the Will, inasmuch as Will can exist only in relation to power. This is why the Will necessarily needs this goal. It is also why a terror of the void essentially permeates all willing. . . . Seen from the perspective of the Will . . . [nothingness] is the extinction of the Will in not-willing. . . . Hence . . . [quoting Nietzsche] our will 'would rather will nothingness than not will.' . . . 'To will nothingness' here means *to will . . . the negation, the destruction, the laying waste*" [italics added].[69]

Heidegger's last word on this faculty concerns the Will's

destructiveness, just as Nietzsche's last word concerned its "creativity" and superabundance. This destructiveness manifests itself in the Will's obsession with the future, which forces men into *oblivion*. In order to will the future in the sense of being the future's master, men must forget and finally destroy the past. From Nietzsche's discovery that the Will cannot "will backwards," there follow not only frustration and resentment, but also the positive, active will to annihilate what was. And since everything that is real has "become," that is, incorporates a past, this destructiveness ultimately relates to everything that is.

Heidegger sums it up in *What Is Called Thinking?*: "Faced with what 'was,' willing no longer has anything to say. . . . The 'it was' resists the Will's willing . . . the 'it was' is revolting and contrary to the Will. . . . But by means of this revulsion, the contrary takes root within willing itself. Willing . . . suffers from it—that is, the Will suffers from itself . . . from . . . the by-gone, the past. But what is past stems from the passing. . . . Thus the Will itself wills passing. . . . The Will's revulsion against every 'it was' appears as *the will to make everything pass away*, hence to will that everything deserve passing away. The revulsion arising in the Will is then the will against everything that passes—*everything*, that is, that comes to be out of a coming-to-be, and that *endures*" (italics added).[70]

In this radical understanding of Nietzsche, the Will is essentially destructive, and it is against that destructiveness that Heidegger's original reversal pits itself. Following this interpretation, technology's very nature is the will to will, namely, to subject the whole world to its domination and rulership, whose natural end can only be total destruction. The alternative to such rulership is "letting be," and letting-be as an activity is thinking that obeys the call of Being. The mood pervading the letting-be of thought is the opposite of the mood of purposiveness in willing; later, in his re-interpretation of the "reversal," Heidegger calls it *"Gelassenheit,"* a calmness that corresponds to letting-be and that "prepares us" for "a thinking that is not a willing."[71] This thinking is "beyond the distinction between activity and passivity" because it is beyond the "domain of the Will," that is, beyond the category of causality, which Heidegger, in agreement with Nietzsche, derives from the willing ego's experience of causing effects, hence from an illusion produced by consciousness.

The insight that thinking and willing are not just two different faculties of the enigmatic being called "man," but are opposites, came to both Nietzsche and Heidegger. It is their version of the deadly conflict that occurs when the two-in-one of consciousness, actualized in the silent dialogue between me and myself, changes its original harmony and friendship into an ongoing conflict between will and counter-will, between command and resistance. But we have found testimony to this conflict throughout the history of the faculty.

The difference between Heidegger's position and those of his predecessors lies in this: the mind of man, claimed by Being in order to transpose into language the truth of Being, is subject to a *History* of Being (*Seinsgeschichte*), and this History determines whether men respond to Being in terms of willing or in terms of thinking. It is the *History* of Being, at work behind the backs of acting men, that, like Hegel's World Spirit, determines human destinies and reveals itself to the thinking ego if the latter can overcome willing and actualize the letting-be.

At first glance, this may look like another, perhaps a bit more sophisticated, version of Hegel's ruse of reason, Kant's ruse of nature, Adam Smith's invisible hand, or divine Providence, all forces invisibly guiding the ups and downs of human affairs to a predetermined goal: freedom in Hegel, eternal peace in Kant, harmony between the contradictory interests of a market economy in Adam Smith, ultimate salvation in Christian theology. The notion itself—namely, that the actions of men are inexplicable by themselves and can be *understood* only as the work of some hidden purpose or some hidden actor—is much older. Plato could already "imagine that each of us living creatures is a puppet made by gods, possibly as a plaything, possibly with some more serious purpose," and imagine that what we take for causes, the pursuit of pleasure and the avoidance of pain, are but "the strings by which we are worked."[72]

We hardly need a demonstration of historical influences to comprehend the stubborn resiliency of the idea, from Plato's airy fiction to Hegel's mental construct—which was the result of an unprecedented re-thinking of world history that deliberately eliminated from the factual record everything "merely" factual as accidental and non-consequential. The simple truth is that no man can act alone, even though his motives for action may be certain designs, desires, passions, and goals of his own. Nor can we ever achieve anything wholly according to plan (even when, as *archōn*, we successfully lead and initiate and hope that our helpers and followers will execute what we begin), and this combines with our consciousness of being *able* to cause an effect to give birth to the notion that the actual outcome must be due to some alien, supernatural force which, undisturbed by human plurality, has provided for the end result. The fallacy is similar to the fallacy Nietzsche detected in the notion of a necessary "progress" of Mankind. To repeat: " 'Mankind' does not advance, it does not even exist. . . . [But since] time marches forward, we'd like to believe that everything that is in it also marches forward—that the development is one that moves forward."[73]

Certainly Heidegger's *Seinsgeschichte* cannot fail to remind us of Hegel's World Spirit. The difference, however, is decisive. When Hegel saw "the World Spirit on horseback" in Napoleon at Jena, he knew that Napoleon himself was unconscious of being the incarnation of the Spirit, knew that he acted out of the usual human mixture of short-term goals, desires, and passions; for Heidegger, however, it is Being itself that, *forever changing,* manifests itself in the thinking of the actor so that *acting and thinking* coincide. "If to act means to give a hand to the essence of Being, then thinking is actually acting. That is, preparing [building an abode] for the essence of Being in the midst of entities by which Being transposes itself and its essence into speech. Without speech, mere doing lacks the dimension in which it can become effective and follow directions. Speech, however, is never a simple expression of thinking, feeling, or willing. Speech is the original dimension in which the human being is able to respond to Being's claim and, responding, belong to it. Thinking is the actualization of that original correspondence."[74]

In terms of a mere reversal of viewpoints, one would be tempted to see in Heidegger's position the justification of Valéry's aphoristic reversal of Descartes: " '*L'homme pense, donc je suis'—dit l'univers*" ("Man thinks, therefore I am, says the universe").[75] The interpretation is indeed tempting since Heidegger would certainly agree with Valéry's "*Les évènements ne sont que l'écume des choses*" ("Events are but the foam of things"). He would not agree, however, with Valéry's assumption that what really is—the underlying reality whose surface is mere foam—is the stable reality of a substantial, ultimately unchanging Being. Nor, either before or after the "reversal," would he have agreed that "the new is by definition the perishable part of things" ("*Le nouveau est, par définition, la partie périssable des choses*").[76]

Ever since he re-interpreted the reversal, Heidegger has insisted on the continuity of his thought, in the sense that *Being and Time* was a necessary preparation that already contained in a provisional way the main direction of his later work. And indeed this is true to a large extent, although it is liable to de-radicalize the later reversal and the consequences obviously implicit in it for the future of philosophy. Let us begin with the most startling consequences, to be found in the later work itself, to wit, first, the notion that solitary thinking in itself constitutes the only relevant action in the factual record of history, and second, that thinking is the same as thanking (and not just for etymological reasons). Having done this, we shall try to follow the development of certain key terms in *Being and Time* and see what happens to them. The three key terms I propose are Care, Death, and Self.

*Care*—in *Being and Time*, the fundamental mode of man's existential concern with his own being—does not simply disappear in favor of the Will, with which it obviously shares a certain number of characteristics; it changes its function radically. It all but loses its relatedness to itself, its concern with man's own being, and, along with that, the mood of "anxiety" caused when the world into which man is "thrown" reveals itself as "nothingness" for a being that knows its own mortality—"*das nackte Dass im Nichts der Welt,*" "the naked That in the Nothingness of the world."[77]

The emphasis shifts from *Sorge* as worry or concern with itself to *Sorge* as *taking* care, and this not of itself but of Being. Man who was the "caretaker" (*Platzhalter*) of Nothing and therefore open to the disclosure of Being now becomes the "guardian" (*Hüter*) or "shepherd" (*Hirte*) of Being, and his speech offers Being its abode.

*Death,* on the other hand, which originally was actual for man only as the utmost possibility—"if it were actualized [for instance, in suicide], man obviously would lose the possibility he has of existing in the face of death"[78]—now becomes the "shrine" that "collects," "protects," and "salvages" the essence of mortals, who are mortals not because their life has an end but because to-be-dead still belongs to their innermost being.[79] (These strange-sounding descriptions refer to well-known experiences, testified to, for instance, by the old adage *de mortuis nil nisi bonum.* It is not the dignity of death as such that puts us in awe but, rather, the curious change from life to death that overtakes the personality of the dead. In remembrance—the way living mortals think of their dead—it is as though all non-essential qualities perished with the disappearance of the body in which they were incarnated. The dead are "enshrined" in remembrance like precious relics of themselves.)

Finally there is the concept of the *Self,* and it is this concept whose change in the "reversal" is the most unexpected and the most consequential. In *Being and Time,* the term "Self" is the "answer to the question Who [is man]?" as distinguished from the question of What he is; the Self is the term for man's existence as distinguished from whatever qualities he may possess. This existence, the "authentic being a Self," is derived polemically from the "Them." ("*Mit dem Ausdruck 'Selbst' antworten wir auf die Frage nach dem Wer des Daseins. . . . Das eigentliche Selbstsein bestimmt sich als eine existenzielle Modifikation des Man.*")[80] By modifying the "They" of everyday life into "being oneself," human existence produces a "*solus ipse,*" and Heidegger speaks in this context of an "existential solipsism," that is, of the actualization of the *principium individuationis,* an actualizing we have encountered in other philosophers as one of the essential functions of the Will. Heidegger had originally ascribed it to Care, his early term for man's organ for the future.[81]

To underline the similarity of Care (before the "reversal") and Will in a modern setting, we turn to Bergson, who—certainly not influenced by earlier thinkers but following the immediate evidence of consciousness—had posited, only a few decades before Heidegger, the co-existence of two selves, the one social (Heidegger's "They") and the other "fundamental" (Heidegger's "authentic"). The Will's function is "to recover this fundamental self" from "the requirements of social life in general and language in particular," namely the language ordinarily spoken in which every word already has a "social meaning."[82] It is a cliché-ridden language, needed for communication with others in an "external world quite distinct from [ourselves], which is the common property of all conscious beings." Life in common with others has created its own kind of speech that leads to the formation of "a second self . . . which obscures the first." The task of philosophy is to lead this social self back "to the real and concrete self . . . whose activity cannot be compared to that of any other force," because this force is sheer *spontaneity* of which "each of us has immediate knowledge" obtained only by the immediate observation of oneself by oneself.[83] And Bergson, quite in line with Nietzsche and also, as it were, in tune with Heidegger, sees the "proof" of this spontaneity in the fact of artistic creativity. The coming into existence of a work of art cannot be explained by antecedent causes as though what is now actual has been latent or potential before, whether in the form of external causes or inner motives: "When a musician composes a symphony, was his work possible before being real?"[84] Heidegger is quite in line with the general position when he writes in volume I of his *Nietzsche* (i.e., before the "reversal"): "To will always means: to bring oneself to one's self. . . . Willing, we encounter ourselves as who we are authentically. . . ."[85]

Yet this is as much of an affinity between Heidegger and his immediate predecessors as can be claimed. Nowhere in *Being and Time*—except for a peripheral remark about poetic speech "as possible disclosure of existence"[86]—is artistic creativity mentioned. In volume I of the *Nietzsche,* the tension and close relationship between poetry and philosophy, the poet and the philosopher, is twice noticed but not in either the Nietzschean or the Bergsonian sense of sheer creativity.[87] On the contrary, the Self in *Being and Time* becomes manifest in "the voice of conscience," which calls man back from his everyday entanglement in the "*man*" (German for "one" or "they") and what conscience, in its call, discloses as human "guilt," a word (*Schuld*) that in German means both being guilty of (responsible for) some deed and having debts in the sense of owing somebody something.[88]

The main point in Heidegger's "idea of guilt" is that human existence is guilty to the extent that it "factually exists"; it does not "need to become guilty of something through omissions or commissions; [it is only called upon] to actualize authentically the 'guiltiness' which it is anyhow."[89] (It apparently never occurred to Heidegger that by making all men who listen to the "call of conscience" equally guilty, he was actually proclaiming universal innocence: where everybody is guilty, nobody is.) This existential culpability—given by human existence—is established in two ways. Inspired by Goethe's "One who acts always becomes guilty," Heidegger shows that every action, by actualizing a single possibility, at one stroke kills all the others among which it had to choose. Every commitment entails a number of defaults. More important, however, the concept of "being thrown into the world" already implies that human existence *owes* its existence to something that it is not itself; by virtue of its very existence it is indebted: *Dasein*—human existence inasmuch as it *is*—"has been thrown; it is there, but *not* brought into the there by itself."[90]

Conscience demands that man accept that "indebtedness," and acceptance means that the Self brings itself to a kind of "acting" (*handeln*) which is polemically understood as the opposite of the "loud" and visible actions of public life—the mere froth on what truly is. This acting is silent, a "letting one's own self act in its indebtedness," and this entirely inner "action" in which man opens himself to the authentic actuality of being thrown,[91] can exist only in the activity of thinking. That is probably why Heidegger, throughout his whole work, "on purpose avoided"[92] dealing with action. What is most surprising in his interpretation of conscience is the vehement denunciation of "the ordinary interpretation of conscience" that has always understood it as a kind of soliloquy, the "soundless dialogue of me and myself." Such a dialogue, Heidegger maintains, can be explained only as an inauthentic attempt at self-justification against the claims of the "Them." This is all the more striking because Heidegger, in a different context—and, it is true, only marginally—speaks of "the voice of the friend that every *Dasein* [human existence] carries with it."[93]

No matter how strange and, in the last analysis, unaccounted for by phenomenological evidence Heidegger's analysis of conscience may prove to be, the tie with the sheer facts of human existence implicit in the concept of a primordial indebtedness certainly contains the first hint of his later identification of thinking and thanking. What the call of conscience actually achieves is the recovery of the individualized (*vereinzeltes*) self from involvement in the events that determine men's everyday activities as well as the course of recorded history—*l'écume des choses*. Summoned back, the self is now turned to a thinking that expresses gratitude that the "naked That" has been given at all. That the attitude of man, confronted with Being, should be *thanking* can be seen as a variant of Plato's *thaumazein*, the beginning principle of philosophy. We have dealt with that *admiring* wonder, and to find it in a modern context is neither striking nor surprising; we have only to think of Nietzsche's praise of the "Yes-sayers" or turn our attention from academic speculations to some of this century's great poets. They at least show how suggestive such affirmation can be as a solution for the apparent meaninglessness of an entirely secularized world. Here are two lines by the Russian Osip Mandelstam, written in 1918:

> We will remember in Lethe's cold waters
> That earth for us has been worth a thousand heavens.

These verses can easily be matched by a number of lines by Rainer Maria Rilke in the *Duino Elegies,* written at about the same time; I shall quote a few:

> *Erde du liebe, ich will. Oh glaub es bedürfte*
> *Nicht deiner Frühlinge mehr, mich dir zu gewinnen.*
> *Einer, ach ein einziger ist schon dem Blute zu viel.*
> *Namenlos bin ich zu dir entschlossen von weit her,*
> *Immer warst du im recht. . . .*

> Earth, you darling, I will. Oh, believe me, you need
> Your spring-times no longer to win me; a single one,
> Just one, is already more than my blood can endure.
> I've now been unspeakably yours for ages and ages.
> You were always right. . . .

> Ninth Elegy

And finally, as a reminder, I cite again what W. H. Auden wrote some twenty years later:

> That singular command
> I do not understand,
> *Bless what there is for being,*
> Which has to be obeyed, for
> What else am I made for,
> Agreeing or disagreeing?

Perhaps these examples of non-academic testimony to the dilemmas of the last stage of the modern age can explain the great appeal of Heidegger's work to an elite of the intellectual community despite the almost unanimous antagonism it has aroused in the universities ever since the appearance of *Being and Time.*

But what is true of the coincidence of thinking and thanking is hardly true of the merging of acting and thinking. With Heidegger, this is not just the elimination of the subject-object split in order to desubjectivize the Cartesian Ego, but actual fusion of the changes in the "History of Being" (*Seinsgeschichte*) with the activity of thinking in the thinkers. "Being's History" secretly inspires and guides what happens on the surface, while the thinkers, hidden by and protected from the "Them," respond and actualize Being. Here the personified concept whose ghostlike existence brought about the last great enlivenment of philosophy in German Idealism has become fully incarnated; there is a Somebody who *acts out* the hidden meaning of Being and thus provides the disastrous course of events with a counter-current of wholesomeness.

This Somebody, the thinker who has weaned himself from willing to "letting-be," is actually the "authentic Self" of *Being and Time,* who now listens to the call of Being instead of the call of Conscience. Unlike the Self, the thinker is not summoned by himself to his Self; still, to "hear the call authentically signifies once again bringing oneself into factually acting" (*"sich in das faktische Handeln bringen"*).[94] In this context the "reversal" means that the Self no longer acts in itself (what has been abandoned is the *In-sich-handeln-lassen des eigensten Selbst*[95]) but, obedient to Being, enacts by sheer thinking the counter-current of Being underlying the "foam" of beings—the mere appearances whose current is steered by the will-to-power.

The "They" reappear here, but their chief characteristic is no longer "idle talk" (*Gerede*); it is the destructiveness inherent in willing.

What has brought about this change is a decisive radicalization of both the age-old tension between thinking and willing (to be resolved by the "Will-not-to-will") and of the personified concept, which appeared in its most articulate form in Hegel's "World Spirit," that ghostly Nobody that bestows meaning on what factually, but in itself meaninglessly and contingently, *is.* With Heidegger, this Nobody, allegedly acting behind the backs of acting men, has now found a flesh-and-blood incarnation in the existence of the thinker, who acts while he does nothing, a person, to be sure, and even identifiable as "Thinker"—which, however, does not signify his return into the world of appearances. He remains the *"solus ipse"* in "existential solipsism," except that now the fate of the world, the History of Being, has come to depend on him.

Thus far we have been following Heidegger's own repeated demands to pay due attention to the continuous development of his thinking ever since *Being and Time,* despite the "reversal" that took place in the middle thirties. We have relied, too, on his own interpretations of the reversal during the later thirties and early forties—interpretations closely and coherently borne out by his numerous publications of the fifties and sixties. But there is another, perhaps even more radical, interruption in his life as well as his thought to which, as far as I know, no one, Heidegger included, has paid public attention.

This interruption coincided with the catastrophic defeat of Nazi Germany and his own serious difficulties with the academic community and the occupation authorities immediately thereafter. For a period of roughly five years he was so effectively silenced that among his published works there exist only two longer essays—the *Letter on Humanism*, written in 1946 and published in Germany and France in 1947, and "The Anaximander Fragment" ("*Der Spruch des Anaximander*"), also written in 1946 and published as the last essay of *Holzwege* in 1950.

Of these, the *Letter on Humanism* contains an eloquent summing-up and immense clarification of the interpretive turn he had given the original reversal, but "The Anaximander Fragment" is of a different character: it presents an altogether new and unexpected outlook on the whole posing of the problem of Being. The main theses of this essay, which I shall now try to outline, were never followed up or fully explicated in his later work. He does mention, in a note to its publication in the *Holzwege*, that the essay was taken from a "treatise" (*Abhandlung*) written in 1946, which unfortunately has never been published.

To me it seems obvious that this new outlook, so isolated from the rest of his thought, must have emerged from another change of "mood," no less important than the change that happened between the first and the second volumes of the work on Nietzsche—the turn from the "Will-to-Power" as Will-to-will to the new *Gelassenheit*, the serenity of "letting-be" and the paradoxical "Will-not-to-will." The changed mood reflected Germany's defeat, the "point zero" (as Ernst Jünger called it) that for a few years seemed to promise a new beginning. In Heidegger's version: "Do we stand in the very twilight of the most monstrous transformation our planet has ever undergone . . . ? [Or] do we gaze into the evening of a night which heralds another dawn? . . . *Are* we the latecomers . . . at

the same time precursors of the dawn of an altogether different age, which has already left our contemporary historiologi-
cal representations of history behind?"[96]

It was the same mood that Jaspers expressed at a famous
symposium in Geneva in the same year: "We live as though
we stood knocking at gates that are still closed. . . . What
happens today will perhaps one day found and establish a
world."[97] This mood of hope disappeared quickly in the
rapidity of German economic and political recovery from
"point zero"; confronted with the reality of Adenauer's Germany, neither Heidegger nor Jaspers ever expounded systematically what must very soon have appeared to them as a
complete misreading of the new era.

Still, in Heidegger's case, we do have the Anaximander
essay with its haunting hints at another possibility of ontological speculation, hints that are half hidden in the highly technical philological considerations of the Greek text (which is
rather obscure and probably corrupt), and from them I shall
risk an exegesis of this fascinating variant of his philosophy. In
Heidegger's literal and provisional translation the short Greek
text reads: "But that from which things arise [*genesis*] also
gives rise to their passing away [*phthora*], according to what is
necessary; for things render justice [*dikēn didonai*] and pay
penalty [*tisin*] to one another for their injustice [*adikia*], according to the ordinance of time."[98] The subject, then, is the
coming-to-be and passing-away of everything that is. While
whatever is *is*, it "lingers" in the present "between a twofold
absence," its arrival and its departure. During the absences it
is hidden; it is unconcealed only for the short duration of its
appearance. Living in a world of appearances, all we know or
can know is a "movement which lets every emerging being
abandon concealment and go forward into unconcealment,"
lingering there for a while, till it "in its turn abandons unconcealment, departing and withdrawing into concealment."[99]

Even this non-speculative, strictly phenomenological description is clearly at variance with Heidegger's usual teaching
of an ontological difference according to which *a-lētheia,* truth
understood as Un-hiddenness or Unconcealment, is always on
the side of Being; in the world of appearances, Being reveals

itself only in the thinking response of man in terms of language. In the words of the *Letter on Humanism*, "Language is the house of Being" (*"Die Sprache [ist] zumal das Haus des Seins und die Behausung des Menschenwesens"*).[100] In the exegesis of the Anaximander fragment, unconcealment is not truth; it belongs to the beings that arrive from and depart into a hidden Being. What can hardly have caused but certainly facilitated this reversal is the fact that the Greeks, especially the pre-Socratics, often thought of Being as *physis* (nature), whose original meaning is derived from *phyein* (to grow), that is, to come to light out of darkness. Anaximander, says Heidegger, thought of *genesis* and *phthora* in terms of *physis*, "as ways of luminous rising and declining."[101] And *physis*, according to a much quoted fragment of Heraclitus, "likes to hide."[102]

Although Heidegger does not mention the Heraclitus fragment in the Anaximander essay, its main theses read as though it had been inspired by Heraclitus rather than by Anaximander. Of central importance is the speculative content; there the relation in the ontological difference is reversed, and this is spelled out in the following sentences: "The unconcealment of beings, the brightness granted them [by Being], obscures the light of Being"; for *"as it reveals itself in beings, Being withdraws"* (*"Das Sein entzieht sich indem es sich in das Seiende entbirgt"*).[103] The sentence I have italicized is stressed in the text by being emphatically repeated. Its immediate plausibility in the German original rests entirely on the linguistically cognate relation of *verbergen* (hide, conceal) with *bergen* (shield and shelter) and *entbergen* (disclose). If we try to explicate the speculative content of that cognateness as construed by Heidegger, we may sum it up as follows: the coming and going, appearing and disappearing, of beings always begins with a disclosure that is an *ent-bergen,* the loss of the original shelter (*bergen*) that had been granted by Being; the being then "lingers for a while" in the "brightness" of disclosure, and ends by returning to the sheltering shield of Being in its concealment: "Presumably, Anaximander spoke of *genesis* and *phthora* [generation and decline] . . . [that is] *genesis estin* (which is the way I should like to read it) and *phthora ginetai,* 'coming-to-be *is,*' and 'passing-away comes to be.' "[104]

In other words, undoubtedly there is such a thing as becoming; everything we know has become, has emerged from some previous darkness into the light of day; and this becoming remains its law while it lasts: its lasting is at the same time its passing-away. Becoming, the law that rules beings, is now the opposite of Being; when, in passing-away, becoming ceases, it changes again into that Being from whose sheltering, concealing darkness it originally emerged. In this speculative context, the ontological difference consists of the difference between Being in the strong durative sense and becoming. It is through withdrawal that "Being holds to its truth" and shields it; it shields it against the "brightness" of beings that "obscures the light of Being" even though, originally, Being has granted this brightness. This leads to the seemingly paradoxical statement "As [Being] provides the unconcealment of beings, it [establishes] the concealment of Being."[105]

In the course of this speculation, the reversal of Heidegger's common approach to the "quest for Being" (*die Seinsfrage*) and "the oblivion of Being" (*Seinsvergessenheit*) becomes manifest. It is no longer genuine inauthenticity or any other particularity of human existence that causes man to "forget" Being in his abandonment to the *"man"* (German for the plurality of "Them"); nor does he do so because he is distracted by the sheer superabundance of mere entities. "Oblivion of Being belongs to the self-veiling essence of Being . . . the history of Being [and not the history of men in philosophy in general or metaphysics in particular] begins with the oblivion of Being, since Being—together with its essence, its distinction from beings—keeps to itself."[106] Through Being's withdrawal from the realm of beings, these entities, whose unconcealment has been caused by it, are set "adrift in errancy," and this *errancy* constitutes "the realm of error . . . the space in which history unfolds. . . . *Without errancy there would be no connection from destiny to destiny: there would be no history*" (italics added).[107]

To sum up: We are still confronted with the ontological difference, the categorical separation of Being and beings, but this separation has acquired, as it were, a kind of history with a beginning and an end. In the beginning, Being discloses itself in beings, and the disclosure starts two opposite movements: Being withdraws into itself, and beings are "set adrift" to constitute the "realm (in the sense of a prince's realm) of error." This realm of error is the sphere of common human history, where factual destinies are connected and form a coherent shape through "erring." In that scheme, there is no place for a "History of Being" (*Seinsgeschichte*) enacted behind the backs of acting men; Being, sheltered in its concealment, has no history, and "every epoch of world history is an epoch of errancy." However, the very fact that the time continuum in the historical realm is broken up into different eras indicates that the casting adrift of entities also occurs in epochs, and in Heidegger's scheme there seems to exist a privileged moment, the transitional moment from one epoch to the next, from destiny to destiny, when Being qua Truth breaks into the continuum of error, when the "epochal essence of Being lays claim to the ecstatic nature of *Da-sein*."[108] To this claim, thinking can respond, recognizing "the claim to destiny": that is, the spirit of a whole age may become "mindful of what is destined" instead of getting lost in the erring particularities of human day-to-day affairs.

Nowhere in this context does Heidegger mention a connection between thinking and thanking and he is quite aware of the possible pessimistic, "not to say nihilistic," conclusions to be drawn from an interpretation that would fit only too well with Burckhardt's and Nietzsche's understanding of the Greek experience at its deepest level.[109] Also, it may be worth noting that here he seems not at all interested in stressing the tension of the very close relation between philosophy and poetry. Instead he concludes the essay with something he has said nowhere else: "If the essence of man consists in thinking the truth of Being [N.B., now a Being that has withdrawn, that veils and hides itself], then thinking must poetize on the riddle of Being" ("*am Rätsel des Seins dichten*").[110]

I have mentioned in passing the radical change the concept of death underwent in Heidegger's late writings, where death appears as the ultimate savior of man's essence, the *Gebirg des Seins in dem Spiel der Welt*, the "shelter of Being in the play of the world."[111] And I have tried to explicate and, in a way, justify the strangeness of this by some well-known testimony to certain familiar experiences which, as far as I know, have never been conceptualized. In the Anaximander essay, the word "death" does not occur, but the concept is of course transparently present in the notion of life between two absences, before it arrives in birth and after it passes away in death. And here we do have a conceptual clarification of death as the shelter for the essence of human existence, whose temporal, transitory presence is understood as the lingering between two absences and a sojourn in the realm of errancy. For the source of this "erring"—and here of course we can see to what an extent this variant remains a mere variation of Heidegger's basic and enduring philosophical convictions—is the fact that a being that "lingers a while in presence" between two absences and has the ability to transcend its own presence can be said to be actually "present [only] insofar as it lets itself belong to the non-present."[112]

It has a chance of achieving that if it seizes on the epochal moment in the transition between epochs when historical destinies change and the truth underlying the next era of errancy becomes manifest to thought. The Will as destroyer appears here, too, though not by name; it is the "craving to persist," "to hang on," the inordinate appetite men have "to cling to themselves." In this way they do more than just err: "Lingering as persisting . . . is an insurrection on behalf of sheer endurance."[113] The insurrection is directed against "order" (*dikē*); it creates the "disorder" (*adikia*) permeating the "realm of errancy."

These statements take us back to familiar territory, as becomes evident when we read that the disorder is "tragic" and not a thing for which man can be made accountable. To be sure, there is no longer any "call of conscience" summoning man back to his authentic self, to the insight that, no matter what he has done or omitted to do, he was already *schuldig* ("guilty") since his existence was a debt he "owed" after having been thrown into the world. But, just as, in *Being and Time,* this "guilty" self could salvage itself by anticipating its death, so here the "erring" *Dasein,* while "lingering a while" in the present realm of errancy, can, through the thinking activity, join itself to what is absent. There is the difference, though, that here the absent (Being in its enduring with-drawal) has no history in the realm of errancy, and thinking and acting do not coincide. To act is to err, to go astray. We should consider, too, how the early definition of being-guilty as a primary trait of *Dasein,* independent of any specific act, has been replaced by "erring" as the decisive mark of all hu-man history. (Both formulations, incidentally, for the German reader are curiously reminiscent of Goethe's *"Der Handelnde wird immer schuldig"* and *"Es irrt der Mensch solang er strebt."*[114])

To these distinct self-echoes we may then add the following sentences from the Anaximander essay: "Every thinker is de-pendent upon the address of Being. The extent of this de-pendence determines the freedom from irrelevant influences"[115] —by which Heidegger clearly means the factual day-to-day events brought about by erring men. When we put these cor-respondences together, it does seem as though we are dealing here with a mere variation of Heidegger's basic teaching.

However that may be, it is obvious that my present inter-pretation is tentative in the extreme; it cannot possibly be a substitute for the unpublished treatise of which the Anaximan-der essay was originally a part. In our present state of textual knowledge the whole thing remains very doubtful. But whether we see it as a variant or a variation, Heidegger's denunciation of the instinct of self-preservation (common to all living things) as a willful rebellion against the "order" of Creation as such is so rare in the history of ideas that I should like to quote here the only similar utterance of which I am aware, three little-known lines of Goethe in a poem written about 1821 under the title *"Eins und Alles":*

> *Das Ewige regt sich fort in allen:*
> *Denn alles muss in Nichts zerfallen,*
> *Wenn es im Sein beharren will.*

> The Eternal works and stirs in all;
> For all must into Nothing fall,
> If it will persist in Being.

## 16  *The abyss of freedom and the* novus ordo seclorum

Very early in these deliberations I warned of an inevitable flaw in all critical examinations of the willing faculty. It is a rather obvious one but easy to overlook in discussing the particular arguments and counter-arguments: simply that every *philosophy* of the Will is conceived and articulated not by men of action but by philosophers, Kant's "professional thinkers," who in one way or another are committed to the *bios theōrēti-kos* and therefore by nature more inclined to "interpret the world" than to "change it."

Of all the philosophers and theologians we have consulted, only Duns Scotus, we found, was ready to pay the price of contingency for the gift of freedom—the mental endowment we have for beginning something new, of which we know that it could just as well not be. No doubt the philosophers have always been more "pleased" with necessity than with freedom because for their business they needed a *tranquillitas animae* (Leibniz), a peace of mind, which—relying on Spinoza's *acqui-escentia sibi*, one's agreement with oneself—could be effectively guaranteed only by an acquiescence in the arrangement of the world. The same self that the thinking activity disregards in its withdrawal from the world of appearances is asserted and en-sured by the Will's reflexivity. Just as thinking prepares the self for the role of spectator, willing fashions it into an "enduring I" that directs all particular acts of volition. It creates the self's *character* and therefore was sometimes understood as the *principium individuationis*, the source of the person's specific identity.

Yet it is precisely this individuation brought about by the Will that breeds new and serious trouble for the notion of freedom. The individual, fashioned by the will and aware that it could be different from what it is (character, unlike bodily appearance or talents and abilities, is not given to the self at birth) always tends to assert an "I-myself" against an indefinite "they"—all the others that I, as an individual, am *not*. Nothing indeed can be more frightening than the notion of solipsistic freedom—the "feeling" that my standing apart, isolated from everyone else, is due to free will, that nothing and nobody can be held responsible for it but me myself. The will with its projects for the future challenges the belief in necessity, the acquiescence in the arrangement of the world which it calls complacency. Yet isn't it clear to everyone that the world is not, and has never been, what it *ought* to be? And who knows, or has ever known, what this "ought" should be? The "ought" is utopian; it has no proper *topos* or place in the world. Isn't trust in necessity, the conviction that everything is as "it was to be," infinitely preferable to freedom bought at the price of contingency? Under these circumstances, doesn't freedom look like a euphemism for the burnt-over area marked by the "forsakenness with which [human existence, the *Dasein*] has been abandoned to itself" (*"die Verlassenheit in der Überlassenheit an es selbst"*)?[116]

These difficulties and anxieties are caused by the Will insofar as it is a mental faculty, hence reflexive, recoiling upon itself—*volo me velle, cogito me cogitare*—or, to put it in Heideggerian terms, by the fact that, existentially speaking, human existence has been "abandoned to itself." Nothing of the sort disturbs our intellect, the mind's capability of cognition and its trust in truth. The cognitive abilities, like our senses, do not recoil upon themselves; they are totally intentional, namely, totally absorbed by the intended object. Hence at first glance it is surprising to find a similar bias against freedom in the great scientists of our century. As we know, they became greatly disturbed when their demonstrable discoveries in astrophysics, as well as in nuclear physics, gave rise to the suspicion that we live in a universe which, in Einstein's words, is ruled by a God who "plays dice" with it or, as Heisenberg suggested, that what we regard as the "outer world [may be] only our inner world turned inside out" (Lewis Mumford).

Such thoughts and after-thoughts are, of course, not scientific statements; they do not claim to deliver demonstrable truths or tentative theorems that their authors can hope to translate eventually into propositions susceptible of proof. They are reflections inspired by a quest for meaning and therefore no less speculative than other products of the thinking ego. Einstein himself, in a much quoted remark, very clearly drew the line between cognitive statements and speculative propositions: "The most incomprehensible fact of nature is the fact that nature is comprehensible." Here we can almost watch how the thinking ego intrudes on the cognitive activity, interrupts and halts it by its reflections. It puts itself "out of order" with the scientist's ordinary activity by recoiling upon itself and musing on the fundamental incomprehensibility of what he is doing—an incomprehensibility that remains a riddle worth thinking about even though it cannot be solved.

Such reflections may yield various "hypotheses," and some may even turn out to yield knowledge when tested; in any case, their quality and weight will depend on the cognitive achievements of their authors. Still, it is hardly deniable that the reflections of the great founders of modern science—Einstein, Planck, Bohr, Heisenberg, Schrödinger—have brought about a "crisis in the foundations of modern science" (*Grundlagenkrise*), "and their central question" (What must the world be like in order that man may know it?) "is as old as science itself and it remains unanswered."[117]

It seems only natural that this generation of founders, on whose discoveries modern science was based and whose reflections on what they were doing have brought about the "crisis in the foundations," should have been followed by several generations of less distinguished epigones who find it easier to answer unanswerable questions because they are less aware of the line separating their ordinary activities from their reflections on them. I have spoken of the orgy of speculative thinking that succeeded Kant's liberation of reason's need to think beyond the intellect's cognitive capacity, the games played by German Idealists with personified concepts and the claims made for scientific validity—a far remove from Kant's "critique."

From the point of view of scientific truth, the Idealists' speculations were pseudo-scientific; now, at the opposite end of the spectrum, something similar seems to be going on. Materialists play the game of speculation with the help of computers, cybernetics, and automation; their extrapolations produce, not ghosts like the game of the Idealists, but materializations like those of spiritualist séances. What is so very striking in these materialist games is that their results resemble the concepts of the Idealists. Thus Hegel's "World Spirit" has recently found materialization in the construction of a "nervous system" fashioned on the model of a Giant Computer: Lewis Thomas[118] proposes to understand the world-wide community of human beings in the form of a Giant Brain, exchanging thoughts so rapidly "that the brains of mankind often appear functionally to be undergoing fusion." With mankind as its "nervous system," the whole earth thus "becomes . . . a breathing organism of finely meshed parts," all growing under the "protective membrane" of the planet's atmosphere.[119]

Such notions are neither science nor philosophy, but science fiction; they are widespread and demonstrate that the extravagances of materialist speculation are quite equal to the follies of Idealist metaphysics. The common denominator of all these fallacies, materialist or Idealist, apart from being historically derived from the notion of Progress and its concomitant, the undemonstrable entity called Mankind, is that they fulfill the same emotional function. In Lewis Thomas' words, they do away with "the whole dear notion of one's own self—the marvelous old free-willed, free-enterprising, autonomous, independent, isolated island of a Self," which is "a myth."[120] The proper name of this myth, which we are admonished from all sides to get rid of, is Freedom.

Professional thinkers, whether philosophers or scientists, have not been "pleased with freedom" and its ineluctable randomness; they have been unwilling to pay the price of contingency for the questionable gift of spontaneity, of being able to do what could also be left undone. Let us put them aside therefore and fasten our attention on men of action, who ought to be committed to freedom because of the very nature of their activity, which consists in "changing the world," and not in interpreting or knowing it.

Conceptually speaking, we turn from the notion of philosophical freedom to political liberty, an obvious difference which, as far as I know, only Montesquieu spoke of, and that in passing, when he used philosophical freedom as a backdrop against which political liberty could be more sharply outlined. In a chapter entitled *"De la liberté du citoyen"* ("Of the citizen's liberty") he said: *"La liberté philosophique consiste dans l'exercise de sa volonté, ou du moins (s'il faut parler dans tous les systèmes) dans l'opinion où l'on est que l'on exerce sa volonté. La liberté politique consiste dans la sûreté, ou du moins dans l'opinion que l'on a de sa sûreté"*—"Philosophic liberty consists in the exercise of the will, or at least (if we must take account of all systems) in the opinion that we exert our will. Political liberty consists in safety, or at least in the opinion of being safe."[121] The citizen's political liberty is "that tranquillity of mind that comes from the opinion that everybody has of his safety; and in order to be in possession of this liberty the government must be such that one citizen could not be afraid of another."[122]

Philosophic freedom, the freedom of the will, is relevant only to people who live outside political communities, as solitary individuals. Political communities, in which men become citizens, are produced and preserved by laws, and these laws, made by men, can be very different and can shape various forms of government, all of which in one way or another constrain the free will of their citizens. Still, with the exception of tyranny, where one arbitrary will rules the lives of all, they nevertheless open up some space of freedom for action that actually sets the constituted body of citizens in motion. The principles inspiring the actions of the citizens vary in accordance with the different forms of government, but they are all, as Jefferson rightly called them, "energetic principles";[123] and political freedom *"ne peut consister qu'à pouvoir faire ce que l'on doit vouloir et à n'être point contraint de faire ce que l'on ne doit pas vouloir"*—"can consist only in the power of doing what we ought to will and in not being constrained to do what we ought not to will."[124]

The emphasis here is clearly on Power in the sense of the I-can; for Montesquieu, as for the ancients, it was obvious that an agent could no longer be called free when he lacked the capacity to do what he wanted to do, whether this was due to exterior or interior circumstances. Moreover, the Laws which, according to Montesquieu, transform free and lawless individuals into citizens are not God's Ten Commandments or the voice of conscience or reason's *lumen rationale* enlightening all men alike, but man-made *rapports*, "relations," which, since they concern the changeable affairs of mortal men—as distinguished from God's eternity or the immortality of the cosmos—must be "subject to all the accidents that can happen and vary in proportion as the will of man changes."[125] For Montesquieu, as for pre-Christian antiquity and for the men who at the end of the century founded the American Republic, the words "power" and "liberty" were almost synonymous. Freedom of movement, the power of moving about unchecked by disease or master, was originally the most elementary of all liberties, their very prerequisite.

Thus political freedom is distinct from philosophic freedom in being clearly a quality of the I-can and not of the I-will. Since it is possessed by the citizen rather than by man in general, it can manifest itself only in communities, where the many who live together have their intercourse both in word and in deed regulated by a great number of *rapports*—laws, customs, habits, and the like. In other words, political freedom is possible only in the sphere of human plurality, and on the premise that this sphere is not simply an extension of the dual I-and-myself to a plural We. Action, in which a We is always engaged in changing our common world, stands in the sharpest possible opposition to the solitary business of thought, which operates in a dialogue between me and myself. Under exceptionally propitious circumstances that dialogue, we have seen, can be extended to another insofar as a friend is, as Aristotle said, "another self." But it can never reach the We, the true plural of action. (An error rather prevalent among modern philosophers who insist on the importance of communication as a guarantee of truth—chiefly Karl Jaspers and Martin Buber, with his I-thou philosophy—is to believe that the intimacy of the dialogue, the "inner action" in which I "appeal" to myself or to the "other self," Aristotle's friend, Jaspers' beloved, Buber's Thou, can be extended and become paradigmatic for the political sphere.)

This We arises wherever men live together; its primal form

is the family; and it can be constituted in many different ways, all of which rest ultimately on some form of consent, of which obedience is only the most common mode, just as disobedience is the most common and least harmful mode of dissent. Consent entails the recognition that no man can act alone, that men if they wish to achieve something in the world must act in concert, which would be a platitude if there were not always some members of the community determined to disregard it and who in arrogance or in despair try to act alone. These are tyrants or criminals, depending on the final goal they aim at; what they have in common and what sets them apart from the rest of the community is that they put their trust in the use of the instruments of violence as a substitute for power. This is a tactic that only works for the short-range goals of the criminal, who after completing his crime can and must return to membership in the community; the tyrant, on the other hand, always a sheep in wolf's clothing, can last only by usurping the rightful seat of leadership, which makes him dependent on helpers to see his self-willed projects through. Unlike the mind's will power to affirm or negate, whose ultimate practical guarantee is suicide, political power, even if the tyrant's supporters consent to terror—that is, the use of violence—is always limited power, and since power and freedom in the sphere of human plurality are in fact synonyms, this means also that political freedom is always limited freedom.

Human plurality, the faceless "They" from which the individual Self splits to be itself alone, is divided into a great many units, and it is only as a member of such a unit, that is, of a community, that men are ready for action. The manifoldness of these communities is evinced in a great many different forms and shapes, each obeying different laws, having different habits and customs, and cherishing different memories of its past, i.e., a manifoldness of traditions. Montesquieu was probably right in assuming that each such entity moved and acted according to a different inspiring principle, recognized as the ultimate standard for judging the community's deeds and misdeeds—virtue in republics, honor and glory in monarchies, moderation in aristocracies, fear and suspicion in tyrannies—except that this enumeration, guided by the oldest distinction between forms of government (as the rule of one, of a few, of the best, or of all) is of course pitifully inadequate to the rich diversity of human beings living together on the earth.

The only trait that all these various forms and shapes of human plurality have in common is the simple fact of their genesis, that is, that at some moment in time and for some reason a group of people must have come to think of themselves as a "We." No matter how this "We" is first experienced and articulated, it seems that it always needs a beginning, and nothing seems so shrouded in darkness and mystery as that "In the beginning," not only of the human species as distinguished from other living organisms, but also of the enormous variety of indubitably human societies.

The haunting obscurity of the question has hardly been illuminated by recent biological, anthropological, and archaeological discoveries, whatever success they have had in extending the time span which separates us from an ever more distant past. And it is unlikely that any factual information will ever throw light on the bewildering maze of more or less plausible hypotheses, all of which suffer from the incurable suspicion that their very plausibility and probability may well turn out to be their undoing since our whole real existence—the genesis of the earth, the development of organic life on it, the evolution of man out of the countless animal species—occurred against statistically overwhelming probabilities. All that is real in the universe and in nature once was an "infinite" improbability. In the everyday world where we spend our own exiguous quotient of reality we can only be sure of a shrinkage of time behind us that is no less decisive than the shrinkage of spatial distances on the earth. What only a few decades ago, remembering Goethe's "three thousand years" (*"Wer nicht von dreitausend Jahren / Sich weiss Rechenschaft zu geben, / Bleib im Dunkel, unerfahren / Mag von Tag zu Tage leben"*), we still called antiquity is much closer to us today than it was to our ancestors.

This predicament of not-knowing is all too likely never to be resolved, corresponding, as it does, to other manifest limitations inherent in the human condition, which sets definite insurmountable boundaries to our thirst for knowledge—for example, we know *of* the immensity of the universe and nevertheless we shall never be able to know it—and the best we can do in the quandary is turn to the legendary tales that in our tradition have aided former generations to come to grips with the mysterious "In the beginning." I mean the foundation legends, which clearly had to do with a time antecedent to any form of government and to any particular principles that set governments in motion. Yet the time they dealt with was human time, and the beginning they recounted was not a divine creation but a man-made set of occurrences that memory could reach through an imaginative interpretation of old tales.

The two foundation legends of Western civilization, the one Roman and the other Hebrew (nothing comparable, Plato's *Timaeus* notwithstanding, ever existed in Greek antiquity), are utterly different from each other, except that both arose among a people that thought of its past as a story whose beginning was known and could be dated. The Jews knew the year of the creation of the world (and reckon time to this very day from it), and the Romans, as contrasted with the Greeks, who reckoned time from Olympiad to Olympiad, knew (or believed they knew) the year of the foundation of Rome and reckoned time accordingly. Much more striking, and fraught with much more serious consequences for our tradition of political thought, is the astounding fact that both legends (in sharp contradiction with the well-known principles allegedly inspiring political action in constituted communities) hold that in the case of foundation—the supreme act in which the "We" is constituted as an identifiable entity—the inspiring principle of action is love of freedom, and this both in the negative sense of liberation from oppression and in the positive sense of the establishment of Freedom as a stable, tangible reality.

Both the difference and the connection between the two— the freedom that comes from being liberated and the freedom that arises out of the spontaneity of beginning something new —are paradigmatically represented in the two foundation legends that have acted as guides for Western political thought. We have the Biblical story of the exodus of Israeli tribes from Egypt, which preceded the Mosaic legislation constituting the Hebrew people, and Virgil's story of the wanderings of Aeneas, which led to the foundation of Rome—*"dum conderet urbem,"* as Virgil defines the content of his great poem even in its first lines. Both legends begin with an act of liberation, the flight from oppression and slavery in Egypt and the flight from burning Troy (that is, from annihilation); and in both instances this act is told about from the perspective of a new freedom, the conquest of a new "promised land" that offers more than Egypt's fleshpots and the foundation of a new City that is prepared for by a war destined to undo the Trojan war, so that the order of events as laid down by Homer could be reversed. Virgil's reversal of Homer is deliberate and complete.[126] This time it is Achilles in the guise of Turnus ("Here too shalt thou tell that a Priam found his Achilles") who flees and is killed by Hector in the guise of Aeneas; in the center, "the source of all that woe" is again a woman, but this time she is a bride (Lavinia) and not an adulteress; and the end of the war is not triumph for the victor and utter destruction for the vanquished but a new body politic—"both nations unconquered join treaty under equal laws forever."

No doubt if we read these legends as tales, there is a world of difference between the aimless desperate wanderings of the Israeli tribes in the desert after the Exodus and the marvelously colorful tales of the adventures of Aeneas and his fellow Trojans; but to the men of action of later generations who ransacked the archives of antiquity for paradigms to guide their own intentions, this was not decisive. What was decisive was that there was a *hiatus* between disaster and salvation, between liberation from the old order and the new freedom, embodied in a *novus ordo saeclorum,* a "new order of the ages" with whose rise the world had structurally changed.

The legendary hiatus between a no-more and a not-yet clearly indicated that freedom would not be the automatic result of liberation, that the end of the old is not necessarily the beginning of the new, that the notion of an all-powerful time continuum is an illusion. Tales of a transitory period—

from bondage to freedom, from disaster to salvation—were all
the more appealing because the legends chiefly concerned the
deeds of great leaders, persons of world-historic significance
who appeared on the stage of history precisely during such
gaps of historical time. All those who, pressed by exterior circumstances or motivated by radical utopian thought-trains,
were not satisfied to change the world by the gradual reform
of an old order (and this rejection of the gradual was precisely what transformed the men of action of the eighteenth
century, the first century of a fully secularized intellectual
elite, into the men of the revolutions) were almost logically
forced to accept the possibility of a hiatus in the continuous
flow of temporal sequence.

We remember Kant's embarrassment in "dealing . . . with
a power of spontaneously beginning a series of successive
things or states," i.e., with an *"absolute* beginning," which,
because of the unbreakable sequence of the time continuum,
will nevertheless always remain "the continuation of a preceding series."[127] The word "revolution" was supposed to dissolve this embarrassment when, during the last decades of the
eighteenth century, it changed its old astronomical meaning
and came to signify an unprecedented event. In France this
even led to a short-lived "revolution" of the calendar: in
October 1793, it was decided that the proclamation of the
Republic was a new beginning of human history; as this had
happened in September 1792, the new calendar declared September 1793 to be the inauguration of the Year Two. This
attempt to localize an absolute beginning in time was a failure,
and probably not only because of the strong anti-Christian
cast of the new calendar (all Christian holidays, including
Sunday, were abolished, and a fictitious division of a thirty-
day month into units of ten days was instituted; the tenth day
of each decade was to replace the weekly Sunday as a day of
rest). Its usage fizzled out around 1805, a date hardly remembered even by professional historians.

In the case of the American Revolution, the old legendary
notion of a temporal hiatus between the old order and a new
era seemed much better suited than a calendar "revolution" to

bridge the gap between a time continuum of ordered succession and the spontaneous start of something new. Indeed, it would be tempting to use the rise of the United States of America as a historical example of the truth of old legends, like a verification of Locke's "in the beginning all the world was America." The colonial period would be interpreted as the transition period from bondage to freedom—the hiatus between leaving England and the Old World and the establishment of freedom in the New.

The parallel with the tales is astoundingly close: in both instances the act of foundation had come about through the deeds and the sufferings of exiles. This is true even of the Biblical tale as told in Exodus; Canaan, the promised land, is by no means the original Jewish home, but the land of the Jews' former "sojourn" (Exodus 6:4). Virgil insists still more strongly on the theme of exile: Aeneas and his companions were "driven . . . to distant places of exile in waste lands," weeping at leaving "the shores and the havens . . . where once was Troy," exiles "uncertain whither the fates carry us or where a resting-place is given."[128]

The founders of the American Republic were well acquainted with Roman as well as Biblical antiquity and they may have taken from the old legends the decisive distinction between mere liberation and actual freedom, but nowhere do they use the hiatus as a possible basis for explaining what they were doing. There was a simple factual reason for that: though the land eventually was to become a "resting-place" for many and an asylum for exiles, they themselves had not settled there as exiles but as colonists. Up to the last, when conflict with England proved to be inevitable, they had no trouble recognizing the political authority of the mother-country. They prided themselves on being British subjects, until the momentum of their rebellion against an unjust government—"taxation without representation"—had carried them into a full-fledged "revolution," a change in the form of government itself, and the constitution of a Republic as the only government, they now felt, fit to rule in the land of the free.

This was the moment when those who had started as men of action and had been transformed into men of revolution changed Virgil's great line *"Magnus ab integro saeclorum nascitur ordo"* ("the great order of the ages is [re]born as it was in the beginning")[129] to the *Novus Ordo Seclorum* (the *"new* order"), which we still find on our dollar bills. For the Founding Fathers, the variation implied an admission that the great effort to reform and restore the body politic to its initial integrity (to found "Rome anew") had led to the entirely unexpected and very different task of constituting something entirely new—founding a "new Rome."

When men of action, men who wanted to change the world, became aware that such a change might actually postulate a new order of the ages, the start of something unprecedented, they began to look to history for help. They set about rethinking such thought-things as the Pentateuch and the *Aeneid*, foundation legends that might tell them how to solve the problem of beginning—a problem because beginning's very nature is to carry in itself an element of complete arbitrariness. It was only now that they confronted the abyss of freedom, knowing that whatever would be done now could just as well have been left undone and believing, too, with clarity and precision, that once something is done it cannot be undone, that human memory telling the story will survive repentance as well as destruction.

This applies only to the realm of action, the "many-in-one of human beings,"[130] that is, to communities where the "We" is properly established for its journey through historical time. The foundation legends, with their hiatus between liberation and the constitution of freedom, indicate the problem without solving it. They point to the *abyss* of nothingness that opens up before any deed that cannot be accounted for by a reliable chain of cause and effect and is inexplicable in Aristotelian categories of potentiality and actuality. In the normal time continuum every effect immediately turns into a cause of future developments, but when the causal chain is broken—which occurs after liberation has been achieved, because liberation, though it may be freedom's *conditio sine qua non*, is never the *conditio per quam* that causes freedom—there is nothing left for the "beginner" to hold on to. The thought of an absolute beginning—*creatio ex nihilo*—abolishes the sequence of temporality no less than does the thought of an absolute end, now rightly referred to as "thinking the unthinkable."

We know the Hebrew solution for this perplexity. It assumes a Creator-God who creates time along with the universe and who as legislator remains outside His creation, and outside of time as the One "who is who he is" (the literal translation of "Jehovah" is "I am who I am") "from eternity to eternity." This concept of eternity, having been framed by a temporal creature, is the absolute of temporality. It is what is left of time when time is "absolved"—liberated from its relativeness—time as it would appear to an outside observer not subject to its laws and by definition unrelated by virtue of his Oneness. To the extent that the universe and everything in it can be traced back to the region of this absolute One-ness, the Oneness is rooted in something that may be beyond the reasoning of temporal men but still possesses a kind of rationale of its own: it can *explain,* give a logical account of, the existentially inexplicable. And the need for explanation is nowhere stronger than in the presence of an unconnected new event breaking into the continuum, the sequence of chronological time.

This seems to be why men who were much too "enlightened" to still believe in the Hebrew-Christian Creator-God turned with rare unanimity to pseudo-religious language when they had to deal with the problem of foundation as the beginning of a "new order of the ages." We have the "appeal to God in Heaven," deemed necessary by Locke for all who embarked on the novelty of a community emerging from "the state of nature"; we have Jefferson's "laws of nature and nature's God," John Adams' "great Legislator of the Universe," Robespierre's "immortal Legislator," his cult of a "Supreme Being."

Their explanations clearly work by analogy: just as God "in the beginning created the heavens and the earth," remaining outside His Creation and prior to it, so the human legislator—created in God's own image and therefore able to imitate God—when he lays the *foundations* of a human community, creates

*The abyss of freedom and the novus ordo seclorum*

the condition for all future political life and historical development.

To be sure, neither the Greeks nor the Romans knew anything of a Creator-God whose unrelated One-ness could serve as the paradigmatic emblem for an absolute beginning. But the Romans at least, who dated their history from the foundation of Rome in 753, seem to have been aware that the very nature of this business demanded a transmundane principle. Otherwise Cicero could not have held that "human excellence nowhere so closely approaches the paths of the gods as in the founding of new and the preserving of already founded communities."[131] For Cicero as for the Greeks, from whom he derived his philosophy, the founders were not gods but divine men, and the greatness of their deed was to have established a law that became the font of authority, an immutable standard against which all positive laws and decrees enacted by men could be measured and from which they received their legitimacy.

Harking back to religious beliefs right in the middle of the Age of Enlightenment might have sufficed if there had been no more at stake than the authority of a new law; and indeed it is striking to find explicit mentions of a "future state of rewards and punishments" inserted into all American state constitutions, although we find no allusion to a hereafter in the Declaration of Independence or the Constitution of the United States. The motives for such desperate attempts to hold fast to a faith that in reality would be unable to survive the co-temporaneous emancipation of the secular realm from the Church were entirely pragmatic and highly practical. In his speech on the Supreme Being and the immortality of the soul to the National Convention on May 7, 1794, Robespierre asks *"Quel avantage trouves-tu à persuader l'homme qu'une force aveugle préside à ses destins, et frappe au hasard le crime et la vertu?"* ("What advantage do you see in persuading men to believe that a blind force presides over their destinies, striking crime and virtue at random?"), and in the *Discourses on Davila,* John Adams speaks in the same curiously rhetorical way of "the most disconsolate of all creeds, that men are but fireflies, and that this *all* is without a father . . . [which would] make murder itself as indifferent as shooting a plover, and the extermination of the Rohilla nation as innocent as the swallowing of mites on a morsel of cheese."[132]

In brief, what we find here is a short-lived effort on the part of secular government to retain not the Hebrew-Christian faith but political instruments of rule that had been so very effective at protecting the medieval communities against criminality. In retrospect it may look almost like a tricky device of the educated few to persuade the many not to follow on the slippery road to enlightenment. In any case, the attempt totally failed (at the beginning of our century few indeed were left who still believed in "a future state of rewards and punishments") and was probably foredoomed to failure. Nevertheless the loss of belief and, with it, of a good deal of the old panic-stricken fear of death has certainly contributed to the massive invasion of criminality into the political life of highly civilized communities that our own century has witnessed. There is an odd built-in helplessness about the legal systems of entirely secularized communities; their capital punishment, the death penalty, only gives a date to and accelerates a fate all mortals are subject to.

In any event, wherever men of action, driven by the very momentum of the liberation process, began to prepare in earnest for an entirely new beginning, the *novus ordo seclorum,* instead of turning to the Bible ("In the beginning God created the heavens and the earth"), they ransacked the archives of Roman antiquity for "ancient prudence" to guide them in the establishment of a Republic, that is, of a government "of laws and not of men" (Harrington). What they needed was not only an acquaintance with a new form of government but also a lesson in the art of foundation, in how to overcome the perplexities inherent in every beginning. They were quite aware of course of the bewildering spontaneity of a free act. As they knew, an act can only be called free if it is not affected or caused by anything preceding it and yet, insofar as it immediately turns into a cause of whatever follows, it demands a justification which, if it is to be successful, will have to show the act as the continuation of a preceding series, that is, renege on the very experience of freedom and novelty.

*The abyss of freedom and the novus ordo seclorum*

And what Roman antiquity had to teach them in this respect was quite reassuring and consoling. We do not know
why the Romans, in the third century B.C. or perhaps even
earlier, decided to trace their descent not from Romulus but
from Aeneas, the man from Troy who had brought "Ilium and
her conquered household gods into Italy" and thus became
"the fount of the Roman race." But it is obvious that this fact
was of great importance not only to Virgil and his contemporaries in Augustus' time, but also to all those who, starting
with Machiavelli, had gone to Roman antiquity to learn how
to conduct human affairs without the help of a transcendent
God. What men of action were learning in the archives of
Roman antiquity was the original purport of a phenomenon
with which, curiously enough, Western civilization had been
acquainted ever since the end of the Roman empire and Christianity's definite triumph.

Far from being new, the phenomenon of re-birth or renaissance, from the fifteenth and sixteenth centuries onward, had
dominated the cultural development of Europe and had been
preceded by a whole series of minor renascences that terminated the few centuries of what really were "dark ages," between the sack of Rome and the Carolingian renaissance. Each
of these re-births, consisting in a Revival of Learning and
centering on Roman and to a lesser degree Greek antiquity,
had altered and revitalized only the rather restricted milieus of
the educated elite inside and outside monasteries. It was not
till the Age of Enlightenment—that is, in a now completely
secularized world—that the revival of antiquity ceased to be a
matter of erudition and responded to highly practical political
purposes. For that enterprise the only predecessor had been
the lonely figure, Machiavelli.

The problem men of action were being called upon to solve
was the perplexity inherent in the task of *foundation,* and
since for them the paradigmatic example of a successful
foundation was bound to be Rome, it was of the greatest
importance to them to find that even the foundation of Rome,
as the Romans themselves had understood it, was not an absolutely new beginning. According to Virgil, it was the resurgence of Troy and the re-establishment of a city-state that had

preceded Rome. Thus the thread of continuity and tradition, demanded by the very continuum of time and the faculty of memory (the innate lest-we-forget, which seems to belong to a temporal creature as much as the ability to form projects for the future) had never been broken. Seen in this light, the foundation of Rome was the re-birth of Troy, the first, as it were, of the series of re-nascences that have formed the history of European culture and civilization.

We need only recall Virgil's most famous political poem, the Fourth Eclogue, to understand how vital it was for the Roman view of their state to interpret constitution and foundation in terms of the re-establishment of a beginning which, as an absolute beginning, remains perpetually shrouded in mystery. For if in the reign of Augustus "the great cycle of periods is born anew" (as all standard modern-language translations render Virgil's great line *"Magnus ab integro saeclorum nascitur ordo"*), it is precisely because this "order of the ages" is not *new* but only the return of something antecedent. To Augustus, who in the *Aeneid* is supposed to start this re-birth, a promise is even given that he will lead the way still further back and "again establish the ages of gold in Latium over the fields that once were the realm of Saturn," i.e., the Italic land before the arrival of the Trojans.[133]

At any rate, the order invoked in the Fourth Eclogue is great by virtue of going back to and being inspired by an earlier beginning: "Now returns the Maid, returns the reign of Saturn." And yet the way *back*, seen from the viewpoint of those now living, is a true beginning: "now from high heaven a new generation is sent down."[134] This poem, no doubt, is a nativity hymn, a song in praise of a child's birth and the arrival of a *nova progenies,* a new generation. It has long been misunderstood as a prophecy of salvation through a *theos sōtēr,* a savior god, or at least as the expression of some pre-Christian religious yearning. But, far from predicting the arrival of a divine child, the poem is an affirmation of the divinity of birth as such; if one wishes to extract a general meaning from it, this could only be the poet's belief that the world's potential salvation lies in the very fact that the human species regenerates itself constantly and forever. But that meaning is not explicit:

all the poet himself says is that every child born into the continuity of Roman history must learn *"heroum laudes et facta parentis,"* "the glories of the heroes and the deeds of the fathers," so as to be able to do what all Roman boys were supposed to do—help "rule the world that his fathers' virtues have set at peace."[135]

In our context, what matters is that the notion of foundation, of counting time *ab urbe condita,* is at the very center of Roman historiography along with the no less profoundly Roman notion that all such foundations—taking place exclusively in the realm of human affairs, where men enact a tale to tell, to remember, and preserve—are re-establishments and re-constitutions, not absolute beginnings.

This becomes quite manifest if one reads Virgil's *Aeneid*— the story of the foundation of the city of Rome—side by side with the *Georgics,* the four poems in praise of husbandry, of "the tending of fields and flocks and trees," and of the "quiet earth" assigned to the care of "the circling toil of the husband-man, [which] returns even as the year rolls back on itself along the familiar track": "she abides unstirred, and outlives many children's children, and sees roll by her many genera-tions of men." This is Italy before Rome, the "land of Saturn, mighty of men"; he who lives in it, "who knows the gods of the country, Pan and old Silvanus and the Nymphs' sisterhood" and remains true to the love of "stream and woodland," is "lost to fame." "Him fasces of the people or purple of kings sway not . . . not the Roman state or realms destined to decay; nor may pity of the poor or envy of the rich cost him a pang. What fruits the . . . gracious fields bear of their own free will, these he gathers, and sees not the iron of justice or the mad forum and the archives of the people." This life "in sacred purity" was "life golden Saturn led on earth," and the only trouble is that in this world full of wonders and a superabundance of plants and beasts, "there is no *tale* of the manifold kinds or of the names they bear, nor truly were the tale worth reckoning out; whoso will know it, let him . . . learn likewise how many grains of sand eddy in the west wind on the plain of Libya, or count . . . how many waves come shoreward across Ionian seas."

Those who sing of the origin of this pre-Roman and pre-Trojan world, whose circling years produce no tales worth telling, while at the same time they produce all the wonders of nature that never cease to delight men, those who in Virgil praise "the realm of Saturn" and creation-myths (in the Sixth Eclogue or in the first book of the *Aeneid*) are chanting of a fairy-tale land and are themselves marginal figures. Dido's "long-haired" bard and Silenus, "his veins swollen as ever with yesterday's wine," entertain a youthful, playful audience with old tales of the "wandering moon and the sun's travail; whence is the human race and the brute, whence water and fire," "how throughout the vast void were gathered together the seeds of earth and air and sea, and withal of fluid fire, and how from these all the beginnings of things and the young orbed world itself grew together."

Still—and this is decisive—this utopian fairy-tale land outside of history is sempiternal and survives in the indestructibility of nature; husbandmen or shepherds who tend the fields and the flocks still testify, in the midst of Roman-Trojan history, to an Italic past when the natives were "Saturn's people whom no laws fettered to justice, upright of their own free will and the custom of the god of old."[136] Then no Roman ambition was charged "to rule the nations and ordain the law of peace" (*"regere imperio populos . . . pacisque imponere morem"*), and no Roman morality was necessary to "spare the conquered and beat the haughty down" (*"parcere suiectis et debellare superbos"*).

I have dwelt on Virgil's poems at some length for several reasons. To sum up: men, when they emerged from the tutelage of the Church, turned to antiquity, and their first steps in a secularized world were guided by a revival of ancient learning. Confronted with the riddle of foundation—how to re-start time within an inexorable time continuum—they naturally turned to the story of the foundation of Rome and learned from Virgil that this starting-point of Occidental history had already been a re-vival, the resurgence of Troy. That could tell them no more than that the hope of founding a "new Rome" was an illusion: the most they could hope for was to repeat the primeval foundation and found "Rome anew." Whatever lay prior to this first foundation, itself the resurgence of some definite past, was situated outside history; it was nature, whose cyclical sempiternity might provide a refuge from the onward march of time, the vertical, rectilinear direction of history—a place of leisure, *otium*—when men tired of the busy-ness of citizenship (*nec-otium* by definition), but whose own origin was of no interest because it was beyond the scope of action.

To be sure, there is something puzzling in the fact that men of action, whose sole intent and purpose was to change the whole structure of the future world and create a *novus ordo seclorum*, should have to go to that distant past of antiquity, for they did not "deliberately [reverse] the time-axis and [bid] the young 'walk back into the pure radiance of the past' (Petrarch) because the classic past *is* the true future."[137] They looked for a paradigm for a new form of government in their own "enlightened" age and were hardly aware of the fact that they were looking backward. More puzzling, I think, than their actual ransacking of the archives of antiquity is that they did not rebel against antiquity when they discovered that the final and certainly profoundly Roman answer of "ancient prudence" was that salvation always comes from the past, that the ancestors were *maiores,* the "greater ones" by definition.

It is striking, besides, that the notion of the future—precisely a future pregnant with final salvation—bringing back a kind of initial Golden Age, should have become popular at a time when Progress had come to be the dominant concept to explain the movement of History. And the most striking example of the resilience of that very old dream is of course Marx's fantasy of a classless and warless "realm of freedom" as prefigured in "original communism," a realm that has a more than superficial resemblance to Saturn's aboriginal Italic rule, when no laws "fettered [men] to justice." In its original ancient form as the inception of history, the Golden Age is a melancholy thought; it is as though, thousands of years ago, our ancestors had a foreboding of the eventual discovery of the entropy principle in the midst of the progress-drunk nineteenth century—a discovery which, if it had gone unchallenged, would have deprived action of all meaning.[138] What actually disposed of the entropy principle for the men who made the revolutions of the nineteenth and twentieth centuries was less Engels' "scientific" refutation than Marx's turning—and, of course, Nietzsche's too—to a cyclical time concept where the prehistoric innocence of the beginning would finally return, no less triumphant than the Second Coming.

But this does not concern us here. When we directed our attention to men of action, hoping to find in them a notion of freedom purged of the perplexities caused for men's minds by the reflexivity of mental activities—the inevitable recoil on itself of the willing ego—we hoped for more than we finally achieved. The abyss of pure spontaneity, which in the foundation legends is bridged by the hiatus between liberation and the constitution of freedom, was covered up by the device, typical of the Occidental tradition (the only tradition where freedom has always been the *raison d'être* of all politics) of understanding the *new* as an improved re-statement of the old. In its original integrity, freedom survived in political theory —i.e., theory conceived for the purpose of political action— only in utopian and unfounded promises of a final "realm of freedom" that, in its Marxian version at any rate, would indeed spell "the end of all things," a sempiternal peace in which all specifically human activities would wither away.

No doubt to arrive at such a conclusion is frustrating, but I know of only one tentative alternative to it in our entire history of political thought. If, as Hegel believed, the philosopher's task is to catch the most elusive of all manifestations, the spirit of an age, in the net of reason's concepts, then Augustine, the Christian philosopher of the fifth century A.D., was the only philosopher the Romans ever had. He was a Roman by education rather than birth, and it was his learning that sent him back to the classical texts of Republican Rome of the first century B.C., which even then were alive only in the form of erudition. In his great work on the *City of God,* he mentions, but does not explicate, what could have become the ontological underpinning for a truly Roman or Virgilian philosophy of politics. According to him, as we know, God created man as a temporal creature, *homo temporalis;* time and man were created together, and this temporality was affirmed by the fact that each man owed his life not just to the multiplication of the species, but to birth, the entry of a novel creature who *as* something entirely new appears in the midst of the time continuum of the world. The purpose of the creation of man was to make possible a *beginning:* "That there be a beginning man was created, before whom nobody was"—"*Initium . . . ergo ut esset, creatus est homo, ante quem nullus fuit.*"[139] The very capacity for beginning is rooted in *natality,* and by no means in creativity, not in a gift but in the fact that human beings, new men, again and again appear in the world by virtue of birth.

I am quite aware that the argument even in the Augustinian version is somehow opaque, that it seems to tell us no more than that we are *doomed* to be free by virtue of being born, no matter whether we like freedom or abhor its arbitrariness, are "pleased" with it or prefer to escape its awesome responsibility by electing some form of fatalism. This impasse, if such it is, cannot be opened or solved except by an appeal to another mental faculty, no less mysterious than the faculty of beginning, the faculty of Judgment, an analysis of which at least may tell us what is involved in our pleasures and displeasures.

# Notes

## Chapter I

1. See *Sophist*, 253–254 and *Republic*, 517.
2. Hermann Diels and Walther Kranz, *Die Fragmente der Vorsokratiker*, Berlin, 1960, vol. I, frag. B4.
3. *Confessions*, bk. XI, chap. 13.
4. *La Pensée et le Mouvant* (1934), Paris, 1950, p. 170.
5. *Ibid.*, p. 26.
6. 1174b6 and 1177a20. See also Aristotle's objections to Plato's concept of pleasure, 1173a13–1173b7.
7. *Op. cit.*, p. 5.
8. For the following, see *Metaphysics*, bk. VII, chaps. 7–10.
9. *De Anima*, 433a30.
10. Bruno Snell, *The Discovery of the Mind*, New York, Evanston, 1960, pp. 182–183.
11. *The Spirit of Medieval Philosophy*, New York, 1940, p. 307.
12. "Whether whatsoever comes to pass proceed from *necessity*, or some things from *chance*, has been a question disputed amongst the old philosophers long before the incarnation of our Saviour. . . . But the third way of bringing things to pass . . . namely *freewill*, is a thing that never was mentioned amongst them, nor by the Christians in the beginning of Christianity. . . . But for some ages past, the doctors of the Roman Church have exempted from this dominion of God's will the will of man; and brought in a doctrine, that . . . [man's] will is free, and determined . . . by the power of the will itself." "The Question concerning *Liberty, Necessity and Chance*," *English Works*, London, 1841, vol. V, p. 1.
13. See *Nicomachean Ethics*, bk. V, chap. 8.
14. *Ibid.*, bk. 3, 1110a17.
15. Gilbert Ryle, *The Concept of Mind*, New York, 1949, p. 65.
16. Henry Herbert Williams, article on the Will in *Encyclopaedia Britannica*, 11th ed.

17. *De Generatione,* bk. I, chap. 3, 317b16–18.
18. *Ibid.,* 318a25–27 and 319a23–29; *The Basic Works of Aristotle,* ed. Richard McKeon, New York, 1941, p. 483.
19. *Meteorologica,* 339b27.
20. Bk. I, 1100a33–1100b18.
21. *De Caelo,* 283b26–31.
22. *The Will to Power,* ed. Walter Kaufmann, Vintage Books, New York, 1968, no. 617.
23. *De Civitate Dei,* bk. XII, chap. 20.
24. *Ibid.,* chap. 13.
25. Our present calendar, which takes the birth of Christ as the turning-point from which to count time both backward and forward, was introduced at the end of the eighteenth century. The textbooks present the reform as prompted by scholarly needs to facilitate the dating of events in ancient history without having to refer to a maze of different time reckonings. Hegel, as far as I know the only philosopher to ponder the sudden remarkable change, saw in it a clear sign of a truly Christian chronology because the birth of Christ now became the turning-point of world history. It seems more significant that in the new scheme we can count backward and forward in such a way that the past reaches back into an infinite past and the future likewise stretches out into an infinite future. This twofold infinity eliminates all notions of beginning and end, establishing mankind, as it were, in a potentially sempiternal reality on earth. Needless to add that nothing could be more alien to Christian thought than the notion of an earthly immortality of mankind and its world.
26. See the article on the Will in the *Encyclopaedia Britannica,* mentioned above, in n. 16.
27. See Dieter Nestle, *Eleutheria. Teil I: Studien zum Wesen der Freiheit bei den Griechen und im Neuen Testament,* Tübingen, 1967, pp. 6 ff. It seems to be noteworthy that modern etymology inclines to derive the word *"eleutheria"* from an Indo-Germanic root signifying *Volk* or *Stamm,* with the result that only those who belong to the same ethnic unity can be recognized as "free" by their fellow-ethnics. Does not this piece of erudition sound rather uncomfortably close to the notions of German scholarship during the nineteen-thirties, when it first saw the light of day?
28. *Critique of Pure Reason,* B476. For this and other citations, see Norman Kemp Smith's translation, *Immanuel Kant's*

*Critique of Pure Reason,* New York, 1963, which the author frequently relied on.

29. *Uber die ästhetische Erziehung des Menschen in einer Reihe von Briefen,* 1795, 19th letter.

30. *The World as Will and Idea* (1818), trans. R. B. Haldane and J. Kemp, vol. I, pp. 39 and 129. Quoted here from Konstantin Kolenda's Introduction to Arthur Schopenhauer, *Essay on the Freedom of the Will,* Library of Liberal Arts, Indianapolis, New York, 1960, p. viii.

31. *Of Human Freedom* (1809), trans. James Gutmann, Chicago, 1936, p. 24.

32. *Beyond Good and Evil* (1885), trans. Marianne Cowan, Chicago, 1955, sect. 18.

33. "Also Sprach Zarathustra," in *Ecce Homo* (1889), no. 1.

34. *Ibid.,* no. 3.

35. See Karl Jaspers, *Nietzsche: An Introduction to the Understanding of His Philosophical Activity* (1935), trans. Charles F. Wallraff and Frederick J. Schmitz, Tucson, 1965; and Martin Heidegger, *Nietzsche,* 2 vols., Pfullingen, 1961.

36. *Philosophy* (1932), trans. E. B. Ashton, Chicago, 1970, vol. 2, p. 167.

37. "*Das primäre Phänomen der ursprünglichen und eigentlichen Zeitlichkeit ist die Zukunft.*" In *Sein und Zeit* (1926), Tübingen, 1949, p. 329; *Gelassenheit,* Pfullingen, 1959, English translation: *Discourse on Thinking,* trans. John M. Anderson and E. Hans Freund, New York, 1966.

38. Editor's note: we have been unable to find this reference.

39. *English Works,* vol. V, p. 55.

40. Letter to G. H. Schaller, dated October 1674. See Spinoza, *The Chief Works,* ed. R. H. M. Elwes, New York, 1951, vol. II, p. 390.

41. *Ethics,* pt. III, prop. II, note, in *ibid.,* vol. II, p. 134; Letter to Schaller, in *ibid.,* p. 392.

42. *Leviathan,* ed. Michael Oakeshott, Oxford, 1948, chap. 21.

43. *Essay on the Freedom of the Will,* p. 43.

44. *An Examination of Sir William Hamilton's Philosophy* (1867), chap. XXVI, quoted from *Free Will,* eds. Sidney Morgenbesser and James Walsh, Englewood Cliffs, 1962, p. 59.

45. See Martin Kähler, *Das Gewissen* (1878), Darmstadt, 1967, pp. 46 ff.

46. See *Laws,* bk. IX, 865e.

47. *Op. cit.*, pp. 63–64.

48. *Notebooks 1914–1916*, bilingual ed., trans. G. E. M. Anscombe, New York, 1961, entry under date of August 5, 1916, p. 80e; cf. also pp. 86e–88e.

49. Augustine, *On Free Choice of the Will* (*De Libero Arbitrio*), bk. III, sect. 3.

50. In the Reply to Objection XII against the First Meditation: "that the freedom of the will has been assumed without proof." See *The Philosophical Works of Descartes*, trans. Elizabeth S. Haldane and G. R. T. Ross, Cambridge, 1970, vol. II, pp. 74–75.

51. Meditation IV, in *ibid.*, 1972, vol. I, pp. 174–175. Author's translation.

52. *Principles of Philosophy*, in *ibid.*, pt. I, prin. XL, p. 235.

53. *Ibid.*, prin. XLI, p. 235.

54. *Critique of Pure Reason*, B751.

55. *Op. cit.*, pp. 98–99.

56. *Critique of Pure Reason*, B478.

57. See Hans Jonas, "Jewish and Christian Elements in Philosophy," in *Philosophical Essays: From Ancient Creed to Technological Man*, Englewood Cliffs, 1974.

58. Henri Bergson, *op. cit.*, p. 13.

59. *Ibid.*, p. 15.

60. Thus wrote Wilhelm Windelband in his famous *History of Philosophy* (1892), New York, 1960, p. 314. He also calls Duns Scotus "the greatest of the Scholastics" (p. 425).

61. John Duns Scotus, *Philosophical Writings: A Selection*, trans. Allan Wolter, Library of Liberal Arts, Indianapolis, New York, 1962, pp. 84 and 10.

62. Hans Jonas, *op. cit.*, p. 29.

63. *Op. cit.*, p. 10.

64. *Ibid.*, p. 33.

65. *Time and Free Will: An Essay on the Immediate Data of Consciousness* (1889), trans. F. L. Pogson, Harper Torchbooks, New York, 1960, p. 142.

66. *Ibid.*, pp. 240 and 167.

67. *Principles of Philosophy*, prin. XLI, in *The Philosophical Works of Descartes*, p. 235.

68. Reply to Objections to Meditation V, *op. cit.*, p. 225.

69. Duns Scotus, *op. cit.*, p. 171.

70. See his exhaustive examination of the fatalist argument, " 'It Was to Be,' " in *Dilemmas*, Cambridge, 1969, pp. 15–35.

71. *Ibid.*, p. 28.

72. *De Fato*, xiii, 30–14, 31.

73. *Ibid.*, V, 35.

74. As Chrysippus had already pointed out. See *ibid.*, xx, 48.

75. *Confessio Philosophi*, bilingual ed., ed. Otto Saame, Frankfurt, 1967, p. 66.

76. *Jenenser Logik, Metaphysik und Naturphilosophie*, Lasson ed., Leipzig, 1923, p. 204, in *"Naturphilosophie I A: Begriff der Bewegung."*

77. See Friedrich Nietzsche, *Thus Spoke Zarathustra*, pt. II, "On Redemption": "The will cannot will backwards. . . . That time does not run backwards, that is his wrath; 'that which was' is the name of the stone he cannot move," in *The Portable Nietzsche*, trans. Walter Kaufmann, New York, 1954, p. 251.

78. See chap. III, p. 142 and n. 89.

79. *Op. cit.*, p. 110.

80. *Ibid.*, p. 122.

81. *Ibid.*, pp. 42, 44, 76, 92, 98, 100.

82. Quoted by Walter Lehmann in his Introduction to an anthology of the German writings, *Meister Eckhart*, Göttingen, 1919, sent. 15, p. 16.

83. The essay is now available in *Etudes d'Histoire de la Pensée Philosophique*, Paris, 1961.

84. Now available in English: *Introduction to the Readings of Hegel*, ed. Allan Bloom, New York, 1969, p. 134.

85. *Op. cit.*, p. 177.

86. *Philosophy of Right*, Preface; *Encyclopedia*, no. 465 in 2nd ed.

87. *Op. cit., loc. cit.*

88. *Ibid.*, pp. 177 and 185, note.

89. *Ibid.*, p. 188.

90. *Jenenser Logik*, p. 204.

91. Koyré, *op. cit.*, p. 183, quoting Hegel, *Jenenser Realphilosophie*, ed. Johannes Hoffmeister, Leipzig, 1932, vol. II, pp. 10 ff.

92. Koyré, *op. cit.*, p. 177.

93. Plato, *Republic*, 329b–c.

94. Koyré, *op. cit.*, p. 166.

95. *Ibid.*, p. 174.

96. Koyré, "La terminologie hégélienne," in *op. cit.*, p. 213.

97. Martin Heidegger, *Sein und Zeit*, no. 65, p. 326.

224

98. Koyré, *op. cit.*, p. 188, quoting *Phänomenologie des Geistes.*
99. Koyré, *op. cit.*, p. 183, quoting *Jenenser Realphilosophie.*
100. Koyré, "Hegel à Iéna," in *op. cit.*, p. 188.
101. Koyré, *op. cit.*, p. 185, quoting *Jenenser Realphilosophie.*
102. The passage in Plotinus is a commentary on Plato's *Timaeus,* 37c–38b. It occurs in *Ennead,* III, 7, 11: "On Time and Eternity." I have used the translation by A. H. Armstrong in the Loeb Classical Library, London, 1967, and Emile Bréhier's translation into French in the bilingual edition of the *Ennéades,* Paris, 1924–38.
103. An excellent and detailed report of the literature about Hegel is now available in Michael Theunissen, *Die Verwirklichung der Vernunft. Zur Theorie-Praxis-Diskussion im Anschluss an Hegel,* Beiheft 6 of the *Philosophische Rundschau,* Tübingen, 1970. The main works for our context are: Franz Rosenzweig, *Hegel und der Staat,* 2 vols. (1920), Aalen, 1962; Joachim Ritter, *Hegel und die französische Revolution, Frankfurt/ Main,* 1965; Manfred Riedel, *Theorie und Praxis im Denken Hegels,* Stuttgart, 1965.
104. *The Philosophy of History,* trans. J. Sibree, New York, 1956, pp. 446, 447; *Philosophie der Weltgeschichte,* Hälfte II, "Die Germanische Welt," Lasson ed., Leipzig, 1923, p. 926.
105. In a letter to Schelling of April 16, 1795. *Briefe,* Leipzig, 1887, vol. I, p. 15.
106. Quoted from Theunissen, *op. cit.*
107. *The Philosophy of History,* p. 442.
108. *Ibid.,* p. 446.
109. *Ibid.,* pp. 30 and 36.
110. *Ibid.,* p. 442.
111. *Ibid.,* p. 443. Author's translation.
112. *Ibid.,* p. 36.
113. *Ibid.,* p. 79. Author's translation; cf. *Werke,* Berlin, 1840, vol. IX, p. 98.
114. *Op. cit.,* p. 189.
115. *The Phenomenology of Mind,* trans. J. B. Baillie (1910), New York, 1964, p. 803.
116. Koyré, *op. cit.*, p. 164, quoting *Encyclopedia,* no. 258.
117. Hegel, *The Phenomenology of Mind,* pp. 801, 807–808. Italics added.
118. *Ibid.,* p. 808.
119. "Uberwindung der Metaphysik," in *Vorträge und Aufsätze,* Pfullingen, 1954, vol. I, sect. xxii, p. 89.

120. Hegel, *Science of Logic*, trans. W. H. Johnston and L. G. Struthers, London, New York, 1966, vol. I, p. 118.
121. *Toward a Genealogy of Morals* (1887), no. 28.
122. Heidegger, "Uberwindung der Metaphysik," *op. cit.*, sect. xxiii, p. 89.
123. *Science of Logic*, vol. I, pp. 95, 97, 85.

## Chapter II

1. *Concept of the Mind*, pp. 62 ff.
2. See the marvelously illuminating study by E. H. Gombrich, *Art and Illusion*, New York, 1960.
3. *De Anima*, 433a21–24 and *Nicomachean Ethics*, 1139a35.
4. For this and the following, see *De Anima*, bk. III, chaps. 9, 10.
5. *Meister Eckhart*, ed. Franz Pfeiffer, Göttingen, 1914, pp. 551–552.
6. Quoted from Werner Jaeger, *Aristotle*, London, 1962, p. 249. Jaeger also notices that "the third Book *On the Soul*," from which I have quoted here, "stands out as peculiarly Platonic" (p. 332).
7. *Nicomachean Ethics*, 1168b6.
8. *Ibid.*, 1166b5–25.
9. See the last lines of *Antigone*.
10. *Nicomachean Ethics*, 1139b1–4.
11. Quoted from Andreas Graeser, *Plotinus and the Stoics*, Leiden, 1972, p. 119.
12. *Nicomachean Ethics*, 1139a31–33, 1139b4–5.
13. *Ibid.*, 1134a21.
14. *Ibid.*, 1112b12.
15. *Eudemian Ethics*, 1226a10.
16. *Ibid.*, 1223b10.
17. *Ibid.*, 1224a31–1224b15.
18. *Ibid.*, 1226b10.
19. *Ibid.*, 1226b11–12. Cf. *Nicomachean Ethics*, 1112b11–18.
20. For an excellent discussion of Will and Freedom in Kant, see Lewis White Beck, *A Commentary on Kant's Critique of Practical Reason*, Chicago, London, 1960, chap. XI.
21. *Op. cit.*, p. 551.
22. Hans Jonas, *Augustin und das paulinische Freiheitsproblem*, 2nd ed., Göttingen, 1965; see especially app. III, published as "Philosophical Meditation on the Seventh Chapter of

Paul's Epistle to the Romans" in *The Future of Our Religious Past,* ed. James M. Robinson, London, New York, 1971, pp. 333–350.

23. *Metamorphoses,* bk. VII, ll. 20–21: *"Video meliora proboque, / deteriora sequor."*

24. Chagigah II, 1. Quoted from Hans Blumenberg, *Paradigmen zu einer Metaphorologie,* Bonn, 1960, p. 26, n. 38.

25. Bk. XI, chaps. xii and xxx.

26. See *Discourses,* bk. II, chap. xix.

27. *Fragments,* 23.

28. *The Manual,* 23 and 33.

29. *Discourses,* bk. II, chap. 16.

30. All the works we have, including the *Discourses,* are "apparently almost a stenographic record of his lectures and informal discussions taken down and compiled by one of his pupils, Arrian." See Whitney J. Oates, General Introduction to his *The Stoic and Epicurean Philosophers,* Modern Library, New York, 1940, whose translation I often follow.

31. *Discourses,* bk. I, chap. xv.

32. *Ibid.,* bk. II, chap. xviii.

33. *Ibid.,* bk. I, chap. xxvii.

34. *Ibid.,* bk. II, chap. i.

35. *Ibid.,* bk. II, chap. xvi.

36. *The Manual,* 23 and 33.

37. *Discourses,* bk. II, chap. xvi.

38. *Ibid.,* bk. I, chap. i.

39. *Ibid.*

40. *Ibid.,* bk. I, chap. xvii.

41. *Physics,* 188b30.

42. *Discourses,* bk. I, chap. xvii.

43. *Ibid.,* bk. II, chap. xi.

44. *Ibid.,* bk. II, chap. x.

45. *Ibid.,* bk. III, chap. xiv.

46. *The Manual,* 1.

47. *Fragments,* 1.

48. *Ibid.,* 8.

49. *Discourses,* bk. I, chap. i.

50. *The Manual,* 30.

51. *Discourses,* bk. I, chap. xxv.

52. *Ibid.,* bk. I, chap. ix.

53. *Ibid.,* bk. I, chap. xxv. Italics added.

54. *Le Mythe de Sisyphe,* Paris, 1942.

55. *De Trinitate*, bk. XIII, vii, 10.

56. *Ibid.*, viii, 11.

57. *Discourses*, bk. II, chap. x.

58. *Ibid.*, bk. II, chap, xvii.

59. *The Manual*, 8.

60. *Fragments*, 8.

61. In *De Libero Arbitrio*, bk. III, v–viii.

62. *Discourses*, bk. II, chap. xviii.

63. *Ibid.*, bk. II, chap. viii.

64. *The Manual*, 51, 48.

65. Frag. 149; *Enarrationes in Psalmos, Patrologiae Latina*, J.-P. Migne, Paris, 1854–66, vol. 37, CXXXIV, 16.

66. Paul Oskar Kristeller, a bit more cautiously, calls Augustine "probably the greatest Latin philosopher of classical antiquity." See *Renaissance Concepts of Man*, Harper Torchbooks, New York, 1972, p. 149.

67. *On the Trinity*, bk. 13, iv, 7: "*Beati certe, inquit* [Cicero] *omnes esse volumus.*"

68. "*O vitae philosophia dux,*" *Tusculanae Disputationes*, bk. V, chap. 2.

69. Quoted with approbation from a Roman writer (Varro) in *The City of God*, bk. XIX, i, 3: "*Nulla est homini causa philosophandi nisi ut beatus sit.*"

70. For the importance and depth of this question, see especially *On the Trinity*, bk. X, chaps iii and viii: "How the mind may seek and find itself is a remarkable question: whither does it go in order to seek, and whence does it come in order to find?"

71. *Confessions*, bk. XI, especially chaps. xiv and xxii.

72. Peter Brown, *Augustine of Hippo*, Berkeley and Los Angeles, 1967, p. 123.

73. *Ibid.*, p. 112.

74. *On Free Choice of the Will*, bk. I, chaps. i and ii.

75. *Ibid.*, chap. xvi, 117 and 118.

76. *Confessions*, bk. VIII, chap. v.

77. *Ibid.*, chap. viii.

78. A detailed explanation deriving *voluntas* from *velle* and *potestas* from *posse* occurs in *The Spirit and the Letter*, arts. 52–58, a late work, concerned with the question "Is faith itself placed in our power?" in Morgenbesser and Walsh, *op. cit.*, p. 22.

79. *On Free Choice of the Will*, bk. III, chap. iii, 27; cf. *ibid.*, bk. I, chap. xii, 86 and *Retractationes*, bk. I, chap. ix, 3.

80. *Epistolae*, 177, 5; *On Free Choice of the Will*, bk. III, chap. i, 8–10; chap. iii, 33.
81. See Etienne Gilson, *Jean Duns Scot: Introduction à ses positions fondamentales*, Paris, 1952, p. 657.
82. *On Free Choice of the Will*, bk. III, chap. xxv.
83. *Ibid.*, chap. xvii.
84. *On Grace and Free Will*, chap. xliv.
85. *Confessions*, bk. VIII, chap. iii, 6–8.
86. *On Free Choice of the Will*, bk. III, chaps. vi–viii; Lehmann, *op. cit.*, sent. 14, p. 16.
87. *On Free Choice of the Will*, bk. III, chap. v.
88. "Precious Five," *Collected Poems*, New York, 1976, p. 450.
89. *Confessions*, bk. VIII, chap. viii.
90. *Ibid.*, chap. ix.
91. *Ibid.*, chaps. ix and x.
92. *Ibid.*, chap. x.
93. *Epistolae*, 157, 2, 9; 55, 10, 18; *Confessions*, bk. XIII, chap. ix.
94. In *An Examination of Sir William Hamilton's Philosophy*, "On the Freedom of the Will" (1867), quoted from Morgenbesser and Walsh, *op. cit.*, pp. 57–69. Italics added.
95. *Confessions*, bk. III, chap. vi, 11.
96. Bk. IX, chap. iv.
97. Bk. XIII, chap. xi.
98. Bk. X, chap. xi, 18.
99. *Ibid.*, bk. XI, chap. iii, 6.
100. *Ibid.*, chap. ii, 2.
101. *Ibid.*, chap. iv, 7.
102. *Ibid.*, chap. v, 8.
103. *Ibid.*, bk. XII, chap. iii, 3.
104. Efrem Bettoni, *Duns Scotus: The Basic Principles of His Philosophy*, trans. Bernardine Bonansea, Washington, 1961, p. 158. Italics added.
105. *On the Trinity*, bk. XV, chap. xxi, 41.
106. *Ibid.*, bk. VIII, chap. x.
107. *Ibid.*, bk. X, chap. viii, 11.
108. *Ibid.*, bk. XI, chap. ii, 5.
109. *Ibid.*, bk. X, chap. v, 7. Italics added.
110. *Ibid.*, chap. xi, 17.
111. *Ibid.*, bk. XI, chap. v, 9.
112. *Ibid.*, bk. X, chap. v, 7.
113. *Ibid.*, chap. viii, 11.

114. *Ibid.*, chap. v, 7. Cf. bk. XII, chaps. xii, xiv, xv.
115. *Ibid.*, bk. XII, chap. xiv, 23.
116. *Ibid.*, bk. X, chap. xi, 18.
117. *Ibid.*, bk. XI, chap. xi, 18.
118. *The City of God*, bk. XI, chap. xxviii.
119. William H. Davis, *The Freewill Question*, The Hague, 1971, p. 29.
120. In its extreme form, as held by Augustine at the end of his life, the doctrine maintains that children are eternally damned if they die before receiving the sacrament of baptism. This cannot be justified by referring to Paul because these children cannot yet have known faith. Only after grace has materialized in a sacrament, dispensed by the Church, and when faith has been institutionalized, can this version of predestination be justified. Institutionalized grace is no longer a datum of consciousness—an experience of the inward man—and therefore not interesting for philosophy; nor is it a matter of faith, strictly speaking. No doubt, this is among the most important *political* factors in the Christian creed, with which we are not concerned here.
121. *The City of God*, bk. XI, chap. xxi.
122. *Confessions*, bk. XI, chap. xiv.
123. *Ibid.*, chaps. xx and xxviii.
124. *Ibid.*, chap. xxi.
125. *Ibid.*, chaps. xxiv, xxvi, and xxviii.
126. See especially bks. XI–XIII of *The City of God*.
127. *Ibid.*, bk. XII, chap. xiv.
128. *Ibid.*, bk. XI, chap. vi.
129. *Ibid.*, bk. XII, chap. xiv.
130. *Ibid.*, chaps. xxi and xx.
131. *Ibid.*, bk. XI, chap. xxxii.
132. *Ibid.*, bk. XII, chaps. xxi and xxii.
133. *Ibid.*, chap. vi.
134. *Ibid.*, bk. XIII, chap. x.
135. B478.

## Chapter III

1. *The Spirit of Medieval Philosophy*, pp. 207 and 70.
2. *Summa Theologica*, I, qu. 82, a. 1.
3. *Ibid.*, qu. 81, a. 3, and qu. 83, a. 4.

4. Duns Scotus as quoted by Gilson, *The Spirit of Medieval Philosophy*, p. 52.
5. Gilson, *The Spirit of Medieval Philosophy*, p. 437.
6. In "What Is Authority" in *Between Past and Future*, I tried to show the importance of the past for any strictly Roman understanding of politics. See especially the explication of the Roman triad: *auctoritas, religio, traditio.*
7. *De Civitate Dei*, bk. XII, chap. xiv.
8. *Op. cit.*, I, qu. 5, a. 4.
9. *Ibid.*, I–II, qu. 15, a. 3.
10. *Ibid.*, I, qu. 5, a. 1, and I–II, qu. 18, a. 1.
11. *Ibid.*, I, qu. 48, a. 3.
12. *Ibid.*, qu. 5, a. 5; qu. 49, a. 3.
13. Quoted in *ibid.*, qu. 49, a. 3.
14. *History of Christian Philosophy in the Middle Ages*, New York, 1955, p. 375.
15. *Summa Theologica*, I, qu. 75, a. 6.
16. *Ibid.*, qu. 81, a. 3.
17. *Ibid.*, qu. 82, a. 4.
18. Gilson, *History of Christian Philosophy in the Middle Ages*, p. 766.
19. *Summa Theologica*, I, qu. 29, a. 3, Resp.
20. Augustine, *De Civitate Dei*, bk. XII, chap. xxi.
21. *Summa Theologica*, I, qu. 82, a. 4.
22. *Ibid.*, qu. 83, a. 3.
23. Raised by Thomas in the *Summa contra Gentiles*, III, 26.
24. Quoted from Wilhelm Kahl, *Die Lehre vom Primat des Willens bei Augustin, Duns Scotus und Descartes*, Strassburg, 1886, p. 61 n.
25. *The Divine Comedy*, Paradiso, Canto xviii, line 109 f., trans. Laurence Binyon, New York, 1949.
26. Quoted from Gustav Siewerth, *Thomas von Aquin, Die menschliche Willensfreiheit. Texte . . . ausgewählt & mit einer Einleitung versehen*, Düsseldorf, 1954, p. 62.
27. *Summa Theologica*, I, qu. 79, a. 2.
28. *Ibid.*, I–II, qu. 9, a. 1.
29. *Nicomachean Ethics*, bk. X, 1178b18–21; 1177b5–6.
30. *Summa Theologica*, I–II, qu. 10, a. 2; *Summa contra Gentiles*, loc. cit.
31. *Metaphysics*, 1072b3.
32. *Summa Theologica*, I–II, qu. 11, a. 3. Cf. *Commentary on St. Paul's Epistle to the Galatians*, chap. 5, lec. 3.

33. *Grundlegung zur Metaphysik des Sitten,* Akademie Ausgabe, vol. IV, 1911, p. 429.

34. See, for instance, sect. IV of the bilingual edition of Duns Scotus: *Philosophical Writings,* ed. and trans. Allan Wolter, Edinburgh, London, 1962, pp. 83 ff.

35. Quoted from Kahl, *op. cit.,* pp. 97 and 99.

36. See Efrem Bettoni, "The Originality of the Scotistic Synthesis," in John K. Ryan and Bernardine M. Bonansea, *John Duns Scotus, 1265–1965,* Washington, 1965, p. 34.

37. *Duns Scotus,* p. 191. In a different context, however, though in the same book (p. 144), Bettoni maintains that "to a great extent . . . the originality of the Scotistic demonstration [of the existence of God lies] in being a synthesis of St. Thomas and St. Anselm."

38. In addition to the items quoted above, I have used chiefly: Ernst Stadter, *Psychologie und Metaphysik der menschlichen Freiheit,* München, Paderborn, Wien, 1971; Ludwig Walter, *Das Glaubensverständnis bei Johannes Scotus,* München, Paderborn, Wien, 1968; Etienne Gilson, *Jean Duns Scot;* Johannes Auer, *Die menschliche Willensfreiheit im Lehrsystem des Thomas von Aquin und Johannes Duns Scotus,* München, 1938; Walter Hoeres, *Der Wille als reine Vollkommenheit nach Duns Scotus,* München, 1962; Robert Prentice, "The Voluntarism of Duns Scotus," in *Franciscan Studies,* vol. 28, Annual VI, 1968; Berard Vogt, "The Metaphysics of Human Liberty in Duns Scotus," in *Proceedings of the American Catholic Philosophical Association,* vol. XVI, 1940.

39. Quoted from Wolter, *op. cit.,* pp. 64, 73, and 57.

40. Quoted from Kristeller, *op. cit.,* p. 58.

41. Quoted from Wolter, *op. cit.,* p. 162. Author's translation.

42. *Ibid.,* p. 161. Author's translation.

43. *Ibid.,* n. 25 to sect. V, p. 184.

44. *Ibid.,* p. 73.

45. *Ibid.,* p. 75.

46. *Ibid.,* p. 72. Gilson holds that the very notion of the infinite is Christian in origin. "The Greeks prior to the Christian era never conceived infinity save as an imperfection." See *The Spirit of Medieval Philosophy,* p. 55.

47. See Walter, *op. cit.,* p. 130.

48. Quoted from Stadter, *op. cit.,* p. 315.

49. Quoted from Auer, *op. cit.,* p. 86.

50. Quoted from Vogt, *op. cit.*, p. 34.

51. *Ibid.*

52. Quoted from Kahl, *op. cit.*, pp. 86–87.

53. Bettoni, *Duns Scotus*, p. 76.

54. See Bernardine M. Bonansea, "Duns Scotus' Voluntarism," in Ryan and Bonansea, *op. cit.*, p. 92. "*Non possum velle esse miserum; . . . sed ex hoc non sequitur, ergo necessario volo beatitudinem, quia nullum velle necessario elicitur a voluntate,*" p. 93, n. 38.

55. See *ibid.*, pp. 89–90 and n. 28. Bonansea enumerates the passages "which seem to indicate the possibility for the will to seek evil as evil" (p. 89, n. 25).

56. Quoted from Vogt, *op. cit.*, p. 31.

57. Bonansea, *op. cit.*, p. 94, n. 44.

58. See Vogt, *op. cit.*, p. 29, and Bonansea, *op. cit.*, p. 86, n. 13: "*Voluntas naturalis non est voluntas, nec velle naturale est velle.*"

59. Quoted from Hoeres, *op. cit.*, pp. 113–114.

60. *Ibid.*, p. 151. The quotation is from Auer, *op. cit.*, p. 149.

61. Hoeres, *op. cit.*, p. 120. So long as the definitive edition of Duns Scotus' works is not completed, a number of questions will remain open concerning his teachings on these matters.

62. Bettoni, *Duns Scotus*, p. 187.

63. *Ibid.*, p. 188.

64. See Stadter, *op. cit.*, especially the section on Petrus Johannes Olivi, pp. 144–167.

65. See Bettoni, *Duns Scotus*, p. 193. n.

66. Such phrases occur here and there. For a discussion of this sort of "introspection," see Béraud de Saint-Maurice, "The Contemporary Significance of Duns Scotus' Philosophy," in Ryan and Bonansea, *op. cit.*, p. 354, and Ephrem Longpré, "The Psychology of Duns Scotus and Its Modernity," in *The Franciscan Educational Conference*, vol. XII, 1931.

67. For the "proof" of contingency, Scotus invokes the authority of Avicenna, quoting from his *Metaphysics*: "Those who deny the first principle [i.e., "Some being is contingent"] should be flogged or burned until they admit that it is not the same thing to be burned and not burned, or whipped and not whipped." See Arthur Hyman and James J. Walsh, *Philosophy in the Middle Ages*, New York, 1967, p. 592.

68. Anybody who is acquainted with the medieval disputations between the schools is still struck by their contentious spirit,

a kind of "contentious learning" (Francis Bacon) that aimed at an ephemeral victory rather than at anything else. Erasmus' and Rabelais' satires as well as Francis Bacon's attacks testify to an atmosphere in the schools that must have been quite annoying to those who were doing philosophy in earnest. For Scotus, see Saint-Maurice in Ryan and Bonansea, *op. cit.,* pp. 354–358.

69. Quoted from Hyman and Walsh, *op. cit.,* p. 597.
70. Bonansea, *op. cit.,* p. 109, n. 90.
71. Hoeres, *op. cit.,* p. 121.
72. Bonansea, *op. cit.,* p. 89.
73. Stadter, *op. cit.,* p. 193.
74. *Ibid.*
75. Wolter, *op. cit.,* p. 80.
76. Aristotle, *Physics*, 256b10.
77. Auer, *op. cit.,* p. 169.
78. For the theory of "concurring causes," see Bonansea, *op. cit.,* pp. 109–110. The quotations are chiefly from P. Ch. Balie, "Une question inédite de J. Duns Scots sur la volonté," in *Recherches de théologie ancienne et médiévale,* vol. 3, 1931.
79. Wolter, *op. cit.,* p. 55.
80. Cf. Bergson's insight cited in chap. I of this volume, p. 31.
81. Quoted from Hoeres, *op. cit.,* p. 111, who unfortunately does not give any Latin original for the sentence: *"Denn alles Vergangene ist schlechthin notwendig."*
82. See Bonansea, *op. cit.,* p. 95.
83. Quoted from Hyman and Walsh, *op. cit.,* p. 596.
84. See Vogt, *op. cit.,* p. 29.
85. Auer, *op. cit.,* p. 152.
86. Bettoni, *Duns Scotus,* p. 158.
87. Wolter, *op. cit.,* pp. 57 and 177.
88. Hoeres, *op. cit.,* p. 191.
89. Stadter, *op. cit.,* pp. 288–289.
90. Quoted in Heidegger, *Was Heisst Denken?,* Tübingen, 1954, p. 41.
91. Quoted from Vogt, *op. cit.,* p. 93.
92. Hoeres, *op. cit.,* p. 197.
93. Bettoni, *Duns Scotus,* p. 122.
94. Bonansea, *op. cit.,* p. 120.
95. *Ibid.,* p. 119.
96. *Ibid.,* p. 120.
97. *On the Trinity,* bk. X, chap. viii, 11.

98. Bettoni, *Duns Scotus*, p. 40.
99. I have used for my interpretation the following Latin text from the *Opus Oxoniense* IV, dist. 49, qu. 4, nn. 5–9: "*Si enim accipiatur quietatio pro . . . consequente operationem perfectam, concedo quod illam quietationem praecedit perfecta consecutio finis; si autem accipiatur quietatio pro actu quietativo in fine, dico quod actus amandi, qui naturaliter praecedit delectationem, quietat illo modo, quia potentia operativa non quietatur in obiecto, nisi per operationem perfectam, per quam attingit obiectum.*"

    I propose the following translation: "For if quietude is accepted as following upon the perfect operation, I admit that a perfect attainment of the end precedes this quietude; if, however, quietude is accepted for an act resting in its end, I say that the act of loving, which naturally precedes delight, brings quiet in such a way that the acting faculty does not come to rest in the object except through the perfect operation by which it attains the object."
100. B643–B645, Smith trans., pp. 515–516.

## Chapter IV

1. Lewis White Beck, *op. cit.*, p. 41.
2. For Pascal, see *Pensées*, no. 81, Pantheon ed.; no. 438 [257], Pléiade ed.; and "Sayings Attributed to Pascal" in *Pensées*, Penguin ed., p. 356. For Donne, see "An Anatomy of the World; The First Anniversary."
3. *The Will to Power*, no. 487, p. 269.
4. *Ibid.*, no. 419, p. 225.
5. Heidegger, in "Uberwindung der Metaphysik," *op. cit.*, p. 83.
6. For this and the following, see especially Edgar Zilsel, "The Genesis of the Concept of Scientific Progress," in *Journal of the History of Ideas*, 1945, vol. VI, p. 3.
7. Zilsel thus finds the genesis of the Progress concept in the experience and "intellectual attitude" of "superior artisans."
8. *Préface pour le Traité du Vide*, Pléiade ed., p. 310.
9. VII, 803c.
10. See Kant, *Idea for a Universal History from a Cosmopolitan Point of View* (1784), Introduction, in *Kant on History*, ed. Lewis White Beck, Library of Liberal Arts, Indianapolis, New York, 1963, pp. 11–12.

11. *Ibid.*, Third Thesis. Author's translation.
12. Schelling, *Of Human Freedom*, p. 351.
13. *Ibid.*, p. 350.
14. Trans. F. D. Wieck and J. G. Gray, New York, Evanston, London, 1968, p. 91.
15. *Vorträge und Aufsätze*, p. 89.
16. *The Will to Power*, no. 419, pp. 225–226.
17. *Critique of Pure Reason*, B478.
18. *Human All Too Human*, no. 2, in *The Portable Nietzsche*, p. 51.
19. *The Will to Power*, no. 90, p. 55.
20. *Ibid.*, no. 1041, p. 536.
21. "An Anatomy of the World; The First Anniversary."
22. *The Will to Power*, no. 95, p. 59.
23. *Ibid.*, no. 84, p. 52.
24. *Ibid.*, no. 668, p. 353. Author's translation.
25. *Nietzsche*, vol. I, p. 70.
26. No. 19.
27. *Ibid.* Italics added.
28. *The Will to Power*, no. 693, p. 369.
29. *Ibid.*, no. 417, p. 224.
30. See chap. III, p. 142.
31. In *Aufzeichnung zum IV, Teil von* "Also Sprach Zarathustra," quoted from Heidegger, *Was Heisst Denken?*, p. 46.
32. *The Will to Power*, no. 667, p. 352. Author's translation.
33. *The Gay Science*, trans. Walter Kaufmann, Vintage Books, New York, 1974, bk. IV, no. 310, pp. 247–248.
34. See *Thinking*, chap. II, pp. 98–110.
35. *Toward a Genealogy of Morals*, no. 28.
36. *The Will to Power*, no. 689, p. 368.
37. *The Gay Science*, bk. IV, no. 341, pp. 273–274.
38. *The Will to Power*, no. 664, p. 350.
39. *Ibid.*, no. 666, pp. 351–352. Author's translation.
40. *Thus Spoke Zarathustra*, pt. II, "On Self-Overcoming," in *The Portable Nietzsche*, p. 227.
41. *The Will to Power*, no. 660, p. 349.
42. *Thus Spoke Zarathustra*, pt. II, "On Redemption," in *The Portable Nietzsche*, p. 251.
43. *The Will to Power*, no. 585 A, pp. 316–319.
44. *The Gay Science*, bk. IV, no. 324. Author's translation.
45. See chap. II, pp. 73–84.
46. *The Will to Power*, no. 585 A, p. 318.

47. See *Twilight of the Idols*, especially "The Four Great Errors," in *The Portable Nietzsche*, pp. 500–501.

48. *Thus Spoke Zarathustra*, pt. II, in *The Portable Nietzsche*, p. 252.

49. *The Will to Power*, no. 708, pp. 377–378.

50. *The Gay Science*, bk. IV, no. 276, p. 223.

51. *Thus Spoke Zarathustra*, pt. III, "Before Sunrise," also "The Seven Seals (or: The Yes and Amen Song)," in *The Portable Nietzsche*, pp. 276–279 and 340–343.

52. See the excellent *Index* to Heidegger's whole work up to and including *Wegmarken* (1968) by Hildegard Feick, 2nd ed., Tübingen, 1968. Under *"Wille Wollen,"* the *Index* refers the reader to *"Sorge, Subjekt"* and quotes one sentence from *Sein und Zeit:* "Wollen und Wünschen sind im Dasein als Sorge verwurzelt." I have mentioned that the modern emphasis on the future as the predominant tense showed itself in Heidegger's singling out Care as the dominating existential in his early analyses of human existence. If one rereads the corresponding sections in *Sein und Zeit* (especially no. 41), it is evident that he later used certain characteristics of Care for his analysis of the Will.

53. New York, 1971, p. 112.

54. First edition, Frankfurt, 1949, p. 17.

55. *Die Selbstbehauptung der deutschen Universität* (The Self-Assertion of the German University).

56. Mehta, *op. cit.*, p. 43.

57. "Brief über den 'Humanismus,'" *Platons Lehre von der Wahrheit*, Bern, 1947, p. 57; translation quoted from Mehta, *op. cit.*, p. 114.

58. "Brief über den 'Humanismus,'" p. 47.

59. Vol. II, p. 468.

60. "Brief über den 'Humanismus,'" p. 53; translation quoted from Mehta, *op. cit.*, p. 114.

61. "Brief über den 'Humanismus,'" pp. 46–47.

62. *Nietzsche*, vol. I, p. 624.

63. *The Will to Power*, no. 708. Author's translation.

64. *Nietzsche*, vol. II, p. 272. In Mehta, *op. cit.*, p. 179.

65. *Nietzsche*, vol. I, pp. 63–64.

66. *Ibid.*, p. 161.

67. *Ibid.*, vol. II, p. 462.

68. *Ibid.*, p. 265.

69. *Ibid.*, p. 267.

70. Pp. 92–93. Author's translation.

71. *Gelassenheit,* p. 33; *Discourse on Thinking,* p. 60.

72. *Laws,* I, 644.

73. *The Will to Power,* no. 90, p. 55.

74. *Die Technik und die Kehre,* Pfullingen, 1962, p. 40.

75. Quoted from Jean Beaufret, *Dialogue avec Heidegger,* Paris, 1974, vol. III, p. 204.

76. Valéry, *Tel quel,* in *Oeuvres de Paul Valéry,* Pléiade ed., Dijon, 1960, vol. II, p. 560.

77. *Sein und Zeit,* no. 57, pp. 276–277.

78. *Ibid.,* no. 53, p. 261.

79. *Vorträge und Aufsätze,* pp. 177 and 256.

80. No. 54, p. 267.

81. *Ibid.,* no. 41, p. 187, and no. 53, p. 263.

82. Bergson, *Time and Free Will,* pp. 128–130, 133.

83. *Ibid.,* pp. 138–143; cf. p. 183.

84. Bergson, *Creative Mind,* trans. Mabelle L. Andison, New York,.1946, pp. 27 and 22.

85. Pp. 63–64.

86. No. 34, p. 162.

87. Pp. 329 and 470–471.

88. Nos. 54–59. See especially pp. 268 ff.

89. *Ibid.,* no. 58, p. 287.

90. *Ibid.,* p. 284.

91. *Ibid.,* nos. 59–60, pp. 294–295.

92. *Ibid.,* no. 60, p. 300.

93. *Ibid.,* no. 34, p. 163.

94. *Ibid.,* no. 59, p. 294.

95. *Ibid.,* nos. 59–60, p. 295.

96. I use and quote throughout David Farrell Krell's translation, first published in *Arion,* New Series, vol. 1, no. 4, 1975, pp. 580–581.

97. The whole citation, from which I quote, in my own translation, reads as follows: *"Wir leben . . . als ob wir pochend vor den Toren ständen, die noch geschlossen sind. Bis heute geschieht vielleicht im ganz Intimen, was so noch keine Welt begründet, sondern nur dem Einzelnen sich schenkt, was aber vielleicht eine Welt begründen wird, wenn es aus der Zerstreuung sich begegnet."* I suppose that the speech at Geneva was published in the magazine *Wandlung,* but have drawn on the preface to *Sechs Essays,* Heidelberg, 1948, a collection of essays I wrote during the nineteen-forties.

98. "The Anaximander Fragment," *Arion,* p. 584.

99. *Ibid.,* p. 596.

100. "Brief über den 'Humanismus,'" now in *Wegmarken,* Frankfurt, 1967, p. 191.

101. "The Anaximander Fragment," *Arion,* p. 595.

102. Frag. 123.

103. P. 591.

104. *Ibid.,* p. 596.

105. *Ibid.,* p. 591.

106. *Ibid.,* p. 618.

107. *Ibid.,* p. 591.

108. *Ibid.,* p. 592.

109. *Ibid.,* p. 609.

110. *Ibid.,* p. 626.

111. Unpublished poem, written around 1950.

112. P. 611.

113. *Ibid.,* p. 609.

114. To avoid misunderstandings: both quotations are so well known that they are part of the German language. Every German-speaking person will spontaneously think along these lines without necessarily having been influenced by Goethe.

115. P. 623.

116. Heidegger, *Sein und Zeit,* no. 57.

117. Thomas Kuhn, *The Structure of Scientific Revolutions,* Chicago, 1962, p. 172.

118. *The Lives of a Cell,* New York, 1974.

119. See *Newsweek,* June 24, 1974, p. 89.

120. *Ibid.*

121. *Esprit des Lois,* bk. XII, chap. 2.

122. *Ibid.,* bk. XI, chap. 6.

123. Quoted from Franz Neumann's introduction to Montesquieu's *The Spirit of the Laws,* trans. Thomas Nugent, New York, 1949, p. xl.

124. *Esprit des Lois,* bk. XI, chap. 3.

125. *Ibid.,* bk. I, chap. 1, bk. XXVI, chaps. 1 and 2.

126. See, for instance, R. W. B. Lewis, "Homer and Virgil—The Double Themes," *Furioso,* Spring, 1950, p. 24; "The recurrent explicit references to the *Iliad* in those books [of the *Aeneid*] are there not in way of parallel, but in the way of reversal."

127. *Critique of Pure Reason,* B478.

128. *Aeneid,* bk. III, 1–12, in *Virgil's Works,* trans. William C. McDermott, Modern Library, New York, 1950, p. 44.

129. The Fourth Eclogue.

130. I borrowed this felicitous term for communities from the highly instructive essay "The Character of the Modern European State" in Michael Oakeshott's *On Human Conduct,* Oxford, 1975, p. 199.

131. *De Republica,* I, 7.

132. *Oeuvres,* ed. Laponneraye, 1840, vol. III, p. 623; *The Works of John Adams,* ed. Charles Francis Adams, Boston, 1850–1856, vol. VI, 1851, p. 281.

133. VI, 790–794.

134. The Fourth Eclogue.

135. There exists an enormous literature on this subject; quite instructive is *Die Aeneis und Homer* by Georg Nikolaus Knauer, Göttingen, 1964. Virgil's *"Homerauffassung scheint mir von der spezifisch römischen Denkform persönlicher Verpflichtung geprägt zu sein, die dem Römer auferlegte, nach dem aus der Vergangenheit überkommenen Vorbild der Ahnen Ruhm und Glanz der eigenen Familie und des Staates durch Verwirklichung im Heute für die Zukunft der Nachfahren zu bewahren,"* p. 357.

136. *Aeneid,* bk. VII, 206.

137. Quoted from George Steiner, *After Babel,* New York and London, 1975, p. 132.

138. R. J. E. Clausius (1822–1888), German mathematical physicist, who enunciated the second law of thermodynamics, introduced the entropy concept (energy unavailable for useful work in a thermodynamic system, represented by the symbol $\phi$). "Postulating that the entropy of the universe is increasing continuously, he predicted that it would expire of 'heat death' when everything within it attained the same temperature." *Columbia Encyclopedia,* 3rd ed. (Ed.)

139. *De Civitate Dei,* bk. XII, chap. xx.

# Editor's Postface

Hannah Arendt died suddenly on December 4, 1975. It was a Thursday evening; she was entertaining friends. The Saturday before, she had finished "Willing," the second section of *The Life of the Mind.* Like *The Human Condition,* its forerunner, the work was conceived in three parts. Where *The Human Condition,* subtitled *The Vita Activa,* had been divided into Labor, Work, and Action, *The Life of the Mind,* as planned, was divided into Thinking, Willing, and Judging, the three basic activities, as she saw it, of mental life. The distinction made by the Middle Ages between the active life of man in the world and the solitary *vita contemplativa* was of course present to her thought, although her own thinker, willer, and judger was not a contemplative, set apart by a monkish vocation, but everyman insofar as he exercised his specifically human capacity to withdraw from time to time into the invisible region of the mind.

Whether or not the life of the mind is superior to the so-called active life (as antiquity and the Middle Ages had considered) was an issue she never pronounced on in so many words. Yet it would not be too much to say that the last years of her life were consecrated to this work, which she treated as a task laid on her as a vigorously thinking being—the highest she had been called to. In the midst of her multifarious teaching and lecture commitments, her service on various round tables and panels and consultative boards (she was a constant recruit to the *vita activa* of the citizen and public figure, though seldom a volunteer), she remained immersed in *The Life of the Mind,* as though its completion would acquit her not so much of an obligation, which sounds too onerous, as of a compact she had entered into. All roads, however secondary, on which chance or intention put her in her daily and professional existence, led back to that.

When an invitation came, in June 1972, to give the Gifford Lectures at the University of Aberdeen, she chose to use the occasion for a kind of try-out of the volumes already in preparation. The Gifford Lectures also served as a stimulus. Endowed in 1885 by Adam Gifford, a leading Scottish justice and law lord, "for the purpose of establishing in each of the four cities of Edinburgh, Glasgow, Aberdeen, and St. Andrews . . . a Chair . . . of Natural Theology, in the widest sense of that term," they had been given by Josiah Royce, William James, Bergson, J. G. Frazer, Whitehead, Eddington, John Dewey, Werner Jaeger, Karl Barth, Etienne Gilson, Gabriel Marcel, among others—an honor roll to which she was quite proud to accede. If she was normally superstitious, she must have seen them too as a *porta-fortuna: The Varieties of Religious Experience*, Whitehead's *Process and Reality*, Dewey's *The Quest for Certainty*, Marcel's *The Mystery of Being*, Gilson's *The Spirit of Medieval Philosophy* had first seen the light as Gifford Lectures. . . . Having accepted, she drove herself harder perhaps than she ought to have to get hers ready in the time available; she delivered the first series, on Thinking, in the spring of 1973. In the spring of 1974, she returned for the second series, on Willing, and was interrupted by a heart attack after she had given her first lecture. She was intending to go back, in the spring of 1976, to finish the series; meanwhile she had given most of Thinking and Willing to her classes at the New School for Social Research in New York. Judging, she had not started, though she had used material on Judgment in courses she gave at the University of Chicago and at the New School on Kant's political philosophy. After her death, a sheet of paper was found in her typewriter, blank except for the heading "Judging" and two epigraphs. Some time between the Saturday of finishing "Willing" and the Thursday of her death, she must have sat down to confront the final section.

Her plan was for a work in two volumes. Thinking, the

longest, was to occupy the first, and the second was to contain Willing and Judging. As she told friends, she counted on Judgment to be much shorter than the other two. She also used to say that she expected it to be the easiest to handle. The hardest had been the Will. The reason she gave for counting on Judgment to be short was the lack of source material: only Kant had written on the faculty, which before him had been unnoticed by philosophers except in the field of aesthetics, where it had been named Taste. As for ease, she no doubt felt that her lectures on Kant's political philosophy, with their careful analysis of *The Critique of Judgment,* had pretty well prepared the ground to be covered. Still, one can guess that Judging might have surprised her and ended by taking up a whole volume to itself. In any case, to give the reader some notion of what would have been in the concluding section, an appendix has been joined to the second volume containing extracts from her classroom lectures. Aside from a seminar paper, not included here, on the Imagination, which touches briefly on its role in the judging process, this is all we now have of her thoughts on the subject (though something further may turn up in her correspondence, when that is edited). Mournful that there is not more; anyone familiar with her mind will feel sure that the contents of the appendix do not exhaust the ideas that must already have been stirring in her head as she inserted the fresh page in her typewriter.

*About the editing.* As far as I know, all of Hannah Arendt's books and articles were edited before reaching print. Those written in English, naturally. It was done by publishers' editors, magazine editors (William Shawn on *The New Yorker,* Robert Silvers on *The New York Review of Books,* Philip Rahv, in the old days, on *Partisan Review*), and also by friends. Sometimes several hands, unknown to each other, went to work on her manuscripts, with her consent and usually, though not always, with her collaboration; those she had learned to trust, she tended to leave rather free with the blue pencil. She referred to all this wryly as her "Englishing." She had taught herself to write English as an exile, when she was over thirty-five, and never felt as comfortable in it even as a spoken tongue as she had once felt in French. She chafed against our language and its awesome, mysterious constraints. Though she had a natural gift, which would have made itself felt in Sioux or Sanskrit, for eloquent, forceful, sometimes pungent expression, her sentences were long, in the German way, and had to be unwound or broken up into two or three. Also, like anybody writing or speaking a foreign language, she had trouble with prepositions. And with what Fowler called "cast-iron idiom." And with finding the natural place for adverbs; for that in English there are no rules—only an unwritten law, which appears tyrannous and menacing to a foreigner because it can also, unpredictably, be broken. Besides, she was impatient. Her sentences could be unwieldy not only because her native language was German, with its affection for strings of modifiers and subordinate clauses encumbering the road to the awaited verb, but also because she tried to get too much in at once. The mixture of hurry and generosity was very characteristic.

Anyway, she was edited. I worked on several of her texts with her, sometimes after another editor, amateur or professional, had preceded me. We went over "On Violence" together one summer in the Café Flore, and then I took it home for further attention. We worked on "On Civil Disobedience" in a *pensione* in Switzerland for several days, and we put some finishing touches on her last published article, "Home to Roost," in an apartment she had been lent in Marbach (Schiller's birthplace), handy to the *Deutsche Literaturarchiv*, where she was sorting Jaspers' papers. I worked with her on the Thinking section of *The Life of the Mind* in Aberdeen; in the photostat of the original manuscript, I can make out my penciled changes. The next spring, when she was in a ward in the Aberdeen hospital, for some days under an oxygen tent, I went over bits of Willing by myself, at her request.

When she was alive, the editing was fun, because it was a collaboration and an exchange. On the whole she accepted correction with good grace, with relief when it came to prepositions, for instance, with interest when some point of usage came up that was new to her. Sometimes we argued and continued the argument by correspondence; this happened over her translation of Kant's *Verstand* as "intellect"; I thought it should be "understanding" as in the standard translations. But I never convinced her and I yielded. Now I think we were both right, because we were aiming at different things: she clung to the original sense of the word, and I was after audience comprehension. In the present text it is "intellect." Most of the disagreements we had were settled by compromise or by cutting. But in the process her natural impatience, sooner or later, would reassert itself. She did not like fussing over details. "*You* fix it," she would say, finally, starting to cover a yawn. If she was impatient, she was also indulgent; for her, I figured as a "perfectionist," and she was inclined to humor the tendency, provided no proselytization was in view.

In any case, we never had a substantive difference. If at times I questioned the thought in one of her manuscripts, it was only to point out what seemed to be a contradiction with another thought she had been putting forward several pages back. It would usually turn out that I had failed to perceive some underlying distinction or, conversely, that she had failed to perceive the reader's need for the *distinguo*. Strange as it may seem, our minds were in some respects very close—a fact she often remarked on when the same notion would occur to each of us independently, while an ocean—the Atlantic—lay between us. Or she read some text I had written and found there a thought she had been silently pondering. This convergence of cast of mind, she decided, must have something to do with the theology in my Catholic background, which had given me, she believed, an aptitude for philosophy. Actually I had made far from brilliant marks in the two college courses in philosophy I had taken, bumbling and lethargically taught, it must be added. Otherwise, though, our studies had not been so far apart. In Germany, she had done her doctoral thesis on the Concept of Love in St. Augustine; in America, I had read him in an undergraduate course in Medieval Latin and been exhilarated by *The City of God*—my favorite. Possibly my medieval and Renaissance studies in French, Latin, and English, plus years of classical Latin and later home reading of Plato, had joined with a Catholic girlhood to make up the deficiency in formal philosophical training. There is also

the fact, which she did not consider, that in the course of years
I had learned a great deal from her.

I mention these things now to cite my qualifications for
editing *The Life of the Mind*. It was not a job I had applied
for, and when, in January, 1974, she made me her literary executor, I doubt very much that she foresaw what was coming,
i.e., that she would not live to finish those volumes and that it
would be I, without benefit of her assistance, who would
see them through the press. If finally she did foresee it, at
least as a distinct possibility, after the heart attack a few
months later in Aberdeen, she must have known how I would
set about the work, with all my peculiarities and stringencies,
and have accepted the inevitable in a philosophical spirit.
Knowing me, she may even have foreseen the temptations that
the new freedom from interference would dangle before me,
freedom to do it "my" way, but if she read me as well as that,
she would also have foreseen the resistance the mere glimmer
of such temptations would muster in my still-Catholic conscience. . . . If she divined, in short, that there would be days
when I would become a battlefield on which allegiance to the
prose of my forefathers fought my sense of a duty to her, the
picture of all that furious contention—the contest of the scruples and the temptations—so foreign to her own nature, would
probably have amused her. I must assume that she trusted my
judgment, had faith that in the end no damage would be done,
that the manuscript would emerge unscarred from the fighting; lacking that basic confidence in *her* confidence, I would
have soon had to throw in the sponge.

But whatever she foresaw, or failed to foresee, she is not
here now to consult or appeal to. I have been forced to guess
her reaction to every act of editorial interference. In most cases,
previous experience has made that easy: if she knew me, I
also knew her. But here and there problems have come up
which in the past I would surely not have attempted to solve
on my own, by guesswork. Whenever I was unsure, I would
pepper a manuscript with question marks meaning "What do
you want to say here?" "Can you clarify?" "Right word?"
Today those points of interrogation ("What do you suppose

she means by that?" "Does she intend this repetition or not?")
are leveled at me. Yet not in my own person exactly; rather,
I put myself in her place, turn into a sort of mind-reader or
medium. With eyes closed, I am talking to a quite lively ghost.
She has haunted me, given pause to my pencil, caused erasures
and re-erasures. In practice, the new-found freedom has meant
that I feel less free with her typescript than I would have felt
if she were alive. Now and then I have caught myself leaning
over backwards for fear of some imagined objection and have
had to right myself with the reminder that in normal circumstances the page-long sentence staring at me would never have
been allowed to pass.

Or on the contrary it has happened that I have firmly
crossed out a phrase or sentence whose meaning was opaque
to me and substituted language that seemed to make better
sense; then, on a second reading, I have had misgivings,
gone back to consult the original text, seen that I had missed a
nuance, and restored the passage as written or else made a
fresh effort at paraphrase. Anybody who has done translating
will recognize the process—the repeated endeavors to read
*through* language into the mind of an author who is absent.
Here the fact that several years ago—and mainly, I suppose,
because of my friendship with her—I started taking German
lessons has turned out to be a benign stroke of fate. I know
enough of her native language now to make out the original
structure like a distant mountainous outline behind her English
phrasing; this has rendered many troublesome passages "trans-
latable": I simply put them into German, where they become
clear, and then do them back into English.

In any event, so far as I know, no change has been made
that in any way affects the thought. A few cuts, mostly small,
have been made, usually to eliminate repetitions, when I concluded that these were accidental rather than deliberate. In a
very few places, not more than two or three, I have added
something, for the sake of clarity, e.g., the words "Scotus was
a Franciscan" to a passage that otherwise would be obscure
to a reader lacking that information. But with these minor
exceptions, what has been done is just the habitual "Englishing" that all her texts underwent.

This does not apply to the material from her lectures printed in the appendix. These extracts are given verbatim, except for obvious typing mistakes, which have been corrected. It appeared to me that since the Kant lectures had never been intended for publication but to be delivered viva voce to a class of students, any editorial meddling would be inappropriate. It was not my business to tamper with history. Along with her other papers, the lectures from which the extracts have been taken are in the Library of Congress, where they can be consulted with permission from her executors.

I ought to mention one other group of changes. The manuscripts of both "Thinking" and "Willing" were still in lecture form, unchanged in that respect from the way they had been delivered in Aberdeen and New York, though in other respects much revised and added to (the last chapter of "Willing" was wholly new). Had she had time, obviously she would have altered that, turning listeners into readers, as she normally did when what had been given as a lecture came out in a book or magazine. In the present text, this has been done, except in the case of the general introduction, with its pleasant allusion to the Gifford Lectures. If something of the flavor of the spoken word nevertheless remains, that is all to the good.

A final remark about the Englishing should be interjected. Evidently personal taste plays a part in an editor's decisions. My own notion of acceptable written English is, like everybody's, idiosyncratic. I do not object, for instance, to ending a sentence with a preposition—in fact, I rather favor it—but I am squeamish when I see certain nouns, such as "shower" (in the sense of shower-bath) or "trigger," being used as verbs. So I could not let Hannah Arendt, whom I so greatly admired, say "trigger" when "cause" or "set in motion" would do. And "when the chips are down": I cannot say why the phrase grates on me, and particularly coming from her, who, I doubt, ever handled a poker chip. But I can see her (cigarette perched in holder) contemplating the roulette table or chemin de fer, so it is now "when the stakes are on the table"—more fitting, more in character. Would she have minded these small examples of interference with her freedom of expression? Did she set much store on "triggered"? I hope she would have indulged me in my prejudices. And though personal taste has occasionally marched in as arbiter (where once I would have sought to persuade), much care has been taken throughout to respect her characteristic tone. My own idiom has not been permitted to intrude; there is not a "Mary McCarthy word" in the text. In the one instance when, finding nothing better, I used such a word, it stuck out like a sore thumb from the galley proof and had to be hastily amputated. So that the text that the reader has been reading is hers; it *is* her, I hope, in the sense that the excisions and polishing reveal her, just as cutting away the superfluous marble from a quarried block lays bare the intrinsic form. Michelangelo said that about sculpture (as opposed to painting), and here at any rate there has been no hint of laying on or embellishment.

It has been a heavy job, which has kept going an imaginary dialogue with her, verging sometimes, as in life, on debate. Though in life it never came to that, now I reproach her, and vice versa. The work has gone on till late at night; then, in my dreams, pages of the manuscript are found all of a sudden to be missing or, on the contrary, turn up without warning, throwing everything, including the footnotes, out of kilter. But it has also been, if not fun, as in former days, rewarding. I have learned, for example, that I can understand the *Critique of Pure Reason*, which I had previously thought impenetrable by me. Searching for a truant reference, I have read some entire Platonic dialogues (the *Thaeatetus*, the *Sophist*) that I had never dipped into before. I have learned the difference between an electric ray and a sting ray. I have reread bits of Virgil's Bucolics and Georgics, which I had not looked at since college. Many of my old college textbooks have come down from their shelves, and not only mine but my husband's (he studied philosophy at Bowdoin) and my dear secretary's husband's (he had Rilke, some of the Aristotle we lacked, and more Virgil).

It has been a co-operative enterprise. My secretary, typing the manuscript, has gently interposed on behalf of commas and a sterner way with grammatical lapses: she is a Scruple, doing battle on the side of Temptation. Hannah Arendt's teaching assistant at the New School—Jerome Kohn—has hunted down dozens of references and, quite often, answering the appeal of those anxious question marks, been able to clarify, or else we have pooled our bewilderment and arrived at reasonable certainties. He has even (see the bad dream above) discovered a page that, unnoticed by us, was missing from the photostatted manuscript. Other friends, including my German teacher, have helped. Throughout this travail, there have been times of positive elation, a mixture of our school days revisited (those textbooks, late-night discussions of philosophic points), and the tonic effect of our dead friend's ideas, alive and generative of controversy as well as of surprised agreement. Though I have missed her in the course of these months—in fact more than a year now—of work, wished her back to clarify, object, reassure, compliment and be complimented, I do not think I shall truly miss her, feel the pain in the amputated limb, till it is over. I am aware that she is dead but I am simultaneously aware of her as a distinct presence in this room, listening to my words as I write, possibly assenting with her musing nod, possibly stifling a yawn.

*A few explanations of practical matters.* Since the manuscript, though finished in terms of content, was not in final shape, not every quotation and allusion in the text was accompanied by a footnote. Thanks to Jerome Kohn and to Roberta Leighton and her helpers at Harcourt Brace Jovanovich, many of these have been run down. But as I write, a few are still missing and if they cannot be found in time, the search will have to continue and the results be included in a future edition. Also, even where we do have references, a few of the footnotes are incomplete, chiefly because the page or volume number as given appears to be wrong and we have not yet been able to locate the right passage. This too, I hope, will eventually be rectified. We have been aided by having books from Hannah Arendt's library that were used by her for reference. But we do not have all the books she referred to.

It is clear that she often quoted from memory. Where her memory did not correspond with a cited text, this has been corrected. Except in the case of translations: here we have sometimes corrected, sometimes not. Again it has been a question of trying to read her mind. When she varied from a standard translation of a Greek or Latin or German or French original, did she do so on purpose or from a faulty recollection? Often one cannot be sure. As comparison shows, she did use standard translations: Norman Kemp Smith's of Kant, Walter Kaufmann's of Nietzsche, McKeon's Aristotle, the various translations of Plato in the Edith Hamilton–Huntington Cairns edition. But she knew all those languages well—a fact which prompted her to veer from the standard version when it suited her, that is, when she found Kemp Smith, for example, or Kaufmann imprecise, too far from the original, or for some other, purely literary reason. From an editorial point of view, this has created a rather chaotic situation. Do we credit Kemp Smith and Kaufmann in the footnotes when she has leaned heavily, but not entirely, on their versions? Not to do seems unfair, but in some eventualities the opposite could seem unfair too: Kaufmann, for instance, might not care to be credited with words and expressions that are not his. Kemp Smith is dead, like many of the Plato translators, but that does not mean that feeling for their feelings should die too.

Leaving the puzzles of credit aside for the moment, we have attacked the overall problem of translations in what may be a piecemeal, *ad hoc* way but which does meet the realities of the circumstance, for which no general and consistently applied rule seems to work. Where possible, each passage has been checked against the standard translation, often underlined or otherwise marked by her in the book she owned; when the variation is wide, we have gone back to the original language, and if Kemp Smith seems closer to Kant's German, we have used Kemp Smith. But when there is a shade of meaning overlooked in the standard translation that the Arendt translation brings out, we have used hers; also when the meaning is debatable. With practice, it soon becomes fairly easy to discern when a variant rendering corresponds to an intention on her part as opposed to inadvertence—a slip of memory or mistake in copying; differences in punctuation, for instance, we have treated as inadvertent.

Unfortunately, this common-sense solution does not meet

all contingencies. Unless the text cited was in her library, in English, we have no idea of what translation, if any, she used for reference. In the absence of further clues, I have assumed that she made her own translation and have felt free to alter it slightly, in the interests of English idiom or grammar, just as I would with her own text. (Once in a while, I have retranslated from the original myself. But I have lacked the effrontery to try that much with Heidegger, though I have dared with Master Eckhart.) In the case of classical authors, there is such a wealth of translations to choose among that one could hardly hope to find the one she might have been drawing on—a needle in a haystack. Once, by luck, I happened on a translation of Virgil which—it was apparent in a flash—she had used. My pencil moved (Eureka!) to indicate editor, date, and so on, in a footnote; then I looked again—no. Here, as so often, she had used a translation but had not stuck to it. And it is impossible to show in a footnote in which spots she diverged and which not.

Eventually we arrived at a policy, which has been to cite a translation only when it has been followed to the letter. Where no translator is named, it means that the version used is entirely or largely the author's or that we could not find the translation she drew on, if one exists. Yet even that policy requires qualification. The reader should know that some standard translations (McKeon, Kemp Smith, Kaufmann, the Hamilton-Cairns miscellany), even where not specifically mentioned, have served *grosso modo* as the author's guides.

The Bible has been a special problem. It seemed hard to tell at first whether she was using the King James version, the Revised Standard version, the Douai version, a German version which she then translated into English, or a mixture of all these. I even amused myself with the fond hypothesis that she had gone back to St. Jerome's Vulgate and done her own rendering from the Latin. My inclination was to use the King James version; aside from personal preference, there was the argument that the "thou shalt"s in the author's voice that appear repeatedly in the "Willing" volume should be matched by Biblical "thou" and "thee"s of the older version—otherwise it would sound peculiar. But Roberta Leighton has demonstrated to me that careful comparison shows that the manuscript is closest to the Revised Standard version; hence, that has been used, with a few exceptions, where the beauty of the King James language proved irresistible to us, as it evidently had to our author. At any rate, sticking on the whole to the Revised Standard has done away with one difficulty: the fact that the old version translates "love" (*agape*) as "charity." Since for modern ears, the word has a mainly tax-deductible connotation, or refers to "taking a charitable view" of something, it would have had to be changed to "love," in surrounding brackets, each time it occurred, which would have made awkward reading.

Such preoccupations with consistency and mirror-fidelity of reference will seem curious to the general reader. They are an occupational infirmity of editors and academics. Or they are the game-rules that scholarly writing agrees to and by their very strictness they add to the zest of the pursuit—a zest that cannot be shared by non-players. Hunting-the-slipper in the guise of an elusive footnote must be taken with dead seriousness, like any absorbing sport or game. Yet if it matters only to a few, mainly those engaged in it, where is the sense? What difference does it make whether God is "He" on one page and "he" on the next? Maybe the author just changed her attitude, which is her right. Why seek to divine her underlying preference and lock her, a free spirit, into a uniform "He" or "he"? Well, it is "He." And the will is "Will" when it is a concept and "will" when it is acting in a human subject.

I apologize to the general reader for mentioning these details of footnotes, capitalization, brackets, and so on, as devoid of interest to an outsider as a sportsman's pondered choice of trout-fly when a worm will catch the fish. That the fish is the point tends to be lost sight of by specialists, as Hannah Arendt would be the first to agree. She cared for the general reader, who for her remained a student in adult form. That was why she especially loved Socrates. Still, being a teacher and scholar, she knew about the game-rules and by and large accepted them, though more in the spirit of tolerance one brings to chil-

# Appendix / Judging

## Excerpts from Lectures on
## Kant's Political Philosophy

. . . We know from Kant's own testimony that the turning-point of his life was the discovery of the human mind's cognitive faculties and their limitations (in 1770), which took him more than 10 years to elaborate and publish as *Critique of Pure Reason*. We also know from his letters what this immense labor of so many years signified for his other plans and ideas. He writes of this "main subject" that it kept back and obstructed like "a dam" all the other matters which he had hoped to finish and publish, that it was like "a stone in his way" on which he could only proceed after its removal. . . . Prior to the event of 1770, he had intended to write and publish soon the *Metaphysics of Morals* which was then written and published nearly 30 years later. But at this early date, the book was announced under the title of *Critique of Moral Taste*. When Kant turned finally to the third *Critique*, he still called it to begin with Critique of Taste. Thus two things happened: Behind taste, a favored topic of the whole eighteenth century, he had discovered an entirely new human faculty, namely, judgment. But at the same time, he withdrew moral propositions from the competence of the new faculty. In other words: It now is more than taste that will decide about the beautiful and the ugly; but the [moral] question of right and wrong is to be decided neither by taste nor judgment but by reason alone.

. . . . . .

The links between [the] two parts [of *The Critique of Judgment*] . . . are closer connected with the political than with anything in the other Critiques. The most important of these links are *first* that in neither of the two parts Kant speaks of man as an intelligible or cognitive being. The word truth does not occur. The first part speaks of men in the plural . . . as they live in societies, the second speaks of the human species. . . . The most decisive difference between the *Critique of Practical Reason* and the *Critique of Judgment* is that the moral laws of the former are valid for all intelligible beings whereas the rules of the latter are strictly limited in their validity to human beings on earth. And the 2nd link lies in that the faculty of judgment deals with particulars which "as such, contain something contingent in respect to the universal" which normally is what thought is dealing with. These particulars . . . are of two kinds; *the first part* of the *Critique of Judgment* deals with objects of judgment properly speaking, such as an object which we call "beautiful" without being able to subsume it under a general category. (If you say, What a beautiful rose! you don't arrive at this judgment by first saying, all roses are beautiful, this flower is a rose, hence it is beautiful.) The other kind, dealt with in *the second part,* is the impossibility to derive any particular product of nature from general causes: "Absolutely no human reason (in fact no finite reason like ours in quality, however much it may surpass it in degree) can hope to understand the production of even a blade of grass by mere mechanical causes." (Mechanical in Kant's terminology means natural causes; its opposite is "technical," by which he means artificial, i.e. something fabricated with a purpose.) The accent here is on "understand": How can I understand (and not just explain) why there is grass at all and then this particular blade of grass.

. . . . . .

Judgment of the particular—*this* is beautiful, this is ugly, this is right, this is wrong—has no place in Kant's moral philosophy. Judgment is not practical reason; practical reason "reasons" and tells me what to do and what not to do; it lays down the law and is identical with the will, and the will utters commands; it speaks in imperatives. Judgment, on the contrary, arises from "a merely contemplative pleasure or inactive delight [*untätiges Wohlgefallen*]." This "feeling of contemplative pleasure is called taste," and the *Critique of Judgment* was originally called Critique of Taste. "If practical philosophy speaks of contemplative pleasure at all it mentions it only in passing, and not as if the concept were indigenous to it." Doesn't that sound plausible? How could "contemplative pleasure and inactive delight" have anything to do with practice? Doesn't that conclusively prove that Kant . . . had decided that his concern with the particular and the contingent was a thing of the past and had been a somewhat marginal affair? And yet, we shall see that his final position on the French Revolution, an event which played a central role in his old age when he waited with great impatience every day for the newspapers, was decided by this attitude of the mere spectators, of those "who are not engaged in the game themselves," only follow it with "wishful," "passionate participation," which . . . arose from mere "contemplative pleasure and inactive delight."

. . . . . .

The "enlargement of the mind" plays a crucial role in the *Critique of Judgment*. It is accomplished by "comparing our judgment with the possible rather than the actual judgment of others, and by putting ourselves in the place of any other man." The faculty which makes this possible is called imagination. . . . Critical thinking is possible only where the standpoints of all others are open to inspection. Hence, critical thinking while still a solitary business has not cut itself off from "all others." . . . [By] force of imagination it makes the others present and thus moves potentially in a space which is public, open to all sides; in other words, it adopts the position of Kant's world citizen. To think with the enlarged mentality—that means you train your imagination to go visiting. . . .

I must warn you here of a very common and easy misunderstanding. The trick of critical thinking does not consist in an enormously enlarged empathy through which I could know what actually goes on in the mind of all others. To think, according to Kant's understanding of enlightenment, means

*Selbstdenken,* to think for oneself, "which is the maxim of a never-passive reason. To be given to such passivity is called prejudice," and enlightenment is first of all liberation from prejudice. To accept what goes on in the minds of those whose "standpoint" (actually, the place where they stand, the conditions they are subject to, always different from one individual to the next, one class or group as compared to another) is not my own would mean no more than to accept passively their thought, that is, to exchange their prejudices for the prejudices proper to my own station. "Enlarged thought" is the result of first "abstracting from the limitations which contingently attach to our own judgment," of "disregarding its private subjective conditions . . . by which so many are limited," that is, of disregarding what we usually call self-interest and which according to Kant is not enlightened or capable of enlightenment but is in fact limiting. . . . [The] larger the realm in which the enlightened individual is able to move, from standpoint to standpoint, the more "general" will be his thinking. . . . This generality, however, is not the generality of concept—of the concept "house" under which you then can subsume all concrete buildings. It is on the contrary closely connected with particulars, the particular conditions of the standpoints you have to go through in order to arrive at your own "general standpoint." This general standpoint we mentioned before as impartiality; it is a viewpoint from which to look upon, to watch, to form judgments, or, as Kant himself says, to reflect upon human affairs. It does not tell you how *to act.* . . .

In Kant himself this perplexity comes to the fore in the seemingly contradictory attitude in his last years of almost boundless admiration for the French Revolution, on one side, and his equally almost boundless opposition to any revolutionary undertaking from the side of the citizens, on the other. . . .

Kant's reaction at first and even at second glance is by no means equivocal. . . . He never wavered in his estimation of the grandeur of what he called the "recent event," and he hardly ever wavered in his condemnation of all those who prepare such an event.

This event consists neither in momentous deeds nor misdeeds committed by men whereby what was great among men is made small or what was small is made great, nor in ancient splendid political structures which vanish as if by magic while others come forth in their place as if from the depths of the earth. No, nothing of the sort. It is simply the mode of thinking of the spectators which reveals itself publicly in this great game of transformations. . . .

The revolution of a gifted people which we have seen unfolding in our day may succeed or miscarry; it may be filled with misery and atrocities to the point that a sensible man, were he boldly to hope to execute it successfully the second time, would never resolve to make the experiment at such cost—this revolution, I say, nonetheless finds in the hearts of all spectators (who are not engaged in this game themselves) a wishful participation that borders closely on enthusiasm . . . with what exaltation the uninvolved public looking on sympathized then without the least intention of assisting.

. . . Without this sympathetic participation, the "meaning" of the occurrence would be altogether different, or simply nonexistent. For this sympathy is what inspires hope:

the hope that after many revolutions, with all their transforming effects, the highest purpose of nature, a *cosmopolitan existence,* will at last be realized within which all the original capacities of the human race may be developed.

From which, however, one should not conclude that Kant sided in the least with future men of revolutions.

These rights . . . always remain an idea which can be fulfilled only on condition that the means employed to do so are compatible with morality. This limiting condition must not be overstepped by the people, who may not therefore pursue their rights by revolution, which is at all times unjust.

. . . And:

If a violent revolution, engendered by a bad constitution, introduces by illegal means a more legal constitution, to lead the people back to the earlier constitution would not be permitted but, while the revolution lasted, each person who openly or covertly shared in it would have justly incurred the punishment due to those who rebel.

. . . What you see here clearly is the clash between the principle according to which you act and the principle according to which you judge. . . . Kant more than once stated his *opinion* on war . . . and nowhere more emphatically than in the *Critique of Judgment* where he discusses the topic, characteristically enough, in the section on the Sublime:

What is it which is, even to the savage, an object of the greatest admiration? It is a man who shrinks from nothing, who fears nothing, and therefore does not yield to danger. . . . Even in the most highly civilized state this peculiar veneration for the soldier remains . . . because even by these it is recognized that his mind is unsubdued by danger. Hence . . . in the comparison of a statesman and a general, the aesthetical judgment decides for the latter. War itself . . . has something sublime in it. . . . On the other hand, a long peace generally brings about a predominant commercial spirit and, along with it, low selfishness, cowardice, and effeminacy, and debases the disposition of the people.

This is the judgment of the spectator (i.e., aesthetical). . . . Yet, not only can war, "an unintended enterprise . . . stirred up by men's unbridled passions," actually serve because of its very meaninglessness as a preparation for the eventual cosmopolitan peace—eventually sheer exhaustion will impose what neither reason nor good will have been able to achieve—but

In spite of the dreadful afflictions with which it visits the human race, and the perhaps greater afflictions with which the constant preparation for it in time of peace oppresses them, yet is it . . . a motive for developing all talents serviceable for culture to the highest pitch.

. . . These insights of aesthetic and reflective judgment have no practical consequences for action. As far as action is concerned, there is no doubt that

moral-practical reason within us pronounces the following irresistible veto: *There shall be no war.* . . . Thus it is no longer a question of whether perpetual peace is possible or not, or whether we are not perhaps mistaken in our theoretical judgment if we assume that it is. On the contrary, we must simply act as if it could really come about . . . even if the fulfillment of this pacific intention were forever to remain a pious hope . . . for it is our duty to do so.

But these maxims for action do not nullify the aesthetic and reflective judgment. In other words: Even though Kant would always have acted for peace, he knew and kept in mind his judgment. Had he acted on the knowledge gained as a spectator, he would in his own mind have been a criminal. Had he forgotten because of this "moral duty" his insights as a spectator, he would have become what so many good men, involved and engaged in public affairs, tend to be—an idealistic fool.

. . . . . .

Since Kant did not write his political philosophy, the best way to find out what he thought about this matter is to turn to his *Critique of Aesthetic Judgment* where, in discussing the production of art works in their relations to taste which judges and decides about them, he confronts a similar, analogous problem. We . . . are inclined to think that in order to judge a spectacle you must first have the spectacle, that the spectator is secondary to the actor—without considering that no one in his right mind would ever put on a spectacle without being sure of having spectators to watch it. Kant is convinced that the world without man would be a desert, and a world without man meant for him: without spectator. In the discussion of aesthetic judgment, the distinction is between genius which is required for the production of art works, while for judging them, and deciding whether or not they are beautiful objects, "no more" (we would say, but not Kant) is required than taste. "For judging of beautiful objects *taste* is required . . . for their production *genius* is required." Genius according to Kant is a matter of productive imagination and originality, taste a . . . matter of judgment. He raises the question, which of the two is the "more noble" faculty, which is the condition sine qua non "to which one has to look in the judging of art as beautiful art?"—assuming of course that though most of the judges of beauty have not the faculty of productive imagination which is called genius, the few endowed with genius, lack not the faculty of taste. And the answer is:

Abundance and originality of ideas are less necessary to beauty than the accordance of the imagination in its freedom with the conformity to law of the understanding [which is called taste]. For all the abundance of the former produces . . . in lawless freedom nothing but nonsense; on the other hand, the judgment is the faculty by which it is adjusted to the understanding.

*Appendix: Judging*

Taste, like the judgment in general, is the discipline (or training) of genius; it clips its wings . . . gives guidance, brings clearness and order . . . into the thoughts [of genius], it makes the ideas susceptible of being permanently and generally assented to, and capable of being followed by others, and of an ever progressing culture. If, then, in the conflict of these two properties in a product something must be sacrificed, it should be rather on the side of genius—without which nothing for judgment to judge would exist.

But Kant says explicitly that "for beautiful art . . . *imagination, intellect, spirit,* and *taste* are required" and adds in a note that "the three former faculties are united by means of the fourth," that is, by taste—i.e., by judgment. Spirit, moreover, a special faculty apart from reason, intellect, and imagination, enables the genius to find an expression for the ideas "by means of which the subjective state of mind brought about by them . . . can be communicated to others." Spirit, in other words, namely, that which inspires the genius and only him and which "no science can teach and no industry can learn," consists in expressing "the ineffable element in the state of mind [*Gemütszustand*]" which certain representations arouse in all of us but for which we have no words and could therefore, without the help of genius, not communicate them to each other; it is the proper task of genius to make this state of mind "generally communicable." The faculty that guides this communicability is taste, and taste or judgment is not the privilege of genius. The condition sine qua non for the existence of beautiful objects is communicability; the judgment of the spectator creates the space without which no such objects could appear at all. The public realm is constituted by the critics and the spectators and not by the actors or the makers. And this critic and spectator sits in every actor and fabricator; without this critical, judging faculty the doer or maker would be so isolated from the spectator that he would not even be perceived. Or to put it another way, still in Kantian terms: The very originality of the artist (or the very novelty of the actor) depends on his making himself understood by those who are not artists (or actors). And while you can speak of genius in the singular because of his originality, you can never speak . . . in the same way of *the* spectator: spectators exist only in the plural. The spectator is not involved in the act, but he is always involved with his fellow-spectators. He does not share the faculty of genius, originality, with the maker, or the faculty of novelty with the actor; the faculty that they have in common is the faculty of judgment.

As far as making is concerned, this insight is at least as old as Latin (as distinguished from Greek) antiquity. We find it expressed for the first time in Cicero's *On the Orator:*

> For everybody discriminates [*diiudicare*], distinguishes between right and wrong in matters of art and proportion by some silent sense without any knowledge of art and proportion: and while they can do this in the case of pictures and statues [and] in other such works for whose understanding nature has given them less equipment, they display this discrimination much more in judging the rhythms and pronunciations of words, since these are rooted [*infixa*] in common senses and of such things nature has willed that no one should be altogether unable to sense and experience them [*expertus*].

And he goes on to notice that it is truly marvellous and remarkable

> how little difference there is between the learned and the ignorant in judging while there is the greatest difference in making.

Kant quite in the same vein remarks in his *Anthropology* that insanity consists in having lost this common sense which enables us to judge as spectators; and the opposite of it is a *sensus privatus,* a private sense which he also calls: "logical *Eigensinn*," implying that our logical faculty, the faculty which enables us to draw conclusions from premises, could indeed function without communication—except that then, namely, if insanity has caused the loss of common sense, it would lead to insane results precisely because it has separated itself from that experience which can be valid and validated only by the presence of others.

The most surprising aspect of this business is that common sense, the faculty of judgment and of discriminating between right and wrong, should be based on the sense of taste. Of our five senses, three give us clearly objects of the external world and therefore are easily communicable. Sight, hearing, touching deal directly and, as it were, objectively, with objects; smell and taste give inner sensations which are entirely private and incommunicable; what I taste and what I smell cannot be expressed in words at all. They seem to be the private senses by definition. Moreover, the three objective senses have in common that they are capable of *re*presentation—to have something present which is absent; I can recall a building, a melody, the touch of velvet. This faculty is called in Kant: Imagination—of which neither taste nor smell are capable. On the other hand, they are quite clearly the discriminatory senses: You can withhold judgment from what you see and, though less easily, you can withhold judgment from what you hear or touch. But in the matters of taste or smell, the it-pleases or displeases me is immediate and overwhelming. And pleasure or displeasure again are entirely private. Why then should taste—not only with Kant but since Gracian—be elevated to and become the vehicle of the mental faculty of judgment? And judgment in turn, that is, judgment that is not simply cognitive and residing on the senses which give us the objects which we have in common with all living things that have the same sensual equipment, but judgment between right and wrong, why should it be based on this private sense? Is it not true that about matters of taste we can so little communicate that we cannot even dispute about them—*de gustibus non disputandum est?*

. . . . . .

. . . We mentioned that taste and smell are the most private of the senses, that is, those senses where not an object but a sensation is sensed, where this sensation is not object-bound and cannot be recollected. You may recognize the smell of a rose or the taste of a dish if you sense it again, but you cannot have it present as you can have present any sight you ever saw or any melody you heard. . . . At the same time, we saw why taste rather than any of the other senses, became the vehicle for judgment; only taste and smell are discriminatory in their very nature *and* only these senses relate to the particular qua particular: all objects given to the objective senses share their properties with other objects; they are not unique. Moreover, the it-pleases or displeases me is overwhelmingly present in taste and smell. It is immediate, nonmediated by any thought or reflection. . . . And the it-pleases or displeases is almost identical with an it-agrees or disagrees with me. The point of the matter is: I am directly affected. For this very

reason, there can be no dispute about right or wrong here.
. . . No argument can persuade me to like oysters if I do not
like them. In other words, the disturbing thing about matters
of taste is that they are not communicable.

The solution of these riddles can be indicated by the names
of two other faculties—imagination and common sense. 1)
Imagination . . . transforms an object into something with
which I do not have to be directly confronted but which in
some sense I have internalized, so that I now can be affected
by it as though it were given to me by a nonobjective sense.
Kant says: "That is beautiful which pleases in the mere act of
judging it." That is: It is not important whether or not it
pleases in perception; what pleases merely in perception is
gratifying but not beautiful. It pleases in representation: The
imagination has prepared it so that I now can reflect on it:
"the operation of reflection." Only what touches, affects, you in
representation, when you can no longer be affected by immediate presence—uninvolved as the spectator is uninvolved
in the actual doings during the French Revolution—can then
be judged to be right or wrong, important or irrelevant, beautiful or ugly or something in-between. You then call it judgment and no longer taste because, though it still affects you
like a matter of taste, you have now, by means of representation, established the proper distance, the remoteness or unin-
volvedness or disinterestedness requisite for approbation and
disapprobation, or for evaluating something at its proper
worth. By removing the object, you have established the condition for impartiality.

And 2) *common sense:* Kant was very early aware that
there was something non-subjective in what seems to be the
most private and subjective sense; this awareness is expressed
as follows: There is the fact that matters of taste, "the beautiful, interests only in *society.* . . . A man abandoned by himself on a desert island would adorn neither his hut nor his
person. . . . [Man] is not contented with an object if he cannot feel satisfaction in it in common with others," whereas we
despise ourselves when we cheat at play, but are ashamed
only when we get caught. Or: "In matters of taste we must
renounce ourselves in favor of others" or in order to please
others (*Wir müssen uns gleichsam anderen zu gefallen*

*entsagen*). Finally, and most radically: "In Taste egoism is overcome," we are considerate in the original meaning of the word. We must overcome our special subjective conditions for the sake of others. In other words, the non-subjective element in the non-objective senses is intersubjectivity. (You must be alone in order to think; you need company to enjoy a meal.)

Judgment, and especially judgments of taste, always reflect upon others and . . . take their possible judgments into account. This is necessary because I am human and cannot live outside the company of men. . . . The basic other-directedness of judgment and taste seems to stand in the greatest possible opposition to the very nature, the absolutely idiosyncratic nature of the sense itself. Hence, we may be tempted to conclude that the faculty of judgment is wrongly derived from this sense. Kant, being very aware of all the implications of this derivation, remains convinced that it is a correct one. And the most plausible phenomenon in his favor is his observation, entirely correct, that the true opposite to the Beautiful is not the Ugly but "that which excites *disgust.*" And do not forget that Kant originally planned to write a Critique of Moral Taste. . . .

. . . The operation of the imagination: you judge objects that are no longer present . . . and no longer affect you directly. Yet while the object is removed from your outward senses, it now becomes an object for your inward senses. When you represent something to you that is absent, you close as it were those senses by which objects in their objectivity are given to you. The sense of taste is a sense in which it is as though you sense yourself, like an inner sense. . . . This operation of imagination prepares the object for "the operation of reflection." And this operation of reflection is the actual activity of judging something.

. . . By closing your eyes you become an impartial, not directly affected, spectator of visible things. The blind poet. Also: By making what your external senses perceived an object for your inner sense, you compress and condense the manifold of the sensually given, you are in a position to "see" by the eyes of your mind, i.e., to see the whole that gives meaning to particulars. . . .

The question that now arises is: What are the standards of the operation of reflection? . . . It [the inner sense] is called taste because, like taste, it *chooses*. But this choice itself is once more subject to another choice: You can approve or disapprove of the very fact of *pleasing*, it is subject to "approbation or disapprobation." Kant gives examples: "The joy of a needy but well-meaning man at becoming the heir of an affectionate but penurious father"; or, conversely, "a deep grief may satisfy the person experiencing it (the sorrow of a widow at the death of her excellent husband; or . . . a gratification can in addition please (as in the sciences that we pursue); or a grief (e.g., hatred, envy, revenge) can moreover displease." All these approbations and disapprobations are after-thoughts; while you are doing scientific research you may be vaguely aware that you are happy doing it, but only in reflecting on it later . . . will you be able to have this additional "pleasure"— of approving it. In this additional pleasure, it is no longer the object that pleases but that we judge it pleasing: If you relate this to the whole of nature or the world, you can say: We are pleased that the world of nature pleases us. The very act of approbation pleases, the very act of disapprobation displeases. Hence the question: How do you choose between approbation and disapprobation? One criterion you may guess if you consider the examples: the criterion is communicability or publicness. You will not be over-eager to announce your joy at the death of your father or your feelings of hatred and envy; you will on the other hand have no compunctions to tell that you enjoy doing scientific work and you will not hide your grief at the death of an excellent husband.

The criterion is communicability, and the standard of deciding about it is Common Sense.

*On the Communicability of a Sensation.*

It is true that the sensation of the senses is "generally communicable because we can assume that everyone has senses like our own. But this cannot be presupposed of any single sensation." These sensations are private, also no judgment is involved: we are merely passive, we react, we are not spontaneous as we are when we at will imagine something or reflect on it.

At the opposite pole we find moral judgments: these, according to Kant, are necessary; they are dictated by practical reason . . . even if they could not [be communicated] they would remain valid.

We have, third, judgments or pleasure in the beautiful: "this pleasure accompanies the ordinary apprehension [*Auffassung*, not perception] of an object by the imagination . . . by means of a procedure of the judgment which it must also exercise on behalf of the commonest experience." Some such judgment is in every experience we have with the world. This judgment is based on "that common and sound intellect [*gemeiner* and *gesunder Verstand*] which we have to presuppose in everyone." How does this "common sense" distinguish itself from the other senses which we also have in common and which nevertheless do not guarantee agreement of sensations?

*Taste as a Kind of* Sensus Communis.

The term is changed. The one, common sense, meant a sense like our other senses—the same for everybody in his very privacy. By using the Latin term, Kant indicates that he means something different: He means an extra sense—like an extra mental capability (the German: Menschen*verstand*)—which fits us into a community. The "common understanding of men . . . is the very least to be expected from anyone claiming the name of man." . . .

The *sensus communis* is the specifically human sense because communication, i.e., speech, depends on it. . . . "The only general symptom of insanity is the loss of the *sensus communis* and the logical stubbornness in insisting on one's own (*sensus privatus*). . . ."

Under the *sensus communis* we must include the idea of a sense *common to all*, i.e. of a faculty of judgment which, in its reflection, takes account (*a priori*) of the mode of representation of all other men in thought, in order, as it were, to compare its judgment with the collective reason of humanity. . . . This is done by comparing our judgment with the possible rather than the actual judgment of others, and by putting ourselves in the place of any other man, by abstracting from the limitations which contingently attach to our own judgment. . . . Now this operation of reflection seems perhaps too artificial to be attributed to the faculty called *common sense*, but it only appears so when expressed in abstract formulae.

In itself there is nothing more natural than to abstract from charm or emotion if we are seeking a judgment that is to serve as a universal rule.

After this follow the maxims of this *sensus communis:* To think for oneself (the maxim of enlightenment); to put ourselves in thought in the place of everyone else (the maxim of the enlarged mentality); and the maxim of consistency (to be in agreement with oneself, *mit sich selbst einstimmig denken*).

These are not matters of cognition; truth compels you, you do not need any "maxims." Maxims apply and are needed only for matter of opinions and in judgments. And just as in moral matters your maxim of conduct testifies to the quality of your Will, so the maxims of judgment testify to your "turn of thought" *(Denkungsart)* in the worldly matters which are ruled by the community sense.

However small may be the area or the degree to which a man's natural gifts reach, yet it indicates a man of *enlarged thought* if he disregards the subjective private conditions of his own judgment, by which so many others are confined, and reflects upon it from a *general standpoint* (which he can only determine by placing himself at the standpoint of others).

. . . Taste is this "community sense" *(gemeinschaftlicher Sinn)* and sense means here "the effect of a reflection upon the mind." This reflection affects me as though it were a sensation. . . . "We could even define taste as the faculty of judging of that which makes generally communicable, without the mediation of a concept, our feeling [like sensation] in a given representation [not perception]."

If we could assume that the mere general communicability of a feeling must carry in itself an interest for us with it . . . we should be able to explain why the feeling in the judgment of taste comes to be imputed to everyone, so to speak, as a duty.

. . . The validity of these judgments never [has] the validity of cognitive or scientific propositions, which are not judgments, properly speaking. (If you say, the sky is blue or two and two are four, you do not "judge"; you say what is, compelled by the evidence either of your senses or your mind.) In this way, you can never compel anybody to agree with your judgments—this is beautiful, this is wrong (Kant

however does not believe that moral judgments are the product of reflection and imagination, hence they are not judgments strictly speaking)—you can only "woo, court" the
agreement of everybody else. And in this persuasive activity
you actually appeal to the "community sense." . . . The less
idiosyncratic your taste is the better can it be communicated;
communicability again is the touchstone. Impartiality in Kant
is called "disinterestedness," the disinterested delight in the
Beautiful. . . . If, therefore, #41 [in the *Critique of Judgment*] speaks of an "Interest in the Beautiful," it actually
speaks of having an "interest" in disinterestedness. . . . Because we can call something beautiful, we have a *"pleasure in
its existence"* and that is "wherein all interest consists." (In
one of his reflections in the notebooks, Kant remarks that the
Beautiful teaches us to love without self-interest [*ohne Eigen-
nutz*].) And the peculiar characteristic of this interest is that it
"interests only in society."

. . . Kant stresses that at least one of our mental faculties,
the faculty of judgment, presupposes the presence of others.
And not just what we terminologically call judgment; bound
up with it is . . . our whole soul apparatus, so to speak. . . .
By communicating your feelings, your pleasures and disinterested delights, you tell your *choices* and you choose
your company. "I'd rather be wrong with Plato than right with
the Pythagoreans" [Cicero].

Finally, the larger the scope of men to whom you could
communicate, the greater the worth of the object:

Although the pleasure which everyone has in such an object is in-
considerable [that is, so long as he does not share it] and in itself
without any marked interest, yet the idea of its general communicability increases its worth in an almost infinite degree.

At this point, the *Critique of Judgment* joins effortlessly
Kant's deliberation about a united mankind, living in eternal
peace. . . . If

everyone expects and requires from everyone else this reference to
general communication [of pleasure, of disinterested delight, then
we have reached a point where it is as though there existed] an
original compact dictated by mankind itself.

. . . It is by virtue of this idea of mankind, present in every single man, that men are human, and they can be called civilized or humane to the extent that this idea becomes the principle of their actions as well as their judgments. It is at this point that actor and spectator become united; the maxim of the actor and the maxim, the "standard," according to which the spectator judges the spectacle of the world become one. The, as it were, categorical imperative for action could read as follows: Always act on the maxim through which this original compact can be actualized into a general law.

In conclusion, I shall try to clear up some of the difficulties: The chief difficulty in judgment is that it is "the faculty of thinking the particular"; but to *think* means to generalize, hence it is the faculty of mysteriously combining the particular and the general. This is relatively easy if the general is given—as a rule, a principle, a law—so that the judgment merely subsumes the particular under it. The difficulty becomes great "if only the particular be given for which the general has to be found." For the standard cannot be borrowed from experience and cannot be derived from outside. I cannot judge one particular by another particular; in order to determine its worth I need a *tertium quid* or a *tertium comparationis,* something related to the two particulars and yet distinct from both. In Kant we find actually two altogether different solutions of this difficulty:

As a real *tertium comparationis* two ideas appear in Kant on which you must reflect in order to arrive at judgments: This is *either,* in the political writings and, occasionally, also in the *Critique of Judgment,* the idea of an original compact of mankind as a whole and derived from this idea the notion of humanity, of what actually constitutes the humanness of human beings, living and dying in this world, on this earth that is a globe, which they inhabit in common, share in common, in the succession of generations. In the *Critique of Judgment* you also find the idea of purposiveness: Every object, says Kant, as a particular, needing and containing the ground of its actuality in itself, has a purpose. The only objects that seem purposeless are aesthetic objects, on one side, and men, on the other. You cannot ask *quem ad finem*—for what purpose?—since they are good for nothing. But . . . purposeless art objects as well as the seemingly purposeless variety of nature have the "purpose" of pleasing men, making them feel at home in the world. This can never be proved; but Purposiveness is an idea to regulate your reflections in your reflective judgments.

*Or* Kant's second and I think by far more valuable solution is the following. It is *exemplary validity*. ("Examples are the go-cart of judgments.") Let us see what that is: Every particular object, for instance a table, has a corresponding concept by which we recognize the table as a table. This you can conceive of as a Platonic "idea" or Kantian schema, that is, you have before the eyes of your mind a schematic or merely *formal table shape* to which every table somehow must conform. Or: if you proceed conversely from the many tables which you have seen in your life, strip off them all secondary qualities and the remainder is a table in general, containing the minimum properties common to all tables. *The abstract table.* You have one more possibility left, and this enters into judgments which are not cognitions: You may meet or think of some table which you judge to be the best possible table and take this table as the example of how tables actually should be—*the exemplary table*. (Example from *eximere*, to single out some particular.) This is and remains a particular which in its very particularity reveals the generality which otherwise could not be defined. Courage is like Achilles. Etc.

We were talking here about the partiality of the actor who, because he is involved, never sees the meaning of the whole. . . . The same is not true for the beautiful or for any deed in itself. The beautiful is, in Kantian terms, an end in itself because all its possible meaning is contained within itself, without reference to others, without linkage, as it were, to other beautiful things. In Kant himself, there is this contradiction: Infinite Progress is the law of the human species; at the same time man's dignity demands that he is seen, every single one . . . in his particularity, reflecting as such, but without any comparison and independent of time, mankind in general. In other words the very idea of progress—if it is more than a mere change of circumstances and an improvement of the world— contradicts Kant's notion of man's dignity.

# Index / Thinking

# Index / Willing

282

## Index